THE UNITED NATIONS AND THE UNITED STATES

Twayne's International History Series

Akira Iriye, Editor
Harvard University

THE UNITED NATIONS
AND THE UNITED STATES

Gary B. Ostrower

Alfred University

TWAYNE PUBLISHERS • NEW YORK
AN IMPRINT OF SIMON & SCHUSTER MACMILLAN

NEW YORK • LONDON • MEXICO CITY • NEW DELHI
• SINGAPORE • SYDNEY • TORONTO

Twayne Publishers
An Imprint of Simon & Schuster Macmillan
1633 Broadway
New York, NY 10019

Library of Congress Cataloging-in-Publication Data

Ostrower, Gary B., 1939–
    The United Nations and the United States / Gary B. Ostrower.
        p.   cm. — (Twayne's international history series)
    Includes bibliographical references and index.
    ISBN 0–8057–1661–0 (alk. paper)
    1. United States—Foreign relations—1945–1989. 2. United States—
Foreign relations—1945– 3. United Nations—History. I. Title.
II. Series.
E744.083   1998
327.73—dc21
                                                        98–14079
                                                          CIP

This paper meets the requirements of ANSI/NISO Z3948–1992 (Permanence of Paper).

10 9 8 7 6 5 4 3 2 1

Printed in the United States of America

CONTENTS

FOREWORD

Twayne's International History Series seeks to publish reliable and readable accounts of post-World War II international affairs. Today, more than 50 years after the end of the war, and already nearly a decade since the end of the Cold War, the time seems opportune to undertake a critical assessment of world affairs in the second half of the twentieth century. What have been the major themes and trends in international relations since 1945? How have they evolved and changed over time? What have been the connections between international and domestic affairs? How have states and non-state actors (such as intergovernmental organizations and multinational corporations) as well as individuals defined and pursued their objectives, and what have they contributed to the world at large? How have conceptions of warfare and visions of peace changed in the last 50 years?

These questions must be raised in any attempt to understand the contemporary world. That understanding must be both international—with an awareness of the linkages among different parts of the globe—and historical—with a keen sense of what the immediate past has brought to humankind. Hence the *International History* series. It is hoped that the volumes in the series will help the reader explore important events and movements since 1945 and develop the global awareness and historical sensitivity required for confronting today's problems.

Most volumes thus far published in the series have examined the United States's relations with other countries, groups of countries, or regions. The focus on the United States is justified in part because of the nation's predominant position in postwar international relations, and also because far more documentation is available on United States foreign affairs than is for those of other countries. These volumes address not only readers who are interested in the recent history of international relations, but also those who seek useful guides and fresh insights into the contemporary world. Now more than ever it is imperative to understand the linkages between national and international history.

This volume is unique for the series in that Professor Gary Ostrower, a leading scholar of the League of Nations, examines the complicated and often tortuous relationship between the United States and the United Nations since the latter's founding in San Francisco in 1945, just before the end of World War II. Based on his intimate knowledge of international organizations and on extensive examination of published and archival documents, the author presents a vivid portrait of the world organization as it has evolved during the last half-century and as it has coped with the often contradictory attitudes on the part of the United States government, Congress, and public opinion. The lively presentation of the increasingly difficult relationship between the United Nations and the United States enables us to understand some of the most important aspects of post-1945 international affairs, for both the United Nations and the United States in many ways have symbolized and responded to humankind's aspirations for a more peaceful, humane world. It is to be hoped that many people and organizations around the globe will read this book to ponder the question of how best to bring about a more stable and cooperative relationship between the only universal and all-purpose international organization and the only remaining superpower.

Akira Iriye
Harvard University

PREFACE

The United Nations limps into the 21st century bigger and more ambitious than the UN constructed by the World War II coalition that defeated the Axis powers. It is also more controversial. Only occasionally has the UN lived up to the expectations of its founders. Then again, it has reshaped itself dramatically and has tackled challenges that its founders only dimly recognized. The cloud over Hiroshima obscured much of the coming 50 years.

During its early days, the UN's most vocal champions had been Americans. Many of them believed that Washington's absence from the League of Nations, the UN's predecessor, had made World War II almost inevitable. These Americans, therefore, placed the UN's goal to prevent war at the center of its life. "We the Peoples of the United Nations determined to save succeeding generations from the scourge of war . . ." begins the Charter. Yes, the UN had humanitarian and economic responsibilities, but no one doubted its primary purpose.

Americans, whose newly discovered internationalism camouflaged a deeply cherished isolationism, desperately wanted to avoid a third World War. They also wanted to avoid a repeat of the economic catastrophe called the Great Depression. The UN, they believed, could help them do both, and they therefore encouraged their own government to play the lead role in the UN's new life. The founders of the UN located the organization in the United States, relied on U.S. financing, and accepted U.S. direction.

Some governments welcomed this state of affairs. Others resented it. Most simply viewed it as they viewed the weather: they could do little about it. Then came the 1970s. With the UN doubling, then tripling in membership, the United States lost its favored position within the organization. In addition, the UN was not preventing wars it was supposed to prevent—in Vietnam, for instance, and Afghanistan. Anti-UN campaigns within the United States capitalized on the resulting frustration. Congressional reductions in U.S. financial contributions to the UN reflected it.

Still, the UN continued to become more active. Its peacekeeping activity witnessed explosive growth by the 1990s. In addition, the UN stepped up its efforts in fields ranging from population control to biodiversity preservation to womens' rights. American neoisolationists and nationalists—they were not the same—might hate the UN, but they could not ignore it.

Like it or not, the UN has transformed the world. It may have failed to guarantee peace or even to guarantee its own existence, but it has redefined the way that the world does business. Has it destroyed the old international system of sovereign states? Of course not. Has it modified it? For certain. The simple fact that the 21st century will open without a colonial problem—at least a colonial problem as the term has been defined for three hundred years—is testimony to just how important the UN has become. And the bumpy American experience with decolonization from Indonesia to Vietnam reflects the rocky road the United States has traveled with the UN. But travel that road, Washington did . . . and does . . . and will continue to do.

Books are written by authors . . . and editors, friends, colleagues, librarians. My thanks to these people. Certainly I could not have completed this work without the assistance of Alfred University, which granted me an ulcer-saving sabbatical leave during 1996–97. Alfred's NEH Committee offered financial assistance. Lana Meissner, vice president for information technology, and Ann Finger of the University of Rochester's Rush Rhees Library, made it possible for me to do most of my research in the remote southern tier of New York state; I owe them and their staffs my gratitude. The archivists at the Truman, Eisenhower, Kennedy, and Johnson presidential libraries, and especially Martin Elzy of the Carter Library in Atlanta, equally deserve my thanks. So, too, the patient Twayne editors who extended more than one deadline for me.

I owe special thanks to five people: Akira Iriye, who three decades ago helped to steer me toward the history of international organizations and who asked me to contribute this volume to the Twayne series; Carla Coch, whose editorial assistance helped turn these chapters into a readable manuscript; Joel Blatt, who critiqued chapters and offered me his insight into European history; Joseph Baratta, whose work for the Society for the Study of Internationalism, and whose edited works on UN affairs, proved invaluable; and Tom Peterson, who set a standard for colleagueship that I hope I can repay.

Others, too, deserve thanks, including Nancy Freelove, the members of AU's NEH Committee that provided financial support, and my colleagues in AU's Division of Human Studies. Dean Christine Grontkowski, now at Frostburg State, backed up her moral support by providing me with computer hardware that speeded up this project by six months. Thanks, too, to AU's provost, Rick Ott, who believes that faculty should be free to do what faculty are hired to do. The organizers of various conferences dealing with UN affairs also aided me, especially Paul Kennedy, who invited me to the best conference I've ever attended, Yale's 1996 workshop on international affairs. Douglas Brinkley and Fredrik Logevall graciously permitted me to read prepublication versions of their own work, as did Amy Staples, Bill McAllister, and Rowland Brucken. Joyce Rosenblum, librarian for the Photo Unit at the UN, very generously aided me in securing historical photographs dating back to 1941. Finally, I wish to acknowledge my introduction to cyber-communications: listmembers of H-Diplo and ACUNS-IO, especially Michael Friedland and Gian Luca Burci, who offered a number of suggestions that found their way into this book.

But no one deserves more credit than my wife, Judy, and my children, Sarah and Pete. They may never want to hear the initials U.S. or UN again. A bear hug to all three of them.

ILLUSTRATIONS

Chapter 1

ROOSEVELT

One of the twentieth century's great love affairs has involved the United Nations. From its founding in 1945, many millions of people, frightened by the prospect of serial wars and super weapons, approached the UN with both passion and hope. As in many love affairs, the passion camouflaged the dangers, and the emotional highs would eventually give way to as much disillusionment as satisfaction.

Of course, the story of the United Nations—and of America's courtship with it—begins long before 1945. It is really part of a much larger story involving a global tug-of-war between the forces of nationalism and internationalism. This competition can be traced back to the French Revolution of the late eighteenth century, when modern nationalism first emerged. Internationalism appeared later, a product of the carnage of the First World War, known as the Great War until an even greater war broke out less than a generation later. If modern nationalism posed the threat of political and economic disintegration, internationalism offered the hope of cooperation and integration. Terms like *Balkanization* and *self-determination* became synonyms for nationalism; while phrases such as *Common Market* and *collective security*, not to mention the acronymn *UN*, referred to internationalism. Even today, historians are uncertain about the relative weight in world affairs of nationalism and internationalism. Sometimes one, sometimes the other, has seemed to be in the ascendant.

Like most large-scale historical movements, the origins of both nationalism and internationalism are somewhat obscure. If a vaguely defined national consciousness appeared during the seventeenth and eighteenth centuries, leading to, among other things, the birth of the United States during the American Revolution, so too did an even more vaguely defined internationalist impulse emerge during the nineteenth century. This early internationalism took many

Churchill and FDR preparing to draft the Atlantic Charter on the HMS
Prince of Wales. September 14, 1941.
(UN/DPI Photo)

forms, from the organization of post-Napoleonic states into the Holy Alliance and Congress System as a means to maintain peace and stability in Europe, to what some scholars call "functional" organizations, such as the General Postal Union (founded 1875) and the International Health Office (1907). Internationalists hoped that the anarchy inherent in a system of sovereign states might be reduced by a system of international cooperation, and they designed agencies to encourage and facilitate such cooperation.

They succeeded, up to a point. But their efforts were all but forgotten when Europeans, and then others, went to war in 1914. The men who made that war and the masses who irrationally supported it soon discovered that their system of power was so perfectly balanced that neither side could win the conflict. What most observers thought would be a small and manageable war turned into a long and uncontrollable conflagration. Militaristic competition overwhelmed the agencies of peace. And yet, just as epidemic disease can provide immunity for the survivors, so too would a near-suicidal war generate ideas and institutions to reform the system of sovereign states that helped to cause the war.

THE LEAGUE OF NATIONS

Even before the war ended, statesmen like American president Woodrow Wilson, French socialist Leon Bourgeois, British aristocrats Lord Phillimore and Viscount Robert Cecil, South African general Jan Smuts, and many lesser-known men and women initiated planning for what eventually emerged at the Paris Peace Conference as the League of Nations. They designed the League to prevent future war and, less important, to foster cooperation in social and economic matters. The League would prevent war by creating what later came to be called the system of "collective security." Social, economic, and technical cooperation, which internationalists believed might eliminate the conditions that cause conflict, would be facilitated by placing the functional organizations under the administrative and financial umbrella of the League. Although the League's collective security activity would fail, its economic, social, and technical cooperation, which really became the heart of post-1919 internationalism, witnessed some striking successes.

Collective security failed for many reasons, but the two most important were that no nation was willing to subordinate its own authority—its own sovereignty—to the new League organization, and that the United States, which had emerged in 1918 as the leading economic and military power in the world, was unwilling to renounce its own freedom of action for the common good. The result was that, within just two years of the League's birth, many governments, led by the Scandinavians and the Canadians, modified their new collective security obligations. And although a collective-security-minded American secretary of state nudged the United States toward political cooperation with the League during the early thirties after Japan violated a number of agreements—including the League's covenant—by illegally occupying Manchuria, the president, as well as Congress, refused to back him up in a meaningful way. As a result the Great Powers at the League's home in Geneva, fearful that they might have to actually fight a war without the support of Washington, offered China, which held nominal title to Manchuria, nothing but windy resolutions.

The consequence was not just Tokyo's triumph in Manchuria but exposure of the League's impotence just when international stability was most threatened. By the end of 1933, both Germany and Japan had announced their intention to depart from Geneva. Less than three years later, following Mussolini's assault against Ethiopia, Italy also quit the League. Nor did Americans at this time welcome new international obligations, for the U.S. Senate in 1935 rejected membership on the Permanent Court of International Justice (the World Court), membership that every American president and secretary of state had supported since 1920. American refusal to cooperate in the area of collective security understandably reinforced the fear of war among the democracies while indirectly encouraging expansionist sentiments among the fascist leaders in Germany, Italy, and Japan. Reforms proposed between 1937 and 1939 aimed to strengthen the League but instead advertised that the League had become a hollow shell. The League stood by impassively in July 1937, when World War II began in the Far East after Japanese troops stormed into Shanghai. By 1939, Europe, too, was at war. The following year, fearing possible Nazi occupation of Switzerland, a skeletal League secretariat fled to safety across the Atlantic. For the duration of World War II, the League resided quietly in Princeton, New Jersey.[1]

There is a doleful irony in knowing that the League spent its last days under the protection of the Stars and Stripes. Twenty years earlier, when the League was still in its infancy, the American secretary of state would not even answer routine mail or verbal inquiries from Geneva.[2] By 1940, although the United States and President Franklin Roosevelt were still many months from Pearl Harbor, more intimate U.S. contact with the League—more accurately, with the ghost of the world's first collective-security organization—became politically permissible.

Whether or not Washington took advantage of what was permissible, contact with the League by private citizens was already occurring in ways that would eventually revolutionize the American role in collective security. Shortly after Hitler's attack on Poland, the American president of the League of Nations Association, James T. Shotwell, resigned his position in order to found the Commission to Study the Organization of Peace.[3] Planning for this somewhat pompously named group actually began before Germany invaded Poland, a sign that many internationalists had already accepted the inevitability of war. The members of the commission, all dedicated internationalists, saw their organization as an unofficial version of Woodrow Wilson's Inquiry, the group that had shaped the American approach to the peace following the

1918 Armistice. Although the commission's efforts during the two years preceding Pearl Harbor would be eclipsed in the public eye by organizations supporting America's European allies, especially William Allen White's Committee to Revise the Neutrality Laws (a precursor to his more well-known Committee to Defend America by Aiding the Allies), the members of Shotwell's commission hardly objected. Not only did the leadership of the two organizations overlap, but they even shared office space. Indeed, the success of White's committee in persuading the president and Congress to repeal the arms embargo provisions of the Neutrality Act on November 4, 1939, cleared the deck for the commission's very first meeting, held the following day.[4] For the next two months, the commission worked quietly; not until early 1940 did its existence become known to the general public.

The Commission to Study the Organization of Peace expected a short life: six months, perhaps a year. Hitler, of course, expected a short war. Both were wrong. The commission would last (its critics might say "linger") for decades, though its most important achievements occurred in the years leading up to the San Francisco Conference of 1945. No private organization expended more energy in an effort to shape the postwar peace, and none contributed more to mobilizing popular support for what eventually became the United Nations. From its earliest days, the commission organized radio broadcasts, public meetings, and college study sessions. If its initial efforts aimed to join the United States to a reformed and invigorated League of Nations, after Pearl Harbor the commission increasingly accepted the need for a wholly new organization. Central to the commission's work was not just designing the mechanics of a new collective-security organization but also securing American membership. And toward this latter goal, the war contributed mightily. In 1937, only 26 percent of the American public favored U.S. membership in the League; by May 1941, seven months *before* Pearl Harbor, half of those polled favored membership in the League, while 87 percent supported U.S. participation in some kind of postwar organization.[5]

It is impossible to say with precision how much the commission's efforts contributed to that 87 percent. Many of the group's leading members, like Shotwell, Commission Director Clark M. Eichelberger (who became acting chairman of the Committee to Defend America during 1941), legalist Clyde Eagleton from New York University, former Johns Hopkins president Isaiah Bowman, William Allan Neilson from Smith College, who headed the commission's executive committee, and future secretary of state John Foster Dulles, had not exactly been effective as advocates for internationalism before the outbreak of hostilities. Two things made them much more successful after 1940: public reaction to the frightening intensity of warfare (especially when newsreels conveyed the drama of Hitler's attack on France), and a much more sympathetic attitude toward international organization on the part of Washington policy makers. Both of these developments helped to discredit isolationism and neutrality.

Nor did the Commission work alone in those early years of World War II. By 1942, according to a future American representative to the UN, Charles Yost, 36 private groups had offered to assist the State Department in shaping postwar policy.[6] The proliferation of such groups threatened to make the task of planning for the peace chaotic. Once State Department officials recognized the problem, they sought to channel internationalist energy into constructive directions.

But who would decide what was constructive? Before Pearl Harbor, the Roosevelt administration was hardly of one mind in respect to postwar planning. When the president himself met with British prime minister Winston Churchill off Newfoundland in August 1941, he refused to embrace the idea of a postwar security organization. Preliminary drafts of what eventually became the Atlantic Charter principles, submitted by Churchill and by Roosevelt advisers Harry Hopkins and Undersecretary of State Sumner Welles, urged unambiguous support for an "effective [postwar] international organization." FDR demurred. Although he eventually compromised by accepting a disarmament clause linked to "a wider and permanent system of general security," he refused to endorse the League of Nations or a successor organization. According to the most recent account of FDR's UN policy, he greatly feared isolationist sentiment at home; he may also have been disillusioned with the League (which he had personally championed until his election campaign in 1932).[7] While some internationalists, like Eichelberger, praised the Atlantic Charter, others, including the clearheaded John Foster Dulles, noted its "striking omission" about international organization.

THE GOVERNMENT STEPS IN: AMERICA PLANS FOR PEACE DURING WORLD WAR II

It was not in the White House, but rather in the State Department and the Senate, that American officials initiated serious postwar planning. Even in these organizations, such planning did not get a high priority before Pearl Harbor. Nevertheless, officials like Leo Pasvolsky, a special assistant to Secretary of State Cordell Hull, were encouraged by the support among clerics for John Foster Dulles's Commission to Study the Basis of a Just and Durable Peace, founded under the auspices of the Federal Council of Churches. Nor did the State Department disregard the popularity of Clarence Streit's global federalism, which he outlined in *Union Now* and institutionalized in a group called, by 1941, Federal Union, Inc.[8] While many internationalists, like Pasvolsky, remained skeptical about the narrow Anglo-American emphasis of Streit's plan, the appearance of scores, then hundreds, of local Federal Union chapters signaled that the era of isolationism was ending.

The State Department had begun postwar planning as early as 1940 when Secretary Hull approved the formation of the Advisory Committee on Problems of Foreign Relations. Unfortunately for its members, the committee was as neglected as its title was nondescript. Not until February 1941, when

Pasvolsky became chief of another new and blandly named unit called the Division of Special Research, did real planning begin. Pasvolsky, a Russian immigrant who specialized in economic affairs, was aided by a man whom historian Robert Divine calls the "most eloquent prophet of a new world order," Undersecretary Sumner Welles, who served much of that critical year, 1941, as the acting secretary when Hull fell ill.[9] Both Pasvolsky and Welles were uncompromising in their commitment to international order through organization. Welles took the public road. Pasvolsky traveled more quietly, rarely making public statements, all the while assembling an impressive and skillful group of journalists and social scientists to shape the State Department's position. A plan for the UN would eventually evolve out of all this activity. Still, the most critical development during 1941 leading to America's reconsideration of international responsibilities occurred 5,000 miles from the site of the old State Department building where Pasvolsky and Welles worked. On December 7, the Japanese navy jolted the United States into the war by attacking Pearl Harbor, and the widespread belief that isolationism could somehow insulate the country from global problems disappeared along with the lives of 2,400 American sailors and airmen. Two weeks later, Winston Churchill left London for a meeting with President Roosevelt. Both leaders quickly drafted the terms of their grand alliance. On December 26, Churchill addressed a joint session of Congress, reminding the Americans that if, after World War I, "we had kept together . . . , if we had taken common measures for our safety, this renewal of the curse need never to have fallen upon us."[10] His audience cheered lustily, fully understanding his reference to "common measures." On New Year's Day, 1942, Churchill and Roosevelt, along with officials from 24 (eventually 34) other countries, signed the Declaration of the United Nations. Vowing not to stop fighting until they had defeated "Hitlerism," they introduced the term "United Nations" to the American public. They also gave it vitality. Even the League of Nations Association, which had stubbornly refused to change its name, summoned the United Nations to win the military victory and "guide the world during the period of reconstruction and become the nucleus of a universal society of nations."[11] "United Nations" gradually became more than a name; it came to represent a conception of world organization that included a more universal and more security-minded arrangement than the League had ever been.

With the United States now directly involved in the war, President Roosevelt and the American public naturally became preoccupied with military affairs. These included not only battlefield developments but the complex issues of domestic mobilization that altered the routine of most Americans for the next three and one-half years. FDR also had to create a strategy to keep his allied coalition together, a task that led him to places such as Casablanca, Cairo, Teheran, and Yalta. During many of these months, the president was only marginally concerned with shaping the postwar peace. Not until after the battle of Stalingrad, which ended in the late winter of 1943, did the Allies conclude that Hitler would lose the war. Until then, postwar planning was a secondary affair, confined to private groups such as the Commission to Study the Organization of Peace, to some relatively low-profile congressional sub-committees, and to the State Department.

This postwar planning highlighted differences of opinion over not just means but ends, and involved rivalries that had as much to do with personal-ity as grand strategy. Perhaps the most important of these rivalries involved Secretary of State Hull and Undersecretary of State Welles. Welles, who shared FDR's aristocratic background (both men had been schooled at Groton and Harvard), genuinely believed that American abstention from the League of Nations was a major reason for the outbreak of World War II, and he placed international organization at the forefront of his interests in the State Depart-ment. The Tennessee-born Hull did not enjoy the same direct access to FDR that Welles did, despite being a member of the president's cabinet, and was less impressed with the collective-security idea. The key to peace, Hull long believed, lay more in economic interdependence than in the collective use of force. "Ages of civilization," he wrote shortly before his death, "have taught us that international commerce promotes material welfare, peace, and advance-ment."[12] Still, as an old-line Wilsonian, he was not unsympathetic to the con-cept of international organization, and it is difficult to say even today whether his disagreements with Welles during 1942 and 1943 were more personal than professional.

What is clear is that the two men often disagreed. Welles's earlier work in the State Department had mainly involved Latin American matters, and his support for the Pan American Union made him highly sympathetic to a collective-security approach that emphasized regionalism. As a result, he ini-tially advocated an organization composed of geographically organized coun-cils; they, in turn, would elect representatives to a global executive committee including delegates from the Great Powers. Another outspoken international-ist, Vice President Henry Wallace, supported Welles, adding a proposal for an international air force that could be used against potential aggressors.

Hull found neither proposal particularly attractive, although he knew that both FDR and Churchill favored a regional approach.[13] Fearing that his own influence was being undermined by Welles's and Wallace's direct access to FDR, he removed Welles as chairman of the State Department's Subcommit-tee on Political Problems, which had been working on postwar planning. Hull further ordered the Special Subcommittee on International Organization, which Welles still headed, to route all proposals through his own office. These changes may have clipped Welles's wings, but they did not end what Hull con-tinued to view as a threat to his own authority. Consequently, in July 1943, Hull suspended the work of *all* subcommittees working on the subject of post-war organization. In their place, he would rely almost exclusively on the recently created Informal Agenda Group, composed of men, including Pasvol-sky, who were reliably loyal to Hull himself, and which produced the first draft

"Charter of the United Nations" in August 1943.[14] As Robert Divine concludes about these rivalries, Hull had finally broken Welles's "domination" of postwar planning in the State Department.

The jockeying for position within the State Department went unnoticed by the outside world. Other than Vice President Wallace and former Republican presidential candidate Wendell Wilkie, few nationally known political figures had offered more than vague generalities about a successor organization to the League. Wallace had already announced his support of an international league with an air force, and Wilkie, an Indiana internationalist who sought to rid his party of its isolationist legacy, proposed that all Republicans pledge, among other things, to "set up institutions of international political and economic cooperation" containing "some system of joint international force."[15] Beyond this, politicians said little. FDR actually discouraged Wilkie from becoming more specific when Wilkie returned from a highly publicized world tour. Even as late as January 1943, the president, in his State of the Union message, charged the League of Nations with unrealistic idealism. He suggested that any successor organization must have not only good intentions but the power to force aggressor nations to disarm. And while some elected officials, such as Vermont's internationalist Republican senator, Warren Austin, and Texas's New Deal senator and chairman of the Foreign Relations Committee, Tom Connally, quietly served on the State Department's nonpartisan Advisory Committee on Postwar Foreign Policy, it was not until after the 1942 congressional campaign that the subject of postwar organization became part of a congressional debate.[16]

Isolationists in the House of Representatives launched their attack in early 1943 when they sponsored resolutions to place members of Congress on postwar planning commissions to advise the president. Internationalists, understandably, were unwilling to see their opponents shape the legislative terrain. Led by West Virginia representative John Kee and Iowa senator Guy Gillette, they counterattacked. When the administration attempted to prevent this skirmishing in order to maintain its own freedom of action, Senator Joseph H. Ball of Minnesota, later joined by Senators Harold Burton of Ohio, Carl Hatch of New Mexico, and Lister Hill of Alabama, introduced a resolution that called on the United Nations to form a postwar organization with police powers, social and economic responsibilities, and the authority to settle disputes.[17] Known as B2H2, the resolution initiated the first serious congressional debate over shaping the peace. The president, who wanted desperately to avoid controversy, was finally forced to endorse B2H2's general principles. While the administration did manage to prevent a full floor debate, many senators and representatives, determined to reverse the Senate's 1919 verdict on the League of Nations, continued to press the issue. Moreover, these members of Congress were influenced by the growing public perception that Allied military success from Sicily to Stalingrad had made the subject of postwar planning more urgent than ever. By the summer of 1943, a rapid increase in the

number of internationalist groups across the country signaled, even to isolationists, that this issue would not go away, and the July 1943 transmutation of
the League of Nations Association into the United Nations Association
advertised the change. Predictably, passage of the B2H2 resolution became
the first order of business for the UNA.

Neither the Senate nor the administration, however, showed real enthusiasm for B2H2, and Senator Tom Connally's Foreign Relations Committee
refused to schedule it for debate. Consequently, others stepped into the picture. Arkansas's J. William Fulbright, a young freshman congressman who,
according to one biographer, viewed national sovereignty as a deadly anachro-
nism, submitted a series of resolutions in order to nudge the administration
toward a commitment to international organization. The resolutions were less
detailed than B2H2, the most important of them calling only for "appropriate
international machinery with power adequate to prevent future aggression,
and to maintain future peace." When this vague resolution went nowhere,
Fulbright's colleagues on the House Foreign Affairs Committee watered it
down even further, eliminating the phrase "to prevent aggression" so as not to
raise the specter of military action and thereby invite isolationist counterattack.[18] And while the administration wasn't much more enthusiastic about
the Fulbright resolution than B2H2, the Arkansas representative's appeals to
FDR and Welles, combined with the resolution's nonthreatening generalities,
elicited a White House promise to work for passage at some unspecified date.
The administration did not exactly display courage or leadership over this
issue, but neither did it seek to derail the resolution. Perhaps FDR's knowledge
that Republican internationalists, led by New York representative James
Wadsworth, supported the measure made it more palatable to him.

With both houses of Congress beginning to address the subject and with
public opinion out in front of both the Congress and the White House, the
last six months of 1943 saw more movement toward international organization than the previous four years combined.[19] The president's fear that the
Republicans would attack administration support for international cooperation as they had done in 1919 began to fade after the Republican Postwar
Advisory Council adopted its Mackinac Declaration in early September. The
product of give-and-take between moderate isolationists who followed Senator Arthur Vandenburg of Michigan, and outright internationalists led by
Senator Austin, New Jersey representative Charles Eaton, and California governor Earl Warren, the declaration committed the Republican Party to promote an international organization to "prevent military aggression and attain
permanent peace." It included some fine print to assuage isolationist sensibil-
ities, but for the most part it ended the specter of partisanship. From September 1943 until the San Francisco Conference of 1945, the quarrels would be
over not whether the United States should join a postwar organization, but
what the shape of that organization should be.

FDR himself contributed very little to defining that shape during the remainder of 1943, but he did commit himself more publicly to some kind of an organization. His commitment was a process more than a single decision, a process fashioned in Quebec, where the president met with Prime Minister Churchill; in Moscow, where Hull met with his British and Soviet counterparts, Anthony Eden and V. I. Molotov; and in Teheran, where Roosevelt met with Churchill and Soviet dictator Joseph Stalin. The president still had not fully thought out his position. He had little sympathy with Wallace's concept of a "people's" organization that would stress humanitarian activities, although he liked Wallace's proposal for an international air force, and he initially sympathized more with Welles's regional approach than with Hull's more universal concept of organization. Still, his disillusionment with the League of Nations was real, and he often returned to the belief that the Great Powers must assume ultimate responsibility for the peace, an idea that he would later articulate as the Four Policemen.

ROOSEVELT'S FOUR POLICEMEN

Even as early as the Quebec Conference, FDR permitted Hull to draft a "four power declaration" that placed responsibility on the United States, Great Britain, the USSR, and China to maintain the peace until they could create a permanent international organization. While the shape of this permanent organization was left undefined, it was not to be the regional organization that Welles had advocated. Indeed, Welles's influence effectively came to an end just before the conference when Hull gave FDR a him-or-me ultimatum. The press reported (almost accurately) that the undersecretary had "resigned," forced out of the State Department by Hull, who considered him personally disloyal and who deeply resented his potential influence in the White House.[20] The departure of Welles must have pained the president, for FDR was as fond of Welles as he was uneasy with Hull, a man for whom FDR did not have high regard. Still, the president had little choice. Welles, with plenty of enemies, had already become a political liability. Unlike Hull, he had little support in Congress. Moreover, the Washington rumor mill spread news of his alleged homosexuality at the same time that at least one national columnist accused FDR of allowing the State Department to be weakened by the Hull-Welles rivalry.[21] The president, forced to choose between the two, abandoned his friend. Hull had proved to be tougher than many officials had thought. He had mastered the State Department bureaucracy, and he had powerful friends in the press and on Capitol Hill. These assets aided his campaign for a universal—as opposed to a regional—international organization, particularly since FDR, who had earlier consigned Hull to a secondary role in the diplomacy of the Grand Alliance, now allowed him primary authority in the creation of the postwar organization.

Nowhere would this new role be more evident than at the Moscow Conference of October 1943. After some hard bargaining, Hull, aided by Eden, persuaded the Soviets to accept the general terms of the four-power declaration that had been drafted at Quebec. For the first time, representatives of the Great Powers, including China, committed themselves to forming, "at the earliest practicable date," a general international organization composed of "all peace-loving states . . . for the maintenance of international peace and security."[22] The "peace-loving" language meant that, at least initially, Hull's dreams of universality would be disappointed. This, however, would prove to be but a minor glitch at a conference where Hull would otherwise enjoy his most heralded moment as secretary of state.

The secretary's success in Moscow clearly influenced the Senate. It is less clear that it actually influenced the president. In the upper house of Congress, where the B2H2 resolution stalled and where Senator Tom Connally's alternative resolution in support of a postwar organization had not satisfied the more ardent internationalists, the news from Moscow spawned new activity. With B2H2 supporters trying to strengthen Connally's resolution while the Texas senator jealously guarded both his own handiwork and the Senate's foreign policy prerogatives (he deeply resented House passage of the Fulbright resolution), an impasse loomed. It would be avoided when both sides agreed to append the text of the Moscow declaration to Connally's resolution. It was a simple yet brilliant compromise not only drawing FDR's approval but uniting the internationalists and the moderates enjoying the afterglow from Moscow. Its proponents touted it as a means to honor Hull, a tribute that even moderate isolationists could not resist in the wake of the secretary's triumphant return. And so the Connally resolution passed overwhelmingly. Only five isolationists, including three who had voted against the League in 1919, voted no.

As Robert Divine reminds us, however, the nearly unanimous support for the resolution testifies to just how ambiguous it really was.[23] The resolution did not spell out much at all: no mention of a Great Power veto, no mention of international police, no mention of a conference structure. Internationalists, celebrating its passage, predictably exaggerated its importance, although they were justified in believing that, after the Connally resolution, the Senate would not—could not—retreat back into 1920s-style isolationism.

The vagueness of both the Fulbright and Connally resolutions in some ways mirrored the vagueness of FDR's own thinking. The president actually supported both resolutions *because* they were so imprecise. The Connally resolution, after all, barely went beyond the administration's own position as spelled out in Moscow, and the even more platitudinous Fulbright resolution said only that the United States should participate in an organization with power to preserve peace. To this day, historians are hard-pressed to define the president's position. Because even isolationists such as North Dakota senator Gerald Nye and New York representative Hamilton Fish supported the resolutions, FDR's endorsement tells us little. The president's disillusionment with the League and his general support for international organization suggests that he wanted something stronger. But what was it? He often swerved to one side or the other during 1943, at times sympathetic to Sumner Welles's vision of an international organization based on regional groupings, at other times dropping the regional emphasis, and finally, of course, concurring with Hull's dismissal of Welles. FDR met with Churchill and, for the first time, Stalin, at Teheran from November 27 to December 1, and he spoke to the Soviet dictator at length about international organization. Though drawing in part on plans earlier drafted by Welles, particularly in regard to an organization containing a general conference composed of all nations but without the power to act, the president nevertheless retreated from Welles's emphasis on regional authorities. To oppose aggressive governments, FDR would rely not on the proposed new organization but rather on the Four Policemen, an idea he had first broached to Churchill at Quebec. Apparently, though, he told Stalin that the decisions of the executive council would not bind the Four Policemen.[24] It needs to be emphasized again that the president had not given a great deal of thought to this matter. Indeed, he told Stalin that it needed a lot more consideration. In contrast to the recent foreign ministers' meeting at Moscow, the three leaders at Teheran nearly ignored the subject of international organization when drafting their concluding statement, saying only that the postwar world should witness the active cooperation of all countries, large and small. By floating such generalities, they left themselves plenty of room to maneuver.

Much has been made of the Four Policemen concept. Certainly it offered evidence that FDR, less than two years after Pearl Harbor, would approach the postwar world by resurrecting a very un-Wilsonian plan for "spheres of influence," though the degree to which he embraced the concept has been debated.[25] FDR refused to trifle with the concept of national sovereignty, at least not that of the major powers. He pursued an approach congenial to Realists like Walter Lippmann and Nicholas Spykman, who never shared the Wilsonian faith that world public opinion, international law, and a new morality could replace the military and economic resources of the Great Powers as the key to global peace.[26] Yet worth repeating once again is that FDR had not systematically thought out his approach to this subject. Friends and critics alike noted that in both foreign and domestic policy, the president drew liberally from advisers of very different persuasions, such as Rex Tugwell and Raymond Moley during the 1930s and Welles and Hull during the forties. Many historians have noted the "administrative disarray" of Roosevelt's White House. Some have suggested that, at least in part, Roosevelt deliberately cultivated bureaucratic disorder so that no single subordinate could seriously challenge the president's authority. They add that disorder might, of course, also allow the president to blame mistakes on others.[27] Perhaps, but two other explanations are also plausible: (1) what looked to outsiders like bureaucratic indecision and/or disarray allowed FDR to keep his options open; and (2) it was *not* purposeful, instead resulting from the degree to which FDR remained uncertain about some very taxing and complex issues, including postwar organization.

In a way, White House disarray did not make much difference. Preoccupied with military affairs, FDR's murky approach to the subject of postwar organization paralleled that of Congress and the public. With hindsight, we see that 1943 was the year when Washington declared in principle its willingness to join a postwar security organization. That was all it declared, though admittedly that was a lot. It wasn't until 1944 that U.S. officials—beyond a small group in the State Department already working on the problem—began giving serious thought to the shape of that organization.

Before 1944, a few developments, such as the administration's sponsorship of a 1943 Hot Springs, Virginia, conference that led to the UN Food and Agriculture Organization (FAO), and administration support for the formation of the UN Relief and Rehabilitation Administration (UNRRA), suggest that more was involved than simply the principle of American membership in a postwar UN that would work to keep the peace. Both the FAO meeting and UNRRA remind us that, like the old League of Nations, the new postwar organization would incorporate social and humanitarian functions.[28] The food and agriculture conference, which met during May and June, created an interim organization that included not only the states signing the Declaration of the United Nations but "associated states." Membership in UNRRA was expected to follow a similar pattern. While reminiscent of membership on technical agencies affiliated with the League (the United States, for instance, although not a League member, joined the International Labor Organization and the disarmament conferences), FAO and UNRRA membership helped to establish an important precedent when, in 1945, the Allies inched toward organizational universality.

The origins of the FAO and the UNRRA are notable for two other reasons. The first is the leadership role of the Americans. The FAO conference not only convened in the United States, but FDR addressed its delegates. UNRRA, meanwhile, emerged specifically from an agreement among the Big Four; American influence was demonstrated by the appointment of former New York governor Herbert H. Lehman, chief of the State Department's office of refugee relief, to head the agency. The second is the way that formation of these agencies, particularly UNRRA, contributed to additional executive-legislative tension. When the president sought to join the United States to UNRRA by means of an executive agreement, Senator Connally and the Foreign Relations Committee protested following objections by the Republican minority leader, Arthur Vandenberg. After some unusually harsh words between Connally and Hull, the administration agreed to ask for a joint resolution of Congress, requiring a majority vote of both houses, following the signing of the executive agreement.[29] The compromise worked. UNRRA began functioning by year's end, and FDR had been given another lesson in senatorial sensitivities.

SHAPING THE UN VISION

The State Department's Informal Agenda Group, which had begun function-ing in 1943 under Pasvolsky's direction, became the real center of American efforts to design the UN. The group contained old League of Nations men like Isaiah Bowman; internationalist business executives like Myron Taylor and Edward Stettinius from U.S. Steel (Stettinius had become undersecretary when Hull dismissed Welles); two trusted FDR advisers, Ben Cohen from the White House staff and Wall Street financier Norman H. Davis; as well as Jimmy Dunn and Stanley K. Hornbeck from the State Department. These were, for the most part, practical men who fully understood that FDR would not risk his political future for a collective-security organization during a presidential elec-tion year. They had learned from 1919 that never again should the State Department propose grand plans that the public or Congress would likely reject. While internationalists became increasingly excited following the pub-lication of Sumner Welles's *A Time for Decision*,[30] as well as works by League of Nations Association activists such as James T. Shotwell and Philip Nash advocating League-inspired schemes of organization, the Informal Agenda group worked quietly, producing its first concrete proposal for the new organi-zation by the end of the year. Hull sent it to the president, who approved it a month later.

Despite their skepticism about the League, the Informal Agenda Group sketched out an organization that was clearly its descendant. Like the old Geneva-based organization, the proposed UN would have two main bodies: a deliberative assembly, corresponding to the old League assembly, and a smaller executive council, reminiscent of the League Council. The latter would con-tain the Big Four holding permanent seats (and possibly an absolute veto). Its main responsibility would be to keep the peace. In other ways, too, the plan looked leaguelike, for the new organization would incorporate a world court as well as technical and social agencies. Yet its differences from the League helped to explain its appeal to FDR, particularly in the way the proposed structure reduced assembly power and elevated Big Four power. Moreover, it did nothing to abridge national sovereignty.[31] During the next 18 months, culminating in the San Francisco Conference of 1945, American and other officials would spill much more ink over the subject of UN authority, but the Informal Agenda Group's outline would remain intact.

During early 1944, neither the White House nor the State Department said much publicly about the plan. The Informal Agenda Group—by now renamed the Informal Political Agenda Group (its name would change two more times before it disbanded)—continued its labors, producing a more detailed design in March and then sending it to Hull and other officials for review. By then, newspaper columnists and congressional critics from both sides increased their demands for information. With private groups like the Commission to Study the Organization of Peace favoring UN military units and isolationists like Wisconsin's Senator Robert M. LaFollette denouncing powerful international authority, Secretary Hull, who always worried about releasing too much rather than too little information, resolved to appease Congress by discussing the work of the Agenda Group. Meeting with Connally's Foreign Relations Committee, Hull proposed that the Senate form a new Committee of Eight, which Connally chose to chair himself. It had an influential membership, ranging from LaFollette to internationalist Warren Austin. It also included Senator Vandenberg, who during the next year-and-a-half would become its most important member. Vandenberg, who sometimes resembled former British prime minister David Lloyd George in his opportunism and inconsistency, had been an outspoken isolationist before Pearl Harbor. After the Japanese attack, he moderated his views, although the public still saw him as the quintessential America Firster. His general agreement with the work of the Agenda Group would become a critical ingredient in Hull's campaign to create a united executive-legislative front on the subject of postwar planning.

What made Vandenberg and the other senators so receptive to the Agenda Group's work were the very things that appealed to FDR. The draft plan, which added detail to the Agenda Group's original organization plan of December 1943, contained no radical proposals, no "one world" visions. It lacked even the provision for an air force that Wallace, Clark Eichelberger, and their supporters in CSOP had recommended since 1942. Each of the Big Four would have a permanent seat and a permanent veto, and only the council could ask members for troop contributions in order to keep the peace. State Department officials assured the senators that the United States would confer with Latin American states on issues of hemispheric importance and that no American troops would be committed to action by the "new League" without senatorial approval. After the initial meeting with Hull, the skeptical Vandenberg praised the plan as "*conservative* from a nationalist standpoint." He noted that it would not permit the United States to be brought into war without congressional approval, and viewed it as "anything but a wild-eyed internationalist dream of a world State."[32] Even LaFollette, who had opposed the Connally Resolution, seemed reassured, though he wanted no promises made in advance of a peace conference.

So Hull, despite election-year pressures, had made progress, although it was obscured by senatorial reservations concerning the timing involved in setting up the organization as well as by serious questions about the shape of the peace to be preserved. Hull, therefore, could not persuade the Committee of Eight to endorse the Agenda Group's draft publicly. Neither, though, did any of them denounce it. That was significant, because by June 1944 both Democrats and Republicans were gearing up for their national party conventions.

As they did, the president launched a preemptive political strike. On June 15, he ordered his press secretary to release the broad features of the State Department's plan for the postwar organization in a deliberately low-key manner. Speculation about the plan suddenly ended. The Republicans, with their upcoming party convention scheduled to begin less than two weeks later, could no longer hope to define the terms of the debate. And although the Republicans refused to endorse Hull's plan, preferring instead to follow Vandenberg with a more general restatement of the Mackinac declaration, the Democrats enthusiastically renominated FDR for a fourth term and, with language drawn from the Moscow Declaration, endorsed his approach to postwar organization. It is true that neither party offered unequivocal support for its internationalist wing. The Republicans repudiated Wendell Wilkie, and the Democrats, with FDR's blessing, dumped Vice President Wallace. Nonetheless, neither party did anything to raise the ghost of Henry Cabot Lodge.

By the summer of 1944, the Roosevelt administration could confidently anticipate little partisan warfare over postwar planning. Meetings between Secretary Hull and John Foster Dulles, who served as the foreign policy spokesman for moderate Republican presidential candidate Thomas Dewey of New York, were designed to insulate the subject from what Dewey called "the abyss of power politics." They succeeded; the two men concluded an agreement that virtually erased the issue of collective security from the presidential campaign. Dulles remained an outspoken internationalist who allayed Dewey's fears that the administration might create a permanent alliance of Great Powers with police authority to dictate to the rest of the world. When, just before the election, the issue of using force surfaced in the press, it was not Dewey but rather Republican internationalist Joseph Ball who raised the subject. He quarreled not with FDR but with Dewey. Indeed, the Minnesota senator believed Dewey was too moderate, too unwilling to condemn the isolationists in his own party. Ball threw his support to the president. Poor Dewey found himself damned by both wings of his party, the isolationists and the internationalists. In a way, his cooperation with FDR became a handicap. FDR must have been pleased indeed. Naturally wanting to shield himself from Republican attacks, he successfully depoliticized the issue during one of the most critical periods leading to the birth of the UN—when American, British, Soviet, and Chinese delegations met at Dumbarton Oaks in Washington, D.C. during the late summer of 1944 to hammer together the essentials of the postwar plan. When collective security reemerged as a political issue, it was too late to hurt him.[33]

THE CONFERENCE AT DUMBARTON OAKS

The Dumbarton Oaks Conference defined the limits of U.S. cooperation with the other Big Four powers. American internationalists, both inside and outside Washington, had occasionally approached the issue of postwar organization as if only American views counted. Roosevelt and Hull knew better. Although Hull at the Moscow Conference and FDR at Teheran had discussed postwar designs with their allies, most American planners, including Pasvolsky's Agenda Group and the senatorial Committee of Eight, had been permitted no serious consultation with foreign governments.[34] Dumbarton Oaks changed all that.

Real preparation for the Dumbarton Oaks Conference began as soon as Pasvolsky's draft for a UN reached FDR's desk on December 29, 1943. State Department officials informed their British and Soviet counterparts five weeks later that the time for joint discussions had arrived and asked both to prepare draft plans for mutual circulation. This took longer than expected. Robert Hilderbrand, the leading historian of the Dumbarton Oaks Conference, claims that America's two chief allies were even more tardy than the State Department in formulating postwar plans.[35] Not until the end of 1942 did the British Foreign Office, under the direction of Permanent Undersecretary Alexander Cadogan and chief of the Economic and Reconstruction Department Gladwyn Jebb, begin to formulate working plans. The Soviets, perhaps because Stalin spent so much time on military matters, delayed drafting working documents until after the Americans requested to see their plans in February 1944. Although a group under Ivan Maisky apparently had been studying the subject for some months, it would not be until the opening of the Dumbarton Oaks Conference that Moscow finally circulated its "Memorandum on the International Security Organisation."

The Soviet approach to international organization had been deeply influenced by fear of Germany. Having endured the destruction of thousands of Soviet villages and millions of its citizens, the Kremlin saw a new organization primarily as a means to prevent future German aggression. Stalin had already told FDR that he favored more of a European council than a universal organization, and he found FDR's plans for the Four Policemen understandably attractive because they accented the role of the only countries that could, he believed, maintain order. He valued security, not international law or morality, and only his belated recognition that the Americans would not join a *strictly* European security alliance persuaded him to support a universal organization.

Like Stalin, the British also approached the peace in terms of European security but viewed a successor to the League as more than simply a security organization. Cabinet planning for the postwar period produced plenty of disagreement, especially between Whitehall and Churchill, which may account for the delay in London's consideration of the subject. For the most part, the Foreign Office, headed by Anthony Eden, favored a universal organization that would include not only the United States but the USSR and China in a genuinely cooperative arrangement. The prime minister, on the other hand, an inveterate anticommunist who feared what he occasionally described as Russian barbarism, deeply distrusted the Soviets. For reasons very different than Stalin's, he, too, initially favored a council of Europe that would include the United States to offset Soviet influence (he even flirted with the idea of a council without Soviet membership). Presumably, such a council would be more sympathetic to British colonial interests than an organization dominated by the Russians. Like FDR, Churchill preferred a formula that was based less on universal membership than on regional responsibilities. Regionalism, claims Hilderbrand, was for Churchill a "matter of common sense."[36] Neighbors would be most threatened by a dispute and would therefore be most inclined to prevent disputes from becoming wars. Eventually, American support for a more universal organization, first evidenced at Quebec in 1943, led Churchill to moderate his own support for a regional solution. Britain's need for U.S. assistance, combined with emerging British-Soviet competition, persuaded the prime minister to acquiesce in Hull's insistence (and increasingly FDR's) that any organization must be worldwide.

Still, Churchill's conversion did not come easily. As late as a month before the Dumbarton Oaks Conference, he continued to confound the British Foreign Office and the U.S. State Department with proposals for regional councils (at first for Europe, then for other areas). Foreign Office efforts to compromise the two approaches were far from satisfactory, especially when Churchill, according to Hilderbrand, simply lost interest in the subject during the middle of 1944. Despite position papers produced by the Foreign Office, including a critical aide memoir of July 14, 1943, and interdepartmental committee memoranda in the spring of 1944, the British had established their position less clearly than had the Soviets by the time the conference actually began.

In the weeks preceding the conference, FDR, Stalin, and Churchill dealt with one final question: the status of China. Stalin had been so hostile to Chinese interests that he flatly refused to permit Nanking representation at the Teheran conference. China was not, he asserted, a Great Power, and he would do nothing to help it become one. Moreover, because the USSR was still formally at peace with Japan, the Soviet leader insisted that China not be a part of the Dumbarton Oaks meeting. Churchill, too, never considered China a Great Power; not only did China not warrant the title, but the British leader believed that treating China as a great power might damage Britain's crippled interests in the Far East. Only FDR among the Big Three insisted on China's Great Power status, and therefore only Roosevelt wanted to bring China to Dumbarton Oaks. The British, seeking U.S. cooperation on more important questions, conceded to Roosevelt on this score. Soviet opposition to meeting with China was more serious. The result was that FDR got his way, but only after he finessed the problem by organizing Dumbarton Oaks into two phases: Dumbarton I without China and Dumbarton II with China but without the USSR.

The conference opened on August 21, 1944, and was, ironically, dominated by the country that had rejected the League in 1920. The British and Soviet drafts did not compare in detail or influence with that of the State Department, submitted to the other allies on July 18 in a memorandum called "Tentative Proposals for an International Organization." Evan Luard, the main historian of the UN, notes that only the U.S. proposal, which was itself an elaboration of the Informal Agenda Group's draft of December 29, included a skeletal outline of the organization. As a result, the U.S. plan became the working draft for the conference, providing the main terms of the agenda and forming the basis of what later became the UN Charter.[37]

Dumbarton Oaks, the Georgetown estate of an American diplomat that had been gifted to Harvard University and converted into an elegant museum of Byzantine studies, hosted 39 delegates headed by American Undersecretary of State Stettinius, Britain's Foreign Office Permanent Undersecretary Cadogan, and the 35-year-old Soviet ambassador to the United States, Andrei Gromyko. There was nothing ceremonial about their roles. Along with four of their colleagues—Pasvolsky and Dunn for the United States, Jebb for Britain, and Soviet Arkady Sobolev—they constituted the Joint Steering Committee which made or reviewed all key decisions. They appointed a series of subcommittees and authorized creation of the Formulation Group, which became the analytical heart of the conference, and the lawyer-dominated Drafting Committee, which gave shape to what later became the UN Charter. They also resolved to work in secret, a decision that inevitably raised suspicions among American isolationists. And although the Chinese, who received regular briefings on the conference's first phase, leaked enough information about the proceedings to insure James Reston of the *New York Times* a Pulitzer Prize, the rumors stemming from their policy of secrecy wounded State Department officials caught between their desire to mobilize popular support for the UN and the need for confidentially during sensitive negotiations.[38]

Confidentiality proved necessary. Meeting from August 21 to October 7, the planners tackled plenty of divisive issues, including the Great Power veto, the authority of smaller nations, universal membership, a UN police force, and mandatory court powers. Their frequent disagreements often stemmed from different conceptions about the essential purpose of the new organization. Would it mainly exist to protect their security? To preserve the peace? To create the economic and social conditions that would make war less likely? To guarantee an international rule of law? While wrestling with (and, at times, evading) these fundamental questions, the American, British, and Russian planners who met at Dumbarton Oaks reached quick agreement on the organization's structure. As outlined in the American "Tentative Proposals," it would contain an administrative secretariat, a large assembly, a smaller council including the Great Powers, and a world court. It mirrored the old League, burying the idea of a peace imposed by the Great Powers alone.

By agreeing at the outset to an assembly of (nearly) universal membership, the Big Three avoided a confrontation with the smaller nations that they probably could not have won anyway. Having enjoyed the fruits of international recognition for 20 years at Geneva, the smaller countries that had signed or associated themselves with the United Nations Declaration of January 1, 1942, would not likely have surrendered their organizational voice without a huge fight. No one relished that fight. The assembly-related discussions at Dumbarton Oaks, therefore, focused on subsidiary issues: How universal would the assembly be? What powers would the assembly have in comparison to the smaller council? What size majority would be necessary when the assembly took action?

As they had in outlining the shape of the new organization, the Americans again set the terms of the debate. Although FDR's original Four Policemen scheme would have left no room for an assembly, the Americans now proposed an assembly based on the "sovereign equality" of all "peace-loving states" (the latter term initially proposed by Molotov at the Moscow Conference). There was no resistance to the exclusion of the fascist states, even though, as Hilderbrand notes, these were the states most in need of membership (the term "peace-loving states" would be deleted at the San Francisco conference in June 1945). Much more troublesome was Gromyko's demand that all 16 Soviet republics be admitted to the UN. Stalin undoubtedly saw this as a way to guarantee the USSR a kind of parity with Britain and her dominion partners and with Washington and her client states in Latin America. But Stettinius objected strenuously, taken by surprise even though the Soviets had hinted at the subject some months earlier. FDR, too, had not expected the issue to arise. "My God!" he exclaimed, when informed that the subject had reemerged.[39] He would refer to it as the X matter, fearing that publicity about the Soviet demand might otherwise doom Senate approval of the UN. Because neither side would budge, Stettinius and Gromyko could only agree to defer further consideration of the question.

The issue of assembly authority proved much easier to settle. For the most part, all three delegations, committed to maximize the authority of their own countries while protecting the UN from the League's collective-security paralysis, viewed the assembly as a forum exclusively for discussion. The authority to enforce peace, they agreed, should be located in the smaller executive council (later to be called the Security Council), which would include the Great Powers. The assembly would be given the power to "recommend"—and only to recommend—on the subject of preventing war as well as on economic and social matters.

On some issues of marginal importance, the United States found itself outvoted by the British and Soviets. An American suggestion to incorporate a system of weighted voting in the assembly—especially on budgetary matters—got nowhere; the Americans also backed away from the idea of a Great Power veto in the assembly (an issue that nearly wrecked the conference when later applied to the council). The Americans also failed in their attempt to give the assembly, not the council, primary responsibility for selecting the secretary-general. Nervous about the authority of smaller countries, all three delegations agreed that "important" assembly votes would require a two-thirds majority; other issues, a simple majority.

Precisely because the planners limited the authority of the assembly, they could afford to compromise. Not so when it came to the council. All three powers quickly agreed that the council should contain, like its predecessor in Geneva, a small number of members—they settled on 11—among them the Great Powers holding permanent seats. The UN's authority to prevent aggression and peacefully settle disputes would be centered in the council. Where the League council only had the right to recommend enforcement action, the UN council would have the authority to order it. For this to happen, all three delegations took for granted the importance of Great Power cooperation, but they did not agree on much more. They disagreed, for instance, on the inclusion of France on the council. Reflecting FDR's hostility to French general Charles DeGaulle, the Americans opposed an invitation to Paris until assured of a friendly government, a position overruled by the other two allies. On another matter, too, the British and Russians rebuffed Washington. FDR, backed up by the Latin American specialists in the State Department, remembered that Brazil had left the League in 1926 when denied a permanent council seat. He therefore ordered Hull and Stettinius to support Brazil's claim for a seat in the new council. British and Russian opposition, combined with the fears of Stettinius and Pasvolsky that other Latin American countries might demand seats and that the Brazilian seat would again open the Pandora's box of regionalism, eventually persuaded the president to back down.[40]

The authority of the council, especially as it related to military force, constituted a third important area of Big Three disagreement. With the Soviets demanding mandatory council authority to settle disputes, and the British adamant that the council recommend rather than require peaceful settlement of disputes, the Americans found themselves not just in the middle but divided among themselves. Both FDR and the U.S. delegation first leaned toward mandatory power, then shifted toward the British position as the president retreated from the Four Policemen concept. The Americans also reversed their position on an international air force. At first they supported it, then they abandoned the idea in favor a plan where each nation would maintain control over its own military units (not just air units) that would be made available to the UN. The British had moved in the opposite direction, first opposed to an international force, then favoring it as Churchill became more involved in the work of the conference. The Russians, most disillusioned with the League's impotence, joined Churchill in demanding a genuinely international force but ultimately bowed to American objections that postponed, and then killed, the proposal.

The major dispute by far revolved around the question of council votes and vetoes. Ever since the Four Policemen idea surfaced, all three foreign offices accepted the necessity of a Great Power permanent veto. Great Powers, after all, wanted the privileges of great power. They disagreed, however, on the morality of vetoing UN action—or even about vetoing *consideration* of action—involving disputes to which they were parties. The Soviets, perhaps reflecting an ideology that assumed all capitalist countries to be potential enemies, insisted on an unrestricted veto. The British favored the old League policy that prohibited a veto over action involving oneself, while the Americans were of two minds. Most U.S. officials, led by Pasvolsky, believed that, at least when it came to disputes that threatened the peace, simple justice demanded that the Great Powers apply to themselves the rules pertaining to smaller countries (which meant no veto). These officials were the idealists. Other officials, supporting an implied promise that Hull had already made to Senators Connally and Vandenberg, argued that the Senate would never ratify a UN treaty that denied the United States an ironclad veto. For the most part, the idealists, with FDR's support, prevailed within the U.S. delegation. They refused to compromise with the Russians. Gromyko proved equally uncompromising. By mid-September, the Dumbarton Oaks Conference neared collapse.

Robert Hilderbrand is probably correct in attributing the impasse to events in Eastern Europe. Before Dumbarton Oaks, many important Washington officials agreed with Moscow on the veto; by mid-September, most of these officials had completely reversed themselves. Increasingly, they saw Washington and Moscow less as allies than adversaries; and a quarrel over the composition of the Polish government—that sharply intensified after the tragic 1944 Warsaw uprising—confirmed their worst fears. With Stalin determined to control Eastern Europe and with the West determined to limit Soviet control, the absolute veto became both symbol and instrument of Soviet-American differences.

Ironically, by the end of Dumbarton I, Churchill's suspicions of Stalin swung the British toward favoring the same absolute veto that Stalin demanded. The British bulldog may have done this to protect British interests in Eastern Europe, or to protect his empire against anticolonial sentiment, or both. By siding with the Russians, Churchill isolated the Americans, effectively ending further discussion of the issue at Dumbarton Oaks. To save the UN, the Americans did the only thing they could: they deferred further discussion until 1945.

The Chinese phase of Dumbarton Oaks took only a week. Because the Americans embraced the fiction of China as a Great Power, they insisted on bringing China into the talks. No more than the British and Soviets, however, did they intend to offer the Chinese a role in decision making, especially where Chinese objections might have the effect of overturning hard-won compromises already accepted by the Big Three. The main demands of the Chinese—for an international air force, for a League-style guarantee of territorial integrity, for a definition of aggression, and for compulsory World Court jurisdiction—all pointed in the direction of a UN with much sharper teeth than the Big Three desired. The Chinese may have clarified some important issues, such as the effect of abstentions on calculating council majorities, but they did not substantially alter the framework hammered out in the conference's earlier phase. In a world at war, second-class powers were treated as second-class powers.[41]

Dumbarton Oaks left a number of important issues unresolved: the veto, the size of the council majority, colonial trusteeships, the "X matter" of Soviet membership, the establishment of a world court, the military powers of the UN. While some of these would not be addressed until the San Francisco Conference, the Big Three, meeting at Yalta in February 1945, made enough progress to guarantee that there would in fact be a conference near the Golden Gate. At Yalta, they solved the thorny problem of Soviet representation by compromising on the issue. Instead of 16 Soviet members, Roosevelt and Churchill agreed on three, despite unhappiness among some members of their delegations. According to Stettinius, Stalin and Churchill agreed that the United States could also have additional seats if it proved politically necessary for FDR. It didn't.[42]

A more important issue—the veto—also moved closer to a compromise at Yalta. At Dumbarton Oaks, Pasvolsky had proposed that a Great Power could apply the veto to security and enforcement matters (meaning the application of economic or military force) involving itself, but could not veto procedures related to the peaceful settlement of a dispute to which it was a party. For the latter, a majority of seven votes—half way between a simple and a two-thirds majority—would be necessary. The Soviets had summarily rejected the proposal in September. At Yalta, Stalin reversed himself, with the Americans reluctantly accepting the new three-seat formula on Soviet membership as the price of Soviet compromise on the veto.

The Yalta Conference also saw agreement in principle on granting France a council seat with a permanent veto, and setting up a trusteeship system for former German and Japanese colonies. The Americans, who had rejected any connection to the old League mandate system, nevertheless embraced the trusteeship concept, and the British, reassured once it became clear that Roosevelt would not insist on placing British colonies in trust, accepted it too. They would work on the details at San Francisco.

Unlike Dumbarton Oaks where UN issues took center stage, the leaders at Yalta had other things on their mind. Roosevelt wanted to guarantee Soviet entry into the Pacific War; Stalin wanted to secure Soviet influence in Poland; Churchill sought to protect British interests in the Balkans. With so much to do in such a short time, these men did not follow up their agreement on UN issues with much detail. That left many important questions unanswered. For instance, could a Great Power veto consideration by the council of enforcement action, or just veto the enforcement action itself? No one yet knew (nor did they know that they did not know), leaving plenty of room for haggling at San Francisco. But all agreed that the San Francisco Conference should begin soon, even before the war ended. FDR insisted on March 1945, though it wasn't until April that the San Francisco meeting would occur, and then without FDR.

In the meantime, the State Department continued to study such matters as world court jurisdiction and trusteeship, while Stettinius, now the secretary of state, attended a conference in Mexico City where his Latin American counterparts let him know that at San Francisco they would insist on a regional seat in the proposed UN council, on increased authority for the assembly, and on Argentine membership. This last demand, Stettinius understood, forecast trouble with the Soviets, for Argentina had been the one hemispheric country that had sided with the Axis. But the most important development concerned regional cooperation. The Latin Americans sought to create cooperative military arrangements that would survive the war, but that might conflict with UN enforcement provisions reached at and after Dumbarton Oaks. The State Department, already wary of congressional backing for the Monroe Doctrine, tried to sidestep any final action in this area. It sought to prevent the creation of a Latin American bloc that would undoubtedly intensify Stalin's fear of being isolated at the UN. The final communique from Mexico City noted that any arrangements among the American republics must be not only consistent with the principles of the new UN but subject to review at San Francisco.[43]

FDR died on April 12, 1945. By then, the shape of the proposed organization had changed numerous times. From the Four Policemen to the compromise over the veto, FDR and his subordinates in the State Department had displayed both flexibility and pragmatism. The looming Cold War with the USSR and, to a lesser extent, American uneasiness with British colonial ambitions, had substantially influenced Washington's outlook. As Hilderbrand puts it, American policy makers, especially on the question of voting and vetoes, vacillated "between structuring the new United Nations to further [their] own postwar ambitions and using it to prevent the British and Russians from furthering theirs."[44] Washington's approach reflected a curious mixture of idealism and realism, a pattern that would reappear at the conference in San Francisco, which was now set for April. For the moment, at least, the Americans felt reassured by the general support of their Latin American neighbors. Using the language of universalism while enjoying the support of states within their own sphere of influence, Washington inevitably reinforced Soviet skepticism. Such skepticism would make San Francisco a tough act for the State Department. The new president, Harry S. Truman, would finesse his way through the conference with the help of the British and some influential Senate Republicans. Except for the UN Charter's military instruments and enforcement provisions, and the more powerful council with its permanent vetoes, what he ended up with would look surprisingly like the old League of Nations.

chapter 2

SAN FRANCISCO

No president's first day in office is remembered more vividly than that of Harry Truman: the grief-stricken Mrs. Roosevelt asking the new president, "Is there anything that we can do for you?"; Truman's appeal to the White House reporters to pray for him; Secretary of War Henry L. Stimson solemnly informing him about the Manhattan Project; the new president's first public announcement—that the San Francisco Conference would go on as planned.

Truman, formerly a senator from Missouri with only limited experience in the foreign field, had played no significant role in the making of the UN. FDR's selection of Truman as a vice-presidential running mate in 1944 was based mainly on political and geographical considerations. Truman's chief rival for the post, former South Carolina senator and Supreme Court justice James F. Byrnes, had more prestige and influence; and Byrnes, who sat at Roosevelt's side during the Yalta Conference, also had more foreign experience. The result was a marriage of connivance after FDR's death. Byrnes lent Truman a degree of authority during the new president's first few months in office; in return, the president promised to appoint Byrnes as secretary of state following the San Francisco Conference.[1]

Secretary of State Edward Stettinius, who had replaced Hull the previous November, knew nothing about Truman's plans for Byrnes. Although Stettinius's gifts as a diplomat were decidedly modest, his conspicuous role at Dumbarton Oaks made it difficult for Truman to reduce his participation at the upcoming San Francisco Conference. Moreover, Stettinius offered certain advantages. He was unlikely to challenge a new president who was just learning his way around the world of diplomacy, and he was willing to be an energetic salesman for the president's program.[2]

Indeed, Stettinius's enthusiasm for an international security organization made him fully supportive of the public relations campaign sponsored by internationalists in advance of the San Francisco Conference. He assigned two of his chief assistants, Assistant Secretary Archibald Macleish and MacLeish's aide, Adlai Stevenson, to help coordinate the massive education and advocacy effort in support of the UN, and it was a job they did with relish. Between February and mid-April of 1945, virtually every important agency in Washington (led by the State Department), every important internationalist organization (led by the American Association of the United Nations and the Carnegie Endowment for International Peace), and scores of civic groups, churches, and League of Women Voters chapters, mobilized support for the Dumbarton Oaks proposals. They capped their efforts with a "Dumbarton Oaks Week" in mid-April, perhaps the most ambitious American effort at public education concerning a foreign-policy issue during the twentieth century.[3]

Just as generals plan strategy to fight the last war, so internationalists during the spring of 1945 were planning to prevent the last war. They feared the return of an isolationist resurgence that they believed had torpedoed Wilson's efforts to join the country to the League of Nations. Internationalists overestimated the influence of their adversaries, however; World War II had seriously weakened the kind of isolationist appeal that had motivated Wilson's opponents after World War I. Even so, isolationists inside Washington, such as Robert LaFollette Jr., and those outside Washington, such as Gerald L. K. Smith, were still making plenty of noise. There were even a few internationalist opponents of the Dumbarton Oaks formula who decried the power that the UN would leave in the hands of the Great Powers. These individuals argued that the new world organization would actually undermine collective security. Fearful of both the isolationists and a split among internationalists, the pro-UN coalition continued its campaign not only beyond the April 25 opening ceremony of the San Francisco Conference, but beyond the Charter signing on June 26.

With the public relations campaign sizzling, Washington officials prepared for the San Francisco Conference in other ways. Truman endorsed his predecessor's decision to send a small official delegation to the conference rather than a large one representing many different areas of American life. To mollify the special interests, a group of 42 "consultants" would attend along with the official U.S. representatives.

Stettinius would head the official group. In addition, recalling Wilson's risky 1919 decision to ignore Senate Republicans when appointing delegates to the Paris peace conference, FDR had appointed Republican Senator Arthur Vandenberg to attend along with the Democratic leader of the Senate, Texan New Dealer Tom Connally. The other delegates played less important roles: Dean Virginia Gildersleeve of Barnard College was a link to women's groups and the educational community; Naval Lt. Commander Harold Stassen repre-

The UN Charter at the San Francisco Conference as Egyptian delegates sign. June 26, 1945.
(UN/DPI Photo)

sented, in a sense, the 12 million men and women in uniform; and two individuals represented the lower House, Democratic Congressman Sol Bloom who chaired the Foreign Affairs Committee, and Republican Charles Eaton. Ill health prevented Cordell Hull, originally named to the delegation, from joining his colleagues in San Francisco.

Of the official delegates, Stettinius and Vandenberg were the key players. As General Dwight Eisenhower helped to keep a potentially fractious military coalition together in Europe between 1942 and 1945, so Stettinius maintained harmony among his diplomatic counterparts in San Francisco, a real accomplishment for a man whose talents have been exaggerated by no historian. "A magnificent job," said Vandenberg of the secretary's performance.[4] Stettinius might have said the same of Vandenberg, a former isolationist whose commitment to a world organization grew immensely during the conference and who played a critically important role in reconciling members of his party to the final agreement.

A less visible cast of official delegates played important supporting roles, especially John Foster Dulles, who served as Vandenberg's key adviser; Leo Pasvolsky, who remained the single most knowledgeable American at the conference; and Nelson Rockefeller, whose assistance on Latin American affairs helped to resolve some of the most difficult negotiations. A number of other State Department aides, such as Harley Notter, Charles Taussig, and Jimmy Dunn, also played important roles, as did Alger Hiss, a Pasvolsky assistant named as the secretary-general of the conference.

Precisely because the conference became embroiled in delicate negotiations that, to Stettinius, necessitated great privacy, the 42 consultants had less influence than expected. Nevertheless, they refused to become doormats for the administration. More than a third were already members of Clark Eichelberger's Commission to Study the Organization of Peace. Well-informed, organized, and opinionated, they contributed significantly to a number of decisions left unresolved at Dumbarton Oaks, including those that helped to strengthen the human rights role of the UN and to provide for a separate Economic and Social Council (ECOSOC).[5] The consultants, who insisted that the Great Powers direct their attention to abstract issues like human rights, had some important allies among those powers. Senator Vandenberg, for instance, spoke eloquently on their behalf, and even President Truman, a man not given to flights of abstraction, sympathized with those who wanted a global "bill of rights" included in the Charter.[6]

But the issue of human rights was little more than a sideshow to the real work of San Francisco. Most important, the conference produced a nearly universal organization. As a successor to the League, the UN adhered with surprising consistency to the plans sketched out at Dumbarton Oaks. The organization would place more emphasis than the League had on issues of imperialism and social equality; and the various means to enforce peace would be much more carefully outlined in its charter. Like its predecessor, the UN created great expectations. Its lofty goals, reinforced by the April 1945 public relations campaign in support of the Dumbarton Oaks proposals, made American backing for the organization a virtual certainty despite some bluffing by U.S. officials during the course of the negotiations.

Paradoxically, although the conference was designed to revitalize internationalism, San Francisco subtly reflected an American retreat from internationalism. Just two weeks after the delegates began their conversations in California, Hitler committed suicide and the war in Europe ended. Although Japan's army fought on, the Allied officials who drafted the UN Charter fully understood that they were not redefining the world at war so much as defining the postwar peace. They would not do this in a diplomatic vacuum. The impending defeat of Germany and Japan prepared the ground for the as yet undefined Soviet-American rivalry. Immediately after V-E day, the Truman administration suspended Lend-Lease military aid to the Soviets and failed to grant Moscow agricultural credits. Disagreement over Polish and other Eastern Europe issues continued to fester, although Secretary Stettinius tried to deemphasize them until the San Francisco delegates adjourned. He was only partly successful. Although he managed to place some of these issues on the back burner, the Conference moved others to the forefront.

In short, the U.S.-USSR rivalry profoundly influenced the shape of postwar diplomacy and produced a set of assumptions among American policy makers quite different from those held by Wilsonians in 1919. Those earlier internationalists had created a collective-security organization whose main weapon would be mobilizing the moral sentiment of mankind, not the use of economic or military force. The League's failure, as well as the souring of Soviet-American friendship, made policy makers less sanguine by 1945. They modified their commitment to Wilsonian internationalism at the same time that they designed ways to protect more traditional national interests. Although this turn toward nationalism became an overarching theme of U.S. policy for the entire Cold War, not until 1947 did it become dominant. Until then, American policy was caught in a tug-of-war between nationalism and internationalism and nowhere was this more evident than at the San Francisco Conference itself.[7]

FINDING COMMON GROUND

In actuality, the San Francisco Conference involved less diplomacy than meets the eye. U.S.-Soviet quarrels often masked areas of considerable agreement, while some celebrated disputes contained little disagreement of substance. For instance, the highly publicized dispute over the number of Soviet seats (Stalin first asked for 16 and finally settled for three) was more symbolic than real. FDR had originally promised Stalin the two additional seats (for the Ukraine and Byelorussia) at Yalta. Stettinius realized by early March that FDR had politically blundered, an opinion confirmed by the public hue and cry after the *New York Herald Tribune* broke the story in March 1945. Administration officials scrambled to undo the damage, but it was too late. The Soviets refused to budge, and both Truman and Stettinius concluded that they would do more harm by breaking FDR's promise to Stalin than by accepting the two additional seats. The new Truman administration attempted to mollify its critics by announcing that, contrary to speculation, the United States would *not* request additional seats for itself; it also announced that although the Ukraine and Byelorussia would have membership at the UN, they would not be invited to the San Francisco Conference. Nevertheless, despite all the noise generated by the controversy, the American delegates understood that membership in the Security Council was the critical issue, not the General Assembly where the three Soviet delegations would appear. There is not one single document—official or private—suggesting that U.S. officials feared the extra seats would seriously inconvenience the United States.[8]

Nor was squabbling over the Soviet seats the only quarrel that generated more heat than light. While the Americans wrestled with Moscow over the size of Soviet representation, they simultaneously confronted angry Latin American delegates who demanded the seating of Argentina, the one Western Hemispheric country that had offered the fascists a benevolent neutrality during the war. Indeed, the Latin Americans threatened to block the membership of the Ukraine and Byelorussia if the USSR vetoed Argentina's membership. The Truman administration found itself in the middle of an unanticipated argument, one made even more complicated when the Soviets demanded the admission of their client Communist government based in Lublin, Poland, and not a rival Polish group that had spent the war as exiles in London. This last demand produced opposition from the British and from anticommunist Polish-Americans (including many in Michigan, Senator Vandenberg's home state). With the real issues of the conference not yet even on the table, Stettinius and his colleagues split the difference: they brokered a deal entailing Latin Americans support for the two additional Soviet republics in return for Moscow's acceptance of Argentina. The compromise left Poland temporarily out in the diplomatic cold.

A Soviet-American dispute over the presidency of the conference further delayed the main agenda. Vyaschlev Molotov, the Soviet foreign minister who attended the first two weeks of the conference, insisted that each of the Big Four Powers—the United States, USSR, Britain, and France—supply a president so that each would have equal status at the conference. The Americans balked, arguing that the host country traditionally provided conference leadership. A Solomonic proposal by Britain's Anthony Eden, establishing a rotating chairmanship under Stettinius's overall presidency, resolved the matter. Once again, much ado over nothing, though the dispute deepened a growing sense of American-Soviet mistrust reaffirmed later by more substantive conflicts.[9]

The most vexing of these substantive issues concerned the security council veto. The Dumbarton Oaks proposals had foreseen a small but powerful Security Council, although no final voting formula emerged before San Francisco. While the Soviets insisted on veto authority for each major power, the Americans remained divided. Some argued that the Senate would never accept anything less than an absolute veto, others that a Great Power able to block consideration of its own transgressions would make a mockery of the collective-security ideal. At Yalta, FDR had come close to accepting the Soviet position; he would permit a veto over "enforcement actions," but not, presumably, over procedural issues. Yet the meaning of procedural issues was not at all clear: sending troops to a disputed area was certainly substantive, but what about declaring a country in violation of the Charter or discussing (though not taking) action against such a country? And, as the young Andrei Gromyko asked other delegates, would a veto apply to a vote on whether a matter should be considered substantive or procedural?[10]

The veto issue divided more than the Soviets and the other Great Powers; it also divided the Great Powers from the smaller countries. Almost unanimously the smaller states insisted that the Security Council, unhampered by a Great Power veto, should have the right to authorize "peaceful" measures short of the use of force, a position that the Soviets instinctively resisted and that the Americans initially supported. With the veto issue still unresolved in May 1945, the French government embarrassed the Allies by launching military attacks against Syrian and Lebanese nationalists in order to reestablish colonial influence. Both London and Washington now faced the possibility that an absolute veto might paralyze the new organization. Fortunately for Stettinius, the French did not join the Soviets in demanding an absolute veto. Nonetheless, the issue brought the conference to an impasse while the Republicans, led by Vandenberg, threatened to revolt unless the Russians compromised.

And the Russians did compromise. Rather than continue to negotiate with Gromyko, who had limited authority, Truman had authorized the ailing Harry Hopkins to approach Stalin directly in Moscow. The Americans set out their position so forcefully that Vandenberg, who had been kept in the dark about Hopkins's mission, would later judge the administration's strategy "magnificent."[11] Even more amazing was Stalin's reaction. He accepted the U.S. demand, agreeing to permit discussion of *any* matter in the Security Council free of a veto. But by conceding to the Americans on an issue that Washington considered of paramount importance, Stalin would get his due: American refusal to side with the small powers who opposed a Great Power veto over "peaceful" measures of enforcement (for instance, mandatory arbitration of a dispute). While the American delegation was rarely of one mind during this period, Stettinius's desire to prevent an open break with Moscow led him to reject the justice of the small power position. Stettinius and his colleagues had already threatened to break with Moscow by opposing an absolute veto over *discussion* of matters brought before the Security Council. They now resolved to weaken the veto no further.

In assessing the veto controversy, it is apparent that the administration, whatever its reservations about Soviet policy (as seen in the suspension of Lend-Lease aid), still pursued a strategy of U.S.-USSR cooperation. Historians who claim that the Cold War began before 1945 ignore or deemphasize the desire for cooperation between the two governments at San Francisco. By the same token, it is hard to overlook the degree to which American policy was in a state of transition. The decisiveness that historians often attribute to President Truman did not characterize his San Francisco policy. Truman—indeed his entire delegation at San Francisco—exhibited uncertainty and indecision, much as FDR had in formulating his UN policy during 1943 and 1944. Cooperation with the Soviets remained a high priority, but the Americans had already become more comfortable about having their own veto power in the new organization. Yet just when it appeared that real cooperation might break down over the veto, Stettinius gave an important address at the end of May in which he reasserted the need for harmony. His speech may well have contributed to Stalin's willingness to compromise on the issue.

In office for less than two months, the inexperienced Truman was going through his get-acquainted period. He had never met Stalin. At times, he seemed to think that the Soviet leader was a Red Mussolini, while at other moments he treated Stalin like a Kansas City political boss. His inexperience may have made indecision inevitable during those early months. When Hopkins's mission turned out to be more successful than any of the American policy makers had anticipated, not only regarding the UN but on matters like Poland, Austria, and Germany, Truman had reason to believe that personal diplomacy might yield happy results. The Cold War was but a slight chill in the summer of 1945.

While the Americans and Soviets sparred over the veto, the delegates at San Francisco also struggled over the issue of regionalism. The roots of the problem could be seen in the Hull-Welles rivalry over UN policy during World War II. Some officials, like Hull and Pasvolsky, championed a truly universal collective-security organization; others, like Welles, Churchill, and at times FDR, preferred a confederation of regional units. Nor was the controversy over regionalism unrelated to the East-West debate; to the contrary, for the subject of regional agreements in relation to the UN Charter emerged at San Francisco after the USSR insisted that its treaties with its East European neighbors be untouched by Security Council prerogatives.

Once the USSR introduced the regional issue, it was neither the Americans nor the Russians but rather the Latin Americans, who became its leading proponents. Having recently created a security system with the Act of Chapultetec, the Latin Americans appealed to Stettinius by reminding him that regionalism in the Western Hemisphere meant the Monroe Doctrine. Could any members of the American delegation have forgotten that the Doctrine had become so indispensable to American nationalists in 1919 that Woodrow Wilson refused to sign the League of Nations Covenant without an article protecting Monroe's handiwork?[12] In 1945, however, Stettinius feared that a Charter provision exempting the Doctrine from UN authority would open the door to further Soviet influence in East Europe, and the British, while worried that regional arrangements could destroy the UN ideal, nevertheless looked to protect their own influence in both Europe and the Middle East. No wonder the American delegation split over the issue. Stassen, Notter, MacLeish, and Pasvolsky argued against concessions to regionalism, while Vandenberg, Dunn, Dulles, and especially Rockefeller supported the Latin Americans. The former group saw regional arrangements as subversive of a genuine world organization, while the latter feared that the Senate would kill the Charter unless the Monroe Doctrine was freed from UN authority.[13]

In the final analysis, the Americans resolved the dilemma by modifying that part of the Dumbarton Oaks formula that had recognized regional arrangements but barred armed action by states or regional organizations without the authorization of the Security Council. Understanding that they could not abandon either the Monroe Doctrine or the recent Act of Chapultepec, the Americans sponsored a compromise that, perfected by the British, became Article 51: the Charter *would* permit traditional self-defense *until* such time as the Security Council should act. Although the Latin Americans complained that the new article failed to mention the Act of Chapultepec, they had won a substantial victory. As Evan Luard notes in his history of the UN, Article 51 made it less likely that the UN's own military enforcement machinery would ever be used. Once the delegates at San Francisco recognized the legitimacy of traditional security arrangements, the UN became less "revolutionary" and considerably weaker than it had seemed after Dumbarton Oaks.[14]

To the extent that Soviet-American distrust influenced the debates over both the veto and Article 51, the San Francisco Conference played a small role in shaping the superpower rivalry of the next half century. Nevertheless, this distrust was not sufficient to prevent the compromises necessary to create a UN (the Charter probably could not have been signed and ratified ten years later when the Cold War intensified).

It is also important to note that a number of issues resolved at San Francisco involved U.S.-USSR relations only marginally. American officials, for instance, went beyond the Dumbarton Oaks formula in approving *slightly* expanded powers for the General Assembly. The other allies accepted these modifications because they were so modest. Indeed, the Great Powers resisted small power demands to significantly enlarge the assembly's authority. A New Zealand proposal to make most Security Council enforcement actions dependent on General Assembly approval got nowhere; in fact, the conference approved a Dumbarton Oaks recommendation (which subsequently became Article 12 of the Charter) that specifically prohibited the assembly from making recommendations concerning disputes that came before the Security Council. On the other hand, the American delegation supported a resolution permitting the assembly to make recommendations for the settlement of any dispute likely to threaten the peace except for those already before the Security Council.

When the Soviets opposed another New Zealand resolution that would have permitted the assembly to consider "any" matter within the sphere of international relations (Moscow feared it would inject the UN into domestic matters), Gromyko proposed to limit the assembly's authority *only* to issues of peace and security. The smaller nations, supported by Senator Vandenberg and some of the other U.S. delegates, now protested, arguing that this limitation was *too* restrictive. The Americans helped to resolve the matter by accepting—and persuading Gromyko to accept—discussion of any matter "within the scope of the present Charter" so long as it was not then before the Security Council. This compromise became Article 10 of the Charter.[15]

ECONOMIC JUSTICE AND HUMAN RIGHTS

The Americans also supported the smaller states that wanted to expand the assembly's authority in two other areas: economic activity and human rights. The Charter's broad Article 10 legitimized both areas, for the scope of the Charter extended far beyond conventional issues of peace and security.[16] The San Francisco Conference, however, did more than merely allow the assembly to address problems relating to economic justice and human rights. By creating the Economic and Social Council (ECOSOC) as an arm of the assembly, the conference constructed an institutional foundation for this activity.

The roots of ECOSOC can be traced back to Article 23 of the League Covenant, and the Americans at Dumbarton Oaks joined other delegates to incorporate the council into the UN.[17] But delegates to the San Francisco Conference, responding to small state pressure, went further: they made ECOSOC into a "principal organ" of the UN itself, thereby giving ECOSOC a centrality never granted to the economic and social agencies of the old League of Nations.

The theory behind the establishment of ECOSOC was simple: a recognition that peace and security rested upon a foundation of economic and social justice. In 1945, fully aware of the connection between political stability and economic development, the Americans comfortably embraced the assumptions that underlay ECOSOC. They were not, however, prepared to undermine their own authority. The limits they—and their Soviet counterparts—placed on assembly prerogatives illuminated their uneasiness with the demands of the small states for increased assembly authority. Neither the United States nor the USSR would support a significant expansion of ECOSOC membership, nor did either support ECOSOC representation for states coming from what would later be called the Third World.

This ambivalent attitude toward the UN's economic and social activity paralleled Washington's view of the General Assembly's human rights activity. Responding to the demands of the American consultants in San Francisco, the Truman administration supported not merely the right of the UN to "promote respect" for human rights, but created—under ECOSOC's authority —a separate Commission on Human Rights.[18] Beyond this the Americans refused to go. The 1919 debate over the Covenant, as well as the Senate's rejection of World Court membership during the interwar period, highlighted American concern about permitting international bodies to address "domestic" questions. Was homegrown racial segregation a violation of human rights or a domestic question? The State Department in 1945 was not anxious to find out. The Americans, with Soviet support, persuaded the conference delegates to expand a Dumbarton Oaks prohibition on UN intervention into matters "solely" domestic to include matters "essentially" domestic (this language found its way into Article 2, section 7).[19] In short, American support for human rights, like backing for the assembly in general, had its limits.

A small irony in this area relates to the U.S.-USSR rivalry. Both countries supported the creation of ECOSOC and the establishment of the Commission on Human Rights. The Soviets, however, despite their official ideology that emphasized economic justice and equal rights, were generally less eager than the Americans to support the smaller states wanting to broaden assembly authority in these areas. Indeed, Stalin's only concession to UN activity here was his support for including a right to work and a right to education as part of "human rights." In light of what we know about Stalin's human rights record during the 1930s, perhaps the real surprise is that he did not reject the human rights proposals at San Francisco altogether. Armed with the Security Council veto and with the knowledge that none of the Great Powers would tolerate UN interference in domestic matters, he may not have considered the subject important enough to break with his American allies.

As for the Americans, they too remained uneasy, wanting credit for creating a human rights commission but fearing that any human rights list would not be sufficiently inclusive. Should every item in America's Bill of Rights be enumerated? Would listing some imply that others were of lesser consequence? One American delegate, Congressman Sol Bloom, wanted to eliminate references to human rights altogether, preferring the term "equal rights," which, he believed, would be more acceptable to his countrymen. Bloom lost his argument. The Americans, still worried that no itemized listing of rights would ever be sufficiently complete, opted instead for only a general demand for human rights.[20]

TRUSTEESHIP AND OTHER ISSUES

Whatever the internal disagreement within the American delegation over human rights, it paled before the split concerning trusteeship. The Dumbarton Oaks proposals would extend the old League mandate system by creating a new Trusteeship Council, but the delegates to Dumbarton Oaks did not define the council's powers, leaving the whole subject murky until the San Francisco Conference. When details appeared, it became clear that the old imperial powers would protect their colonies as they had done in 1919 when they created the mandate system (after World War I, the Allies placed only former colonies of the defeated enemy, not their own colonies, into a mandate system designed to promote the independence of these colonial territories).

Between Dumbarton Oaks and San Francisco, controversy surrounding the trusteeship concept led to two kinds of disagreement involving the Americans. The first divided officials in Washington: Roosevelt's political advisers favored placing all dependent territories and colonies under the trust system, while the Pentagon sought to exempt the former Japanese-controlled islands in the Pacific, which were of potential strategic value to the United States. The second controversy arrayed American officials against their colleagues from colonial powers such as France and Great Britain. Led by Churchill and

French general Charles De Gaulle, the Europeans sought to minimize UN influence over their colonies, an effort the Americans protested for economic reasons (American negotiators feared it would lead to the reestablishment of a system of tariff preferences).

The whole controversy over trusteeship—involving interests that were not just strategic and political, but also economic and psychological—became bitter. To resolve the disagreement within the Truman administration, the Americans proposed two types of trusteeship: one would essentially eliminate the authority of the Trusteeship Council over "strategic" areas (like Micronesia), the other would treat more traditional (and nonstrategic) territories as they had been under old League mandates. After acrimonious debate, the San Francisco Conference accepted this arrangement, but the American victory came at a price: the other colonial powers forced the Americans—and the smaller countries—to curtail the authority of the Trusteeship Council. A number of proposals never got past the draft stage, most notably an Egyptian recommendation to permit the council to transfer the administrative title of trust territories from one country to another, an Australian suggestion to permit the General Assembly to determine which colonies would be trust territories, and a recommendation for the council to consider petitions from trust territory populations without first consulting the trust country.[21]

The fundamental goal of independence for trust territories, implied since the Dumbarton Oaks Conference, disappeared from the draft UN Charter after the American plan was adopted. The U.S. delegation, split on so many issues, divided on this one too. Led by Harley Notter and economist Charles Taussig, some delegates argued that retreat from the goal of independence would seriously compromise American leadership among subject peoples. Said Taussig, to deny independence "would sow the seeds of the next world war." Others, led by Harold Stassen, Leo Pasvolsky, and Johns Hopkins president Isaiah Bowman, argued that promoting independence might undermine British and French support for the United States in the developing competition with the Soviets (the USSR, together with China, strongly favored the independence ideal). Predicting war with the Soviets, Bowman asked "who would be our friends?" if the United States refused to champion the colonial interests of the western allies. Such logic led him and others who feared offending the colonial powers to claim that independence was akin to isolationism and nationalism as a cause of war. In other words, they turned Taussig's argument upside down. When the inevitable moment of compromise finally arrived, the Americans agreed to dilute the independence ideal, adopting in Article 76 the elastic notion of promoting the "progressive development toward self-government *or* independence as may be appropriate" to each trust territory's "particular circumstances."[22]

The last major issue left unresolved at Dumbarton Oaks, the authority of the new International Court of Justice (ICJ, often referred to as the World Court), also reflected the American tendency to subordinate ideals to practical considerations. Although the State Department had agreed to give the court "compulsory jurisdiction" over questions that might otherwise be considered "domestic," the congressional delegates objected. They feared that granting the new court compulsory jurisdiction would revive disputes similar to those during the 1930s, which had prompted the Senate to reject American membership in the old World Court. When delegate Harold Stassen argued in favor of the court's compulsory jurisdiction even if it meant the Senate might object during the ratification process, Senators Vandenberg and Connolly dug in their heels. They understood the Senate a lot better than Stassen, and they worried that including the compulsory jurisdiction clause would invite a Senate reservation. Once the Senate adopted one reservation, they argued, hostile senators would declare open season on the UN Charter. In short, they saw compulsory jurisdiction leading to the slippery slope of 1919.[23]

The Americans contributed to the resolution of many other issues discussed at San Francisco, including such things as the admissions process (the Security Council veto would apply to admitting new states), the right of a state to withdraw from the UN (unlike the Covenant, the Charter would include no provision for withdrawal), the veto as it applied to election of a Secretary-General (the Security Council would "recommend" a candidate to the General Assembly, which meant that the Great Powers would possess their right to veto), and the authority of the Security Council to enforce the judgments of the World Court (the Charter gave the Security Council such authority). For the most part, the Americans approached these issues as they did others already discussed: they protected the Dumbarton Oaks formula, which surrendered little authority to the small states, whether in the General Assembly, the specialized councils, or the World Court. In so doing, Washington more often than not sided with (rather than opposed) Moscow. Armed with the veto, the Americans never relinquished real authority. Neither, of course, had the Soviets nor the other permanent members of the Security Council. That is why the UN would never live up to the grand expectations of 1945.

chapter 3

TRUMAN

San Francisco was a beginning. It was also an end, at least in respect to the near-unanimous American support for the new organization.[1] The end of unanimity did not occur with dramatic finality but accompanied the emergence of tensions that, collectively, came to be called the Cold War. In the summer of 1945, these tensions were hidden from most Americans. Not only were disagreements aired in July at the Potsdam Conference camouflaged by the continuing war against Japan, but Stalin's entry into the Pacific War (just two days after Hiroshima) reinforced the appearance of Allied unity at the very time that unity began to unravel.

And unravel it did, seriously affecting UN policy. Three days after Potsdam, where the allies had focused mainly on the postwar status of Germany, Jimmy Byrnes replaced the congenial Stettinius as Truman's secretary of state. Byrnes had little of the former secretary's deep interest in the UN. The president compensated the departing Stettinius by offering him the post of U.S. delegate on the executive committee of the UN Preparatory Commission, a commission assigned the task of converting the Charter into an operating organization. "Converting" meant arranging an agenda for the General Assembly and Security Council, selecting a location for the UN, and choosing its secretary-general. None of these tasks proved easy to do.

Stettinius and his able staff, led by the young Adlai Stevenson, found themselves stymied by disorder among America's allies no less than by policy disorganization in Washington. In London, for instance, the new Labour government confronted economic disarray aggravated by Washington's sudden cut-off of Lend-Lease aid. Elevating domestic reform far above foreign policy, British officials, including the irascible anticommunist Ernest Bevin, would give the Americans no fewer headaches than they gave the Soviets.

Eleanor Roosevelt views a copy of the Universal Declaration of Human Rights. November 1949.
(UN/DPI Photo)

Stettinius's difficulties with the British paralleled U.S. friction with the Soviets. All this became public when the London foreign ministers' conference in September 1945 ended without enough agreement to allow for a joint concluding statement. Nor was the diplomatic disarray confined to the former allies. The Americans themselves divided over a clear definition of U.S. interests in the postwar world, over the pace of demobilization, and over the relationship between military strength and international objectives.

Interdepartmental rivalry between the State Department and the War and Navy Departments was shadowed by disagreements over UN policy within the State Department itself. For instance, the department divided over locating the UN in the United States. Some officials backed the Soviet desire to place the new organization in North America (Stalin had rejected a return to Geneva from which the USSR had been expelled following its 1939 attack on Finland). Others supported the policy of most European governments, including

Britain and France, who lobbied for a European home. American indecision on this issue prevailed not only through the meetings of the Provisional Commission, but even into the first days of the General Assembly. Although Stevenson had announced that the United States would host the UN if the membership desired an American location, the United States did not oppose a resolution favoring a European site (Washington abstained). When the resolution lost by two votes, the Provisional Commission approved, with Washington's support, a UN home in the eastern part of the United States.[2]

Selection of a secretary-general for the infant UN also revealed ambiguity and inconsistency. Many internationalists had favored an American site for the UN as a way to secure U.S. support for the new organization; so too their thinking about the nomination of an American to serve as secretary-general. General Dwight D. Eisenhower initially became the most conspicuous candidate, though the Soviets at one point proposed Alger Hiss (a Soviet agent?), who had played so prominent a role as secretary of the San Francisco Conference. Most governments, however, favored a candidate from a country not holding a permanent seat on the Security Council, and even Washington came around to this view. The Americans then joined with London to support Canada's Lester Pearson, while the Soviets recommended Yugoslav Stanhoe Simic.

Neither survived the final vote. Although the Soviets had originally proposed Norway's Trygve Lie as the president of the first session of the General Assembly, they preferred Simic as secretary-general. And although the Americans promoted Lie's candidacy for the General Assembly post as early as August 1945, they eventually abandoned him in favor of Belgium's Paul Henri Spaak, whose anticommunism did not endear him to Moscow. The backstage maneuvering left Lie embarrassed and bitter. He rightly believed that Washington's continued support almost certainly would have assured his election to the assembly post. What he could not have known in January 1946 was that his defeat as assembly president prepared the way for his election as secretary-general. He remained everyone's number two choice. When the Great Powers stalled over Pearson, Simic, and some lesser-knowns, Lie became their compromise candidate.[3]

It is risky to read too much into U.S. decision making concerning the UN during late 1945 and early 1946, but the politics of site-selection and election of a secretary-general reveal a few elements of Washington's approach that bear attention. What is notable about the former issue was Washington's reluctance to stake out a position for fear of appearing too self-interested. As for the latter issue, three things are noteworthy: the degree to which U.S.-USSR relations so dimly reflected Cold War tensions (the Soviets not only favored a North American site for the UN, but joined Washington in supporting Lie as secretary-general); the degree to which the Americans badly fumbled Lie's election as president of the General Assembly; and the degree to which the State Department placed relatively little importance on the selection of a secretary-general. State Department officials simply underestimated the Secretariat's political significance. The Americans could have mobilized strong support for either Pearson or Spaak, both men of recognized ability. The Truman administration chose not to do so. By supporting Spaak for the assembly presidency, the United States, perhaps unintentionally, nullified his candidacy for secretary-general. Historian James Barros, arguing that the Soviets cleverly maneuvered the United States into doing exactly this in order to kill any possibility of Spaak becoming secretary-general, calls American policy "contradictory" and "amateurish," terms that are, even absent the Soviet angle, close to the mark.[4]

Despite giving lip service to the importance of the secretary-general's office, the State Department knew little about Trygve Lie. He had been a relatively obscure foreign minister from a small country, certainly not among the more eminent internationalists like Czechoslovakia's Thomas Masaryck or France's Jean Monnet. Acting Secretary of State Dean Acheson, one of the department's more perceptive observer's, considered him unimpressive. As usual, Acheson proved right.

What became readily apparent during 1945 was that Washington's overall foreign policy was as undeveloped as UN policy. Just as the Americans had not analyzed their use of the UN in the months following the war, so they had not clarified either their Far Eastern policy or their European objectives. The Americans demobilized yet maintained military bases and personnel in remote corners of the world, including Japan, Germany, Korea, and China. They condemned old-fashioned colonialism (and prepared to lower their own flag in the Philippines) while lending their former allies political and economic support in colonial theaters—like the Middle East—that Washington considered of strategic importance. They heralded Great Power cooperation in the postwar world yet ended economic support to the war-devastated Soviet Union; they also barred the Russians from joint occupation of Japan.

This untidiness expressed itself at the UN no less than in London or Paris. Along with many other developments, including the domestic preoccupation of European statesmen and national rivalries intensified by ideological conflicts, Washington's zig-zag direction crippled the UN in its most formative period. It is important to recognize that the Americans were not alone in groping for a consistent and effective postwar policy. Still, America's enhanced power at the end of the war, coupled with its leadership at San Francisco, necessarily amplified its influence during the coming months.

THE MILITARY STAFF COMMITTEE

The UN's first year witnessed a number of important developments, including the appointment of key officials to assist Secretary-General Lie, the establishment of a working bureaucracy and a means to finance the organization, efforts to curb Soviet influence in Iran, and a UN plan to control the production and use of atomic weapons. But the most important development—or non-development—may have been the failure to implement effectively the terms of the Charter's Article 47, which called for the creation of a Military Staff Committee (MSC).[5]

Composed of the chiefs of staff of the permanent Security Council members, the Charter assigned the MSC responsibility "for the strategic direction of any armed forces placed at the disposal of the Security Council." The Charter had not created an independent UN force, but it clearly gave the Security Council authority to determine the existence of a threat to—or breach of—peace and to determine what measures—including the use of "air, sea, or land forces"—might be necessary to restore peace. By the same token, it mandated that member states "undertake to make available to the Security Council . . . armed forces, assistance, and facilities . . . necessary for the purpose of maintaining international peace and security."[6] These military articles, found in chapter VII of the Charter, constituted the heart of the postwar collective-security system. The MSC was designed to be its brain, coordinating not only enforcement action, but arms control. All this seemed possible while the Grand Alliance still functioned in 1945.

The MSC held its first meeting just one month after the inaugural session of the Security Council. Within two years, it was virtually dead, a victim of the clash between UN ideals and ideological realities. The few areas of agreement outlined by the military chiefs paled before the many points of friction. The MSC, reflecting the interest that all five Security Council permanent members had in protecting their own authority, quickly resolved that a UN force must not be independent of the veto. The permanent Security Council members also agreed that any UN force must be derived mainly from units of their own armed services rather than from troops of smaller countries.[7] Control, in other words, would remain at home.

But agreement ended there. From that point, the MSC became mired in so many quarrels that, by July 1948, it effectively ceased to function.[8] The most important areas of disagreement revolved around practical issues: the absolute size of military forces, the relative size of each country's contribution, the location of military bases, the length of missions, and the rights of passage for UN forces. The American position on each of these matters reflected Washington's role as leader of the UN majority. The Americans favored a force containing more than 300,000 men and 3,800 planes, while the Soviets argued in favor of a much more limited force, perhaps 125,000 men and fewer than 1,000 planes. The Americans rejected Soviet demands that each country contribute units of similar size and strength. They also argued that all members of the UN must make military bases available on demand. To this last demand, the Soviets as well as the French objected: The Soviets asserted that the American position would compromise national sovereignty, while the French sought a compromise that would allow UN units to be stationed in far-flung outposts of the French empire. Moscow also demanded a strict time limit for employing UN forces, which the Americans rejected.[9]

In short, while the Americans staked out positions that confidently anticipated the use of a UN force and a UN-majority sympathetic to American objectives, the Soviets were much more cautious. Years later, when the Americans found themselves leading a minority rather than a majority bloc at the UN, they would likely have embraced the Soviet position; indeed, in 1994, they effectively repudiated the authority of the MSC.[10] From 1946 to 1948, however, they embraced an activist role for UN-sponsored military units, especially when those units would largely be composed of American soldiers and sailors serving ends consistent with U.S. policy.

The degree to which American policy makers in 1946 believed that United States and UN purposes were identical seems remarkable in retrospect. "The fundamental principles of U.S. foreign policy find their expression . . . in particular in the Charter of the United Nations," wrote a high State Department official to the State-War-Navy Coordinating Committee. President Truman publicly lauded the organization. "A cause for profound thanksgiving to Almighty God," he said at the conclusion of the San Francisco Conference. "The plain fact is that civilization was saved in 1945 by the United Nations," he noted in his State of the Union message in January 1946, a statement consistent with his private views.[11] Others shared these sentiments. Cordell Hull believed the UN would end forever the need for alliances and power balances. Real military authority would be centralized in the new organization, which helps to explain the American enthusiasm for a sizable UN force with the MSC serving as linchpin. The post-1946 fate of the MSC, therefore, mirrors the diminishing role of the UN as an instrument of collective security, a development made inevitable once allied unity faded after the war.

PREPARING TO MONITOR THE ATOMIC AGE

If U.S. aims regarding the MSC never materialized, neither did early American efforts to have the UN regulate the development of atomic energy.

Few events contributed more to postwar insecurity than the atomic explosions that ended World War II. They served as exclamation points to the realization that modern weaponry had converted the earth into a perilous planet. The Americans, who had led in developing atomic weapons, enjoyed a temporary nuclear monopoly; knowledgeable Washington officials knew that the Soviets would end it within a few years. Some, like influential Senators Arthur Vandenberg and Tom Connally, Undersecretary of State Dean Acheson, Navy Secretary James Forrestal, and Manhattan Project Director General Leslie Groves, either flatly opposed sharing atomic secrets with Moscow or recommended placing such strict conditions on cooperation—particularly in regard to inspection of atomic facilities—that the Soviets would likely demur. Others, most notably Secretary of War Henry Stimson and Secretary of State

Byrnes (sometimes), counseled cooperation with the Soviets, believing that the alternative would lead inevitably to an arms race that would increase global instability.

But how should cooperation be achieved? Stimson argued that the stakes were so enormous that only three-power cooperation involving the United States, the USSR, and the United Kingdom could resolve the issue. Others, including the president, who was supported by the British and Canadian prime ministers, wanted to drop the matter into the lap of the UN; indeed, Vandenberg, who opposed sharing atomic secrets with Moscow, argued somewhat inconsistently that the bomb made the UN "more essential to the hopes of mankind than ever before."[12]

The evolution of American policy during the coming months was not pretty. The creation of congressional committees like the Joint Congressional Committee on Atomic Energy, combined with the preoccupation of Truman with domestic matters, tended to diffuse responsibility at the very time that the UN was establishing its own committee to consider international control. The result was indecision and drift. Administration suspicion of Soviet intentions had not yet hardened into a consistent anti-Soviet strategy. The recommendations of Truman and Byrnes proved so erratic that even their chief subordinates complained: Acheson protested that neither man had an understanding of the atomic energy issue.[13]

Not until Byrnes appointed a committee under Acheson's direction, composed of some of the major names in American atomic development (Groves, James Conant, John J. McCloy, Vannevar Bush), did a pattern emerge from the clutter. With help from the "father" of the bomb, J. Robert Oppenheimer, the committee produced the Acheson-Lilienthal report, which became the touchstone of U.S. policy for the next two years. The report, issued in March 1946, called not only for international sharing of atomic secrets, but also for international control of atomic procedures from mining uranium to the production—and eventual destruction—of weapons and other atomic devices. The men who wrote the report were hardly starry-eyed internationalists. They proposed a process that would protect America's atomic monopoly until the plan's final phase.

Any international plan for atomic energy in 1946 would likely require UN supervision, leading the Truman administration to request Security Council consideration of the matter. Truman asked former Wall Street financier Bernard Baruch to present the American plan to the council. Although Baruch cultivated a reputation as a distinguished elder statesman (he had advised presidents since Woodrow Wilson), he had plenty of detractors. Lilienthal, for instance, minced no words when he said the appointment made him sick.[14] Acheson shared the sentiment. The Kremlin may have agreed. Even Truman would later call him "an old conniver" and a "counterfeit."[15] Baruch's pomposity and his ignorance of atomic energy did not help matters, but the main problem was substantive, revolving around his reservations about the Great Power veto. Baruch proposed that no country have the right to veto sanctions (punishment) against a country violating the terms of the plan. On this issue, Truman backed Baruch against Acheson, but Acheson understood what Truman did not: that the Soviets would *never* surrender their veto, particularly during years when the United States—and not the Soviets—possessed deliverable weapons.

Moreover, the plan that Baruch presented to the UN was defined by stages during which the United States would retain its atomic monopoly until inspection provisions could guarantee that international control posed no security risk. During this staged process, the Soviets, without their own bomb, would be placed in a second-class position, a position that Stalin never considered seriously. The Soviets therefore played for time: developing their own atomic program, all the while tying the UN committee into interminable technical knots and calling for general atomic disarmament. It may be true that, as Baruch's main biographer claims, Truman backed the unworkable plan because he was a prisoner of Baruch's prestige; more likely, Truman was a prisoner of his own exaggerated faith in the UN.[16] He would not be for long, however. By mid-1947, it had become clear to the president that the negotiations were going nowhere. They dragged on for another year before expiring of fatigue.

Bernard Baruch had left his post as the American representative to the UN's Atomic Energy Committee in January 1947. President Truman replaced him with Vermont's Senator Warren R. Austin, whom Truman had nominated some months earlier to be Stettinius's replacement as the American permanent representative to the UN. Austin served in the latter capacity for six of the UN's most formative years. The senator had been one of the leading internationalists in the Republican Party. Truman's decision to nominate him rather than a fellow Democrat was clearly designed to deflect Republican criticism of administration foreign policy, but it also reflected the president's respect for Austin's deep-seated commitment to internationalist principles. Indeed, Austin, who was up for reelection in November 1946, surrendered a relatively safe Senate seat to take up his duties. What he gained in public recognition he must have lost in sleep, for his tenure was not an easy one. Serving during years when the emerging nationalism of the Cold War eclipsed the cooperative ideal of Dumbarton Oaks, Austin, more than any other administration official, had to witness the evisceration of his own work. With containment replacing cooperation as the cornerstone of U.S. policy, Austin became increasingly marginal in the making of Truman administration policy. A more forceful personality might have resigned in protest. Austin remained the faithful servant, enduring a relationship with the State Department in which he was often left uninformed about important foreign policy initiatives.[17]

Austin did not have one thing that many of his successors enjoyed: cabinet status. Stettinius had earlier requested it but without success. Lacking direct access to the White House, the voice of the country's chief UN representative was frequently muffled by the State Department bureaucracy, a problem that became more serious after Secretary of State Dean Acheson, who succeeded George C. Marshall in that post, took over in 1949. Until then, Austin headed a one-hundred-member American mission to the UN that reported directly to the State Department's Office of Special Political Affairs (renamed the Office of United Nations Affairs). In 1949, the department converted the office into a bureau headed by an assistant secretary of state, John Hickerson, who had taken over from Dean Rusk.[18] The bureaucratic changes did not stem Austin's declining influence; his new boss, Dean Acheson, had less sympathy for the UN than any other secretary of state between 1945 and 1998.

The American mission to the UN, headquartered in New York, has always had a peculiar relationship to the foreign policy apparatus in Washington. Both the mission and the State Department have, at various times, considered the other a rival, the mission often believing that Washington officials are too far removed from the UN to understand its subtleties. Because Austin had established a reputation predating his appointment to the UN post, and because he was not a career foreign service official whose job evaluations depended on pleasing his superiors, he had considerable flexibility. Nevertheless, the State Department officials to whom he reported never seriously entertained the idea that he or his mission had autonomy, and his able staff suffered in prestige as the focus of U.S. foreign policy increasingly shifted away from the UN.

EARLY UN INTERVENTIONS

This development was not yet evident in 1946. With the new organization still enjoying the afterglow from San Francisco, American officials promptly referred a number of early disputes to the UN for resolution. The first of these became a messy test of Soviet intentions and UN capabilities. In the months after VE Day, the USSR and the British had agreed to withdraw their troops from Iran in order to reestablish Iranian independence. While the British kept their part of the bargain, the Soviets, by early 1946, had increased, not decreased, their military presence in the northern Iranian provinces of Azerbaijan and Kurdistan, part of a plan to prevent the Iranian army from crushing Soviet-encouraged separatist movements in those provinces. U.S. officials initially resorted to watchful waiting, hoping that the Soviets would withdraw their troops by March 1946 as Molotov had earlier promised. When the Soviets instead increased their units in Iran in early 1946, American officials worried that Moscow might extend its influence southward toward the Persian Gulf oil fields. Such fears converted this situation into one of the earliest Cold War disputes. Indeed, the Iranian affair came to dominate the proceedings of the first Security Council.[19]

These Iranian developments led Washington into an increasingly cozy relationship with the prowestern shah of Iran (it would not end until Islamic militants overthrew the shah in January 1979). But what Washington increasingly denounced as Soviet expansionism, the Kremlin viewed as a defensive response to potential Anglo-American threats to Soviet oil facilities at Baku following the construction and consolidation of western naval and air bases from Suez to Dhahran.[20] Nor was the issue simply strategic: the Soviets also demanded Iranian oil concessions to balance British oil interests in southern Iran. These Soviet demands hardly pleased the Iranians, the British, or the Americans. Pressured not only by Moscow but by a Soviet-supported political movement within Iran led by the Tudeh Party, the Iranians appealed to the Security Council under the Charter's Article 33 in January 1946.

Perhaps quiet diplomacy might have settled the dispute. But the UN sometimes offered public confrontation rather than quiet negotiation, especially after London's foreign minister, Ernest Bevin, accused Soviet delegate Andrei Vishinsky of using the UN to justify the USSR's hostile occupation of Iranian territory. Vishinsky then charged the British with similar behavior in Greece. The United States, in what some historians consider the last effort to mediate between America's wartime allies, brokered an agreement promising talks in Moscow to end the dispute.[21]

The State Department, which had mildly protested the Soviet position before this confrontation, now gave the Iranians full support both in Teheran and New York. The shift in U.S. policy reflected Truman's own fear that the Soviets might invade Turkey and seize all territory from the Black Sea to the Mediterranean.[22] During the next two months, the Security Council rejected Soviet claims that the council had no authority to discuss the issue. The Iranian case became not only the first dispute formally addressed by the council, but the first to divide the Americans and the Soviets in the new organization.

Having ordered the American 6th Fleet into the Persian Gulf in March 1946, Truman and his advisers later concluded that their strong stand, *including* the use of the UN, had forced Moscow to withdraw its troops from Iran within two months of the original March withdrawal date. Perhaps it was true that "the only thing the Communists understand is force." Perhaps, though, U.S. officials overlooked an equally important development: Iran and the USSR concluded an agreement guaranteeing Moscow a 51 percent interest in a joint Soviet-Iranian oil concession; in return, Russian troops would leave Iran.[23]

That the Americans likely overestimated their own contribution to settling the crisis is of some importance to an historical understanding of the early Cold War. More important, however, is the way that the UN affected American policy. By backing Iran's appeal to the Security Council, American officials legitimized Washington's involvement in a remote country against a former ally. The UN, in other words, allowed Washington to universalize its policy and therefore disregard isolationist warnings about the risk of foreign entanglement. The Charter helped to convert entanglement into a moral imperative. Britain, meanwhile, already fearful that the USSR might undermine London's extensive oil interests in southern Iran, appreciated such strong U.S. support. Whitehall understood that the Charter made it easier for the Truman administration to threaten action against the Soviets. Instead of viewing America's "obsession" with the UN as "escapism," British policy makers began to see it as a useful weapon of diplomacy.[24]

For all the attention to Iran, it remains true that use of—and the usefulness of—the UN was modest. If the UN served a lasting purpose during the affair, it was mainly because the new organization served to spotlight what might otherwise have been an obscure confrontation between Moscow and the west. As a spotlight, it provides a parallel with UN involvement in the Greek civil war following World War II.

Conflict in Greece

Events in Greece during the second half of the 1940s were, to say the least, more complex than in Iran. Where the Iranian affair involved mainly a competition for resources, the Greek civil war was a genuine civil conflict pitting communists against a highly disorganized and occasionally repressive coalition of anticommunist groups.[25] The war was not just a clash of ideologies. It also involved political and territorial interests among Greece's communist neighbors (Yugoslavia, Albania, and Bulgaria, and, many claimed, the USSR) who, especially after 1948, did not always get along themselves. Moreover, Greek politics after World War II spilled over into Turkey—traditionally a Greek rival, but also threatened by the Soviet Union—and affected the future of British colonialism.

The UN forum offered both sides of the conflict in Greece opportunities to vilify their ideological opponents. The Soviets demanded that the British, who had sent troops to defend what the Soviets called the "Monarchist-Fascist" government in Athens, end their occupation of Greece. The British replied that they had been "invited" into Greece, while Athens asked the Security Council to condemn armed interference from guerrillas infiltrating into Greece from Bulgaria and Yugoslavia.[26] Yugoslav support for "self-determination" in the Greek portion of Macedonia, a land containing ethnic Slavs, met with fierce Greek resistance, while the USSR condemned the Greek government for holding elections (the Soviets called them rigged) that the left-wing parties had boycotted. Combine all this with calls from both sides for border adjustments resulting from ancient national and ethnic conflicts, and the mix of historic and ideological antagonisms is difficult to sort out even today.

To Americans in 1946 and 1947, these complexities faded before their fear, reinforced by Iranian developments, that the Soviets would use the Greek civil war to expand into the eastern Mediterranean. The Truman administration, therefore, anxiously sought to use UN machinery in order to restore the status quo, which meant protecting the Greek government against the communist insurgency. After an abortive effort to establish an investigatory commission, and following American and British advice to Trygve Lie not to do so on his own authority (the State Department feared that he would undermine his authority if he probed what the Security Council had already refused to investigate), the United States finally sponsored a resolution in December 1946 that the Council unanimously adopted. It created a commission to review the international phase of the conflict. Composed of representatives from each country sitting on the Security Council, the commission issued a report in June 1947 critical of border incursions from Greece's communist neighbors and calling for the creation of the UN Special Committee on the Balkans (UNSCOB), the first of what would be a long line of UN watchdog groups.[27]

Because the committee would observe violations of border security, the communist states infiltrating guerrillas into Greece refused to cooperate or participate. There is no evidence that the State Department expressed regret over this development, but the committee, reflecting its western majority, strongly denounced infiltration and warned against diplomatic recognition of a communist-led rival government in Greece. The warning may have succeeded: the USSR did not recognize the communist faction. Many commentators believe, however, that UNSCOB's warning not to extend diplomatic recognition to the communist faction may have been less important than Stalin's 1944 promise to the British to view Athens as part of Britain's sphere of influence.[28] Stalin may have denounced British influence in Greece, but he did little to genuinely challenge it.

The real news concerning Greece came not from UN headquarters in New York, however; it came from the White House when the president proclaimed his Truman Doctrine in March 1947 following Britain's announcement that London no longer had the resources to militarily aid either Greece or Turkey. The doctrine committed the Americans to both economic and military support far beyond the capabilities of the British. It was foreign entanglement with a vengeance. What is remarkable about Washington's internal debate over the Truman Doctrine is the nearly complete absence of comment about the UN.

Significantly, Warren Austin had not been consulted about the shift in policy and did not even see a copy of Truman's famous March 12 speech to Congress until the day before it was delivered. Nor had the Bureau of Special Political Affairs been consulted. Dean Acheson, who was responsible for this omission and who had never been fond of the UN, wryly called it "a fortunate error."[29] Of course it was no error at all. Truman and his advisers acted from a sense of urgency. Less than two years after San Francisco, they had concluded that the UN simply was not up to the task of protecting the west from Soviet expansionism.

But they could not avoid public criticism for disregarding the world organization. Columnists like Anne O'Hare McCormick and Walter Lippmann called for reinvigorated cooperation with the UN, and the public, according to pollster George Gallup, overwhelmingly agreed. When Congress finally passed the Greek and Turkish aid bills two months later, about one-quarter of the membership voted no, including not just old-line isolationists but internationalists who scorned the administration for abandoning the UN.

Challenges in the Third World

If the emerging competition with the USSR prompted Washington to relegate the UN to a secondary role, the emergence of what would later be called Third World nationalism had just the opposite effect. In some areas, such as Algeria and Indochina, the Truman administration discreetly kept its counsel. Reluctant to alienate the French, who remained pivotal to American plans for a revived Europe, Washington offered no serious support to nationalists demanding their independence. Remaining on the sidelines was not so easy to do in the Dutch East Indies where World War II had breathed life into a dormant nationalist insurgency that declared independence just three days after the Japanese surrender. The British, with a small number of occupation forces in Indonesia, were caught in the middle: as colonialists themselves, they refused to grant formal recognition to the new government, although they urged the Dutch to begin negotiations with the nationalists. American policy makers hoped the situation would resolve itself. After the Ukrainian delegate to the UN brought the matter to the Security Council in January 1946, charging the Dutch *and* British with interference in the internal affairs of a sovereign state, the Americans no longer had the luxury of sidestepping the issue. Caught between their ideological anticolonialism and their desire to mollify the Dutch for reasons mainly related to European policy, the Americans, first cautiously, then more vigorously, fostered UN efforts to broker the emergence of newly independent states. Although this process was not entirely free of Cold War rivalries (the Ukraine, after all, had brought the resolution to the Security Council), such factors played a strictly secondary role in the chronicle of Third World independence.

Israeli Independence

Similar to the American role in the Indonesian issue was the American role in the even more explosive story of Israel's independence. Here, too, although the issue did not directly involve an American confrontation with communism, it indirectly related to developing Cold War political and strategic themes, and here, too, the Americans became deeply involved only after it became clear that the situation would not resolve itself.

The political history of modern Israel goes back to World War I when Lord Balfour, then British foreign minister, promised an independent Palestinian homeland for the Jews. His famous declaration advanced Britain's wartime strategy of weakening the Central Powers because the Turks, then allied with Britain's European enemies, included Palestine within their Ottoman empire.

After the armistice, however, Britain increasingly regretted Balfour's promise while administering Palestine as a League of Nations mandate. The conflicting claims of the Jewish minority in Palestine who embraced the Balfour policy, and of the majority Palestinian Arabs who rejected it, left the British in an unenviable position. As Jewish immigration to Palestine increased, occasional riots pitting Jews against Arabs warned of greater violence to come. By 1939, London, seeking to keep the peace, sharply ("cruelly," said the Zionists) limited Jewish immigration into Palestine at the very moment that Nazi persecution intensified demands for opening the door. The escalation of anger wearied and weakened British determination for what, until then, had been their main goal: an independent and unified Palestine containing both Jews and Arabs.

To complicate matters, World War II brought with it the further growth of both Arab and Jewish nationalism. It also brought news of the Holocaust, which dramatically intensified demands by both Jews and non-Jews to open Palestine to Jewish immigration. In October 1945, British Foreign Secretary Ernest Bevin unexpectedly proposed to increase Jewish immigration into the Holy Land. His purpose was political, not humanitarian; he would use the prospect of higher immigration numbers to induce the Americans—who strongly favored relaxing immigration quotas—to cooperate with Britain in order to maintain order in the region. Unfortunately for Bevin, the political crosscurrents in Palestine and the United States doomed his efforts to forge an Anglo-American consensus. Jewish and non-Jewish opinion in the United States moved the Truman administration to support partition of Palestine in order to create a separate Jewish state, while the British, who in 1939 had repudiated Balfour's promise, remained committed to a single Palestine in which Jews and Arabs would share authority. By February 1947, an exhausted and isolated London, surveying the wreckage of its mandate, announced that it would walk away from Palestine and hand the problem to the United Nations—"without recommendations."[30] Britain would terminate its mandate on May 15, 1948.

The British announcement effectively tossed the problem into American and UN laps. With memories of the Holocaust still fresh, Americans, along with officials from most other western states, increasingly favored the idea of partitioning Palestine. Nevertheless, the Truman administration was not anxious to take the lead in this admittedly delicate area. It therefore deferred to the UN, hoping that a resolution of the problem would increase the prestige of the UN itself. This was not to be.

Three things made the Truman administration skittish about the British government's intention to leave Palestine and London's April 2 request for the UN General Assembly to address the partition issue. First, President Truman had unambiguously informed Arab governments that he would support no solution without consulting them in advance. Second, British Foreign Secretary Bevin's hostility to a Jewish homeland, combined with a formal recommendation from the Joint Chiefs of Staff who warned against any policy that might jeopardize American oil interests in the area, meant that Truman would have very little room to maneuver even within his own government. Finally, the beginning of Jewish terrorism in Palestine and Arab warnings that a Jewish state would be met with force meant that Washington's influence might be quite limited no matter what the president wished.

Truman, therefore, welcomed UN leadership in this area. He claimed that the Palestine issue "was just the kind of problem that we had the U.N. for," and he ordered the State Department to support the creation of the UN's Special Committee on Palestine (UNSCOP).[31] Although the committee included no permanent members of the Security Council (in order to exclude the Soviets), it did contain a number of governments aligned with the superpowers, effectively giving each a voice. On August 31, with Trygve Lie's endorsement, UNSCOP issued a majority report strongly favoring partition, with the UN as the administering authority. President Truman eagerly supported it.

On November 29, the General Assembly endorsed the majority report by a vote of 33 to 13 with 10 abstentions. The UN had spoken. But the UN had no army to enforce its voice. With Arab governments now sending troops to the Palestinian border and Jews arming in self-defense, violence in the region escalated.

If the United States had shielded itself behind UN resolutions during the coming months, American diplomacy might have faced only charges of timidity. In fact, it suffered worse: charges of fecklessness, betrayal, and ignorance. Truman never admitted in his memoirs that the State Department's leadership almost unanimously opposed creating a separate Jewish state. Secretary Marshall, his assistants such as Dean Acheson, Charles Bohlen, Loy Henderson, and George Kennan, along with their counterparts in the military including Secretary of the Navy James Forrestal, acutely feared the loss of Arab support should the United States continue its present course. Forrestal, for instance, believed that the Soviets would be the only winners in an Arab-Jewish conflict over Palestine; others, led by Kennan, stressed less the Soviet threat than the belief that any UN-imposed settlement would be "unworkable."[32] To most of them, the loss of Arab support meant not only the loss of oil and military bases, but the entry of the Soviet Union into a strategic area from which it had previously been absent.

The American delegation at the UN, led by Warren Austin and Eleanor Roosevelt, was more sympathetic to the Zionist cause. So, too, was the chief of the International Organization section at the State Department, Dean Rusk. These UN proponents had very limited influence, however. Policy was mainly made in and around Secretary Marshall's office and in the White House where the president and his chief adviser, Clark Clifford, continued to favor partition against the advice of the State Department. But the rising level of violence in Palestine, combined with increasing Cold War tensions following the February 1948 Communist coup in Czechoslovakia, led even Truman to soften his support for partition. Whatever his sympathy for the Jews, who exasperated him, the president refused to quarrel with the advice of Marshall and the Joint Chiefs when they asserted that only with soldiers could partition be enforced.[33] Because he refused to approve the use of American troops, Truman agreed to permit a UN trusteeship over Palestine *if* partition proved unworkable.

President Truman had *not* abandoned partition. But to State Department officials who never favored partition in the first place, Truman's agreement on March 8 permitting trusteeship as a fallback position was the green light they needed. Three days later, Truman secretly met with Chaim Weizman, the Zionist leader (soon to be the first president of Israel), assuring him of support for partition. Unbeknownst to the president, just 24 hours later, Warren Austin, on State Department orders, announced at the Security Council that the United States would drop its support for partition in favor of the trusteeship proposal. "Every articulate Jew in the United States," wrote one Truman biographer, "except Weizman, who wisely held his counsel, accused the President of gross betrayal."[34]

Truman's fury at the way that the State Department had publicly undercut his policy did not prevent him from reluctantly approving the trusteeship concept; he did so to stem the disarray within his administration, but his efforts were in vain. The bigger issue, however, was the shape of the Mideast, and here the UN, not Truman's own sentiments or those of advisers like Clifford, eventually bailed him out. Fortuitously for Truman, the UN's Palestine Committee rejected the trusteeship option (the Zionists would have repudiated it if the Palestine Committee had not). Neither did Lie nor the General Assembly favor trusteeship. The success of Jewish soldiers on the battlefield, not the confused policy of the American government, defined the future.

American policy continued to exhibit uncertainty right up to the deadline for British withdrawal on May 15, 1948. Although the State Department still opposed a separate Jewish state (Marshall warned that Arab armies would destroy it anyway), Clifford persuaded Truman to grant it diplomatic recognition. Truman equivocated after the trusteeship coup in March. In mid-May he finally exhibited his legendary decisiveness, recognizing the new state of Israel minutes after it declared independence.

Historians have long debated whether Truman acted from considerations of domestic politics or national interest. Both undoubtedly influenced him. He was in the midst of an election year in 1948 and he certainly needed Jewish support in states like New York and California. By the same token, Clifford and others argued that an independent Israel would help to limit Soviet influence in the Middle East (State Department officials argued the opposite). The president was not much influenced by the threat of losing Arab oil; the United States only imported 8 percent of its oil at that time, and the Arabs, Truman knew, needed American markets. Was he influenced by the arguments of Trygve Lie that a UN failure in Palestine would seriously weaken the organization? Possibly. Lie had threatened to resign in March after Marshall ordered Austin to back the trusteeship proposal (Truman did not know this). Lie, who often argued that the Great Powers must support the UN, viewed the U.S. retreat from partition as tantamount to a personal betrayal.

Yet the fact of the matter is that the UN never resolved the Palestinian issue. Quite the contrary: Palestine turned out to be a UN failure, a failure that not only led to decades of on-again, off-again warfare, but one that discredited the UN at a critical moment in its young history. Britain's surrender of its mandate responsibilities cannot be divorced from this failure, although it is tempting to argue that London's withdrawal was more a result than a cause of the problem. What British officials understood in 1946, which many American and UN officials did not understand until 1948, was that the gap separating the two sides in Palestine had already become nearly unbridgeable.

But was it absolutely unbridgeable? The UN never found out. Evan Luard argues that the greatest liability of the UN in Palestine was that the organization substituted votes and resolutions for real solutions. In fact, says Luard, the controversy could only be resolved by getting the two sides to negotiate and compromise. The UN never really tried to do this.[35]

Others, too, must share the blame for the mess. Trygve Lie, for instance, sided with the Zionists from an early date, therefore surrendering his own claim to impartiality and making it less likely that the Arabs would rely on UN diplomacy for a solution.[36] The Americans, too, must take some of the responsibility. U.S. policy was confused and inconsistent. Once the British announced in February 1947 that they would withdraw, the Americans found themselves in a situation where they sought three incompatible goals: (1) to strengthen the UN; (2) to protect U.S. economic and strategic interests in the Middle East against Soviet expansion (February 1947, remember, was the same month that London notified Washington of its inability to defend Greece and Turkey); and (3) to assure peace between Arabs and Jews. By 1948, American policy toward Palestine and toward the UN had become so erratic that at one critical moment, Warren Austin, America's chief UN delegate, simply left the UN building in embarrassment rather than explain changes in Washington's directives.[37]

Perhaps American confusion was inevitable. The president, after all, was quite ignorant about the intricacies of Middle East politics. He was intolerant of, exasperated by, and yet sympathetic to the Jews. He virtually worshipped Secretary of State George Marshall, who opposed partition, while he was predisposed to dismiss the recommendations of the "striped-pants boys" in the State Department, who also opposed partition. And, of course, he was mindful of the need for Jewish support in the upcoming presidential election.[38] Moreover, because the UN and Truman staked out positions that, after 1946, favored the establishment of a Zionist state, Jews both inside and outside of the United States had little reason to compromise. By the same token, the Arabs exaggerated their oil influence and therefore believed that they, too, need not compromise. Without compromise, the UN stumbled from resolution to resolution until Jewish military victories, not diplomacy, guaranteed the existence of a new Israeli state.

It should be noted that the birth of Israel did not end the UN's Middle East involvement during the remainder of the Truman administration. One day after the American recognition of Israel, full-scale war broke out between the new state and her Arab neighbors. Having brokered partition, UN officials, including Trygve Lie, now believed the organization had a mandate to resolve the fighting. To do this would require American help. From the perspective of Washington, this task would be complicated by the the Soviet Union's decision to recognize Israel on May 18. American leaders reasonably viewed Moscow's action as an attempt to increase Soviet influence in the Middle East. Fearing that Mideast instability would work to the advantage of the USSR, the Truman administration proved willing to support UN efforts to arrange an armistice, efforts that led the Security Council in April 1948 to appoint Sweden's Count Folke Bernadotte to mediate the conflict.

Mediation works best when both sides are willing to negotiate. When neither side wants negotiation, the mediator may need an instrument of persuasion. That instrument, Bernadotte thought, might best be a U.S. marine battalion, which he requested during the summer of 1948. American officials balked. Echoing the reservations of the Joint Chiefs, they refused to dispatch any American troops to the region. The Berlin crisis, which began in May 1948, reinforced the administration's reluctance to meet Bernadotte's request. Nor was opposition limited only to the use of American troops. Reflecting the MSC's recent history, Washington spurned proposals to authorize any international force under UN auspices, fearing that the Soviets would otherwise use it to gain militarily what they had been unable to gain diplomatically. On the other hand, the administration did not rule out the future use of American troops. Fearing that the Red Army might eventually enter the region by befriending either the Israelis or the Arabs, the Joint Chiefs and the State Department would keep their own options open.[39]

Bernadotte's assassination by an Israeli in September 1948 and the appointment of American Ralph Bunche as his successor had little direct effect on American policy. The United States did join an international team of observers, making certain that Bunche, and not the Security Council, selected the participants in order to exclude Soviet representatives. The observer team had little effect. Bunche helped to negotiate a series of truces that soon broke down. Continued hostilities brought many more council resolutions.

More troublesome for the Americans was establishing a policy in regard to Israeli boundaries. The UN had initially defined boundaries consistent with the General Assembly resolution of November 29, 1947. The fighting threw these plans into question as Israeli army victories expanded the Jewish areas of control. Count Bernadotte, however, had produced a plan that generally ignored these victories; most importantly, he had refused to recognize Israel's title to the Negev Desert. That left Truman in the middle, especially when his sympathy for the Israelis was neutralized by strong British support for the Bernadotte Plan. London had interests quite separate from the Americans, especially in wanting to enhance Transjordan, a British client, at the expense of Israel. Foreign Minister Ernest Bevin argued that because Israel might not survive, giving disputed territory to Transjordan would protect western strategic interests (mainly oil and military bases). Although Truman and the State Department initially supported Bevin, Zionist political pressure in Washington soon persuaded the White House to fudge the American position. In any case, the Israelis continued to demand boundaries that included areas never recognized by the UN, including parts of the Negev and the western Galilee.

The debate turned out to be quite academic. Once again, Jewish military success proved decisive. And the Americans, fearing that continued conflict might so weaken the Arabs as to invite Soviet influence into the region, supported a truce that included the boundaries demanded by the Israelis. The truce lasted until 1956.[40]

BEHIND-THE-SCENES DIPLOMACY

In some ways, the story of the U.S.-UN relationship involves what did *not* happen at UN headquarters (which, in 1949, moved to its present quarters on New York's East River). Perhaps the most important of these developments was the signing of the North Atlantic Treaty establishing the NATO alliance. Like the UN itself, NATO would also be called a collective-security organization. It wasn't. It was an old-fashioned alliance, guaranteeing that each of its twelve original members would come to the defense of the others in the event of a Soviet attack on any one of them. The creation of NATO was a visible reminder that the UN, crippled by the Security Council's permanent veto, could not do what it was supposed to do: prevent war when great power interests were at risk.

But if the UN could not prevent war (at least where the Great Powers were involved), it could help others who wanted to prevent war. For example, following the Soviet blockade of Berlin in 1948, U.S. policy makers divided over whether to submit the issue to the UN. They all understood that the Soviets could veto enforcement action to end the blockade. Nevertheless, Secretary of State George Marshall strongly favored bringing the dispute to the UN, in part to preempt a Soviet propaganda campaign, in part to avoid having to choose between war or appeasement.

When in October 1948 the United States asked that the matter be placed before the Security Council, the Soviets objected. And although the council permitted discussions (this was a procedural matter), the UN could do little but make recommendations. Despite the UN's limitations, however, the final breakthrough might not have materialized without the UN. Marshall's successor, Dean Acheson, proposed that a private approach to Moscow might succeed where more formal diplomacy had failed, and that the approach be made at the

UN. He instructed the deputy American representative to the UN, Philip Jessup, to seek out Soviet delegate Jacob Malik informally. Their behind-the-scenes talks led to a breakthrough, vindicating use of the UN if not as a collective-security organization then as a practical forum for backroom diplomacy.[41]

COMMUNISM AND THE LOYALTY ISSUE

For all the inconsistencies in the American use of the UN during the Truman years, the thread that best ties together U.S. policy is anticommunism. It helps to explain American acceptance of the permanent veto. It helps to explain American diplomacy in both Iran and Greece in the year before the Truman Doctrine appeared. It helps to explain why the State Department opposed a separate Jewish state and, oddly, why the president supported it. And it also helps to explain why American officials challenged the loyalty and independence of UN civil servants from 1947 to 1953.

It is ironic that just when the Cold War began to enfeeble collective security, American officials increasingly worried that disloyal UN employees holding U.S. citizenship might subvert American goals at the organization. This was McCarthyism before McCarthy. The Truman administration commenced its surveillance of American citizens at the UN at the same time that it initiated its loyalty program in Washington. No matter that the UN Charter, as had the League Covenant, sought to insulate UN employees from the politics of their home countries. Article 100 specified that the staff shall be "responsible only to the Organization," that it "shall not seek or receive instructions from any government or from any other authority external to the Organization." The same article obligated every signatory of the Charter "not to seek to influence [the staff] in the discharge of their responsibilities."

For the next six years, the U.S. government would violate Article 100. A 1949 written agreement between the State Department and the secretary-general permitted U.S. agents systematically to screen American employees (eventually, non-Americans as well) who served in the Secretariat. Over 40 were fired, many of whom had taken the Fifth Amendment during administrative hearings but otherwise had unblemished performance records and were charged with no offense. Others saw their jobs abolished.[42]

In a tragic footnote to this story, Abraham Feller, an American who served as Lie's very capable legal officer and who was increasingly distrusted by both the "witch-hunters" and "the hunted," committed suicide one day before a special tribunal appointed by Lie was scheduled to hear charges against him. No one doubts that the secretary-general was grief stricken. Still, he refused to change course.[43] Former UN official Shirley Hazzard would charge Lie with "covert subservience" to American pressure.

Lie did not act alone. He had the strong support—more accurately, guidance—of the assistant secretary-general for administrative and financial services, American Byron Price. According to Hazzard, Price was a secret U.S. agent who cleverly played upon Lie's vulnerability.[44] Because Lie needed U.S. support much more than the United States needed him, especially after the Soviet Union turned against him in 1950, he continued to subvert the ideal of an impartial civil service even to the point of permitting the establishment of an FBI office at UN headquarters. Hazzard claims that not even Dag Hammarskjold, Lie's unusually independent successor, protested this policy, nor did any high UN official denounce the firing of the only junior American staff member who did object. But Hazzard is *too* critical of Hammarskjold. The future UN chief deeply resented the FBI's intrusion into UN affairs. After becoming secretary-general in 1953, Hammarskjold closed the FBI office at UN headquarters by taking advantage of a foolish comment by bureau director J. Edgar Hoover.[45]

THE KOREAN CONFLICT

The anticommunist hysteria that precipitated America's violation of Article 100 was heightened not only by the politics of Wisconsin's Senator Joe McCarthy, but by events in Korea where the Cold War was turning exceedingly hot.

Korean civilians seek safety from the continuous fighting.
(UN/DPI Photo)

From 1905 until Hiroshima, Korea had been a Japanese protectorate. Following World War II, the United States and the USSR divided Korea at the 38th parallel, the Soviets occupying the northern half, the United States the southern half. Occupation presented some discomfiting choices. Although many American officials considered Korea to be of only limited interest, leftist political unrest in the south meant that the United States might have to beef up its military presence, which the Truman administration opposed, or leave altogether. This last option risked seeing the Soviets step into the vacuum at a time of increasing U.S.-Soviet tension in other areas. The State Department therefore adopted a third course: turning Korea over to the UN. The UN would be asked to supervise free elections in both zones and prepare them for unification. Warren Austin presented this plan to the General Assembly in early October 1947. On November 14, the General Assembly recognized Korea's independence and called for the withdrawal of all occupation troops.[46]

Within a year, North Korea and South Korea separately proclaimed their independence, the North led by Kim Il Sung and the South by Singman Rhee, an anticommunist nationalist. By the end of 1948, the last Soviet troops left North Korea; American troops completed their withdrawal from the south six months later.

The withdrawal of troops camouflaged deep unrest, and on September 2, 1949 the UN commission on reunification admitted failure and warned about the possibility of civil war. American officials were privately pessimistic. Even before the last U.S. troops sailed home, the author of a key State Department memo, probably George Kennan, had written "There is no longer any real hope of a genuinely peaceful and free democratic development in that country. . . . Since the territory is not of decisive importance to us, our main task is to extricate ourselves without too great a loss of prestige."[47]

Had Mao Zhedong not succeeded in overthrowing the Nationalist government in China during the summer of 1949, it is unlikely that the United States or the UN would have become involved in the Korean War. The success of the Chinese communist revolution, however, combined with recent communist gains in Czechoslovakia, the Berlin Blockade, and the end of America's nuclear monopoly, made it nigh impossible for Washington to pursue what the memo had called "our main task." U.S.-Soviet competition had become U.S.-Soviet confrontation. The Truman administration's most famous Cold War memo, NSC-68, came to memorialize this state of affairs. It foresaw the "new fanatic faith" of the communists leading to a Soviet attempt to establish "absolute authority over the rest of the world." This threat required from Washington not conventional compromise but unlimited American strength, for any further gains by the Soviets would mean that "no coalition adequate to confront the Kremlin with greater strength could be assembled." A "defeat of free institutions anywhere is a defeat everywhere."[48]

Translated into layman's language, this meant that every corner of the globe (including remote Korea) became a crucial testing ground.[49] To prevent what U.S. officials portrayed as a looming catastrophe would take money, lots of it, and the mobilization of all military and diplomatic instruments. Those instruments included the UN.

There was no great debate about this recommendation precisely because the danger of communism seemed so familiar by early 1950. Yet, quite at odds with the expectations of 1945, the UN no longer played a major role in U.S. thinking. Officials like George Kennan and Secretary of State Acheson privately disdained the UN while offering it public praise.[50] An example of this praise appears in the Secretary's famous "perimeter" speech of January 12, 1950 where he noted that military aggression beyond America's Pacific defense perimeter (Korea sat beyond that perimeter) would meet "the commitments of the entire civilized world under the Charter of the United Nations which so far has not proved a weak reed" against aggression.[51] This was nonsense. The UN had indeed proved itself a weak reed, as in the Berlin crisis, and Acheson knew it better than anyone else.

But Korea would be different. What made it different was that the Soviet Union was absent from the Security Council. Since January 1950, Moscow had boycotted the UN to protest the UN's refusal to replace the Chinese Nationalist representatives with those from the new revolutionary regime.[52] Therefore, when North Korea unexpectedly attacked its southern neighbor on June 25, 1950, the Russians were in no position to block collective action at the UN. From the perspective of Washington, the boycott could not have come at a more opportune moment.

Once word of the North Korean attack arrived in Washington, the Truman Administration, acting on the recommendation of Assistant Secretary of State for United Nations Affairs John Hickerson, took just two hours and 40 minutes to call for a meeting of the Security Council. The State Department requested the meeting even before the president, who was in Missouri, learned about the attack.[53] For the next week, Acheson, rather than White House or Pentagon officials, led in formulating the American response.

With Warren Austin recuperating from illness in Vermont, his assistant, Ernest Gross, requested to meet with Trygve Lie in New York. Like Acheson, Gross saw the North Korean invasion as part of a broad communist strategy and approached Lie in this spirit.[54] Lie agreed immediately to convene the Security Council. He had initially expected to act under Article 99 (giving the secretary-general authority to bring issues threatening peace to the Security Council), but Gross's proposal freed Lie from having to act on his own authority. Washington's request for UN action was further strengthened when the UN Commission on Korea (UNCOK), based on reports from two Australian observers, confirmed the American version of the attack. Not only did UNCOK reports help to mobilize activity at the UN's temporary headquarters in Lake Success; they fortified Acheson's bold (and legally questionable) decision to bypass Congress in seeking authority for a military response.[55]

The Security Council met twice during the next three days. On June 25, with the USSR absent and Yugoslavia abstaining, the council passed a resolution calling for a North Korean withdrawal, and urging all governments to desist from aiding North Korea while supporting the UN in executing the resolution.[56] Two days later, the council passed a more important resolution, this time with Egypt and India not voting. It authorized "such assistance . . . as may be necessary to repel the armed attack and restore international peace and security. . . . "

During this initial period of activity, American policy makers flatly rejected any appeal to the moribund Military Staff Committee for fear of involving the Soviets. Because they also fretted about the appearance of taking unilateral action, they made it clear that the UN, not the United States, would ask for offers of assistance. Secretary-General Lie would front for the State Department in this diplomatic shadow dance. It is not surprising, therefore, that the Soviets charged Lie with complicity in an American plot. He had "outlived his usefulness," as one Eastern bloc diplomat put it.[57] Needless to say, the very things that made him persona non grata to the Soviets made him exceedingly useful to the Americans.

The formalization of the U.S.-UN relationship in respect to Korea came quickly. Both Washington and Secretariat officials, including Lie and his chief assistant, American Andrew Cordier, recognized the need to establish a command structure for UN troops in Korea. They proposed a resolution that created a unified command under a UN flag. American officials were happy to oblige. The Pentagon objected, however, to creation of a coordinating committee that Lie hoped would place the UN—and not just the United States—in a position to oversee the military phase of the war. The Joint Chiefs insisted on their own command and control. An amended resolution, formally sponsored by the United States and Great Britain, passed on July 7.[58] It created a unified UN command under American direction.

Not until July 27 when the Soviets ended their Security Council boycott did the UN role change. Why did Stalin end the boycott? Conventional wisdom holds that the boycott had become too costly in a diplomatic sense, particularly with the USSR soon scheduled to take over the council presidency. This is likely correct. Once the USSR returned to the Security Council, meetings concerning Korea became arid propaganda debates. Washington turned its attention to the General Assembly where no permanent veto could frustrate the American-led majority.

As in Palestine, it was battlefield developments, not diplomats, that defined what the UN would do during the remainder of the year. In September when UN forces broke out of their defensive perimeter around Pusan and began a steady advance northward, American and UN officials could no longer postpone asking whether their units should advance across the 38th parallel. According to U.S. officials, not only would the destruction of the communist government in North Korea eliminate the military problem, it would facilitate the UN's long-term goal: a unified Korea under a freely elected government. Perhaps NSC-68—or the assumptions that produced

NSC-68—made it unlikely that Washington would recommend anything else. Soviet protests and the reservations of a few Asian countries, led by India, were ignored as the Americans forcefully pressed their case in the General Assembly. The assembly overwhelmingly endorsed the decision to cross the 38th parallel on October 7, 1950.[59] American ambition had overwhelmed UN caution.

Within weeks, the first troops from the People's Republic of China (PRC) crossed the Yalu River separating North Korea from Manchuria. Great Britain, followed by others who should have raised serious questions about the October 7 resolution *before* it passed, expressed alarm about a full-scale Chinese intervention. Even the United States proposed a Security Council resolution that promised to respect the integrity of the North Korean-Chinese border. The USSR vetoed it. In any case, General MacArthur dismissed his own government's belated concerns about Chinese intervention. On November 25, the Chinese attacked massively. They proved Acheson right: the war was no longer a civil conflict.

Even before the Chinese attack, the USSR's return to the Security Council had prompted Washington to sponsor the Uniting for Peace Resolution in the General Assembly.[60] It formalized the shift of authority over collective-security matters from the council to the assembly whenever the veto deadlocked the council. As Evan Luard stated, this provision was "emphatically not contained in the Charter."[61] A key 1945 assumption—that the UN should *not* act when the Great Powers stood in opposition to each other—had now been discarded. The Uniting for Peace Resolution also challenged the assumption that compromise among the Great Powers was necessary for the UN to operate effectively; after its passage, compromise was no longer necessary.

This rejection of the need to compromise led the United States, in February 1951, to insist on UN condemnation of the PRC as an aggressor. China, of course, routinely hurled the same charge at the United States and its allies. When the United States formalized the "aggression" language in a UN resolution, Washington achieved a short-term victory but created a long-term problem. Reflecting anti-Chinese sentiment along with anticommunism the resolution passed by the usual large majority (44–7, with 9 abstentions) despite uneasiness among America's European allies.[62]

Labeling the PRC as an "aggressor" was not merely international name-calling. The Charter permits UN members to punish aggressors. Within two weeks, the General Assembly established the Additional Measures Committee to explore sanctions against China. When the PRC launched its next offensive after ignoring appeals to negotiate, Washington shortcut the deliberations of the Additional Measures Committee by recommending an embargo of raw materials to China, along with all goods of military importance. On May 18, with eastern bloc states refusing to vote, the General Assembly approved the embargo overwhelmingly.[63]

In sponsoring the resolutions of February 1 and May 18, Washington ignored the possibility—indeed, the probability—that settlement of the Korean conflict would require negotiations with the Chinese. The two resolutions—together with the UN's refusal to seat the new communist regime in Beijing—convinced Chinese officials that the UN was anything but neutral. To the extent, then, that the UN became identified with the United States, the resolutions may have ironically postponed a settlement; they continued to be a bone in China's throat well into the 1970s.

Certainly these resolutions did not hasten the end of the conflict, which continued for two more years. Nor did collective security—in which *all* UN members join to prevent aggression—approach universality. Of the 60 UN members, only 16 sent ground troops to Korea. Except for Filipinos and Thais, all were western. Of the total UN ground forces in Korea, half were American, 40 percent were South Korean, and the remaining 10 percent came from other states. Casualties reflected these percentages: over 30,000 Americans died in Korea. Of air units, 93 percent came from the United States, the rest from South Korea. Thirty other UN members contributed economic, medical, or technical assistance.[64]

The UN played the role of bystander during the final two years of the war. Truman's removal of General MacArthur as UN commander undoubtedly reassured many governments that the United States would continue a sane military policy. America's allies sought no wider war, certainly no war that would involve the USSR. Truman administration officials shared these sentiments.

By the summer of 1951 the war had become a stalemate. Peace negotiations began after Acheson and Soviet representative Jacob Malik made it known that both Washington and Moscow would welcome a truce. Helping them was a report by Abraham Feller, Trygve Lie's legal counsel, who concluded that a military armistice could be negotiated without additional UN consideration of the matter (new political conditions would have required UN approval). A number of UN members proposed resolutions to facilitate a settlement. Modified by the United States, the assembly approved an Indian resolution.[65] It created only false hopes.

Not until 1953 did the two sides agree to an armistice. McCarthyism in the United States, and Chinese resentment of the General Assembly's resolution naming the PRC as an aggressor, undoubtedly limited the flexibility of officials on both sides. And when a settlement became more likely after Stalin's death in March 1953, a bitter quarrel over the repatriation of POWs delayed matters for months. When, out of mutual exhaustion, the negotiators signed a truce on July 27, 1953, they ignored political issues, such as unification or free elections. A political settlement was postponed until the Geneva Conference of April 1954. By that time, global attention had shifted to Indochina. Fearful that free elections might work to their disadvantage, both Koreas shunned meaningful political concessions so that the Korean peninsula looks, at least politically, much the same in the 1990s as during the late 1940s.

In some ways, wrote Evan Luard, "the Korean episode can be regarded as the UN's finest hour." Yet even Luard understood that only the fortuitous Soviet boycott permitted the use of the force provisions of the Charter, and that the United States dominated the organization in a manner that compromised the real meaning of collective security.

If the Truman years had proved anything, it was that the UN could not live up to the hopes of its founders. Those hopes were built on expectations of Great Power cooperation. The veto protected those powers in the event that rivalry replaced cooperation which, of course, occurred with startling rapidity after the San Francisco Conference. The Americans could afford to give the UN plenty of lip service precisely because of U.S. influence at UN headquarters, but Realists like Kennan, Marshall, and Acheson never thought for a minute that the UN should be anything but another instrument for asserting U.S. interests abroad. Those instruments might include economic aid to Europe, or American occupation of Japan, or NATO, or covert activities among foreign labor unions. They might also include UN resolutions and embargoes and, when necessary, private negotiations with the Soviets as occurred at the UN between Jessup and Malik over Berlin.

A few Americans were genuine idealists. Austin was one, at least until the Korean War. By 1950, however, he too sounded like a Cold War warrior. Like so many liberal internationalists, he maintained his credibility with the State Department by telling his superiors what they wanted to hear. Eleanor Roosevelt's case was more complex. She had the kind of status that made her exceptionally independent. When she threatened to resign over U.S. Mideast policy in 1948, the administration worried about a political avalanche. Marshall refused to accept her resignation "however much it may complicate matters to have you criticizing the attitude of the administration."[66]

But even Mrs. Roosevelt was rendered safe. Refusing to assign her to the Security Council, the administration appointed her to the Human Rights Commission. Here she did monumental work drafting the UN's famous Declaration on Human Rights. The Senate ratified the measure despite opposition by southern segregationists. The Declaration stood in marked contrast to the Genocide Convention also favored by Mrs. Roosevelt and Assistant Secretary of State Ernest Gross. The convention would be held hostage by supporters of Senator John Bricker, who sought to limit the treaty-making power of the president. (see chapter 4).[67]

The Truman years were not friendly to idealists. By the time the UN moved into its new headquarters on the East River in 1950, it had lost much of its stature. That may be why the most important recent general history of American foreign policy during the Truman era, Melvin Leffler's 689-page *A Preponderance of Power*, contains only four index references to the UN.

chapter 4

EISENHOWER

General Dwight Eisenhower's 1952 victory in the presidential election, heralded by Republicans as a political revolution, meant only a meager change at the UN. Not only was the new president an internationalist, but both his secretary of state and his ambassador to the UN embraced the approach of the previous administration.

John Foster Dulles, the new State Department chief, was the grandson of one former secretary of state and the nephew of another. During the interwar period, Dulles had been among the most outspoken American advocates of collective security. As a representative of the Federal Council of Churches, he had organized support for American membership in a postwar organization during World War II. Despite Dulles's membership in the Republican Party, Truman named him to the U.S. delegation at the San Francisco Conference and to the General Assembly during 1946, 1947, 1948, and 1950. David Wainhouse, who served under Acheson and, later, Dulles in the Office of UN Affairs, considered Dulles much more supportive of the UN than Acheson.[1]

Joining Dulles in support of the UN, not always harmoniously, was Henry Cabot Lodge Jr. Lodge's father may have fought Woodrow Wilson over ratification of the League of Nation's Covenant, but he had been an internationalist and had strongly favored an Anglo-American security treaty to defend France in the wake of World War I (the treaty died when the Senate rejected the Covenant). Lodge Jr. continued the family's support of internationalism. From 1953 to 1960, he would serve his country as chief delegate to the UN, longer than any other American.

In that capacity, Lodge had plenty of influence. Unlike Austin, Lodge received formal cabinet-level status as America's UN representative. Combined with his personal connection to the president (Lodge helped Eisenhower launch his 1952 campaign), he enjoyed direct entree to the White House. Such access did not endear him to the new secretary of state, who worried that Lodge would circumvent the normal diplomatic chain of command. Dulles had reason to worry, though the sheer complexity of foreign policy forced Lodge, on routine matters, to approach Washington not only via Dulles, but through the Division of UN Affairs. Indeed, after an initial year filled with suspicion and even resentment, Lodge and Dulles forged a respectful relationship. "I'm a good soldier," Lodge protested in self defense.[2] In fact, the day-to-day need for bureaucratic efficiency helped to create an increasingly harmonious relationship; so, too, did the extent to which both Lodge and Dulles agreed on the ideological shape of collective security.

The president himself was no stranger to the challenges of foreign affairs. As commander of Allied forces in Europe during World War II and then as NATO commander, Eisenhower deepened his own commitment to international cooperation. One of the earliest themes in his memoirs reflects his fear about a postwar return to isolationism, and although he lacked Truman's enthusiasm for the UN, he clearly sympathized with its aims.[3]

Eisenhower, Dulles, and Lodge served a political party that had not fully come to terms with the demands of Cold War foreign policy. The Republicans in 1953 may have included out-and-out internationalists like Dulles and Lodge, but not all Republicans shared their outlook. The party also included a vocal faction, led by senators like William Jenner of Indiana and John W. Bricker of Ohio, who were spiritual descendants of the interwar isolationists, and another faction, led by Senate majority leader Robert Taft, that supported collective security intellectually but not emotionally. Perhaps the only thing that held this diverse group together was anticommunism and its corollary, contempt for the Soviet Union.

The new president reflected mainstream Republican thinking. He shared the widespread belief that Moscow's aims were illegitimate. The United States faced a "Soviet conspiracy to achieve world domination," he wrote in his memoirs, and he meant it.[4] The stakes were monumental, the competition global. The new administration made Truman's NSC-68 thoroughly bipartisan.

Yet despite the continuity with Truman administration thinking, the Republicans had trouble with bipartisanship. Republican attacks on Truman often equated the Democratic policy with simple treason. Anticommunists like Dean Acheson found themselves forced to defend their loyalty and patriotism. Republican extremists, led by Wisconsin's junior senator, Joe McCarthy, shifted the political center of gravity sharply to the right. Even Republicans like Eisenhower and Taft, who had the kind of integrity that never rubbed off on the Wisconsin demagogue, feared that a public quarrel with McCarthy might splinter the party and weaken their own influence.[5] It would have been surprising indeed if McCarthy's mischief did not affect American relations with the UN.

Sinai Desert. Yugoslav troops of the United National Emergency Force
on patrol. January 1957.
(UN/DPI Photo)

THE LOYALTY ISSUE CONTINUES

Perhaps the earliest manifestation of Republican anticommunism at the UN
was the intensification of loyalty issues pertaining to UN employees. Dulles's
approval of Scott McLeod as chief security officer for the State Department
augured trouble. McLeod proved to be an intemperate and intolerant zealot,
more loyal to McCarthy than to Dulles himself. But it was not the security
apparatus in Washington so much as the way that Ambassador Lodge imple-
mented security in New York that wounded the UN. From Yalta to the events
in China, the State Department had long been a target of fanatical anticommunists. By 1949, they increasingly turned their attention to the UN as a
hotbed of Red subversion (see chapter 3). American magazines, most notably
US News and World Report, fanned charges that UN stood for "Un-American,"
while congressional investigators, led by Nevada senator Pat McCarran and
Pennsylvania representative Francis Walter, mined them for political
(fools)gold.

After Eisenhower's inauguration, the pace of accusation increased. Perhaps
because he really believed the charges against UN personnel, though more

likely because he had sensitive political antennae, Ambassador Lodge unambiguously supported the loyalty program after assuming his post. According to historian Jeff Broadwater, Lodge asked the FBI director to undertake "full-field investigations of all employees at the U.S. Mission" just hours after taking over his UN post. By the time the FBI finished its work, it roamed far beyond the mission, fingerprinting nearly two thousand employees at UN headquarters.[6] The Eisenhower administration then issued executive order 10459, creating a new International Organizations' Employees Loyalty Board to advise the secretary-general on personnel issues. Ideological purity enjoyed its heyday, though in truth 10459 merely continued an expired directive from the previous administration.

Dag Hammarskjold, who assumed the post of secretary-general in March 1953, gave the Loyalty Board less support than had Lie. Nevertheless, the inexperienced secretary-general reluctantly acquiesced in the firing of Americans who took the Fifth Amendment before Senator McCarran's Internal Security subcommittee. He even refused to reinstate them after appeals. But when a UN tribunal granted them compensation, leading to strong protests from Lodge and Vice President Richard Nixon, Hammarskjold backed up the tribunal. The controversy did not end there. The fever pitch of domestic anti-communism prompted the State Department to seek to overturn the tribunal's judgment by appealing directly to the General Assembly. Although the Americans usually had their way in the UN during these years, they overreached on this issue. With the United States on the verge of losing its appeal—and therefore its face—Britain and France sought to defuse the issue by asking the World Court to adjudicate the matter. The State Department unwisely protested. Nevertheless, the court had its say, ruling against the Americans in July 1954.

It is difficult even today to judge the degree to which the Americans—especially Dulles and Lodge—were motivated by ideological zeal or political self-interest. Their critics, like Shirley Hazzard, emphasize the former; their defenders, like Dulles's biographer Frederick W. Marks III, emphasize the latter.[7] Undoubtedly both motives were important. Important, too, is a point made by Marks but often ignored by Dulles's harshest critics: that the secretary of state responded to cues sent from the White House. No one came out of this episode with honor. It should also be remembered that the Eisenhower-Dulles investigation of communists at the UN was no worse (though no better) than that of their Truman administration predecessors. Finally, it should be noted that the Senate's censure of Senator McCarthy in December 1954 ended the worst abuses.

The degree to which Trygve Lie had cooperated with the State Department's loyalty program (much more than had Hammarskjold) may well be related to the politics of his efforts to continue as secretary-general. Lie's five-year term had expired in 1951. Although the USSR had initially vowed to back his reappointment, Lie's support for UN operations in Korea led the Soviets to repudiate him. Shortly thereafter, when the United States announced that it would reject anyone other than Lie, Moscow announced that it would use the veto to block him. That meant deadlock when the United States vowed to veto a Soviet-backed candidate. Because the Charter required that the Security Council recommend appointment or reappointment of a secretary-general to the General Assembly, the United States proposed that the General Assembly simply extend Lie's tenure, though not as a formal reappointment, thus bypassing the Security Council. The assembly concurred in November 1950; it rarely disregarded American cues during this period.[8]

Thus did Lie gain another term . . . and more Soviet enmity. Denouncing his reappointment as illegal, Moscow refused to have anything to do with him.[9] This made Lie even more dependent on the Americans than previously, accounting in part for his cooperation with the U.S. government on the loyalty issue. Unfortunately, his cavalier treatment of his staff, especially in light of the investigations, virtually destroyed the morale of the Secretariat. By 1952, the situation had become impossible. Denounced by the Soviets, disdained by his own staff, distrusted by American officials who increasingly questioned his competence, and attacked by the nationalist right in the United States, Lie announced his resignation in the same month as the American presidential election.

The political maneuvering surrounding the selection of his successor made the intricacies of papal politics look quaint. Washington initially backed Carlos Romulo of the Philippines, while the British backed Canada's Lester Pearson or, as a backup, Netherland's Foreign Minister Dirk Stikker. Other candidates, too, came and went: India's Madame V. L. Pandit and Benegal Rao, Poland's Stanislaw Skreszewski, Lebanon's Charles Malik, Mexico's Pablo Nervo, and Sweden's foreign minister Erik Boheman. A predictable impasse developed, with the United States and USSR still vowing to veto each other's choices. Only after Soviet dictator Stalin died on March 5 and Lie ungraciously announced that he would be willing to withdraw his resignation did the situation begin to resolve itself. Word that the Americans would support no one but Lie probably helped persuade the Kremlin to consider a compromise candidate.[10] That candidate was Hammarskjold. Only the Nationalist Chinese government, resentful of Sweden's recognition of the PRC, stood in the way with its own veto. This obstacle disappeared when China agreed to abstain.

On March 31, 1953, Hammarskjold, an economist who served as Sweden's Minister of State and had formerly headed the European section of Sweden's foreign ministry, received his appointment. U.S. officials greeted him warmly, less because they knew him than because they welcomed the departure of Lie and the end of the succession controversy. Internationalists, after all, had other things to worry about. In early 1953, American isolationists and nationalists increasingly attacked the UN, using the loyalty issue and the UN's inability to end the stalemate in Korea as a substitute for a direct attack on the UN itself.

The bloom had worn off the UN rose. Anti-UN sentiment crystallized around a campaign organized by conservative Republican senator John W. Bricker of Ohio to curb the president's authority in the foreign policy area. In the new Republican congress of 1953, Bricker reintroduced a constitutional amendment to limit the treaty-making power of the executive branch and to reduce presidential authority to make executive agreements. His proposed amendment would itself be amended a number of times during the next year, eventually garnering support from most Senate Republicans and many southern Democrats. It drew much of its strength from anticommunists who believed that FDR and Truman had sold out U.S. interests to Stalin at Yalta and Potsdam. But it fed equally on anti-UN sentiment. At issue were a number of sections of the Charter. Bricker singled out those articles that called for member nations to promote social and economic progress.[11] He argued that UN economic programs would turn the United States into a "socialistic state." He also aimed his guns at the Declaration of Human Rights and a companion agreement, the 1948 Genocide Convention drafted to outlaw state-sponsored mass slaughter falling outside the legal framework of war. Southern segregationists led the campaign for the Bricker Amendment as a way to protect the system of white supremacy.

The Bricker Amendment required that international agreements, including treaties, be subordinate to congressional legislation and even state law. Not only would the amendment threaten NATO and UN commitments, but it would leave virtually all international agreements vulnerable to legislative and legal challenge. As the implications of the amendment became clear, especially after Bricker refused to consider a substitute amendment stating that no treaty could violate the constitution, President Eisenhower came out in full opposition. He dismissed the American Bar Association's support for the amendment (he accused the ABA of trying to "save the constitution from Eleanor Roosevelt"), called Bricker "almost psychopathic" on the subject, and argued that passage of the amendment would cripple the president's constitutional authority in the area of foreign affairs.[12] Debate over the Bricker Amendment lasted for more than a year. In the spring of 1954, by just a single vote, the Senate denied the amendment the two-thirds majority it needed for further congressional consideration.

Regardless of the outcome, the amendment's widespread support deterred the Eisenhower administration from drafting additional covenants related to the Universal Declaration of Human Rights, which the Senate had ratified in 1948, and ended the administration's interest in ratifying the UN's Genocide Convention. (The Senate would not ratify the Genocide Convention until 1986; it finally became law when the Reagan administration and Senate majority leader Robert Dole, neither known for their UN sympathies, forced

Senate action to advertise American support for human rights).[13] Dulles, who had previously exhibited a moralistic concern about human rights, claimed that government reports would provide more effective protection for oppressed groups than UN covenants. Some historians argue that he genuinely believed that the time was not yet ripe for these covenants, but the truth is more prosaic: In the wake of Bricker's campaign, Dulles sought to shield the administration from growing anti-UN sentiment at home. He paradoxically backed away from public support for the UN as a way to slow the campaign in favor of the Bricker Amendment. It is impossible to know for sure whether this strategy succeeded. What is certain, however, is that he derailed American support for the human rights declaration and the Genocide Convention for more than two decades.[14]

DISPUTES OVER CHINA

At the same time that the Eisenhower administration battled Bricker, it engaged in several skirmishes at the UN. All related to the Cold War, and all helped to refashion the UN as a weapon in the East-West conflict. The Cold War, according to historian H. W. Brands, "marginalized" the UN, turning it into less a system of collective security than a "truncated system of selective security."[15] Nowhere is this more evident than in the Eisenhower administration's efforts to preserve UN representation for Nationalist China.

During Truman's presidency, the Chinese communists, having defeated the Nationalists who fled to Taiwan in 1949, had demanded the Chinese seat on the Security Council. The Charter covered seating new members but said nothing about replacing representatives from a state already holding membership. Most UN officials believed that the procedure would resemble that for admitting new members, with the Security Council making a recommendation to the General Assembly. Any permanent member, including China and the United States, could, therefore, exercise its veto. When the United States unsurprisingly protected the Nationalist seat, the Soviets stormed out of the UN, not to return until August 1950.

The hardening of U.S. policy toward the PRC (officials in Washington never said "PRC," only "Red China") had been substantially influenced by the China Lobby, which charged ad nauseam that Truman had "lost" China. And although the State Department was privately uncertain about whether the PRC, if it were a UN member, would chart an independent line from Moscow (as had Tito's Yugoslavia), the department became a prisoner of both its public and private assertions that communism was monolithic. Unwilling to abandon the Nationalists on Taiwan and increasingly nervous about the end of the U.S. atomic monopoly, the Truman administration had extended no hand to the new Chinese leadership. When the Korean War erupted in June 1950, followed by Chinese intervention in November, American policy toward China froze.

Eisenhower continued Truman's policy after moving into the White House. Anything less would have been politically perilous at a time when editors like Henry Luce and writers like William Bullitt advocated that the United States unleash Chiang Kai-shek for an invasion of the Chinese mainland. McCarthyism fertilized this kind of thinking. In June 1953, congressional Republicans attached a rider to an appropriations bill mandating a cutoff of funds to the UN if the General Assembly seated Beijing (Peiping, they called it). Indeed, Senate majority leader William Knowland, one of the most prominent spokesmen for the China lobby, threatened to resign his seat in order to seek U.S. withdrawal from the UN if the General Assembly seated a PRC representative, while lobby loyalists like William Jenner and Walter Judd equated talk of a policy change with treason.[16] The new administration had no inclination to argue publicly.

Privately, however, a few officials, notably the special ambassador to Korea, Arthur Dean, did suggest a shift in policy. Stalin's death and the Quemoy-Matsu crisis subsequently encouraged others to consider a two-China policy, hoping it would loosen China's alliance with the USSR. Most officials, however, believed that the best way to break the Moscow-Beijing alliance was to take a hard line, including military threats and a trade embargo.

Interestingly, Dulles never entirely ruled out the possibility of a two-China policy. Historians like Gordon H. Chang and Nancy Bernkopf Tucker argue that he positively favored it. Indeed, asserts Tucker, in 1954 he considered removing China from the Security Council in order to eliminate the Chinese veto. This, he believed, would make the PRC entry into the UN "a less fearful prospect."[17] She also claims that Dulles unsuccessfully tried to persuade Chiang not to veto the seating of Outer Mongolia in 1955, and that he privately favored universal membership. But whatever he said behind closed doors was not necessarily said publicly. Dulles certainly did *not* promote two-China membership during Security Council debates in 1953 and 1955. (Nor, it should be added, did either Chinese faction exhibit the slightest interest in a two-China policy). In the General Assembly, Dulles opposed formal discussion of PRC representation when, each year, the Soviets proposed to expel the Chinese Nationalists. The Eisenhower administration occasionally placed a higher priority on anticommunism than universal membership.

Because the PRC had no seat, the UN saw little of the U.S.-PRC rivalry. There were three exceptions: the seating issue itself, the return of U.S. airmen captured in China, and the offshore islands dispute. The second of these led to a protest by U.S. ambassador Lodge after the PRC convicted 11 American airmen, plus two other Americans, of espionage.[18] The Chinese claimed the men had been shot down over Manchuria, while the United States retorted they had been downed over North Korea before the end of the Korean War. In other words, the Americans defined the men as POWs, which saddled the dispute with emotional baggage.

The American government argued that the UN, not the United States, should take responsibility for pressing the case against Beijing because the airmen had been part of the UN command in Korea. Hammarskjold did not object. He did, however, tone down the American condemnation of Beijing included in a proposed UN resolution so that the two sides would concentrate on the prisoners without turning the issue into a propaganda circus. He also volunteered to mediate the dispute. On December 10, 1954, the General Assembly passed the amended resolution demanding release of the prisoners and authorizing Hammarskjold to use whatever means he judged appropriate to settle the issue.[19]

The secretary-general would eventually succeed and, in the process, redefine his office. Neither came easily. During late December 1954 and early January 1955, he travelled to Beijing while Washington hardliners denounced his effort. Senator Knowland called it a failure and charged the UN with "a massive propaganda buildup," while the State Department inveighed against "China's gangster role."[20] Such comments may have played well in Peoria, but not in Beijing. With the airman issue further complicated by American opposition to the PRC's shelling of Nationalist offshore islands, Hammarskjold temporarily gave up. He resumed his efforts in February, but even Lodge complained that Hammarskjold exceeded his authority. The secretary-general therefore found himself handicapped by both American critics during the offshore islands crisis and Beijing's refusal to deal with a Security Council that refused to recognize its existence. Nor was his task made easier when the United States refused an offer by Chinese Foreign Minister Zhou Enlai to permit the airmens' families to visit the prisoners.

Hammarskjold refused to give up. By August 1, his exhaustion turned to quiet exhilaration as Beijing released the prisoners. Hammarskjold had taken the December 10 resolution as a personal challenge; as he would do later in the Congo, he displayed extraordinary resourcefulness and imagination in pursuit of a goal that few officials believed achievable. Despite Washington's ambivalent response to his effort (Eisenhower's memoirs, for instance, do not even mention Hammarskjold's role in China), he had won new respect for both himself and his organization.

The last important episode involving the UN, the United States, and the PRC was the offshore islands dispute. Here the stakes were higher and the UN's role less prominent. When the Chinese Nationalists fled to Formosa in 1949, they maintained control of some small islands off the mainland including Quemoy and Matsu (about five miles off the coast), the Tachen group, and the Pescadores. The revolutionary government in Beijing claimed sovereignty over these islands as over Taiwan itself, but the PRC lacked the military capability to enforce its claims. By 1954, with the Nationalists launching irritating raids on the mainland from some of these islands while threatening a military "return," the communists stepped up their own demand for the islands and shelled Quemoy and Matsu as a way to advertise their title. The

Eisenhower administration characterized China's action as another example of Red aggression.

Neither Eisenhower nor Dulles ever believed that the islands were strategically critical to either American or Taiwanese security. Both men feared, however, that loss of the islands would damage Taiwan's morale, and they worried plenty about the domestic political effect of surrendering the islands. Seeking neither another war with China so soon after Korea nor wanting to appear supine, the administration adopted a middle course: it sent the Seventh Fleet to the area but refused to say categorically that it would fight for the islands' defense.

Such deliberate ambiguity did not last long. By early 1955, the administration came out in support of the Formosa Resolution in Congress, which gave the president virtually a free hand to defend Taiwan and "related positions and territories. . . . " With the crisis heating up, Dulles gave Chiang Kai-shek assurances that the United States would indeed defend Quemoy and Matsu in case of a communist military assault. The fall of the islands would be catastrophic, Dulles concluded by March, so much so that the administration apparently resolved to use tactical atomic weapons in their defense.[21]

But the administration did not relish gearing up for a war it really did not want and sought ways to defuse the crisis. The State Department first applied pressure on Chiang to evacuate the Tachens. It then brought the matter to the UN, having already helped to defeat a Soviet resolution before the General Assembly (by a 44–5 vote) calling for the end of U.S.-sponsored acts of aggression against the PRC. But early in 1955, when New Zealand asked the Security Council to consider the question of armed hostilities around the islands, the USSR responded by asking the council to address American aggression against China. A procedural wrangle ensued when the Soviets demanded that a PRC representative attend the session. New Zealand agreed, but only if the agenda were to be limited. In the final analysis, the council voted 9–1 (the Nationalists opposed) to invite a Beijing representative to debate the resolution. The PRC rejected the invitation because the Nationalists continued to occupy the Chinese seat. Under these circumstances, the council decided to postpone discussion of the New Zealand resolution and rejected by 10 to 1 Moscow's demand for a discussion of the Soviet resolution denouncing the U.S. role. As had already proved true over Korea (and would prove true again during the Vietnam War), the UN could do little to negotiate solutions to conflicts so long as Great Power vetoes prevailed and disputing parties were themselves nonmembers.

TENSION IN LATIN AMERICA

At about the same time that the United States isolated the PRC at the UN during the offshore islands controversy, American representatives used the

UN to weaken a leftist government in Latin America. American anticommunism had a global reach.

The target this time was Guatemala. The origins of the controversy extended back to 1944 when a popular revolution in that country overthrew a reactionary government, beginning a process of political and economic reform. In 1950, Jacobo Arbenz Guzman became Guatemala's second elected president. Conservatives in Latin America during the Cold War, no less than many American conservatives, discredited reform by calling it communism. When Truman's advisers drafted NSC-141 in 1952, they called for the kind of orderly development in Latin America that would make the region "resistant to the internal growth of communism and to Soviet political warfare."[22] After Truman left office in January 1953, his successors were, if anything, even more willing than he to pursue an actively anticommunist policy in the region. That meant trouble in Guatemala, for conservative opponents of Arbenz frequently denounced him as a communist. His refusal to disavow communist support seemed to lend validity to these charges.

Because they could not believe that voters anywhere would freely elect communists, many American policy makers viewed Guatemalan radicalism—which they construed to be communism—as a product of Soviet subversion. Put differently, they came to see the politics of Guatemala as, in Dulles's words, "the intrusion of Soviet despotism" challenging "our Monroe Doctrine."[23] As early as the end of 1953, this view led to joint CIA-State Department efforts to organize anti-Arbenz activity. In March of the following year, the State Department supported efforts at the Organization of American States (OAS) conference in Caracas to endorse "appropriate action" against any Western Hemisphere country controlled by "the international communist movement." Once Arbenz began to expropriate the property of the American-owned United Fruit Company, the Eisenhower administration earmarked more and more U.S. military aid for Guatemala's rival neighbors. The result, of course, was that Arbenz increasingly looked to the Eastern bloc for arms, which reinforced the belief that he was a communist. By mid-June 1954, American authorities gave the go-ahead for a counterrevolution.

Within hours, CIA-armed Guatemalan rebels in Nicaragua crossed the border into Guatemala. They advanced toward the capital city while American planes flown by American pilots bombed strategic targets. In desperation, on June 19 Arbenz asked the Security Council to denounce American "aggression" and end the fighting.[24] During the offshore islands controversy, the United States had the consolation of knowing that the PRC had no UN seat. The Guatemalan government, of course, had a seat. What it did not have was influence. Ambassador Lodge, working closely with representatives of friendly Latin American states, argued that the dispute should be considered by the OAS, not the Security Council. Article 52 of the UN Charter, he claimed, authorized the council to refer disputes to regional agencies; he fully understood that the OAS was subject to even more U.S. direction than the UN.

The Guatemalan delegate objected, insisting that Articles 34, 35, and 39 gave each member-state the right to appeal directly to the Security Council.

The validity of his argument was irrelevant. Guatemala never had a chance at the UN. Brazil and Colombia, responding to U.S. suggestions, sponsored a resolution calling for the OAS to consider the matter. It passed 10–1, with the USSR in opposition.[25] On June 20, with the OAS deliberately dragging its feet, the Soviet Union and Guatemala again asked for Security Council consideration. This time, a number of states, including Britain and France, expressed reservations about refusing to place the matter on the council agenda. They began to worry that the precedent might come back to haunt them. The Americans offered them no comfort. An angry Eisenhower complained that the British expected U.S. support regarding Cyprus but would not back the United States on Guatemala; two days later, he ordered Lodge to inform both NATO allies that if they supported Guatemala, "we would feel free to take an equally independent line concerning such matters as Egypt and North Africa."[26] Dulles repeated this threat directly to Prime Minister Churchill and Foreign Secretary Anthony Eden when they visited Washington the next day. With the United States threatening to veto any resolution calling for consideration of the question, Britain and France caved in. The council, by one vote, supported the U.S. position, with both allies abstaining.

Within 48 hours, Arbenz surrendered. The Americans may have enjoyed the fruits of their imperial behavior, but they had further injured the UN, using the organization to promote rather than to prohibit aggression.[27] (Ironically, having strong-armed the British and French by threatening to undermine their Mediterranean interests unless they toed the U.S. line on Guatemala, Dulles undermined them anyhow during the Suez Crisis of 1956. Gratitude was not his strong suit.)

As for the UN, the damage had been done. Hammarskjold, who took the Charter very seriously, protested to the State Department, arguing that Article 103 elevated the UN above any regional agreement. He further insisted (correctly) that not even a permanent veto could prevent consideration of a question at the Security Council.[28] The State Department protested his protest, warning him that he risked grave damage to his impartiality. What the Soviets had done to Lie, the Americans, by implication, threatened to do to Hammarskjold. The United States did not see the secretary-general's independence as a virtue, nor his strength as an asset. American policy makers sought UN compliance, not autonomy.

A number of developments, then, suggest that Washington viewed the UN in 1955 much differently than it had in 1945. The administration's ambivalence about Hammarskjold's initiative over the downed airmen, its retreat from universality over the China question, its sandbagging of efforts to bring the Guatemalan appeal to the Security Council, all point in the direction of using the UN as a Cold War instrument, not a universal peace organization. Historians who have charted U.S. Cold War policy often focus on Secretary of State Dulles as the key to understanding this change. Many emphasize his rigidity, his moralistic approach to international politics, his knee-jerk anticommunism, his tendency to substitute slogans ("liberation, "rollback," "massive retaliation," "brinkmanship") for analysis.

Yet Dulles was hardly one-dimensional. A view of Dulles is emerging that suggests he was simultaneously less ideological and more pragmatic than previously believed. For example, he never ruled out a two-China policy. He did not advocate equipping Chiang Kai-shek for a return to the mainland, nor did he allow the offshore islands dispute to become a hot war. His approach to Indochina in 1954 also exhibited restraint: he opposed sending in American air or ground troops unilaterally in order to help the French stave off defeat against a communist insurgency. The secretary may have feared the wrath of the China lobby and other allies of Joe McCarthy (who didn't?), but he consistently refrained from their worst excesses.

Moreover, Dulles had no use for Senator Knowland's hostility toward the UN, and, in 1955, his State Department authorized Lodge to abstain from, but not veto, a resolution admitting five communist states to the General Assembly (Mongolia and four from Eastern Europe). The United States, claimed Lodge, could not welcome their membership because they were not "independent" states, but by including all but Mongolia as part of a package deal involving 12 other countries, the State Department helped to settle a nettlesome membership issue that had bedeviled the UN since 1951.[29]

At about the same time, therefore, that it weakened the UN by promoting its own agenda on issues like China and Guatemala, the United States strengthened it by inching toward an ideal it did not really support: universality. The president and his secretary of state also strengthened the organization by using the UN to promote other goals that they may not have entirely believed in, such as a world free from atomic holocaust.

THE ATOMIC THREAT

The world had become a more dangerous place at the moment the Soviets broke America's atomic monopoly in 1949. In 1952, the British tested their first A-bomb. A few days later, the United States exploded its first hydrogen bomb. Some months later, the USSR followed suit. In an age when the difference between tactical and strategic weapons remained fuzzy, when American military planners emphasized the virtues of an "inexpensive" nuclear defense rather than a more expensive conventional defense, and when Secretary Dulles announced a policy dubbed "massive retaliation," it seemed rational indeed to worry about atomic incineration. Even Republicans worried about it, which led President Eisenhower to the General Assembly where, in December 1953, he delivered his most celebrated foreign policy address. The United States, he announced to the applause of even Soviet delegates:

pledges . . . its determination to help solve the fearful atomic dilemma—
to devote its entire heart and mind to find the way by which the miraculous
inventiveness of man shall not be dedicated to his death, but consecrated
to his life.[30]

That way, suggested the president, would be creation of an international
atomic agency to store all fissionable materials. With security measures to protect the world against unauthorized use, these materials could then be allocated for peaceful use. "Atoms for Peace," a friendly press called it.

The UN had provided little more than the setting for the president's proposal. The idea had germinated in Washington among presidential advisers
such as propaganda specialist C. D. Jackson and Atomic Energy Commission
chairman Lewis Strauss. UN disarmament forums had been uninvolved.
Because atomic disarmament was akin to motherhood, the Soviets could
hardly snub it. But neither could they endorse a plan requiring them to contribute their limited supply of uranium 235 to an international storehouse.
They knew—and Eisenhower also knew—that for a considerable period, the
United States would retain vastly greater uranium reserves. As the Baruch
Plan would have guaranteed the United States nuclear superiority, so too did
Atoms for Peace.

Nevertheless, Eisenhower's initiative had tapped a source of global ner-
vousness, and it would be wrong to think that he privately disdained what he
publicly promoted. In spite of the degree to which his own administration
increasingly relied on a nuclear defense strategy, the president believed that
the world was "courting disaster" in the armaments race. He viewed his warning as revolutionary.[31] Because Atoms for Peace allowed him to blend his personal convictions with defending the national interest, he approved establishing the Vienna-based International Atomic Energy Agency (IAEA) in 1957.
This UN organ would promote the peaceful use of atomic energy and protect
against the diversion of nuclear materials for purposes of war.

Yet the early history of the IAEA illustrates an element of American thinking that vexed the UN for years. U.S. policy makers, preoccupied with Cold
War rivalries during the 1950s, sought to move the IAEA as far from the UN
as they could. Ostensibly, they sought to shield it from the "political merry-go-
round" in New York. In fact, they wanted to insulate it from the Soviet veto.
Hammarskjold fought this development. He believed that the IAEA (and
others specialized organs) should be UN agencies no less than an organization
like the Food and Agricultural Organization. Of course atomic energy was
political; to pretend otherwise—as Eisenhower implied—was to believe in
fairy tales.[32]

No less political was Eisenhower's "open skies" proposal. At the 1955
Geneva summit meeting with Soviet leaders, the president unveiled his plan
for unrestricted international aerial flight and surveillance. Like Atoms for
Peace, it had broad appeal. If overflights of Soviet or American territory would

inhibit preparation for war, then presumably both countries would be less likely to prepare secretly for conflict. Indeed, the General Assembly gave overwhelming support to the idea: only seven Soviet-bloc states voted against it.[33]

But of course there was more to Open Skies than met the eye. While Lodge told the General Assembly that any country that "truly hates war" would support Open Skies as a way to "outlaw surprise attack," the Soviets demurred. As a closed society, they had much more to lose by opening their skies to the eyes of U.S. intelligence.[34] Consequently, both at the UN and elsewhere, Moscow ignored the issue until, following the 1957 launch of Sputnik and the birth of satellite photography, it faded into the fog of propaganda past.

THE SUEZ CRISIS

During 1956, while the United States called for Open Skies, Middle East developments closed an important waterway. The revolutionary leader of Egypt, Gamal Abdel Nasser, threatened to nationalize the Suez Canal, precipitating the greatest foreign policy crisis of the Eisenhower presidency. Although the crisis initially evolved without much reference to the UN, its resolution deeply involved the American government in UN diplomacy and forever changed the shape of the organization.

The Suez Crisis, as it would be called, had roots that extended back to British construction of the canal in the nineteenth century and Israel's independence in 1948. The truce that ended the Israeli war for independence in 1949 did not bring real peace; and without a peace treaty, Israel and Egypt remained in a state of belligerence. Subsequent Arab commando (fedayeen) raids into Israel from the Gaza strip, usually followed by Israeli retaliatory strikes in Egypt, kept the region in a fervid state. In March 1956, Washington and London proposed that the United States appoint an "agent-general" in the Mideast with broad authority to impose a peaceful settlement, and an American resolution, passed by the Security Council on April 4, authorized Hammarskjold to travel to the region in order to restore, if not peace, at least calm.[35] The resolution, however, did not address such underlying issues as refugees, water rights, or the state of war between the two sides.

Hammarskjold's efforts notwithstanding, the 1949 truce continued to deteriorate during the remainder of 1956. American interest in a regional settlement took second place to growing U.S. anger directed at Nasser. During years when the State Department viewed neutralism with alarm, Nasser's commitment to nonalignment took the form of accepting Soviet military and economic aid no less than Western aid. His socialist rhetoric, the vulnerability of Western oil lines, his uncompromising policy toward Israel, all made Washington increasingly nervous.

To secure Egypt's cooperation to construct what was projected to be the world's biggest dam, the United States, through the efforts of the UN-affiliated World Bank, had agreed to extend to Cairo a $130 million loan (with Britain contributing another $80 million and the bank $200 million). The dam was central to Nasser's plans to develop Egypt's struggling economy. To be located at Aswan, it would serve as the foundation for electric power and agricultural development.

Then came a political earthquake. With the Americans already nervous about the cost, Nasser extended diplomatic recognition to the PRC and concluded an arms deal with communist Czechoslovakia. Dulles and Eisenhower saw red, both figuratively and politically. They withdrew the American offer of financial support. Two days later, Britain followed suit, threatening not just Egypt's future, but Nasser's prestige.[36] The Egyptian then showed that two could play the same game. He not only approached the Soviet Union for financing (rumors that he had done this earlier may have influenced the U.S. decision in the first place), but he unilaterally nationalized the Suez Canal on July 26, 1956. The $100 million in annual tolls that would result would allow him to finance the Aswan project without western aid, and he could control the flow of oil to every corner of industrialized Europe. To the petroleum-rich Americans, this prospect was unpleasant enough. To the oil-dependent British and French, it was an economic death threat.

The West should not have been surprised at Nasser's reaction. For years Egyptians had resented foreign control of the canal (and were slated to take it over in 1968 anyway). Neither, it should be said, should Nasser have been surprised at the European response. Prime Minister Eden viewed the Egyptian action as a criminal betrayal (he titles this section of his memoirs "Theft"). "Some say that Nasser is no Hitler or Mussolini," he wrote. "Allowing for a difference in scale, I am not so sure."[37] Eden, like French Premier Christian Pineau, was a political child of the 1930s. He detested appeasement. It would have been surprising if he had *not* resolved to use force to regain control of the canal.

For Eden, the UN was not much of an option. He had about as much respect for the organization as had Acheson. Both London and Paris understood that the Soviet veto would likely render the Security Council worthless in persuading Nasser to reverse his decision, and they were almost equally skeptical about the General Assembly. They would rely on their own power.

What they had not foreseen, however, was U.S. opposition to threatening Nasser with military measures. Beginning as early as July 31, President Eisenhower clearly warned them against using force; he would repeat himself again and again, both privately and publicly. Unlike the president, Dulles was ambivalent. He abhorred European imperialism and deeply respected the UN's mission to maintain a peaceful world (despite his inconsistency when American interests were involved). By the same token, his fear about a challenge to American control of the Panama Canal, combined with his appreciation of Europe's dependence on oil, left him more tolerant of a military response. For the most part, however, Dulles toed the presidential line.[38] If the

Secretary-General Dag Hammarskjold and UN Undersecretary Ralph
Bunch view Suez Canal salvage operations. March 25, 1957.
(UN/DPI Photo)

British and French did not understand this, it was because they did not want
to understand it.

The failure of a London conference to settle the controversy in August led
to new efforts to achieve a compromise that would satisfy the demands of
Egypt's sovereignty and French and British navigation. For the next month or
two, the United States took the lead. The Americans proposed formation of a
Suez Canal Users' Association (SCUA) to operate the canal, maintain freedom of passage, and negotiate with Egypt over tolls. With Britain and France
already secretly preparing for military action, and with Nasser demanding
more control over the canal than SCUA would allow, the proposal went
nowhere.

Neither did suggestions for UN action. When Britain and France first
called the dispute to the attention of the Security Council, they did not
bother to request an actual council meeting. They did not want the UN to
interfere with their military planning. Not until October 5 did the council
meet to consider the issue. During the next few days, Dag Hammarskjold took
charge of finding a middle ground, and the dispute did seem to move closer—
a *little* closer—to a resolution. During the next two weeks, the secretary-
general authored a set of six principles that he hoped would form the basis of
a settlement.

Hammarskjold should have saved his energy. With Britain and France now joining with Israel to coordinate plans for an attack, they were even less interested in a UN settlement. They would tolerate neither nationalization of the canal nor the continuation of Nasser as Egyptian leader.

American policy makers, meanwhile, were kept in the dark. Although U.S. intelligence saw signs of Israeli mobilization and Anglo-French military movement in the Mediterranean, the Americans, no less than the Egyptians, were unprepared for what happened next. On October 29, the Israelis advanced into the Sinai desert on the pretext of destroying the fedayeen. This was not the kind of retaliatory raid so often launched during the previous few years. This was war. One day later, Britain and France issued an ultimatum to Egypt and Israel to withdraw their forces and permit an Anglo-French occupation of the canal zone. The most serious foreign policy crisis since Korea was about to envelop the UN just days before Premier Nikita Khrushchev ordered Soviet tanks into Budapest to crush a revolutionary challenge to Moscow's authority.

Until the Israeli attack, the UN had played a distinctly secondary role in the Suez affair. No more. Within hours, the State Department announced that it would bring the matter to the UN. Eisenhower and Dulles were hopping mad, in part because they believed the war to be unnecessary and foolish, in part because they felt that the Israelis and French (but not the British) had bamboozled them. On October 30, Ambassador Lodge wasted little time calling for a cease fire and Israeli withdrawal. He acted hastily because the Americans wanted to beat the Soviets to the draw, especially in light of Russian involvement in Hungary. Indeed, the Hungarian developments made Eisenhower, Dulles, and Lodge all the more determined to flaunt their anticolonialist credentials, credentials that they took very seriously. Suez offered them a wonderful opportunity. The center of diplomatic gravity having shifted to the Security Council, Lodge's resolution led Britain and France to exercise their vetoes for the very first time. They likewise vetoed a similar Soviet resolution.

With the Security Council handcuffed by the veto, Yugoslavia moved to invoke the United for Peace Resolution, which Washington immediately backed. Used by Acheson during the Korean War to circumvent the Soviet veto, this brought the dispute to the General Assembly meeting in its first emergency session. Eisenhower ordered Dulles to attend, and the secretary of state, defending his decision to break with America's NATO allies, gave an impassioned speech in defense of "principles which far transcend the immediate issue."[39] Rarely during the next two decades would the United States find itself so enthusiastically supported by the assembly's anticolonial majority. On November 2, just four days before the American presidential election, a U.S.-sponsored resolution passed by a 64–5-6 vote (Australia and New Zealand joined Israel and the two European allies in opposition). It called for a cease-fire, military withdrawal, and reopening of the canal with passage for all ships, including previously banned Israeli shipping. The resolution ignored the underlying problems.[40]

The most important development at the UN during that week did not come at the suggestion of the Americans, however. In the debate over the resolution, British representative Pierson Dixon obliquely suggested creating a UN force to separate Israelis and Egyptians in the canal zone and to take steps to restore freedom of navigation. During the next two days Canada's Lester Pearson picked up on this idea, from which evolved the United Nations Emergency Force, the first genuine UN peacekeeping force. A Canadian/Columbian/Norwegian resolution asking the secretary-general to draft plans for such a force (the idea to enlist Hammarskjold came from Lodge) passed on November 5. Great Britain and France, which by now had bombed targets in the canal zone and were finally landing troops, indicated that they would cease fighting if such a force came into being and canal passage could be assured. On this basis did all parties agree to a cease-fire.

For the next four months, the UN labored to bring things to a conclusion. This meant persuading London, Paris, and Tel Aviv to withdraw their troops and persuading Nasser to reopen the Suez Canal (he had blocked the canal by sinking numerous ships, blaming Israel for the sinkings so as not to violate conventions guaranteeing free navigation). The British and French dragged their feet. They sought to be included in the UNEF in order to retain some control of canal operations while they continued to claim that UNEF was merely a "substitute" for their own forces.[41]

But they had no case, and the State Department made this very clear. Needing to mend fences with Washington, reliant on American financial support to alleviate a severe economic crisis precipitated by the canal crisis, desperate for oil (73 percent of which flowed through the canal), and yielding to American insistence that UN authority would be compromised by anything short of total withdrawal, the two European powers bowed to the inevitable.[42] They completed their retreat one week before the new year.

The Israelis took longer. Not even a series of one-sided General Assembly resolutions condemning Israel's defiance of the truce terms forced the Israelis to follow the French and British lead. Tel Aviv insisted on guarantees that Israeli shipping would have free access through Sharm al Sheikh (which Nasser had closed to Israeli shipping), free navigation through the canal, and some administrative oversight in Gaza, which the fedayeen had used for assaults on Israelis. American anticolonialism may have contributed to Washington's unwillingness to compromise with the Europeans; no such sentiment interfered with U.S. attitudes concerning Israel. Moreover, a perusal of State Department messages during the period shows conclusively that U.S. officials recognized the justice of the Israeli demands.

Consequently, these officials sat on the horns of a proverbial dilemma. They refused to retreat from principle, believing that any weakening of support for Charter guarantees against aggression might haunt them in places like Hungary or Korea. As Dulles said to Israel's Prime Minister Golda Meir, anything less risked the "virtual destruction of the United Nations with the resulting breakdown of world order and the risk of World War III."[43] By the same token, beginning with its UN resolution of February 1, 1957, the United States, for the first time, included unambiguous recognition of Israel's security concerns. For the next five weeks, the United States played good cop/bad cop. The Americans subtlety extended the mandate of UNEF to encompass Tel Aviv's need for security, included in the November 2 resolution; and President Eisenhower apparently promised the Israeli prime minister that the United States would guarantee free navigation through the straits at Sharm al Sheikh. At the same time, Dulles raised the threat of economic sanctions if Israeli troops were not completely withdrawn from the Sinai.[44]

In the final analysis, neither the UN nor the United States offered assurances that, to Israel, meant real security. The Israelis continued to press Hammarskjold and Dulles about the tenure of UNEF. Might it depart from the Sinai if the Egyptians unilaterally insisted on ending its role? Yes. True, Hammarskjold secured a "good faith" pledge from Nasser that UNEF would remain in place until its task had been completed, but Nasser's good faith proved worthless. On March 7, 1957, the Israelis completed their withdrawal, but not because they received meaningful guarantees. Ten years later when Nasser expelled the UNEF in preparation for a new assault on Israel, the justice of Israel's position during the UN debates following the Suez crisis became terribly clear.

THE HUNGARIAN REVOLUTION

The Hungarian Revolution, which was concurrent with the Suez crisis, also involved American use of the UN to prevent what American officials viewed as an illegal use of force. Likewise, it involved a Great Power possessing a Security Council veto. And it also raised some of the same questions that Eisenhower and Dulles considered central to the Suez issue, including the sanctity of borders and the mobilization of world opinion to discourage aggression.

The revolution in Hungary followed a general liberalization of communism during 1956, signalled by Khrushchev's denunciation of Stalin at the 20th Communist Congress in February and a reform movement in Poland leading to a new government under Wladislaw Gomulka in June. Hungarian communists, too, demanded changes. Demonstrations in Budapest beginning on October 22 led to insurrection in a number of Hungarian cities. Although the government called for help from Soviet military units, a new cabinet under Imré Nagy formed a national coalition on October 30 and requested the departure of Soviet troops. The next day, to the surprise of American observers, Moscow struck notes of conciliation. They did not last long. On November 1, Nagy not only protested again the movement of Soviet troops into Hungary, but called for Hungary's withdrawal from the Warsaw Pact. Twenty-four hours later, he asked for a UN guarantee of Hungarian neutrality.

Had all this not occurred at the very moment when the United States and the USSR were mobilizing UN energies during the Suez crisis, Washington might have made Hungary a test case at the UN. But with Dulles already ailing (he would enter the hospital a few days later) and with Washington in no position to call for British and French cooperation, the UN played a very different role.

The United States, together with Britain and France, initially brought the Hungarian issue to the Security Council under Article 34.[45] The Soviets insisted that the council had no jurisdiction, claiming that the revolution was strictly an internal Hungarian affair, and that Budapest had legally (under a 1947 peace treaty) requested Soviet assistance to crush a "fascist" movement. Despite Soviet objections, the council discussed the issue on four separate days. On November 4, only minutes after it created UNEF, the council debated a U.S.-sponsored resolution calling on Moscow to "desist" from using force in Hungary and calling for Soviet military withdrawal. The USSR vetoed it. Under the Uniting for Peace Resolution, Lodge appealed to the General Assembly where, on November 4, the majority approved a resolution "requesting" that the secretary-general investigate and recommend measures to end the "foreign intervention."[46]

Whatever chance the UN might have had to resolve the crisis ended later that day. The Soviets arrested Nagy and replaced him with a government echoing Moscow's claim that Budapest had requested friendly aid from the USSR to suppress a fascist rebellion. Therefore, declared both the Soviets and the Hungarians, a UN role was unnecessary. Although the General Assembly continued to address the question for some months, especially in regard to refugees, the UN played no meaningful part in resolving this crisis. It could denounce the Soviets; it could not change their behavior.

The Americans fully understood. Unlike the situation in Suez where the Egyptians welcomed UN action and where the British, French, and Israelis were sensitive to both world opinion and U.S. economic pressure, the Hungarian government flatly rejected UN interference, and neither Budapest nor Moscow worried about public opinion or economic pressure. And, of course, the geography differed. Not only was Hungary landlocked between neutral and communist neighbors, but it stood as much within the Soviet sphere of influence as Guatemala stood within the U.S. sphere. Washington would protest. It would not risk war.[47]

The Hungarian crisis brought credit to neither the United States nor the UN. Prime Minister Eden claimed that U.S. policy makers deliberately dragged their feet over Hungary, but not over Suez. He complained that Lodge accused Britain of trying to use the Hungarian crisis to obscure British activity in Suez. A "pitiable failure," Eden called the UN's handling of Hungary. Even Dag Hammarskjold's biographer faults the United States over Hungary. He argues, with justification, that the U.S.-sponsored resolution of November 4 set up the secretary-general to be a scapegoat in the event of a UN failure. By shifting responsibility to Hammarskjold, the United States camouflaged its own impotence. An "indignant" Hammarskjold believed that the State Department cynically risked weakening his office to cover its own failure.[48]

TENSION IN THE MIDDLE EAST

No week better illuminates the possibilities and the limitations of UN activity than the first week of November 1956. And no week better illustrates an important shift in UN activity: away from the traditional Cold War rivalry as was played out in Hungary and toward anticolonial involvement as glimpsed in the Suez crisis. It would take years for this shift to become fully evident, but keen observers who counted the numbers of new UN members during the late 1950s had seen the handwriting on the UN wall.

That first week of November would also persuade American officials to avoid in the future the kind of public quarrel they had conducted with some of their closest allies. The Suez quarrel, after all, had threatened to rupture not only the UN, but NATO. When, therefore, radical Iraqi nationalists overthrew the Baghdad government in July 1958, leading to western fears that similar events might threaten the governments of Lebanon and Jordan, U.S. and British officials would make special efforts to cooperate with each other.

For nearly six months, western observers had worried about the stability of friendly regimes in the Middle East. On February 1, 1958, Egypt's Nasser announced the formation of the United Arab Republic, merging his own country with Syria. In response, Jordan federated with Iraq later that month. For the next five months, Nasser-inspired subversion in Lebanon led to an uprising against pro-western governments in both Jordan and Lebanon. By mid-June, appeals to the UN from both Amman and Beirut accusing Nasser of interference in their internal affairs led the Swedish government to propose the dispatch of a UN observer group to Lebanon. Called UNOGIL, it witnessed the escalation of violence but could not prove a link to Nasser. No matter, especially when the Iraqi coup created fears of regional instability. With Washington officials apprehensive about the survival of the two friendly governments, the United States did not wait for conclusive UN reports. To the distress of Hammarskjold, President Eisenhower announced the landing of 8,000 (eventually 14,000) marines in Lebanon. Britain followed suit in Jordan three days later.

These military actions turned a regional problem into an East-West confrontation. For the next few weeks, Soviet and American delegations at the UN, both of which had supported UNOGIL, sponsored competing resolutions on the landings. The Soviets claimed that the United States and Britain violated the Charter by interfering in the domestic politics of the region. The United States argued that the landings were perfectly legal, requested by friendly governments to maintain regional stability. A Soviet resolution condemning the American action failed on July 17. An American counter resolution, proposing a UN force to replace the Americans and British, met a Soviet veto the following day.[49] With Moscow's veto immobilizing the Security Council, the United States turned the issue over to the General Assembly.

Once more, the two superpowers introduced resolutions that looked more to winning the propaganda war than to genuinely resolving a difficult problem. Happily, two things led to a settlement. The Soviet delegate, Arkady Sobolev, although earlier vetoing a Japanese resolution that would have allowed the secretary-general to expand the UN presence in Lebanon, proposed an assembly resolution that would in fact enlarge UNOGIL.[50] This was strange behavior during a period when the Soviets often charged the UN with having a western bias. In a practical sense, Sobolev's proposal legitimized Hammarskjold's desire to strengthen UNOGIL, and Hammerskjold did exactly this. Of equal importance, the enlargement of UNOGIL provided the Americans an excuse to consider withdrawing their troops. Indeed, the American resolution of July 16 had looked to enlarge the UN presence as a way to justify the exit of U.S. troops. On this score the Americans had not changed their tune.

When Khrushchev proposed a summit of Mideast countries along with the USSR, Britain, and the United States, Eisenhower quickly rejected the idea. Ostensibly, the Americans would not meet without Israel being included in the meeting; in fact, the United States feared any opportunity that would permit the Soviets to directly enter the world of Middle East politics. What Eisenhower did do, however, was to authorize the calling of an emergency meeting of the General Assembly where, on August 13, he outlined a six point plan for regional peace.[51] Although Hammarskjold strongly dissented from one of the president's proposals—a UN standby peace force—he saw real promise in the others. Within days, a Norwegian resolution combining a number of elements from Eisenhower's proposal, became the basis for an Arab resolution that received unanimous support in the General Assembly.[52] It called for the secretary-general to make "practical arrangements" to maintain the purposes of the Charter in Lebanon and Jordan (practical arrangements could mean everything from rearranging UNOGIL to economic aid); such arrangements, said the resolution, would "facilitate the early withdrawal of foreign troops . . . "[53] This was a far cry from the Soviet *demand* for the removal of western troops. In short, it offered the Americans a face-saving way out during a congressional election campaign, ending an occupation that, by the end of August, no longer seemed necessary to either Washington or London. The last British and American troops departed Lebanon on November 10, 1958.

Many less consequential issues connected the United States to the UN during the Eisenhower years, including the interminable dispute dividing India and Pakistan over Kashmir, a Greek-Turkish dispute involving the former British colony of Cyprus (to be covered later), escalating protests concerning South African apartheid, and a quarrel that brought the Cold War to remote Laos. Each involved former colonial territories. Although three of the four turned into long-term disputes, and all—to varying degrees—indirectly fed on Cold War rivalries, none of them addressed interests that American policy makers considered vital (at least not yet). Consequently, Washington gave them neither the attention nor the deliberation that other UN-related issues received. Two subjects did get U.S. attention, however: the entry of the UN into the disarmament field, and the Congo crisis, which was easily the most divisive episode in the UN's involvement with anticolonial politics.

DISARMAMENT EFFORTS

The history of UN disarmament efforts is long and exceedingly complex. Initial drafts of the Charter made no reference to the subject. As Evan Luard reminds us, many who drafted the Charter believed that World War II stemmed not from too much armament, but from too little.[54] Moreover, the Charter's collective-security mechanism relied on the enforcers having sufficient arms at their own disposal. Nevertheless, Article 11, though much weaker than the comparable article in the League Covenant, gave the General Assembly the right to "consider" the "principles governing disarmament and the regulation of armaments." A few other articles indirectly addressed the subject.

The founders' inattention to disarmament lasted until Hiroshima. Where officials from many UN member governments initially feared that they could not afford to disarm, the advent of nuclear weapons left them fearing that they could not afford *not* to disarm. This anxiety produced the General Assembly's very first resolution, which urged "control of atomic energy," along with the creation, in January 1946, of a UN Atomic Energy Commission.[55] Within months, the UN sponsored the Acheson-Lilienthal plan, followed by Baruch's proposal for international control of atomic energy.

As explained in the previous chapter, these efforts went unrewarded. With the Cold War obscuring the horror of Hiroshima, U.S. officials viewed the subject of atomic arms control with only lukewarm interest. So long as the United States had an atomic monopoly, and so long as U.S. military officials assumed that a defense of western Europe would necessitate the use of nuclear weapons, American officials approached arms reduction with skepticism. So too did the Soviets for exactly the opposite reasons. Moscow would not seriously consider restraints on the Soviet nuclear program until it had achieved parity with the United States. Indeed, Moscow's belief that the world organization reflected western goals and interests made it distrustful of UN agencies controlling uranium stockpiles (as, for instance, proposed by Baruch). And when the Soviets offered counter proposals, notably the Gromyko Plan, which called for the elimination of atomic weapons but included no effective mechanism to verify or enforce this objective, the United States demurred. Neither side had much inclination to compromise as Cold War tensions increased during the late 1940s. By early 1950, the Soviets walked out of the AEC at the same time and for the same reason that they boycotted the Security Council. Shortly thereafter, the AEC disappeared.

During the early years of the Cold War, conventional arms reduction received even less serious attention. The story of UN disarmament can be traced in part by the appearance (and disappearance) of numerous UN agencies to study the subject. The Commission on Conventional Armaments (1947) achieved no more success than the AEC. As the AEC went out of existence after the Soviets departed, so too did this commission. In 1951, responding to a proposal by President Truman, the UN established another committee, which in turn established a new Disarmament Commission. Its composition mirrored its predecessors: the Security Council's membership plus Canada. The new commission followed Truman's lead in recognizing the relationship between atomic and conventional weapons. It would consider these weapons together and called for reduction, verification, and disclosure of all weapons.

Because the Soviets typically shrouded the details of their weapon programs in secrecy, virtually all American disarmament proposals placed emphasis on the need for verification and inspection. Moscow, convinced that inspection would decrease its security, naturally dissented. It emphasized the need to eliminate weapons *prior* to establishing a system of inspection and control. Distrusting the Soviets, U.S. policy makers routinely dismissed this approach.

Not until Stalin's death did the Soviets begin to move toward the western position. Ironically, U.S. interest in a comprehensive plan began to flag by then. With Secretary of State Dulles articulating the strategy of massive retaliation at the same time that Washington worried about Moscow's recent test of a hydrogen bomb, the Eisenhower administration backtracked despite its lip service to disarmament. When the UN established still another committee to study nuclear weapons in 1954 and the Soviets surprisingly offered to open their budgetary records for inspection, it was the United States that, according to Luard, went into "retreat." Increasingly believing their own propaganda about communist duplicity while becoming ever more reliant on a nuclear strategy for defense, the Americans placed nuclear development, not nuclear (or conventional) disarmament, at the center of their thinking. It is important to remember that 1954 was the year that the United States outlawed the Communist Party. It was the year that Dulles threatened an "agonizing reappraisal" of NATO if the Europeans did not support the creation of a European Defense Community that would integrate German military units into a European force structure. It was the year that Dulles, seeking a "maximum deterrent at a bearable cost," recommended that "local defenses must be reinforced by the further deterrent of massive retaliatory power."[56] In this environment, some U.S. officials welcomed disarmament proposals as warmly as malaria.

But not all U.S. officials felt the same. The president, despite skepticism from both the State and Defense departments, took the subject quite seriously. His Atoms for Peace plan, like his Open Skies proposal, reflected genuine fear of a nuclear future. Atomic weapons, he said more than once, meant that "in any outbreak of general hostilities, regardless of the element of surprise, destruction will be reciprocal and complete." The "era of armaments has ended," he declared, "and the human race must conform its action to this truth or die."[57]

In 1955, Eisenhower approved the appointment of former Minnesota governor Harold Stassen as his special assistant on disarmament. Stassen, who had already coordinated planning for the Open Skies proposal, helped to reorient U.S. disarmament policy at the UN from the abolition of atomic weapons to their control. But Stassen met opposition from Dulles, who not only had less interest in disarmament, but jealously guarded his own bureaucratic turf.

With the United States and the Soviets standing 180 degrees apart, the Soviets announced in 1955 that they would leave the UN's disarmament subcommittee. New bodies were then formed to accommodate Soviet demands for greater communist representation. The General Assembly expanded the Disarmament Commission, first to 25 members, then to include the entire UN membership. This was like placing 75 captains on a ship sailing through a mined channel. Not only did it diminish any real possibility of meaningful discussions, but it actually diluted the Soviet voice. Consequently, the Soviets again walked out, this time to protest the commission's enlargement. Efforts to reconvene the commission in the summer of 1958 failed, temporarily ending the UN's six-year campaign to arrive at a comprehensive treaty to reduce armaments.

Nevertheless, the subject had too much popular appeal to be ignored. Momentum for a test ban kept interest high. By 1959, the General Assembly, seeking to revive UN disarmament activity, created the Disarmament Committee (usually called the Ten-Member Committee), which paralleled the Disarmament Commission. It included five representatives from the Soviet bloc and five from the west. In one very important way, however, the Ten-Member Committee differed from all others: it had no formal connection to the UN. Indeed, Dag Hammarskjold spent countless hours trying to create a link, however tenuous, fearing that separation would weaken the UN even beyond its disarmament activity.[58] Unfortunately for the secretary-general, both the United States and the USSR preferred independence from the UN's disarmament work. When Hammarskjold proposed placing two neutrals on the committee, both superpowers demurred. Washington and Moscow wanted to maximize their freedom of action, the very thing that Hammarskjold feared.

Perhaps Hamarskjold should not have worried. Neither the Disarmament Commission nor the Ten-Member Committee produced much of value. And when in 1959 the British, followed by the Soviets and finally the Americans, proposed "general and complete disarmament," they chose to do so not in small committees with few reporters, but in the highly visible General Assembly. Of course the Soviets knew full well that the United States would not accept its plan, which placed reduction before verification. The Americans equally knew that the Soviets would reject a plan that placed inspection before reduction. Both sought not disarmament so much as a propaganda feast.

But there was also mischief, at least from the perspective of Secretariat officials. In their own counterproposal, the United States included a provision to create a separate disarmament body, to be called the International Disarmament Organization. It was designed to stand apart from the UN, with the Americans arguing that it must not be held hostage to the Soviet veto. Hammarskjold, who already resented the independence of the Ten-Member Committee, feared that the new agency would rob the UN of one of its key duties. He protested directly to the State Department. The Americans abandoned the plan.

Still, general disarmament plans went nowhere. As early as 1955, the State Department had withdrawn its comprehensive disarmament proposals at Geneva. Military planners at both Foggy Bottom (State Department headquarters) and the Pentagon feared Soviet trickery more than thermonuclear weapons. Their influence prevailed in the White House from 1955 until the end of Eisenhower's second term despite the 1959 American comprehensive proposal offered to the UN. And after the USSR downed an American U-2 spy plane in 1960, the Ten-Member Committee, like so many earlier disarmament bodies, collapsed when the five communist states on the committee withdrew in protest.

The record on disarmament, however, was not a complete bust. After American officials began to see a comprehensive proposal as impractical during the mid-1950s the United States increasingly used the UN to try to achieve certain limited goals. These included creating control posts at communications centers, nuclear free (or thinned out) zones in Europe, and mechanisms to reduce the likelihood of surprise attack. They, too, went nowhere. One proposal, however, appealed to enough people to achieve a life of its own: a nuclear test ban. First proposed by India's Jawaharlal Nehru in 1954, it generated worldwide interest within three years. That interest stemmed from a number of sources, including publicity from the contamination of Japanese fishermen after a 1954 Pacific test (one died, others fell ill), the popular anti-bomb film "On the Beach," and campaigning by antinuclear groups like SANE. When scores of scientists warned about the long-term effects of strontium-90, a radioactive isotope released by the tests, even cynical politicians could no longer ignore the subject. Although Eisenhower had rejected a test ban when it was first proposed by his opponent during the presidential election of 1956, he soon changed his mind, especially after it became clear that the United States possessed technology to detect most—though not all—

tests. When in 1958 Khrushchev unilaterally declared a one-year moratorium, Eisenhower responded in kind, in part because the moratorium would freeze the nuclear arms race with the United States in the lead, in part because he genuinely feared a runaway arms race.[59] The two leaders soon extended the moratorium to three years. Although testing resumed in 1961, both super-powers agreed to further talks so long as discussions for a proposed test ban applied only to above-ground and underwater explosions. Such limitations would allow them to eliminate the fallout threat while permitting further weapons development. In 1963, the two countries incorporated this plan into a treaty.

Although the test-ban treaty was mostly negotiated outside of the UN, delib-erations until 1959 fell under UN auspices and owed much to the insistence of Hammarskjold. Perhaps Hammarskjold provided more than just insistence. He had transformed the UN during the years of Eisenhower's presidency. Unlike Lie, who was distrusted and inconsistent, Hammarskjold had integrity and energy that projected the UN into genuinely new roles. UN peacekeep-ing, the routine use of UN observers, the Secretariat's good offices: all gave the UN a voice and a presence that made it an increasingly important agent in the international community. The Cold War had threatened to kill the organiza-tion. Hammarskjold became a one man rescue squad.

But Hammarskjold did not transform the organization alone. Anticolonial-ism contributed too. The UN, with 51 members in 1945 and 60 when Ham-marskjold became secretary-general, had 101 on the day of his death. First India and Pakistan in 1947, then many others joined the organization as the European states granted independence to their former colonies. In 1960 alone, 16 newly independent states joined. The automatic western majority had dis-appeared by the time Eisenhower handed his White House keys to John Kennedy.

Were this transformation merely one of numbers, it would have been sig-nificant enough. But the transformation was equally one of focus. It relegated traditional Cold War issues away from the UN (to NATO, SEATO, or the OAS); in their place, the UN increasingly focused on North-South disputes, most of them related to—or stemming from—the tidal wave of anticolonial-ism that followed World War II. Inevitably, the Security Council, with its per-manent veto became less important; the General Assembly, with its rapidly expanding membership aided by new post-Charter authority (such as the Uniting for Peace Resolution), became the center of UN activity.

THE CONGO CRISIS

All of these developments came together in the last major foreign policy cri-sis of the Eisenhower administration. It materialized not in the usual trouble-spots like eastern Europe, the Middle East, or east Asia, but in the heart of

Africa. Where some European states had prepared their colonies for independence, Belgium had not. And when, in 1960, the government in Brussels reluctantly granted independence to the Congo, chaos led to disintegration, and then war.

The UN's response to the crisis did not emerge in a vacuum. African and Asian states had begun to assert themselves at the UN in 1955, when a group of neutral states forged a coalition at the Bandung Conference. Their goals were negative (*not* to subordinate their interests to the Cold War needs of the United States and USSR) and positive (to dismantle the political, economic, and military legacy of colonialism). Although the United States had little direct interest in preserving the remnants of colonialism, NATO's disarray after the Suez crisis alerted Washington to the delicacy of the subject. Moreover, the United States still enjoyed some indirect benefits from the colonial system, including trade and military bases that made it inexpedient to offer more than lip service to decolonization.

The Soviets, on the other hand, although no happier about nonalignment than the Americans, easily grasped the propaganda appeal of anticolonialism. Furthermore, Leninist anticolonial ideology would challenge the interests of many capitalist states in what would soon be called the Third World. On September 23, 1960, just months after the Congo crisis began, Khrushchev proposed to the General Assembly a Declaration on Decolonization that, among other things, called for immediate independence for remaining colonial territories.[60] The Soviet premier had tapped a very sensitive nerve, and the U.S. delegation at the UN, now led by James J. Wadsworth (Lodge had resigned to run for vice president), strongly supported the declaration.

But Washington did not. Reminiscent of the 1948 confusion over the partition of Palestine, the State Department first approved the resolution, then reversed itself rather than abandon allies who bitterly opposed it. Britain's Prime Minister Harold Macmillan appealed directly to Eisenhower, after which the State Department ordered Wadsworth to abstain.[61]

Perhaps Washington believed the abstention would mollify both sides. The Asians and Africans, however, viewed it as a betrayal. With 89 UN members condemning colonialism, the episode left some American delegates humiliated. One even stood and cheered passage of the resolution; another charged the State Department with "reject[ing] our own history," allowing "the communist bloc to champion the cause of these millions of people who are trying to gain their independence."[62]

Those gaining their independence in the Congo had little time to cheer. Although central Africa was the locale for the messy narrative of Congo independence, the UN provided a stage for its diplomacy. The basic facts bear mention. The Belgians granted Congolese independence on July 1, 1960. Within five days, the army and police, commanded by Belgian officers, mutinied, leading to widespread rioting, looting, killing, and raping. Katanga (today, Shaba) province, rich with copper and other mineral deposits, seceded. Belgian troops returned to restore order without the authorization of the new government. On July 12, Congo authorities, led by President Joseph Kasavubu and Prime Minister Patrice Lumumba, asked for UN troops. They appealed not to restore order, but to protect the Congo against Belgian aggression.

Acting on his own authority under Article 99, Hammarskjold brought the dispute to the Security Council. Within 48 hours, the council, by an 8–0–3 vote, authorized creation of a UN force (ONUC). Britain and France, uneasy about UN interference in their own colonial affairs, abstained. The United States and the USSR voted with the majority.[63] Hammarskjold wasted no time implementing the resolution. Airlifted in U.S. planes, the first troops arrived in Leopoldville (today known as Kinshasa) one day later.

American-Soviet cooperation did not last much beyond the July 14 resolution. That was because, as in Guatemala, a local matter gradually mutated into a Cold War dispute. The Congo's leftist prime minister, Patrice Lumumba, apparently viewed the return of the Belgian troops—and Brussels's support for Katangan secession in which the Union Minière corporation played an important part—as a capitalist effort to subvert Congolese independence. Rather than rely exclusively on UN aid, Lumumba threatened to request Soviet assistance to expel the Belgians.

U.S. authorities, many fearing (others concluding) that Lumumba was a communist, maneuvered to keep the Soviets out of the Congo. In Eisenhower's words, the choice boiled down to a UN "take over" of the Congo or a UN "crack up."[64] Yet Washington officials equally feared unilateral involvement in a remote and unfamiliar country. Worried about complications with their NATO ally in Brussels, they also feared that direct U.S. involvement would lead to charges of neocolonialism. Faced with these hazards, the administration supported UN efforts to defuse the crisis and to check those Congolese factions that Washington viewed as procommunist. When Lumumba visited Washington in late July seeking financial and technical aid, the State Department spurned him, telling him that the UN would handle all assistance.[65] By the same token, the Americans initiated efforts to remove Lumumba from the scene altogether, surmising that even if he were not a communist, his departure would help to end the crisis.

For the remainder of Eisenhower's term, U.S. policy did not deviate. This remained true even when events in the Congo threatened chaos, as when Kasavubu and Lumumba dismissed each other from their posts, leading to Lumumba's arrest on December 1; or when General Joseph Mobutu (president from 1965 to 1997 as Mobutu Sese Seko), over UN objections, expelled officials from communist embassies in Leopoldville. The United States was also aided by allies at the UN. Mongi Slim, a highly respected Tunisian who held the African seat on the Security Council, favored a multilateral approach consistent with U.S. goals. And the UN's influential African-Asian bloc generally supported the ONUC. Even when the Africans divided over recognition of a Congolese delegation to the UN following Lumumba's arrest (a few governments withdrew their troops from the ONUC), nonaligned support for the ONUC remained intact.

Perhaps the most conspicuous feature of America's UN policy during this period was the degree to which the Eisenhower administration came to the defense of the organization. For reasons already mentioned, the administration had been ambivalent toward the UN. The Republican right wing, following Senator Knowland, had never reconciled its nationalism with support for the UN; even Dulles's support for the UN occasionally wavered. Dulles's successor, former Massachusetts governor Christian Herter, was a moderate internationalist, but never a particularly vocal champion of the organization.

That changed during the fall of 1960. The year had been stressful. The presidential election campaign highlighted criticism of the administration's foreign policy. Soviet downing of an American U-2 spy plane near Sverdlosk in May led not only to a huge propaganda victory by Moscow, but the resumption of Soviet pressure on Berlin and the cancellation of a summit meeting in Paris. When Khrushchev proposed that the General Assembly meeting in September become a summit on disarmament, American officials nearly had apoplexy. Already preoccupied with the Congo and licking their wounds over the Paris cancellation, they anticipated nothing but trouble (the secretary of state called the UN summit "ludicrous").[66] Yet they knew that, with most other national leaders attending, Eisenhower could not decline to appear.

Appear, then, he did, delivering a keynote speech to the new General Assembly with a strong defense of the UN. The following day, Khrushchev converted the meeting into perhaps the most memorable in UN history. He not only introduced his anticolonialism resolution and attacked the United States on disarmament and the Congo, which the Americans expected, but also delivered an intemperate attack on Dag Hammarskjold. Eisenhower and the other "colonialists," he proclaimed, "have been doing their dirty work in the Congo through the Secretary-General of the United Nations and his staff." The Russian premier offered no quarter. First demanding that the assembly force the secretary-general to abide by Charter principles, he then called for the elimination of the post altogether, proposing the creation of a three part "troika" that would give separate blocs (the Communist states, the west, the neutrals) a veto over UN action.[67]

Khrushchev left many delegates in a state of shock. Pounding the table with his fists and his shoe to protest the comments of others, the Soviet premier did more than merely attack Hammarskjold. In much the way that the Security Council had been crippled by the permanent veto, his "troika" would have created a new veto that threatened the General Assembly. To the new states whose representation at the UN formalized their independence, Khrushchev's plan looked like an attack on the UN itself. Ten days later, the Soviet premier demanded that Hammarskjold resign.

The secretary-general's defense electrified the organization. Resigning "at this present and difficult juncture," he said, would "throw the Organization to the winds." He claimed that he had no right to resign "because I have a responsibility to all those states-members for which the Organization is of decisive importance, a responsibility which overrides all other considerations."[68]

No secondary account of this speech can do it justice. Hammarskjold was at his best: eloquent, logical, passionate. His commitment to the organization and to the cause of peace was palpable. The long standing ovation he received from the General Assembly echoed in editorials the world over. Probably nothing since the Korean War had unified Americans so much in defense of the UN. The president himself wrote privately that "The UN is working better now, particularly as a moral force, than ever before." He told Jordan's King Hussein that Khrushchev was trying to "destroy the UN."[69] This he would not permit.

It was ironic that Khrushchev made the UN look better than it was. In reality, little had changed. Hammarskjold notwithstanding, it would still take four more years to resolve the Congo mess. On other matters, such as Laos, which was becoming a major headache at the end of Eisenhower's presidency, the UN could do little. Nor had American officials yet fathomed the degree to which the new members would change the character of the organization. Such understanding would be left to Eisenhower's successors.

chapter 5

KENNEDY AND JOHNSON

President John F. Kennedy's inauguration shifted the focus of American politics toward foreign affairs. Under the Republicans, policy makers had emphasized the virtues of a domestic status quo that was characterized by prosperity, the rise of suburbia, TV, and early civil rights activity. Foreign affairs, including the offshore island tension with China, the crises in Hungary and Suez, Vice President Richard Nixon's humiliating 1958 visit to Latin America, Castro's revolution in Cuba, the U-2 incident, and the collapse of the Paris summit, held less campaign promise for the Republicans. Democratic candidate Kennedy spotted political opportunity in these troubled foreign waters.

Moreover, Kennedy, who had written his senior thesis in college about pre-war appeasement, was personally more attracted to the dynamics of international relations than domestic wheeling and dealing. His electrifying inaugural address said much about the world, little about America. He promised ambitious global efforts—to eradicate disease, to cast off the chains of poverty, to explore the stars. And he welcomed American adversaries to join in creating "not a new balance of power, but a new world of law where the strong are just and the weak secure and the peace preserved." He called the UN "our last best hope in an age where the instruments of war have far outpaced the instruments of peace." To the UN organization, he promised to "renew our pledge of support . . . and to enlarge the area in which its writ may run."

Were these empty words? To persuade his critics that he meant business, the new president named Adlai Stevenson to represent the United States at the UN, giving the former Democratic nominee for president cabinet rank. No living American in 1961 better symbolized postwar liberalism than

Stevenson, with the possible exception of Eleanor Roosevelt; certainly no one would bring more prestige to the UN post. But as often is true in the world of Washington politics, appearances were deceiving. Stevenson had desperately wanted to become secretary of state, not UN ambassador. Kennedy, who nursed resentments of Stevenson extending back to the 1956 Democratic Party convention, had no desire to give him real authority.[1] It took years for Stevenson to understand this.

Nevertheless, Stevenson would be the most important U.S. ambassador to the UN since 1945. Not only did he receive cabinet rank, but a number of other bureaucratic concessions were given to him as well, including the right to select his top deputies, an opportunity to meet with the president's National Security Council (NSC) to discuss foreign issues, and regular meetings with the secretary of state. However, the policy conditions he attached to his acceptance of the UN post—including an administration commitment to "preserve the UN as center of our foreign policy" against Soviet attacks— would prove too mushy to be meaningful.[2]

Stevenson certainly brought glitter to both the UN and the Kennedy administration, and his UN assignment protected him from the boredom of political exile in Chicago. Still, he never insulated himself effectively from the problems that his predecessors had faced. Promises notwithstanding, the main decisions affecting U.S. policy at the UN continued to be made in Washington, not New York. His relationship with John Kennedy remained strained; his relationship with the president's brother, Robert, was even more problematic. Where his superiors in Washington (with the exception of the secretary of state) were brusk and bold, Stevenson was reflective and cautious. Where they tended to take risks by threatening the use of force, he took risks by questioning the use of force. Moreover, the competition for authority between the State Department and the U.S. mission at the UN (USUN) involved a troubled relationship that no U.S. ambassador has ever successfully resolved.[3] Foreign service officers often viewed assignment to USUN as a dead-end promotion. It may have killed not only careers, but also morale.

Nor did USUN view its tasks in the same way that officials at Foggy Bottom did. One of Stevenson's UN successors later observed that "The Africans were a nuisance to the State Department, but they meant votes to us."[4] Corralling those votes took political skills never taught in foreign service seminars; indeed, skills devalued by most FSOs. Wrote Stevenson biographer Porter McKeever, the fiction of giving the UN ambassador power to make policy inevitably led to resentment once the fiction was exposed. Oddly, Stevenson understood the fiction—that is why he refused to consider the post until Kennedy denied him appointment as secretary of state—yet he *still* insisted on such authority.

All these things, compounded by Stevenson's tendency to underestimate his superiors—he viewed them as arrogant yet lacking both talent and experi-

U.S. permanent representative Adlai Stevenson displays photos of missile sites in Cuba to the Security Council during the most threatening crisis of the Cold War. October 25, 1962.
(UN/DPI Photo)

ence—contributed to an uneasy relationship. The White House and State Department occasionally deferred to his judgment, but not, as he soon learned during the Bay of Pigs fiasco, when it really counted.

If Stevenson had limited authority, who did make the administration's UN policy? The answer is Secretary of State Dean Rusk and Harlan Cleveland, the assistant secretary for International Organization Affairs. Rusk, formerly director of the International Organization (IO) bureau at the State Department and later head of the Rockefeller Foundation, had been handed the plum that Stevenson really wanted. A committed internationalist, he was an equally committed cold warrior and even less of a risk-taker than Stevenson. A very private man whom his son described as obsessed with confidentiality, Rusk was exceedingly loyal to his president and generally unsympathetic to those, like Stevenson, who desired direct access to the Oval Office.[5] Certainly Rusk was genuinely committed to the ideals of the UN. He was an anticolonialist in an age of anticolonialism whom Realist critics occasionally charged with placing the interests of the UN above those of his own country. The charge was ridiculous. Rusk was paradoxically both a pragmatist and a moralist, and although he became increasingly uneasy with the radicalism of the General Assembly's African-Asian bloc during the 1960s, his pragmatism enabled him to subordinate UN principles to American interests with alacrity.[6]

Harlan Cleveland, who headed the IO bureau of the State Department, shared the secretary's sympathies. A former editor and educator who had administered aid programs for the UN, Cleveland also advocated strong support for UN activity. Nevertheless, he had a sense of the limits of the UN, and he never proposed policy that subordinated U.S. interests to UN goals. He believed that "whenever we can get an international organization to get out in front of us and do things we would otherwise have to do, that is both a better and a cheaper way to operate."[7] A pragmatist who understood that the world was composed of shades of gray, he generally promoted the importance of the Third World and argued the case for both UN and U.S. activism. "Do we really have to be so very much involved, in so many ugly grudge fights, in so many places . . . ? The answer," he wrote, "is yes."[8]

TROUBLE IN THE CONGO CONTINUES

The ugliest of those fights during the early Kennedy years raged in the Congo. The Kennedy administration modified the Congo policy of its predecessor in at least two important ways. After conducting a thorough review of U.S. policy toward that unhappy land, the White House concluded that Eisenhower's strong support for General Mobutu as a means to contain communist (and Lumumbaist) influence would be less likely to guarantee stability than the coalition approach championed by Hammarskjold and other UN officials. Moreover, Kennedy resolved to place greater emphasis on strengthening the UN's military authority. This might limit Soviet influence, but it carried certain dangers. It not only worried the Belgians and their European allies who continued to support a partisan approach elevating Mobuto's authority, it also threatened Congolese factions that wanted to minimize, not increase, UN influence.[9] Oddly, the UN had initially faced its greatest opposition from Lumumba and his supporters in Eastern Europe and the radical African states; it now met increasing criticism from the Western Europeans who feared that a strengthened UN presence—and a more neutral UN policy as it pertained to the authority of the competing factions—would open the way for Lumumba's return.[10]

The Americans, therefore, found themselves at odds with some of their traditional supporters. This schism became even more apparent when events in the Congo threatened to derail Washington's plans. The February 1961 murder of Lumumba by Katangan troops, Soviet accusations charging Hammarskjold with responsibility for the assassination, and the recognition of a Lumumbaist regime in Stanleyville (today, Kisangani) by radical African governments (and perhaps by the USSR) threatened to turn disorder into a genuine civil war.[11] Within days of Lumumba's murder, the main issue in the Congo had become one of constitutional authority, which led to strong U.S.

support for two resolutions—one in the Security Council on February 21, and the other in the General Assembly on April 15—for convening a Congolese Parliament. The parliament, believed the State Department, would provide legitimacy and therefore stability, even at the risk of increasing leftist influence in the Congo. The State Department, and even Hammarskjold, otherwise feared that a fractured Congo would invite direct Soviet intervention as well as the arrival of military forces hostile to the UN. Consequently, UN policy, generally supported by Washington during these months, favored two related aims: the creation of a central Congolese government to provide national unity, and the expulsion of all foreign forces other than those under UN command. The alternative appeared to be civil war.[12]

It is worth emphasizing two points at this juncture. First, the American desire to support the UN was real. Time and again, Rusk, Cleveland, and Stevenson agreed during the crisis that the UN must not be permitted to fail. Washington (correctly) viewed the Soviet attack on Hammarskjold following Lumumba's murder—"the culmination of Hammarskjold's criminal activities," said a Soviet spokesman[13]—as an attack on the UN itself. Even in the months preceding this attack, when Premier Khrushchev proposed his "troika" reform to defang the secretary-general, the Americans swiftly denounced the scheme, knowing full well that it would disable not just Hammarskjold but the organization.

The second point is equally important: if necessary, the Americans would abandon support for the UN to insure that the Congo "not fall into Communist hands. . . . "[14] The Americans desperately hoped to prevent the Congo from becoming a battleground of the Cold War (they had their hands full with Laos, Cuba, and, increasingly, Vietnam), and Washington policy makers were quite prepared to subordinate internationalism to anticommunism.

To the American's relief, Soviet opposition to UN activity in the Congo following Lumumba's death relieved the United States of the need to choose between the two. With Moscow (and Paris) refusing to pay for ONUC activity, the UN became even more dependent on U.S. support. Furthermore, the Security Council resolution of February and the General Assembly resolution of April in support of a parliamentary solution to the crisis did not stand alone. Even more significant in the long run was a Security Council resolution passed on February 21 authorizing the ONUC, if necessary, to utilize military force "in the last resort" to prevent civil war.[15] This resolution, too, had strong American support (the USSR and France abstained), and it highlights the degree to which the United States helped to expand sharply the scope of UN peacekeeping authority. Indeed, journalist Stanley Meisler correctly notes that not until the Somalia and Balkan crises of the 1990s would such authority again be employed.[16]

In sum, the Kennedy administration during its first six months gave strong support to the UN and Hammarskjold in the Congo. Even though the number of African and Asian members of the UN had increased dramatically during the previous decade, and six radical states led by Egypt and Ghana withdrew from ONUC, most African governments continued to support the effort as the surest path to stability. The result was that U.S. leadership in the UN remained intact. American officials, including those such as Stevenson and Cleveland who advocated more attention to African issues, saw no contradiction between the general Cold War interests of the United States and nation-building in the Third World. The Congo may have been confusing and chaotic, but it little challenged the basic framework of American thinking about international cooperation.

American support for the UN during the Congo crisis remained conditional. During the second half of 1961, the Kennedy administration showed that it could be as inconsistent as its Republican predecessor concerning the UN. Certainly the rock-solid support that Rusk and Stevenson gave to Hammarskjold during the February to April 1961 period was missing by September. What led to the turnaround was Moise Tshombe's separatist movement in Katanga province.

The UN role in the Congo since July 1960 had three goals that were not always compatible: (1) the protection of European and other foreigners from undisciplined factions, (2) the maintenance of a stable government (for which the parliamentary process offered promise), and (3) the desire to prevent the Congo (which had been initially patched together by colonialists who largely ignored tribal interests) from fragmenting. Mineral-rich Katanga (western news accounts *always* called it "mineral-rich"), led by the mercurial Tshombe who was supported by Belgium and other copper-interested states, had every intention of seceding. The Congolese government—even Lumumba had agreed with his opponents on this matter—had no intention of permitting this to occur. Little had been done about this matter during 1960 when Americans and the former colonialists were worrying mainly about Lumumba. After Lumumba's death, however, the Americans as well as the Secretariat shifted their concern to Congolese unity. Even Hammarskjold, like the policy makers in Washington, agreed that the loss of Katanga would escalate regional instability. To the secretary-general, Katangan secession threatened to undermine the Charter. To the State Department, it raised the specter of Soviet penetration. For both the department and the secretary-general, therefore, the end of the Katangan secession movement became a top priority, especially after Cyrille Adoula formed a new government of national unity in August 1961.[17]

There were two problems, however. One was within the UN, where Hammarskjold believed that negotiation, not military force, must be used to end the secession; others, including the UN's new representative to Elizabethville (today, Lubumbashi), Irish diplomat Conor Cruise O'Brien, believed that only military measures would succeed. The second problem involved the practical difficulties of dealing with Tshombe. Tshombe's reputation ("No contradiction, no detected lie, caused Mr. Tshombe the slightest embarrassment," wrote O'Brien) didn't help matters.[18] His repeated promises to cooperate with Kasabuvu and Adoula were belied by his refusal to dismantle his army, composed of Katangans but led by a motley though lethal assortment of Belgians and white mercenaries from various countries including Rhodesia and South Africa. Unless this force could be disbanded, the UN would exercise little influence over Tshombe. Even Hammarskjold recognized the importance of removing the Belgians and white mercenaries in Katanga, for which he gave O'Brien authorization. Under pressure, the Belgian government withdrew its forces. Perhaps half of the mercenaries were then rounded up and deported, but others, including many fanatical supporters of Katangan independence, stayed where they were and threatened not only UN officials but even Tshombe if he cooperated with UN officials. From this point, the details become increasingly foggy. O'Brien, without consulting New York and acting independently of Hammarskjold, ordered UN troops into action on September 13 to expel the remaining mercenaries. All accounts agree that the operation turned into a UN disaster. Not only did O'Brien foolishly announce that he had ended the Katangan secession when in fact he had been authorized to do no such thing, but he failed to achieve even his own modest goal of rounding up the mercenaries. Katanga may have been "a lunatic asylum," but it was hardly subdued.[19]

The military mess mirrored the diplomatic mess. European governments damned the operation, focusing their ire on O'Brien. As in Suez, the operation divided the United States and its NATO allies. O'Brien's operation undid in a few hours all the delicate work that Hammarskjold had done to achieve a consensus at the UN paralleling the new unity government in Leopoldville.

In Washington, too, the atmosphere turned sour. State Department support for the UN Congo operation, extending back to the Eisenhower administration, threatened to disintegrate. Europeanists in the department backed their NATO counterparts, while those viewing the Third World as increasingly important accepted the need to control Tshombe, even if this meant using force. This latter group included Stevenson and Cleveland, and, up to a point, Rusk. It did not include the president. Yet even Rusk was appalled at the mess. The secretary of state bitterly complained less about the use of force than the UN's failure to consult Washington in advance (of course, O'Brien had not even consulted Hammarskjold in advance). Rusk viewed the operation as "jeopardizing everything we have attempted to do in Katanga and [the] Congo," and worried about growing domestic opposition to the UN, and to the administration's support for the UN's Congo operation.[20]

That opposition became increasingly vocal. Led by Connecticut's Democratic senator Thomas Dodd, it also included a predictable assortment of right-wingers, including William F. Buckley and Arizona senator Barry Goldwater. Injecting Cold War ideology into the tribal politics of Africa, they equated Tshombe with democracy and freedom; by doing so, they effectively extended Senator Knowland's anti-UN campaign into the 1960s. They knew little, but they still managed to scare an inexperienced Kennedy administration that had already been burned by events in Cuba and Berlin.

Yet Kennedy and his subordinates did understand one critical point: the United States had no vital interests in the Congo. Indeed, this realization was exactly what led both Eisenhower and Kennedy officials to follow the UN lead in the Congo for over a year. But from the fighting in September 1961 to the end of that year, when even more serious fighting broke out between ONUC and the Katanga secessionists, American policy toward the Congo zig-zagged wildly, with Kennedy as well as the State Department fearful that the defeat of Tshombe might produce a Katangan—or even Congolese—Castro. When the September fighting prompted Kennedy to call for a cease-fire under conditions that even Hammarskjold could not tolerate, an exasperated secretary-general damned American influence. Wouldn't it be better, he wrote, "for the UN to lose the support of the US because it is faithful to law and principles than to survive as an agent whose activities are geared to political purposes never avowed or laid down by the major organs of the UN?"[21]

Within days, Hammarskjold was dead, killed in a plane crash while trying to bring the Congolese factions together. For all the lip service given to Hammarskjold and the UN during the memorial service, the Americans continued a highly inconsistent policy. For the most part, the United States aimed to maintain open communications with Elizabethville as a means to pressure Katangan officials to talk to those in Leopoldville, but flatly opposed the use of military force to "crush Tshombe."[22] Still, when the December fighting threatened to destroy the UN mission in the Congo, Kennedy authorized the use of U.S. aircraft to ferry supplies and troops to Katanga. The fighting left the Americans with few options. Either Washington would support the UN, or ONUC would crumble. Whatever the administration's worries about Katangan Castros and domestic critics, both Kennedy and Rusk finally came to understand that they could not fine-tune events in Africa. By January 22, 1962, UN troops had indeed crushed Tshombe.

The Congo had been reunified, but not pacified. Not for another two years would the UN role in the Congo finally end. During that period, civil war continued in different sections of the country and governmental instability remained the norm. With U.S. support, ONUC troops finally withdrew in 1964 and, remarkably, Tshombe became prime minister. Lumumbaist troops took over new sections of the country. Tshombe now served as the spokesman for national unity; he even brought back mercenaries to prevent the disintegration of the country. The chaos in 1964 equalled the chaos of 1961. This was not quite comic opera. When the United States and Belgium intervened to rescue their nationals from the disputed areas, radical African states denounced the operation and demanded a meeting of the Security Council. This time, however, the council produced nothing more than angry rhetoric and the passage of an innocuous resolution for a cease-fire. It was no longer 1961. The Cold War implications of the crisis had disappeared. Both the

United States and the Soviets supported the resolution for a cease-fire, surely a sign that they had wearied of the Congo. It was too confusing, too potentially costly, too insignificant.

In light of the Congo turmoil following withdrawal of ONUC, it is hard to call the UN role a rousing success. Yes, the Belgians had been withdrawn, the mercenaries deported, Katanga reunited with the rest of the country. But there was not much peace to keep, even at the end of what remains perhaps the most important peacekeeping mission ever performed by the UN.

To the extent that the operation did achieve its objectives, it is important to credit both Hammarskjold's single-minded initiative and the willingness of the United States to support the UN even after the strains of August and September 1961. The Americans, without any pressing interest in the area, viewed the UN as an acceptable instrument to serve U.S. aims—mainly, stability and anticommunism. The General Assembly had become less prowestern in 1961 than it had been a few years earlier, but it was still far from the antiwestern agency that it would become in the 1970s. Officials like Rusk and Stevenson recognized the emerging importance of Africa and Asia in the organization. They increasingly believed that the United States must align itself with the forces of Third World nationalism. Not to do this, they reasoned, would allow the Soviets to tie U.S. policy to the corpse of European colonialism. Rusk and Stevenson may have exaggerated the East-West issues at stake in the Congo, but they were not colonialists. And because they detested colonialism, they often found themselves at odds with their Europeanist colleagues at Foggy Bottom.

The Congo left some indelible marks on the UN. Dag Hammarskjold lost his life there; never again would the UN have as dynamic and imaginative a leader. UN peacekeepers found themselves with a remarkable amount of independent initiative; neither the Americans nor the Soviets closely supervised their activity. The Soviets, although they never vetoed a single resolution dealing with the crisis, began, with France, a long tradition of states not paying the expenses of peacekeeping operations with which they disagreed. It constituted what might be called a money veto. It had little effect other than to precipitate the Article 19 crisis that will be discussed later.

CUBA

While the Congo crisis may have been the UN's most frustrating and confusing episode, the Cuban situation was its most dramatic. The roots of the UN's involvement in Cuba grew during 1961 when the American government initiated an attempt to overthrow Cuban premier Fidel Castro by sponsoring a 1,500-man invasion at the Bay of Pigs. Castro, Cuba's revolutionary leader who had overthrown the pro-American dictator Fulgencio Batista in 1959, had become increasingly dependent on the Soviet Union once the Americans decided he was hostile. Flights over Cuba by anti-Castro exiles based in Florida did not help the cause of good relations; neither did Havana's nationalization of American corporations.

Shortly before Kennedy's inauguration, the Eisenhower administration had severed diplomatic relations with the island regime. By this time, Cuban exiles were already being trained by the United States for the Bay of Pigs operation. The United States rejected Cuban allegations regarding the planned invasion during a special session of the Security Council in January 1961.[23] It was not the former general Eisenhower but the former PT-boat captain Kennedy who would take responsibility for what became no less a fiasco than the UN's August 1961 operation in Elizabethville.

The Bay of Pigs invasion, begun on April 17, had been organized by the CIA and supported by the U.S. Navy. At first, Kennedy denied any American involvement. The Cubans again took their case to the UN, this time not to the Security Council where the United States had a veto-proof majority, but to the General Assembly. Four resolutions addressed the crisis. Those from the USSR and Romania never made it to a vote. A troublesome resolution from Mexico (troublesome because it threatened to split OAS members) lacked the two-thirds majority necessary for implementation. Finally, seven Latin American states offered a very mild resolution with U.S. support calling for peaceful action "to remove existing tensions."[24] Ambassador Adlai Stevenson delivered a spirited defense against Cuban charges of American complicity in the attack. The ambassador offered a blanket denial of American participation or involvement, accepting in good faith the CIA's cover story. "My official liar," Kennedy quipped; Stevenson later called this his most humiliating experience in government.[25] At the end of the debate, the U.S.-dominated assembly approved the Latin American resolution.[26] It included no accusations, no condemnation, no identifications. Not even the word "invasion."

The UN's ineffectiveness during the Bay of Pigs affair said much about the influence of the Great Powers—especially Washington's power—within the organization. Is there any doubt that the UN would have treated a Cuban-sponsored invasion of Florida differently? Nor did repeated Cuban efforts to use the UN to protest subsequent American activity prove any more successful. Cuba even turned to the UN in order to protest its being expelled from the OAS during 1962. The UN ignored the appeals. None of these events promised Cuba any comfort for the main event, which began to unfold in October 1962 when the Americans challenged the deployment of Soviet missiles in Cuba.

Historians have identified many possible reasons why the Soviets introduced missiles into Cuba, including Moscow's desire to shift the balance of power, and its efforts to provide Cuba with more effective defense in light of the Bay of Pigs operation and subsequent U.S. threats. Domestic considerations, too, may have influenced the plans of Soviet premier Khrushchev.[27]

Whatever Khrushchev's motives, the deployment of these missiles set off the most serious military confrontation of the entire Cold War, exactly the kind of situation that the UN had been created to prevent. But the UN had limited authority when permanent members of the Security Council could veto unwelcome proposals. If the UN were to help resolve the crisis, it could only do so as a forum for world opinion or as an agency to facilitate communication among governments that otherwise might not talk to each other. In this instance, the UN would perform both tasks, playing a modest part in resolving the Mt. Everest of all Cold War crises.

During the fall of 1962, the Soviets and Americans had routinely traded accusations about Cuba, the Americans denying that they had aggressive intentions against the island (they lied), and the Soviets denying that they were sending missiles to Cuba (they also lied). An American economic embargo of Cuba, covert operations to overthrow Castro, and various hostile activities by Cuban exiles operating from U.S. soil had worsened the atmosphere; so, too, had a Cuban-Soviet announcement of construction of a port facility in Cuba(the Soviets said for a fishing fleet; the Americans guessed for submarines).

By early October, the Cuban-American relationship had become poisonous. When Cuban president Dorticos delivered an anti-American tirade in the General Assembly on October 8, he precipitated not just an ugly anti-Cuban gallery demonstration but a confrontation with Stevenson that threatened to degenerate into a physical altercation.[28] For more than a year, the Cubans had introduced so many anti-American resolutions at the UN that even neutral nations no longer took them seriously. In itself, UN rejection of the Cuban appeals was of small consequence, though it deepened Havana's antagonism not just to the United States but to the UN as well.

One week later, CIA officials examined the first photographs revealing clear evidence of the Soviet missiles. Agency officials notified Kennedy 24 hours later. Within hours, the administration convened a group of high-level NSC officials—ExComm (for executive committee)—to recommend policy; the president's brother Robert and Defense Secretary Robert McNamara were its most influential members. Adlai Stevenson, whose so-called policy making role in the administration had never materialized, was invited to join them. He attended most—but not all—of their meetings.

During the 13 days of crisis, Stevenson played two roles: as adviser and as public spokesman. In the former capacity, he consistently argued in favor of a policy that would emphasize the importance of negotiation over force, that would invite compromise instead of confrontation. After the crisis, reporters, probably prompted by officials (perhaps even the president) who disdained Stevenson, sought to portray the ambassador as "soft," as wanting "a Munich."[29] These charges were as misleading as they were mean-spirited. Stevenson had indeed opposed some of the most hawkish proposals offered during the first days of the crisis. Some Kennedy advisers, including Dean

Acheson, General Maxwell Taylor, and the Joint Chiefs of Staff, had advocated an air strike on the missile bases, even a general assault on Cuba. But others, not just Stevenson, sought a more moderate course. Stevenson had not initially favored a naval blockade but soon accepted its desirability if linked to diplomatic initiatives; indeed, *most* ExComm members softened their advice during the 13 days of crisis. The diplomatic horse trading proposed by Stevenson included, at least for argument's sake (he did not necessarily personally support each suggestion), the case for concessions such as the removal of American missiles in Turkey and Italy and the evacuation of Guantanamo naval base in exchange for the removal of the Soviet missiles. These suggestions were initially rejected by most other advisers; by the end of the crisis on October 28, they seemed much more in line with the final settlement. Kennedy agreed not just to a no-invasion pledge, but to the removal of U.S. missiles from Turkey. Because these terms remained secret, many reporters believed that Stevenson had sought concessions rejected by his superiors.

American use of the UN during the crisis, it is worth noting, did not always involve Stevenson. Hours before the fateful climax of the crisis when the Americans feared that Khrushchev would insist on terms unacceptable to the United States, making an air strike almost inevitable, the president either ordered Secretary Rusk—or approved a Rusk suggestion—to "open a secret conduit to the UN as an *option* for a public deal."[30] This would involve a call to Andrew Cordier, formerly a close aide to Dag Hammarskjold, who would be that conduit. Cordier would be authorized to ask the secretary-general to propose a trade of American missiles in Turkey for Soviet missiles in Cuba, a proposal that the Americans would then publicly accept. It is unclear whether the call to Cordier was ever made or whether Stevenson would have been informed in advance. What the evidence suggests, however, is that the UN remained an instrument that Kennedy hoped to use in a last ditch effort to preclude Soviet-American hostilities, and also that Kennedy's fear of nuclear war overrode his fear of being criticized for weakness. By having U Thant of Burma, who was elected secretary-general following Hammarskjold's death, convey the proposal to Moscow, Kennedy may have hoped to deflect criticism from American hard-liners. In that way, the UN would serve the cause of both peace and public relations.

Stevenson's role as advice-giver paralleled his much more public role as American spokesman in the Security Council. As soon as President Kennedy broke the news of the missile crisis to the world in his now-famous TV speech of October 22, public attention shifted to the UN. Kennedy, in announcing the naval quarantine, noted that the United States would bring the missile issue before the Security Council; Cuba and the USSR immediately announced that they would follow suit, arguing that the "blockade" represented "an act of war." Unbeknownst to outsiders, Kennedy had asked John J. McCloy, a Republican cold warrior who had served as American high commissioner in Berlin, to join Stevenson at the UN. A number of ExComm members, including Robert Kennedy, thought Stevenson too conciliatory, too unreliable. McCloy's job was to stiffen Stevenson's resistance. The president need not have worried. Stevenson's UN work during the coming days reflected plenty of spine. And while Stevenson naturally resented McCloy's presence, the two men apparently got along quite well.

Stevenson's speech to the Security Council would stand as a monument to his UN service and to his own commitment to Cold War principles. Soviet missiles in Cuba, he said, have transformed Cuba "into a base for offensive weapons of sudden mass destruction." While the United States had committed itself "to the world of the Charter," to a community of "freely cooperating independent States bound by the United Nations," the Soviets had committed themselves to "the idea of uniformity," "dogma," "conformity."

"Had the Soviet Union ever really joined the United Nations?" he asked, for Moscow had pursued a "war against the world of the United Nations" as soon as the ink on the Charter had dried. He described Soviet policy as "remorseless expansionism" leading to "a world civil war—a contest between the pluralistic world and the monolithic world—a contest between the world of the Charter and the world of communist conformity." Every nation, he warned, is involved if it wishes to retain its independence. As for the missiles, they were offensive, he argued in one of the more argumentative sections of the speech. "In the Soviet lexicon, all weapons are purely defensive, even weapons that can strike from 1,000 to 2,000 miles away." Such missiles have created a "new and dangerous situation." After reading the text of the American resolution calling for the dismantling and withdrawal of the missiles, he read the text of an OAS resolution—just handed to him—authorizing the use of military force, and calling for the UN to dispatch observers to Cuba to verify a withdrawal of the missiles.[31]

Even Kennedy was impressed. The president must have been even more impressed two days later when Stevenson had his most famous exchange with Soviet ambassador Valerian Zorin. Zorin had previously justified the missiles as defensive. Now Zorin reverted back to the original line that the missiles did not exist, and Stevenson, ever the lawyer, zeroed in on the inconsistency. "Do you, Ambassador Zorin, deny that the USSR has placed . . . missiles . . . in Cuba? Yes or no? Do not wait for the interpretation. Yes or no?" Zorin shot back that he was not in a court of law and would not respond to a question put in the manner of a prosecuting counsel. Stevenson grabbed his opportunity: "You are in the courtroom of public opinion right now, and you can answer 'Yes' or 'No' . . . I am prepared to wait for my answer until Hell freezes over . . ."[32]

Of course the Americans were unwilling to wait for anything to freeze over; they never expected their resolution to pass. The resolution was ritual; it also served as a holding action.[33] Washington was even cool to the idea of a standstill agreement, which was the most important initiative offered by U Thant during this perilous period. Thant had already become the conduit for messages from Washington to Moscow prodding the Soviets to keep their ships out of the quarantine zone. The Soviets agreed, buying time for further negotiations. The Americans did not want to accept Thant's standstill proposal because it did not prevent further construction at the missile sites, but neither did they want to rebuff the secretary-general. Kennedy's ambiguous but clear response, sent through Stevenson, signalled that the missiles must be removed in any case. Khrushchev responded positively to Thant's proposal, which indicated to the Americans that the Soviet leader was looking for a way out of the thicket. This was especially likely since Zorin, two days earlier, had rejected U Thant's approach.[34]

The secretary-general had contributed modestly to the continuation of dialogue. Still, his efforts amounted to little. It would be the direct Kennedy-Khrushchev correspondence that ended the crisis. Nevertheless, the UN continued to play a minor role. The United States proposed that the UN take responsibility for verifying removal of both missiles and Russian bombers, and U Thant visited Cuba on October 30 to orchestrate this last act. Castro, furious at what he considered a Soviet betrayal, refused to cooperate. The Cuban leader had come to see the UN as an American tool, the Soviets as deeply disloyal. Still, Soviet economic and military leverage over Cuba, along with Soviet and American meetings involving Stevenson, McCloy, and the new Soviet negotiator Vassily Kuznetzov, slowly resolved most issues.[35] By January 1963, the United States and the USSR removed Cuba from the Security Council agenda.

CYPRUS, INDIA, AND WEST IRIAN

The Congo and Cuban crises comprised the core of UN activity during the Kennedy years, the Congo crisis highlighting what the UN could do to preserve peace, the Cuban crisis what it could not do. But such generalities should be considered with caution. The expansion of UN peacekeeping and of the role of the secretary-general during the Congo crisis only resulted in partial success. The UN successfully removed the Belgians and ended Katangan secession, but it hardly insured peace; and the UN's inability to apply its collective-security machinery in Cuba did not preclude at least modest diplomatic initiatives by the secretary-general.

Yet the Congo and Cuba hardly tell the entire story of the United States and the UN during the early 1960s. The UN also addressed disputes in Cyprus, India (Kashmir and Goa), and West Irian (Indonesia and the Netherlands). The first of these issues had roots going back to the previous decade when Cyprus, still a British colony, experienced hostilities between its majority Greek and minority Turkish populations. In part, the Cyprus issue involved the politics of decolonization, more in terms of a merger with another state (Greece) than in respect to independence. During the first phase of the controversy, between 1954 and 1958, the United States played a secondary role.

No Cold War issues intruded, and, unlike the Cuban situation, the United States had no direct role on the island. Where the United States did involve itself, it did so to *prevent* UN consideration of the dispute: all three principals were NATO members by 1954, and a brawl in UN chambers between Greece and Turkey threatened to weaken the alliance in the Mediterranean. Between 1954 and 1956, the United States managed to prevent the UN from "inscripting" the dispute (placing it on the agenda). During the next two years as more former colonial states joined the UN, the General Assembly did vote on the Cyprus issue, but in ways that settled little. When the United States could not forestall a formal vote, as in 1958, it sided with Britain rather than Turkey, calling for negotiations so tepid as to be meaningless.[36] When, in 1959, the disputing parties accepted a settlement leading to independence in 1960, it was arranged through NATO, not the UN.

The next round of the Cyprus problem began after Kennedy's assassination. With the Greek Cypriots having granted extensive minority rights to their Turkish neighbors in 1960 in order to achieve independence, and with Turkey pledged to guarantee the treaty, future quarrels were inevitable. When the Cypriots approached the UN demanding either changes to or abrogation of the 1960 treaty, they stood on weak ground. Once again, the United States remained in the background, but, as a status quo power, joined the majority opposing any Cypriot right to alter the treaty. What the United States supported was a March 4, 1964 resolution creating a peace-keeping force for Cyprus. Called UNFICYP, the Security Council extended its original three-month life repeatedly. Still, sporadic fighting on the island continued for the next four years, with the Cypriot government continually trying to annul the Turkish protection clauses of the 1960 constitution. When Turkey threatened to invade Cyprus in 1967 to protect the Turkish minority, the U.S. government sent a mediator, Cyrus Vance, to prevent war, at the same time strongly urging the Security Council to issue a consensus statement in favor of peace and expanding UNFICYP.[37] Nonetheless, small-scale skirmishes between the two communities continued until a major population exchange occurred in 1994. UN action may have avoided war between Greece and Turkey but it certainly did not guarantee peace; and UNICYP in 1998 continues as the longest-lived peacekeeping force in UN history.

The American role in the UN debate over Goa was less restrained. India had long eyed Goa, a Portuguese colony of 800,000 people on India's western coast. As one of the earliest postwar independent states, and certainly the largest, India took a leading role in calling for not just national self-determination, but peace. Americans, in fact, had long been irritated by what many U.S. officials considered the Indian prime minister's moralizing on issues of peace and decolonization. Therefore, when India finally attacked and annexed Goa and two other Portuguese enclaves in December 1962, Washington strongly condemned what it called aggression and called for a cease-fire and further negotiations. Adlai Stevenson argued that the Indians had violated Article 2 regarding a threat to peace. He ignored the underlying issue of colonialism in order to focus on New Delhi's illegal use of force. The U.S.-backed resolution received a narrow majority. Many newly independent countries applauded the Soviet veto.

What makes this episode memorable, however, is not just the degree to which the United States and the other NATO allies elevated the issue of force over decolonization, but also the way that Stevenson responded. The State Department's instructions to Stevenson were straightforward. Not so Stevenson's response to the Indian representative. The U.S. ambassador launched into a scathing condemnation of New Delhi's action, accusing the Indians, who so often advocated nonviolence, of hypocrisy. This "act of force, he said, "mocks the good faith of India's frequent declarations of exalted principle." It was a "lamentable departure" from India's own professions of good faith. Years later, one of Stevenson's former aides would, with sadness, describe his performance as demagoguery.[38] Nevertheless, Stevenson had said what many Americans were thinking. He had exposed a double standard in the anticolonial camp concerning the principle of self-determination, and his successors at USUN would repeatedly denounce what they viewed as Third World hypocrisy during the next two decades.

The American role in the West Irian episode reflected more ambiguity. West Irian—previously known as West New Guinea—was a Dutch colony that the Indonesians claimed to be a part of their own country. Ethnically, it was distinct from Indonesia, a fact ignored by Indonesian authorities. The Jakarta government argued a doctrinaire anticolonial case in their attempt to annex West Irian. The Indonesians during the 1950s resisted UN suggestions for a plebiscite, however, fearing that the West Irians would opt for independence rather than incorporation into Indonesia.

The Americans, generally sympathetic to decolonization, initially distanced themselves from this matter, caught between a desire to support Third World nationalism and sympathy for a NATO ally. After Kennedy's inauguration, the United States quietly supported Dutch efforts to resolve the issue by implementing the principle of self-determination for the West Irians. A General Assembly resolution to this effect passed by a 53–41–21 margin. Nevertheless, the State Department subordinated principle to Cold War expediency. As Evan Luard argues, the Americans not only simplistically interpreted the issue in terms of old-fashioned colonialism (it wasn't), but feared that supporting the Dutch would have the effect of "pushing [Indonesian President] Sukarno into the arms of the Russians."[39] When Sukarno gradually turned to military measures that threatened a wider war, the United States virtually abandoned the Dutch, refusing even to allow Dutch planes to refuel at U.S. bases. The Americans did supply a mediator to work out a settlement that mandated temporary UN administration of the area, but under conditions that gave Indonesia effective control of the territory. Geopolitical considerations, not UN principles, proved crucial in Washington's willingness to surrender any serious support for West Irian self-determination. On this issue, Adlai Stevenson delivered no impassioned speeches.[40]

STRUGGLES WITHIN THE GENERAL ASSEMBLY

It is clear that the American approach to the UN during the first half of the 1960s showed the same kind of unevenness for which the United States condemned others. Numerous developments helped to account for this. The membership of many former colonies made the UN, and especially the General Assembly, less sympathetic to American aims, which produced a more defensive—and less confident—United States at the UN. Nor was there a strong secretary-general like Dag Hammarskjold to call the United States to account, as Hammarskjold had done during the Congo crisis. His successor, Burma's U Thant, lacked Hammarskjold's intellect, confidence, and moral conviction. Hammarskjold had believed that the secretary-general's effectiveness stemmed from his independence; he defended the UN, when necessary, against the Great Powers. Thant believed that the secretary-general's effectiveness rested on the support of the Great Powers. Paradoxically, his reluctance to defy them contributed to a widespread belief that he was a weak leader. In fact, though he was not a Hammarskjold, U Thant was a much more effective secretary-general than men like Lie before him and Kurt Waldheim, his own successor. The negative opinion toward U Thant offered years later by officials such as Dean Rusk ironically stemmed from his occasional willingness—not his unwillingness—to take issue with the Great Powers.[41]

In 1961, U Thant had been no better known than Hammarskjold had been a decade earlier. His election following Hammarskjold's death came with neither great support nor great opposition from the major powers. The Soviets had rekindled their demand for a troika, but President Kennedy rejected it unconditionally when addressing the UN on September 25. For the next two months, debate over Hammarskjold's successor dominated UN politics. The United States initially favored Mongi Slim of Tunisia, but Israeli and Soviet opposition eventually persuaded Stevenson to recommend Thant. As with his predecessors, Thant was everyone's second choice, a man not expected to take imaginative initiatives. Neither he nor his country had important enemies. He corralled Soviet support after Stevenson agreed to make him "acting" secretary-general until the end of Hammarskjold's unexpired term.[42] Because he seemed so much safer than his predecessor, the Soviets dropped their demand for a troika. In 1963, the General Assembly elected Thant to a full term in his own right.

Thant's generally cautious approach fit nicely with what Kennedy's successor, Lyndon Baines Johnson, expected from the UN. Johnson retained Rusk as his secretary of state, but Stevenson's sudden death in 1965 deprived the UN of its most visible American champion. In reality, Stevenson had increasingly lost interest in his official duties during his final two years as ambassador to the UN. "History had passed him by," commented Undersecretary of State George Ball, and the new president from Texas flatly refused to give him the policy role he had so actively sought back in 1961.[43]

Stevenson's successor, Supreme Court Justice Arthur J. Goldberg, never achieved the former Illinois governor's prestige at the UN. As Kennedy had done with Stevenson, Johnson gave Goldberg the post to advertise the importance of the UN in American policy making. This was vintage Johnson, twisting the arm of a highly respected judge to pry him away from the court. As had Stevenson, Goldberg demanded a policy making role. Johnson quickly agreed. Unlike Kennedy, who had reneged on this promise, Johnson allowed Goldberg to set policy on most UN-related matters. In this sense, the locus of authority on UN affairs shifted from Washington to New York (Joseph Sisco, the new assistant secretary of state for international organization, would not enjoy Harlan Cleveland's influence). The new ambassador's superb skill as a negotiator effectively increased the influence of his office within the foreign policy making machinery, though his meager oratorical talent prevented him from rivaling Stevenson's public stature.

The most pressing issue facing the UN during the last months of Kennedy's administration and continuing well into 1965 concerned finances. At the UN's inception, the American government financed 40 percent of the organization's budget. This had been reduced to 33 percent by 1960. The Soviets originally contributed about 6 percent, increasing to 13 percent in later years, with the other permanent members of the Security Council paying smaller amounts. No one withheld the payment of regular dues during this period, but special assessments to fund peacekeeping operations became as controversial as they were expensive; ONUC alone cost about $100 million each year, dwarfing the UN's regular budget. Although neither the USSR nor France had vetoed ONUC in 1960, neither contributed a penny toward its activity. Moreover, it was the vetoless General Assembly, not the Security Council, that approved the original peacekeeping mission (UNEF), which meant that future peacekeeping missions might again be authorized even if the Great Powers objected. Indeed, assessments for both operations had been explicitly made part of the UN's "normal" expenses, a procedure validated in a 1962 advisory opinion by the World Court.[44] Was withholding funds therefore legal? The Charter, written before either special assessments or peacekeeping had been invented, clearly said in Article 19 that a member in arrears for two years would lose its vote in the General Assembly if the amount due exceeded the amount paid. Article 19 said nothing about different categories of assessments.

Between 1962 and 1964, the Americans denounced their Cold War rivals for nonpayment. Neither did they spare the French during these years when

President Charles DeGaulle criticized U.S. policy in Vietnam and removed French forces from NATO command. But denouncing nonpayment was one thing; depriving countries of their vote was another. This really meant driving them out of the UN, and such action would probably destroy the organization. American policy makers were therefore ambivalent. In the meantime, Washington, along with other governments supporting peacekeeping, purchased UN bonds to maintain the organization's solvency. But even the bond issue complicated matters because Stevenson, seeking Congressional support for the plan, promised to be "extremely stubborn" about Soviet payments. Piecemeal solutions would not suffice, however, and in 1964 the Americans resolved to invoke Article 19. A General Assembly resolution endorsing the World Court decision passed overwhelmingly (76–17–8), stiffening American willingness to take a hard line.[45]

There was nothing inevitable about Washington's course. State Department officials fully understood that the legal issue was cloudy: The Charter had not distinguished between regular and special assessments, and UN activity in Korea had been financed outside of the UN framework by allied countries in order to avoid an assessment that all Soviet-bloc governments would have rejected.[46] The American decision had as much to do with election-year tactics as with legal niceties. It reflected Cold War politics more than professions of internationalist faith, as well as White House (and National Security Council) fears that the State Department might be too conciliatory.[47] But the stakes were enormous, and the small countries in the UN, passionately committed to the UN's existence, pleaded with American officials to desist, even postponing the General Assembly session until after the 1964 American presidential election.

Having bought some time, delegates sought ways to head off the crisis. UN officials proposed postponing a showdown on Article 19 by creating the Special Committee on peacekeeping to study the issue. Stevenson, without State Department authorization, then suggested that the General Assembly not record formal votes during its 19th session.[48] Albania, in 1964 as much a maverick state as a Soviet ally, denounced U.S. "blackmail" and tried to block Stevenson's strategy by demanding normal voting procedures. This would require a roll-call vote, thereby precipitating an Article 19 showdown. The Americans dodged the bullet, however, by claiming that because the matter did not involve a "substantive" issue (actually, it involved a *very* substantive issue), the U.S. delegate would not invoke Article 19 on the roll call.[49] Except for the Albanians, all parties supported these stalling tactics. Finally, in August 1965, Arthur Goldberg announced what by then everyone knew— that the United States would no longer press the issue. Perhaps it was just as well. It would have come back to haunt the United States when, years later, the Americans refused to pay what they had damned their Cold War rival for not paying during the 1960s.[50]

THE DOMINICAN REPUBLIC

If there is a single theme that describes the United States's relationship to the UN until this point, it is inconsistency. Events during Lyndon Johnson's last four years in the White House would do nothing to remedy this.

During April 1965 as the Article 19 controversy was fading, President Johnson ordered American marines to occupy the Dominican Republic. He acted ostensibly to protect U.S. citizens following the overthrow of the Dominican government by Dominican army units who then announced they would hold free elections. In reality, Johnson acted to prevent former Dominican president Juan Bosch from returning to power. The White House viewed Bosch as a dangerous leftist. No more Castros, argued Johnson. We "will not permit the establishment of another communist government in the Western hemisphere."[51]

At the UN, Ambassador Stevenson informed the Security Council of the ostensible U.S. purposes and then announced that Washington would convene the OAS to deal with the matter. This would simplify matters. The UN, with its numerous new members, would likely view the occupation as neocolonialist; the OAS, on the other hand, had been more agreeable to U.S. aims, as in Guatemala in 1954 and Cuba eight years later.

When, therefore, the USSR introduced a resolution into the Security Council condemning the U.S. occupation, American policy makers replied with measures designed to secure OAS, not UN, primacy. Although a few Latin American states broke with Washington over this strategy, a majority refused to challenge their influential neighbor to the north. In addition, Cuban attacks on U.S. policy during the crisis had the effect of muting criticism of the United States at the UN, even among countries sympathetic to the Dominican revolutionaries. The result was that Washington succeeded in marginalizing the UN during the crisis. The UN did manage to send an observer team to the island in mid-May, headed by Jose Mayobre of Venezuela. Mayobre, who was sympathetic to the revolution, proved nettlesome to American officials, though he eventually served as a useful conduit between the Americans and their opponents.[52] The Americans also managed to sidetrack demands for UN human rights investigations in the Dominican Republic; these too would be carried out under OAS auspices.

The U.S.-UN relationship during the crisis closely resembled the way that the Americans had used—more accurately, *not* used—the organization during the Guatemalan crisis a decade earlier. Evan Luard suggests another analogy—that American policy toward the UN during this episode resembled Soviet stonewalling of the organization during the Hungarian Revolution of 1956.[53] By the same token, it should be noted that the UN Charter did indeed permit a regional agency like the OAS to step into the picture, although Article 53 stated that such regional agencies could not take enforcement action "without the authorization of the Security Council." Such "enforcement action"—the U.S. occupation, later joined by troops from some OAS states—had already occurred. Washington's tepid support for the UN observer team was in reality a way to mollify those UN members who otherwise criticized the United States for ignoring the Security Council. The Americans had thrown the UN a bone.

CONFLICT IN VIETNAM

The UN did little to end the crisis in the Caribbean; it would do even less to end the war in Vietnam. The Dominican crisis involved foreign (U.S.) intervention in a civil conflict. So, too, did the hostilities in Vietnam, although Washington defined that war as foreign aggression (by the North Vietnamese) rather than civil conflict. With military activity escalating after 1961, the Americans asserted the legality of their position in respect to the UN Charter. They claimed that the Charter permitted a state to act in self-defense, and that South Vietnam's request for American assistance fell into this category. Critics of American involvement saw things differently. They claimed that the Americans were the aggressors, violating, not defending, Charter principles.

Although American military advisers in South Vietnam were involved in infantry skirmishing as early as 1961, it was not until 1964 that UN officials addressed the conflict. By then, those advisers had increased from fewer than a thousand to nearly 25,000. The assassination of the South Vietnamese president, antigovernment rioting in Saigon and other cities, and the first air attacks by the United States against North Vietnamese targets had recently made front page news around the world. To complicate matters, the pressures of the 1964 presidential election placed Johnson in a difficult position. Publicly, he distanced himself from his hawkish opponent, Arizona senator Barry Goldwater, rejecting demands for American military escalation in Vietnam. Privately, he escalated. Indeed, by asking Congress to approve the Tonkin Gulf resolution in August 1964, he laid the legal foundation for a sharp acceleration of American involvement.

The very week that Johnson sent the Tonkin Gulf resolution to Congress, Rusk, Stevenson, and a number of other State Department officials met with U Thant, initiating the first—and the most important—chapter concerning the UN-U.S. relationship over Vietnam. Thant left the meeting wrongly believing that Washington welcomed his good offices to bring North Vietnamese and American leaders together for talks that might lead to a settlement. Because Hanoi was not a UN member, he used Soviet diplomats at the UN to contact North Vietnam president Ho Chi Minh, who responded positively in late September. Thant was jubilant. So, apparently, was Stevenson, but not Stevenson's superiors in Washington. According to Stevenson, President Johnson refused to authorize any direct U.S.-North Vietnam contacts during the presidential campaign. Even afterwards, the Americans threw cold water on the proposal by saying that they believed Ho Chi Minh had no interest in such talks. This was untrue, as Thant soon conveyed to the Americans.[54]

Stevenson therefore found himself in a most awkward position. Personally sharing Thant's goals, he even asked "on his own," according to historian Walter Johnson, that Thant suggest a location for talks. Thant proposed Rangoon. On January 30, 1965, the State Department rejected the plan, claiming that talks could not be kept secret and that leaks would bring down the Saigon government.

Washington assumed that the matter would end there. It did not. Two weeks later, Stevenson, again apparently on his own initiative, asked Thant about Hanoi's reaction to Washington's response. Stevenson's inquiry led Thant to offer an alternative proposal: a multination meeting instead of a bilateral meeting, to include both Vietnams as well China, the USSR, France, and Great Britain. Once again, Stevenson became an advocate for Thant's proposal, forwarding it to both Johnson and Rusk and now arguing that a Hanoi rejection would justify additional American military measures. A week later, with no response from Washington and with Stevenson traveling abroad, Thant announced at a news conference that the American government had withheld "the true facts" about the peace process from the American people.[55]

Thant's relationship with President Johnson and Secretary Rusk never recovered from this episode. Johnson, hardly one to welcome disagreement, would undoubtedly have been irate if Thant had conveyed the charge privately; he was furious that Thant went public. Much the same can be said about the usually circumspect Rusk, who claimed that the secretary-general had "lied like a sailor" about Hanoi's interest in peace.[56]

But had U Thant lied? The accusation is hard to take seriously. Thant, like Rusk, was a man of integrity. He may have been misinformed about Hanoi's interest in talks by his Russian informant in the Secretariat, but it is unlikely he fabricated anything. To defend themselves against his charge, the Americans would later claim that he offered them no written evidence of Hanoi's seriousness (which was true), and that he had actually made no proposal at all (rather, they claimed, he had only offered a "procedure").[57] Both excuses are lame. Years later, Rusk's secretary, a man deeply involved in the minutiae of policy, would tell an interviewer "we put *every* piece of that puzzle together. And I still don't know whether there was any serious North Vietnamese initiative there . . . it really looks less real than almost any of the other [peace] efforts of the period. And I thought then and I think now that it was really much ado about nothing."[58]

Whatever the truth of the matter, Vietnam never became a serious issue at the UN again. Although Stevenson was deeply disappointed, Harlan Cleveland generally supported administration policy and believed that bringing the conflict to the Security Council would be counterproductive: it would force the USSR into a public defense of North Vietnam and therefore end all hopes of using Moscow as an intermediary to Hanoi.[59] Moreover, in spite of occasional proposals from UN advocates like Arthur Goldberg and Oregon's senator Wayne Morse asking the administration to bring the war to the attention of the UN, North Vietnamese and PRC nonmembership made it unlikely that the UN would or could be a useful forum. Even U Thant understood that the Security Council "could not be usefully involved" in a settlement, though he never ruled out using his good offices even after his unhappy experience in 1965.[60] He did reject invoking Article 99 permitting the secretary-general to bring a matter threatening peace to the attention of the world body. Hammarskjold might have used this authority; Thant, whom the CIA characterized as a "minimalist" at the UN, was much more circumspect.[61]

THE SIX-DAY WAR

The UN's impotence concerning Vietnam differs dramatically from its activity during the Arab-Israeli Six-Day War of June 1967. Unfortunately for the secretary-general, this conflict, too, would compare him unfavorably with his activist predecessor.

One of the main legacies of the Suez crisis had been creation of UNEF, separating the Egyptians and Israelis in the Sinai peninsula. The Israelis had rejected a peacekeeping force on Israeli soil, but they accepted the UNEF concept after receiving assurances that the peacekeepers would prevent Egyptian "belligerency" and that Israeli ships would have access to the Gulf of Aqaba. The UN would not order a precipitate withdrawal, promised Hammarskjold.[62] Ten years later, U Thant ignored the quid pro quo. He ordered UNEF peacekeepers to withdraw from their posts after United Arab Republic President Nasser, apparently responding to bogus Soviet reports of an impending Israeli attack, demanded their removal on May 14, 1967.[63] Many observers later damned the secretary-general for ordering the withdrawal. Rusk, who already distrusted Thant, called it "disastrous"; President Johnson called it "shocking."[64]

Within three weeks, Israel and the UAR were at war. Thant's decision discredited both the UN and himself in Israel and, to a lesser degree, in the United States and other western states. Some observers argued that Thant should not have removed the troops at all. "The umbrella was removed at the very moment when it began to rain," protested Israel's foreign minister.[65] Others admitted that the secretary-general stood on firm legal ground, but that he should have played for time, bringing the Security Council into the situation via Article 99, or bringing the issue to the General Assembly, which had created UNEF in the first place. U Thant, in turn, argued that he had no choice: that Nasser's expulsion of UNEF was as valid as Israel's 1956 refusal (reaffirmed in 1967) to allow UNEF units on Israeli soil, and that no UN force could—or should—take up positions without the consent of both sides to a dispute. His legal case was strengthened by practical necessities. The UAR ambassador had flatly told him that any appeal to Nasser for delay would be viewed as "hostile" and "unacceptable," and that Indian and Yugoslavian UNEF units were already leaving the scene as Egyptian troops took their place. "Humbug," "escapism," a "resolute determination not to consider the real facts," says Brian Urquhart about U.S. criticism of Thant.[66]

Urquhart is probably correct, but the American case can't be dismissed quite yet. For one, Nasser had originally promised to accept UNEF in "good faith," which implied that the troops could not be ordered out until their peacekeeping function had been fulfilled. Secondly, Rusk would later write that Nasser had asked for a partial pullout of UN troops, not a complete withdrawal.[67] The distinction is important because Nasser later claimed that the secretary-general's order to withdraw *all* UNEF soldiers left Egypt no choice but to confront the Israelis directly. To Nasser, this included blockading Israeli shipping from the Gulf of Aqaba, an action that Tel Aviv insisted would be an act of war. The Strait of Tiran at the gulf entrance had previously been patrolled by UNEF. "What could I do?" asked Nasser, implying that he had hoped UNEF troops would remain at the strait, thereby avoiding a blockade that made the war nearly inevitable.

Nasser's question is nonsense. If he wanted a way out, he could easily have found it. U Thant, who was already on his way to Cairo when the UAR president ordered the blockade, would certainly have accommodated him. Had Nasser won the war that began less than two weeks later, it is inconceivable that he would have expressed regret and surprise at U Thant's order.[68]

Might the Americans or Soviets have restrained their Mideast allies? Perhaps, but almost surely not through UN measures. The Security Council suffered from paralysis; for both foreign and domestic reasons, neither superpower would permit Security Council condemnation of its Middle East ally. Moreover, once Nasser deployed his army to the Sinai, it is doubtful whether anything could have deterred an Israeli response. As the Americans had discovered a decade earlier, a threatened Israel would act first and ask permission later—despite conversations with Israeli officials that Washington hoped would delay war.[69] In fact, Israelis felt more threatened than ever as Nasser concluded a mutual defense agreement with Jordan identical to his pact with Syria. Surprising even their American friends, the Israelis launched a preventative attack on June 5, obliterating the Egyptian air force and setting the stage for Israel's quick victory over her neighborhood rivals.

Neither the UN nor Washington had played a constructive role in preventing the war. Both, however, would play a major role in ending it. Sensitive to Arab charges that the United States was too pro-Israel, Washington turned to the UN to broker a settlement. Both Rusk and Goldberg were already committed to the Charter's collective-security ideal. The president and his national security adviser, former MIT economist Walt W. Rostow, were less committed; they viewed the organization as a convenience, as useful in the Middle East as it was expendable in Vietnam. Yet even they concluded that the UN could help arrange an armistice once Israeli security was assured after the first few hours of fighting. Consequently, Goldberg backed a resolution calling for a cease-fire. It even got Soviet support after Nasser discredited his own case by claiming that American aircraft had joined in the Israeli attack.

On June 6, the resolution passed unanimously. So did another the following day, and a third, introduced by Ambassador Goldberg, on June 9. Fighting continued. So much for UN resolutions. Arab officials denounced them because they did not condemn Israel. Israel ignored them because Tel Aviv believed victory was in sight. Military developments defined the diplomacy of peace, and the Americans refused to pressure Tel Aviv into a hasty truce. First Jordan, then Egypt, finally Israel and Syria accepted the UN's proposed cease-fire. By June 11, with Nasser's army shattered in the Sinai and Israel wresting control of both Jerusalem (taken from the Jordanians who had marched into East Jerusalem at the outbreak of fighting) and the Golan Heights (taken from the Syrians), the fighting ended.[70]

The war lasted six days. Reconstructing the peace took six months. Neither U Thant nor his trusted assistant, Ralph Bunche, ever fully recovered from the sense of failure—and the stinging criticism—that followed the war. Although Arthur Goldberg's Jewish background made him suspect in Arab capitals, he, more than anyone else, orchestrated UN diplomacy during the months following the war. With the UN discredited in both Israel and Egypt, and with Israelis acutely aware of how territorial concessions made after the 1956 war led to the 1967 conflict, his task took stamina and skill. An American diplomat assigned to the UN for 15 years called him "the best negotiator I have ever seen," praise that his Mideast diplomacy merited.[71] Preoccupied with Vietnam, Washington gave him the kind of leeway it had promised, but denied, to Adlai Stevenson.

The war ended with Israeli soldiers occupying Egypt's Sinai Desert, Jordan's section of Jerusalem, the West Bank of Palestine, which contained nearly one million Arabs, and Syria's mountainous Golan region, which for years had housed artillery used to shell northern Israeli villages. The return of UN troops as part of the UN Truce Supervision Organization (UNTSO) helped to maintain temporary stability, although occasional outbreaks of violence continued through the summer and fall of 1967. The euphoria of victory made Tel Aviv little disposed to return territories paid for with blood. Washington, however, understood correctly that continued Israeli control of these territories would inevitably feed demands for another war, a sentiment heightened by Secretary Rusk's belief that Tel Aviv was betraying two decades of *American* denials regarding Israeli territorial ambitions.[72]

There may have been an even more compelling reason for the Johnson administration's interest in a more permanent peace. A future threat to Israel's existence would certainly raise questions about whether the United States could remain out of the next war. American involvement in a Mideast war would, in turn, inevitably drag the Soviets militarily or diplomatically into the Mideast, which the Americans dearly wanted to avoid.[73] Such speculation added urgency to Rusk's support for Goldberg's efforts. From June to November, the ambassador struggled to design a formula to provide a new foundation for stability. His formula became Security Council Resolution 242.

Although Britain's Lord Caradon formally introduced Resolution 242, authorship was mainly Goldberg's. The resolution contained two main principles, one calling for Israeli return of territories occupied during the war (the Israelis would later note that the resolution did not state "all" territories, and Lord Caradon confirmed that the omission was deliberate), the other calling for "acknowledgment" of Israel's existence and "right to live in peace with secure and recognized boundaries . . . "[74] Unanimous adoption of the resolution once again fed illusions of UN effectiveness. Yet nothing had changed. Skirmishing between Israel and her neighbors continued until war again erupted six years later.

The final year of Johnson's presidency witnessed no significant U.S. initiatives at the UN. The State Department used the Security Council to denounce North Korea's capture of the destroyer USS *Pueblo*, and as the preferred forum to gather support for the Nuclear Non-Proliferation Treaty, approved by the General Assembly in June 1968. Although Goldberg wanted to resign from his post once it became clear that he would have no role in negotiating an end to the Vietnam War, he stayed on until the summer of 1968. Former Undersecretary of State George Ball and then *Washington Post* editor James Russell Wiggins served as permanent representatives during the remaining months of the Johnson administration. Neither had name recognition or international standing. As interim appointees, they brought little stature to the organization. The U.S. mission was marking time.

chapter 6

NIXON AND FORD

Ambassador George Ball resigned from his UN post to campaign against Richard Nixon during the fall of 1968. Like Stevenson, he had little respect for the former vice president who was seeking the White House a second time. Nixon, in turn, had little respect for the UN. His victory during one of the most tumultuous campaigns in American history meant that Washington's reliance on the UN would be terribly modest during the next six years.

Nixon prided himself on his knowledge of foreign affairs. Smart albeit dishonest and conspiratorial, he had built his political career on an anticommunist platform reaching back to the Hiss espionage case of the late 1940s. His conservatism and anticommunism, however, took a back seat to his pragmatism; this became most evident when the man who had done his small part to isolate the revolutionary government in China during 1949 would justifiably take credit for bringing China back into the family of nations a generation later. Nixon worried more about results than principles, and rarely worried about consistency. He viewed concentrations of political power as vastly more important than ideology. And he understood that the UN had no real power.

In order to ensure his own primacy as a foreign-policy maker, Richard Nixon appointed his law partner, William Rogers, as secretary of state. Rogers, a corporation lawyer, knew virtually nothing about foreign affairs and cared little for the UN, which was just the way Nixon liked it. More visible would be Nixon's national security adviser. To revitalize the NSC in a manner that would consolidate the making of foreign policy within the White House, Nixon appointed Henry Kissinger, a Harvard professor who had recently been advising one of Nixon's Republican rivals. Although it is often said that the two men were opposites—one a politician, the other an intellectual; one a WASP, the other a Jew; one a native Californian, the other a refugee from

Hitler's Germany—in fact both shared a penchant for secrecy, manipulation, and self-promotion. Neither had much use for ideology or the sanctity of human rights. Both were geopoliticians, fusing nationalism and internationalism whenever convenient.

Like his predecessors, Nixon initially sought a prestige candidate for the UN. His recent Democratic rival, Senator Hubert Humphrey, rejected the offer, as did the black moderate senator from Massachusetts, Edward Brooke. Nixon finally turned to Charles Yost, a highly respected professional foreign service officer who would loyally—though unhappily—follow White House orders. Yost had worked with the American delegation at the San Francisco Conference and later served both Stevenson and Goldberg at the U.S. Mission to the UN.[1] A reflective man of solid integrity, he believed deeply in the UN even while he remained skeptical of a UN system hampered by the veto and the absence of an international military arm. He accepted the post less out of naive faith in the organization than fear that Nixon would otherwise appoint a critic of the UN during a time when anti-UN rhetoric was increasing in the US.[2]

Yost would not serve for long. Shut out of a policy making role, he resigned within two years. During the remainder of the Nixon and Ford administrations, Yost would be followed by four other men: defeated Texas senate candidate George Bush, reporter John Scali, professor and bureaucrat Daniel Patrick Moynihan, and former Pennsylvania governor William Scranton. The post of permanent U.S. representative became anything but permanent. Such turnover contributed to more inconsistency in America's UN policy and indicated the scant regard held by both Nixon and Kissinger for the organization.

The love affair between the United States and the UN had surely ended by 1969. Actually, this parting can be traced back more than a decade. What intensified it during the Nixon-Ford years, however, was that the UN had failed to resolve America's most unpopular war (for which some observers oddly blamed the UN), and that Americans increasingly viewed the organization as anti-American. There was some truth to this perception. U.S. influence in the organization had declined noticeably. The automatic U.S. majority in the General Assembly had become a thing of the past by 1970. The organization's ballooning membership (76 countries in 1955, 114 in 1965, 145 by 1975) was increasingly composed of former colonies who viewed the West as less a protector than as an adversary. The emerging Third World majority was hardly unified, but neither did Washington find it malleable. On issues concerning decolonization and Israel, the new majority tended to be, from the American perspective, doctrinaire and hostile. The founders of the UN may have emphasized its peaceful purposes in 1945 ("no more World War IIs," was their unstated motto), but the post-1965 majority subordinated peace to its anticolonial definition of justice. In the real world, this meant that many of the most vocal new UN members became increasingly sympathetic to intrastate violence and interstate confrontation.

They also became increasingly sympathetic to a UN "style" that stood at odds with the American approach to the Charter. Lebanese representative Charles Malik noted that the UN might best be viewed not as a collection of individual states with parliamentary voting rights, but rather as an organization containing several competing "cultures": western, communist, African, Asian, and so forth. Americans and their European cousins approached the UN in terms of Roman legalism, emphasizing formal votes, the sanctity of treaties, interstate agreements, and avoiding—or winning—war. But the Third World culture, according to Malik, cared less about formal votes than about popular revolution and the destruction of old elites. Even America's liberal anticolonialism, he argued, could not measure up to the radical and strident anticolonialism of the communist East.[3] The United States, wanting to remain loyal to its NATO (and imperial) allies without alienating the Third World, could hardly compete in such an environment. By the time of Nixon's inauguration, the ultimate UN insider was becoming an uncomfortable outsider. Nothing better symbolized this change than Washington's very first Security Council veto, cast on March 17, 1970, to block an African resolution extending economic sanctions against and severing all contact with white-dominated Southern Rhodesia.[4]

It is fitting that the United States veto came over a debate concerning race and colonialism. And it is instructive that within 24 hours, Ambassador Yost voted with the majority to isolate Rhodesia on an alternative resolution that omitted some of the most objectionable features of the earlier resolution. The U.S. veto signalled a sharp rebuke of the anticolonial majority, but neither Nixon nor Kissinger could completely ignore Third World sentiment. Although both men tended to support their NATO allies more frequently over decolonization than did their predecessors, they often swung the other way when UN debates did *not* involve their NATO allies. As an example of their support for a NATO ally, Nixon and Kissinger refused to condemn Portuguese colonialism in Mozambique and Angola at a time when more powerful European countries had already thrown in the imperial towel. On the other hand, with no NATO ally involved, Nixon and Kissinger joined the anticolonial majority three times in 1970 alone to nullify South Africa's mandate over Southwest Africa (later renamed Namibia).[5]

With the possible exception of Israeli-Arab relations, no issue vexed Washington as much as the colonial question. The halting and inconsistent record of the United States in this area finally led the Nixon administration to quit the most important UN group dealing with the issue, the so-called Committee of Twenty-Four. Created during the early 1960s to implement the General Assembly's Declaration on the Granting of Independence for Colonial Countries and Peoples, the committee increasingly supported armed struggle to eliminate the last vestiges of colonialism. The Nixon White House had enough trouble with verbal denunciations of colonialism; to "render all necessary moral and material assistance to the peoples of colonial Territories

... " was more than it could handle."[6] When the committee's African and Asian majority proved unwilling to compromise on this issue (indeed, it rarely compromised on any issue), the Americans withdrew entirely in January 1971.

THE STRUGGLE FOR PEACE IN THE MIDDLE EAST

In a sense, the Niagara of words directed toward the colonial issue was much ado about nothing. By 1970, most colonies had already been liberated quite peacefully, and the General Assembly's obsession with the issue reflected the triumph of ideology over the practical need for compromise. A bit less ideological would be the UN's approach to the other main issue competing for attention among UN delegates: peace in the Middle East. Here, no settlement was possible without compromise.

Security Council Resolution 242, approved following the Six-Day War, was followed by nothing so much as a gradual escalation of violence. Calling for Israeli withdrawal from occupied territories in return for security for, as well as Arab recognition of, Israel, the resolution accomplished neither. Sweden's Gunnar Jarring, appointed as UN mediator under 242, narrowed the areas of disagreement and succeeded in getting the Israelis to endorse the resolution, but he failed in his main mission: to persuade the Israelis to withdraw from conquered territory they defined as vital to their security. "Constructive ambiguity," says one historian about the resolution's requirements for swapping land for peace.[7] The Arabs had originally demanded "all territories." The French translation read "des territories." The final English text said merely "territories." The resolution's ambiguity allowed each party to believe what it wanted to believe about the timing of withdrawal, inviting the Israelis to drag their feet while they insisted that the Arabs first offer security guarantees. This the Arabs refused to do as Moscow began the process of rebuilding the Egyptian and Syrian armies. The result was frustration on both sides, a deepening resentment among the Palestinians, who until then had played a subordinate role in the conflict, and a low-level war of attrition that left the Israelis ever more determined to hold onto the occupied lands.

The Nixon administration did not seriously try to resolve the Mideast standoff until 1970, when Secretary of State William Rogers authored a plan (without any reference to the UN) that resulted in a shaky cease-fire. By then, Jarring's mission had collapsed. Washington policy makers, preoccupied with escalating domestic opposition to the war in Vietnam, fallout from Moscow's intervention in Czechoslovakia, Chinese-Soviet competition, and Moscow's arms shipments to the Mideast, took few risks for Mideast peace either inside or outside of the UN.[8] Although the so-called Rogers Plan did finally end the war of attrition, it failed to address the deeper rifts separating the two sides. Over the next three years, the United States resupplied the Israeli military to offset the Soviet buildup in Egypt and Syria. With Jerusalem's troops maintaining order in the territories and the war of attrition winding down, the

U.S. ambassador Daniel Moynihan voting against a resolution to condemn Israel for air attacks on Lebanon. December 8, 1975.
(UN/DPI Photo)

Israelis were content with the status quo. Not so the Arabs. Another war became likely.

It began on Yom Kippur (October 6, 1973), the holiest day of the Jewish year, when Egyptian president Anwar Sadat ordered an attack that overran Israeli fortifications constructed along the Suez Canal after the 1967 war. Initial Egyptian and Syrian gains, however, proved temporary; within four days, the Israelis had throttled the Syrian advance and, by October 14, destroyed most Egyptian armored units in the Sinai with a devastating counterattack. A massive "air bridge" resupply effort directly from the United States and from American bases in Europe encouraged the Israelis to reject a cease-fire that they had earlier been ready to accept. Correctly judging time to be on their side, they launched a surprise attack west of the canal, resulting in the encirclement of Egypt's Third Army and effectively ending the military phase of the war by October 23.

Although Secretary-General Kurt Waldheim of Austria, who had been elected in 1971, appealed for peace, neither he nor the Security Council could take action unless the belligerents appealed to the council. This they refused to do, Egypt because it expected further victories, Israel because it would not accept a cease-fire favorable to Cairo.

The UN, too, remained passive, largely because the Secretariat was left uninformed about battlefield developments during the early days of fighting: Egyptian officials had ordered the removal of UN Truce Observers placed at the canal after the 1967 war. Even had the UN had more information, it might not have made any difference, for no Security Council resolution would likely pass in light of the conflicting loyalties of the Soviets and Americans. Only after hostilities threatened to lead to an American-Soviet confrontation did Washington and Moscow consent to UN consideration of the matter. With Moscow increasingly concerned about the turn of the military tide, and with Washington thrown off balance by the prospect of an Arab oil boycott, both superpowers agreed to cosponsor a Security Council resolution calling for a cease-fire.

Unlike 1967, when Ambassador Goldberg at USUN dominated the making of U.S. policy at the UN, in 1973 the secretary of state in Washington orchestrated American policy. With the relatively inexperienced John Scali representing the United States in New York and President Nixon preoccupied by the Watergate scandal (the scandal's infamous Saturday Night Massacre occurred on the very day Kissinger arrived in Moscow to negotiate a Mideast cease-fire proposal that would become Security Council Resolution 338), Kissinger's authority was unrivaled. He used it in typical Kissinger fashion. Ostensibly seeking an immediate truce, he actually stalled to give the Israelis time to consolidate their victory but not so much time as to humiliate their opponents. When Soviet impatience threatened to lead to a unilateral military intervention on behalf of Egypt, Kissinger recommended placing American forces on the highest level of peacetime alert, which in turn threatened to convert a regional conflict into a global cataclysm.

On October 22, Security Council Resolution 338 calling for a cease-fire within 12 hours and direct talks between the belligerents, which the Arabs had rejected for years, passed unanimously. The Israelis, however, ignored it as they advanced on Egypt's Third Army. Resolution 339 passed the next day, reaffirming the intent of the earlier resolution.[9] Still the Israelis advanced. It was at this point that the Soviets threatened unilateral intervention, potentially undermining Kissinger's strategy. With the American response to the Soviet threat signaling to Israel that the United States would indeed protect her existence, Israeli Prime Minister Golda Meir's cabinet accepted a final cease-fire embodied in Resolution 340. This resolution did not "urge" a cease-fire; it "demanded" it.[10]

Resolution 340 also created a successor UN Emergency Force to separate the warring parties (Nasser had terminated the original force in 1967). Called UNEF II, the Americans insisted on—and the Soviets reluctantly accepted—the exclusion from UNEF II of units from both superpowers. Excluding these troops represented a critical element of American planning. Not only would the Soviets be kept from reintroducing their troops into a region from which Sadat had expelled them in 1972, but excluding U.S. troops from UNEF II would be consistent with the so-called Nixon Doctrine. The doctrine, a corollary to the administration's Vietnam policy, warned that the United States would introduce its troops into troubled regions *only* as a last resort.

CHINA POLICY

Interestingly, the PRC refused to support (but did not oppose) all three resolutions, charging that the Security Council was becoming a "tool to be manipulated by the two superpowers."[11] The Chinese doubtless spoke for other states too, but in the Security Council where Beijing offered this complaint, great power still counted.

The PRC voice in the council was quite new and, from the American perspective, hardly welcome. From the moment that Mao Zedong overthrew the Nationalists, Washington had maneuvered to deny the communists a UN seat. If the Americans displayed little consistency in many areas of UN policy, they showed a lot on this issue; and although both Dulles and Rusk had once *privately* favored a two-China policy, both Beijing and Taipei rejected it. Nor was it just Beijing and Taipei that rejected the two-China course. President Kennedy, too, rejected it, courting the China lobby by promising to veto Beijing's admission into the UN.[12] Sino-American relations did not improve under Johnson. Quite the contrary, for the Vietnam War intensified hostility toward Beijing. Even Rusk, an early supporter of a two-China policy, had turned harshly against the idea by the mid-1960s, often comparing the PRC to Nazi Germany.

The PRC delegation is seated at UN. November 15, 1971.
(UN/DPI Photo)

Ironically, the Soviet Union had also become increasingly anti-Chinese, a factor that profoundly affected American thinking toward China. Richard Nixon, in a well-known article in *Foreign Affairs* published shortly before he became president, argued that on grounds of narrow self-interest, it was foolish to isolate China, a sentiment that many Realists (in contrast to those Americans opposing the PRC mainly on ideological grounds) found persuasive.[13] Moreover, each year the ritual of voting on seating Beijing at the UN showed the steady erosion of American influence. Only seven countries endorsed PRC membership in 1952, but 29 did so in 1959, and 48 by 1969. For years, the Americans had used a parliamentary device to buttress their weakening position. Labeling the subject of Chinese membership an "important question" in the General Assembly meant that no action could be taken without a two-thirds majority. The catch was that it took a majority vote to declare the issue "important." In 1971, the Americans finally lost that majority when 59 states voted against the U.S. motion. The tally on the subsequent Albanian resolution to seat the PRC and expel the Nationalists was 76–35–17.[14] The game over, Ambassador George Bush sullenly watched assembly delegates literally dancing in the aisles in a circuslike anti-American demonstration.

American officials from Nixon to Bush publicly denounced the vote and the undiplomatic behavior of assembly delegates, but their reaction was just a charade. In reality, American policy toward the PRC had softened almost from the day of Nixon's inauguration. Informal contacts begat a liberalization of trade, which begat the regularization of Chinese-American communications including the famous ping-pong invitation, and finally the secret visits of Kissinger to Beijing. Once word leaked to the press that Kissinger was in Beijing at the moment the General Assembly prepared to vote on seating the PRC, U.S. opposition to Beijing's seat collapsed: it "pulled the rug" from under us, complained one American delegate.[15] Even Bush, who by now had shifted to support for a two-China policy though still uninformed about Kissinger's visit, understood the futility of further opposition. It was not losing the vote that he resented. It was the celebration.

It is not an exaggeration to say that the assembly majority had done the Americans a favor. Handcuffed to Taiwan by two decades of political promises, Washington had wanted to—but could not—unilaterally break its ties to Taipei. The assembly vote helped to loosen them. And although the initial PRC speech to the assembly damned the United States for its "colonial" policies in Asia, in fact the Chinese spent their next few years vilifying the Soviets more than their western adversaries. In short, the seating of Beijing widened the rift in the communist world, which served American Cold War objectives. This rift contributed to a general redefinition of American Cold War policy, placing more and more emphasis on geopolitical rather than ideological considerations.

The new emphasis on geopolitics was not evident in the election of a new secretary-general, which occurred at approximately the same time as the vote on China's representation. U Thant wanted to run for a third term, but his frosty relationship with the United States made that impossible. The State Department backed Max Jakobson of Finland, a bright and capable delegate who had established a reputation for fairness and compromise. Jakobson's Jewish background, however, made him suspect in the Arab world, and the Soviets, probably in deference to their Arab allies, perhaps because the Americans found Jakobson so attractive, promised to veto his candidacy. As had happened repeatedly since 1945, the Great Powers now had to scurry around for a second choice. "Grey, safe men were positively sought out" for the post ever since 1945, writes one of the UN's more perceptive critics, which made Austria's Kurt Waldheim a popular compromise candidate.[16] "One has to know the limits," said Waldheim, who, even less than U Thant, would rarely display the independence and vision that might have stemmed the UN's eroding prestige in the West. Waldheim, who never even recognized the erosion, was "an ambitious, energetic mediocrity" whose foggy past would eventually disgrace both his own biography and that of the organization he served.[17]

Four years after leaving his post, researchers uncovered Waldheim's real résumé. He had long claimed that he had been a former German infantry officer during the early years of World War II, then left the army for law school after being wounded. In fact, he had been a pro-Nazi officer in the Balkans involved in antiresistance "reprisal and extermination" operations.[18] He concealed that past for fear that it would, if known, destroy any possibility for him to attain a post of high honor. Captured Nazi records, many in the UN itself, contained this hidden history.

Did the Americans or Soviets know about his background when they elected him secretary-general? The answer remains uncertain, though it is likely they did. Historian Robert E. Herzstein has uncovered evidence that the CIA knew plenty about Waldheim's past in 1971. If so, was this information passed on to White House and State Department officials? Did American officials use such information to keep Waldheim on a tight leash? Herzstein argues forcefully:

> Certain facts have become clear. The State Department and the CIA helped to fabricate and disseminate the false biography that enabled Kurt Waldheim to deceive the world and lead the United Nations. In return, Waldheim provided the U.S. with sensitive information, undertook one dangerous mission [to Iran], and kept the Americans informed about attempted Soviet penetration of the Secretariat.[19]

Repeatedly, the State Department praised Waldheim for being cooperative "in promoting U.S. interests." The whole truth may never be known. What is incontrovertible, however, is that, in Shirley Hazzard's words, Waldheim's "appeasement of member governments . . . was eager and obsessive."[20] His main attribute was his compliancy, which fractured his morality. This was the secretary-general who denounced the Israeli rescue of hostages at Uganda's Entebbe Airport as a "serious violation" of sovereignty while ordering the removal of *The Gulag Archipelago* from bookstores at the UN's Geneva offices.[21] He offered no denunciations of Soviet human rights abuses, nor did he criticize those of American clients or, for that matter, even crude Third World despotisms like the Central African Republic or Paraguay. He indeed knew his limits.[22]

AMBASSADOR MOYNIHAN

The same could not be said of Daniel Patrick Moynihan, perhaps the most controversial American representative at the UN since the birth of the organization. Moynihan was a former Harvard economist who had written his doctoral dissertation about the UN-related International Labor Organization. A Democrat who had previously served in both the Kennedy and Nixon administrations as a labor and urban affairs specialist, he displayed unusual interest in both domestic and international affairs. The public knew him as the author of a highly controversial report on instability among black families, and of the Nixon administration's proposal to deemphasize race-based legislation in favor of a policy of "benign neglect." Washington insiders also knew him as the author of Nixon's creative family assistance plan.

Moynihan had declined an appointment to the UN post in 1971, returning to academia for a brief stint after which he became ambassador to India. Before being offered the UN post in 1971, he had served as a delegate to the UN's Third Committee dealing with social and humanitarian issues. The propagandistic character of that committee—it rivalled the Decolonization Committee as a forum for Third World invective—profoundly affected his thinking about the UN. Nor did he believe that the State Department took the UN very seriously, which, of course, it did not. By the time Nixon's successor, Gerald Ford, appointed him permanent representative in 1975, Moynihan had loaded his blunderbuss. It is hard to know exactly what he expected, having seen "Stevenson humiliated. Goldberg betrayed. Ball diminished. Wiggins patronized. Yost ignored. Bush traduced. Scali savaged."[23] Was he a masochist? Along with warnings that Kissinger would routinely lie to him (not "because it is in his interest. He lies because it is in his nature," said a Kissinger associate), one wonders why he accepted the job at all.[24] Given his love of intellectual combat and overstatement, Moynihan would turn out to be the wrong man for the wrong job at the wrong time.

And yet, the American public apparently loved him. More than any other official, Moynihan struck a deeply responsive chord in a land that had lost its confidence in the wake of Watergate, Vietnam, and OPEC's (Organization of Petroleum Exporting Countries) oil embargo. America's automatic majority in the UN had disappeared, replaced by a Third World majority organized and disciplined within the so-called Group of 77 (by 1975 increasing to over a hundred countries). First organized in 1968, the Group of 77 was the incarnation of the cultural change that Charles Malik had described: sympathetic to social and economic radicalism, deeply hostile to what it defined (correctly or not) as imperialism, dogmatic about race and intolerant of western legalism. Not all members of the group agreed privately, but they were reluctant to disagree publicly for fear of losing both their political effectiveness and their newly recognized stature. Even what westerners believed to be most outrageous about the Third World—raw despots like Uganda's Idi Amin, appalling massacres like the Tutsi slaughter of 200,000 Hutus in Burundi—would go unmentioned by the group in the name of Third World solidarity.

To an old-fashioned Jeffersonian like Moynihan, such behavior represented the antithesis of what he believed the Charter to be all about. Resenting what he defined as appeasement by his predecessors, he launched his counterattack on the forces he believed would destroy the UN. He titled his memoir of his

UN years *A Very Dangerous Place*, and he meant dangerous not to himself but to his country, to human rights, and to the UN itself. The threat, he believed, was grave: as Americans ignored the UN, in part out of a "diminishment of liberal conviction," the politics of the organization was increasingly being conducted "on behalf of a totalitarian principle and practice wholly at variance with [the UN's] original purpose."[25]

The sine qua non to save the Charter, believed Moynihan, was a reassertion of American leadership. No longer, he argued, should a state think it could defy the United States at the UN without paying a penalty, be it political or economic. More importantly, he resolved to spotlight what he considered Third World hypocrisy, such as when the General Assembly denounced South African—but not Cuban— military intervention into Angola; or when the "STALINIST SON OF A BITCH FROM CUBA [WENT] ON ABOUT PUERTO RICO . . . " in the Colonialism Committee (Moynihan's caps).[26] Where Kissinger simply dismissed most UN activity as mere words, Moynihan believed such words to be the heart of the modern world order. Indeed, the ambassador argued that it was the General Assembly that mattered most because it was in the Assembly where this new international world was on display. The Security Council, rendered impotent by the veto, had lost its importance.

And so Moynihan fought two fights: one against his own State Department, the other against what he viewed as the totalitarians abroad. If officials like Lodge and Stevenson had boosted their authority because they had their own political base, Moynihan took advantage of the State Department's preoccupation with matters outside of the UN. He criticized Kissinger for allowing the important work of American diplomacy, with the single exception of security, to be handled by persons "the Secretary had mostly never heard of and . . . certainly never met."[27] Moynihan would therefore handle from his own office the UN-related issues dealing with "the symbols of progress for mankind." He urged Kissinger to authorize "active opposition" to Third World mendacity, not (as had happened until then) to just authorize a negative vote.

No one had energized America's UN authority as passionately as Professor Moynihan, not even Eleanor Roosevelt or Stevenson in the 1950s and 1960s. His efforts, however, were often in vain. For instance, he used former ambassador Robert Murphy's report from the Commission on the Organization of the Government for the Conduct of Foreign Policy to lobby for more direct USUN involvement on human rights policy, believing that the State Department "simply [did] not grasp the significance of human rights at this time."[28] Serving an administration that consistently subordinated human rights to the demands of Realpolitik, he was wasting his energy. Perhaps he was a bit ahead of his time. In regard to human rights, history would soon prove that Moynihan was more in tune with the Carter administration's policy than that of the State Department under Ford.

ZIONISM-IS-RACISM

Perhaps no issue better illustrates American UN diplomacy during Moynihan's tenure than the General Assembly's 1975 condemnation of Zionism as a form of racism. Ever since the Six-Day War, the Arab bloc had sought to isolate Israel at the UN. With the formation of the Group of 77, of which 25 percent was originally Arab, this process picked up steam, evolving from criticism of Israeli policy to blunt efforts to delegitimize the Israeli state altogether. By the 1970s, denunciation of Zionism in the General Assembly and the Decolonization Committee had become almost too routine to notice. The Israelis stood accused as both oppressors and colonialists: Zionism was increasingly viewed as an imperialist ideology justifying Israeli occupation of the West Bank and Gaza after the Six-Day War. Moreover, the Six-Day War had brought the Palestinians much more visibly into the politics of the region. As the UN inched toward recognition of the Palestinians between 1970 and 1975, criticism of Zionism and Israel became even more virulent. For instance, the 1975 UN Conference on Women, meeting in Mexico City, first explicitly linked Zionism with racism when it denounced Zionism, apartheid, and racial discrimination (but not gender discrimination); while an American effort at the UN supporting amnesty for political prisoners was eventually withdrawn when it became mired in attacks on Zionism and colonialism.[29]

For observers who may have missed the point, in 1975 the president of the Organization of African Unity, Idi Amin, speaking at the 30th session of the General Assembly, finally made clear what others had not quite said: he called for "the expulsion of Israel from the United Nations and the extinction of Israel as a state." The Zionists, he continued, had "colonized" the United States and turned the CIA into a "murder squad to eliminate any form of just resistance. . . . "[30]

Amin received a standing ovation. His brutal rule in Uganda, where he had already expelled or massacred tens of thousands of Asians, apparently detracted little from the reception of his anti-Israeli comments. But the Third World enemies of Israel had done more than link Zionism and the CIA. Ever since the USSR had called for a condemnation of "anti-semitism, Zionism, Nazism . . . colonialism, national and race hatred and exclusiveness . . . ," Third World critics of Israel had increasingly identified Zionism with racism, Israel with South Africa. Previous Third World efforts to expel South Africa from the UN led inevitably to efforts to expel Israel. By the time that Amin stirred up his followers, the Zionism-is-racism resolution had become merely a matter of time.

That time came on November 10, 1975. Moynihan would later claim that western delegates, including the Israelis, had not seen it coming and therefore had insufficiently organized opposition. His account is self-serving. He had plenty of warning, for the Third Committee had already passed the resolution three weeks earlier. The final vote in the General Assembly tallied 72 states in support of the resolution, 35 in opposition. Another 32 abstained, including many who had fought the resolution in the Third Committee but did not in the assembly. A number of countries from sub-Sahara Africa and Latin America joined the United States and its European allies in opposition, but, as on other issues, few Group of 77 members who were against the resolution publicly expressed their dissent.[31]

Moynihan, however, voiced his mightily. "The United Nations," he thundered, will become known as "a place where lies are told." He asked delegates from small states that derived their independence "in no small measure" from the campaign for human rights how they would be able to defend themselves when the language of human rights "no longer has a power of its own?" His moral outrage filled the General Assembly and the columns of American newspapers. Privately, he complained that Washington had not given him enough support, complaints that his enemies—or Kissinger's enemies—eventually leaked to the press. His eloquence notwithstanding, he managed to alienate almost everyone but the American and Israeli publics. The Libyan delegate most influential in sponsoring the resolution reportedly said afterwards that Moynihan's behavior actually *aided* Israel's enemies by provoking resentment among Third World delegations.[32] British ambassador Ivor Richards, much more sensitive to the divisions among Third World delegations than Moynihan, contrasted his own approach to that of the U.S. ambassador. Wrote Richards testily, "I spend time preventing rows at the UN—not looking for them." Comparing his American counterpart to Wyatt Earp, Richards downplayed the importance of the resolution, which is what the Israeli ambassador had originally done. Like Kissinger, Richards undoubtedly thought the resolution "mere words" and explicitly refused to view the UN as a "confrontational arena in which to 'take on' those countries whose political systems and ideology are different from mine."[33] But once Moynihan had turned the affair into a moral crusade, it achieved a life of its own. Until then, only a few radical groups like the John Birch Society had called for Washington's departure from the UN; after Moynihan's tenure, this became, if not a mainstream demand, at least respectable in conservative circles. The reputation of the UN never fully recovered.

Contributing to the loss of respect for the UN within the United States were two additional elements connected to the Zionism-is-racism resolution. First, Waldheim had exercised little leadership on this matter. Unlike the outspoken Hammarskjold, Waldheim remained discreetly silent. Second, a series of General Assembly votes during the next few months gave the Palestine Liberation Organization formal standing at the UN over United States objections.[34] The United States backed the Israelis without reservation at a time when Jerusalem granted the PLO as much legitimacy as the PLO extended to what it called "the Zionist entity." And because Washington officially defined the PLO as nothing more than a terrorist organization, a position widely applauded in the United States, UN invitations to bring PLO delegates into both the Security Council and the General Assembly further diminished the organization's stature in the eyes of Americans.

These invitations also emphasized dwindling U.S. influence. Despite its best efforts, the American delegation had been unable to block them: a pro-Palestinian majority ruled the General Assembly, while in the Security Council, the majority denied Washington a veto by declaring the invitation to be a procedural matter. When a pistol-packing Yassar Arafat subsequently addressed the General Assembly just two years after the 1972 Munich massacre of Israeli Olympic athletes, Americans were scandalized. And when Arab-sponsored resolutions condemned Israeli reprisals following terrorist raids or PLO shelling of Israeli villages, but routinely ignored the reasons for the Israeli response, Americans became even more convinced that the UN resembled a kangaroo court. To such resolutions, the United States cast ever more frequent vetoes. Yet Washington did not let public opinion dictate its policy. It was in his final address to the General Assembly in 1976 that Kissinger first referred to the "legitimate rights of the Palestinians."[35] This acknowledgment of the Palestinians (still a far cry from recognition) would almost surely never have come from Moynihan, not even under orders.

Moynihan's differences with his superiors in Washington might have remained invisible but for documents leaked to the *New York Times* in January 1976. The leaks may well have originated in Kissinger's office. Advertising Moynihan's belief that the department did not adequately support him, the leaks made his exit inevitable. He departed on February 2. The Ford administration replaced him with a moderate Republican from Pennsylvania, former governor William Scranton, who had sought the Republican nomination for president in 1964. Scranton had no experience in the foreign arena but a fair amount of prestige at home. It was Ford, not Kissinger, who selected Scranton for the UN, and the new permanent representative repaired USUN relations with the State Department. Unlike Moynihan, Scranton brought to his post a habit of conciliation, not confrontation. He deferred to Kissinger even as he revived the practice of having the UN representative attend cabinet meetings on a fairly regular basis. He also helped to revive the authority of the assistant secretary of state for international organization, a post that had withered as a result of Nixon's and Kissinger's indifference to the UN, not to mention Moynihan's activism.[36]

Scranton's short year in New York offered promise of a more patient American policy. The post-Watergate healing that Ford initiated at home Scranton now employed at the UN. Denunciations of General Assembly behavior disappeared. The Americans did register a few vetoes in the Security Council; none involved highly publicized confrontations except when Washington vetoed a UN seat for Vietnam. The Vietnam veto was probably inevitable. The recent war had opened up nasty wounds within America that would take decades to heal, and Kissinger, despite Scranton's recommendation to the contrary, was unwilling during a presidential election year to follow up his China opening with a UN invitation to Hanoi.

SOUTHERN AFRICA

Washington's handling of African issues at the UN reflected the same ambivalence that Kissinger displayed regarding African issues in Washington. The most important area of activity had become southern Africa: not just South Africa, which exploded during the 1976 Soweto uprising, but Angola, Southern Rhodesia, and Namibia.

The most bitter issue centered on Angola, where Cuban and South African troops aided rival factions. Angola possessed modest oil reserves, but it was not oil as much as Soviet backing for Marxist Angolans and for sending Cuban troops to Angola that interested the State Department. To Kissinger, Soviet Premier Leonid Brezhnev had not only propelled Angola into the global Cold War rivalry but had also undermined his earlier commitment to détente.[37] If the Soviets got away with this policy, Kissinger argued, America's position in Africa would be compromised, which in turn would weaken the United States in Europe. Kissinger, here the geopolitical Realist, strongly endorsed covert military aid to a pro-American (though oddly Marxist) Angolan faction.

Congress was not persuaded that the United States should offer *any* more aid to Angola. The liberal Democrats in both the House and the Senate were increasingly uneasy about South African troops opposing the Cubans, for the white government of South Africa by 1976 had become the focus of black African anger. Moreover, even congressional conservatives worried that Washington might step into Vietnam-style quicksand. Led by Senator Dick Clark of Iowa, Congress cut off all aid to Angola. Kissinger was furious: *"It is the first time that the United States has failed to respond to Soviet military moves outside the immediate Soviet orbit,"* he warned.[38] But his protests were to no avail. The Soviet faction in Angola prevailed, and even U.S. oil companies accommodated themselves to the new reality. Kissinger expressed his anger by instructing USUN to veto Angolan membership in the UN.

The UN had played only a minor role in this dispute. Moynihan, as usual, quarreled with Kissinger over tactics. The permanent representative had wanted to place the issue before the Security Council while Kissinger had preferred ignoring the UN in favor of covert aid to the pro-American group in Angola. "Not a day goes by without a cable from Moynihan on Angola," the secretary complained. "Who the hell is Moynihan to get into Angola anyway?"[39] The quarrel contributed to Moynihan's decision to leave his UN post.

The UN connection was much more prominent in respect to South Africa and Southern Rhodesia. Here the issues were not foreign intervention or colonialism, but racism. Walter Isaacson, Kissinger's biographer, notes that U.S. policy toward both regimes had emerged from a 1969 NSC memorandum observing that "the whites are here to stay and the only way that constructive change can come about is through them."[40] In practice, this meant placing little pressure on the two white regimes to adopt a system of majority rule. By 1976, however, with the departure of the last colonial regimes, the fear of more Angola-like Soviet influence in the area, and the unrelenting demand of the Afro-Asian bloc in the UN for reform, the Americans found it increasingly difficult to defend the white governments of both countries. Not even American strategic interests—naval posts and corporate investment in South Africa, strategic materials like nickel and chromium in Rhodesia—justified continued support for the white governments. On Rhodesia, therefore, the United States voted with the Security Council majority on April 6 to extend economic sanctions until the adoption of majority rule, though ironically a nearly unanimous General Assembly condemned the United States for importing chrome and nickel from that country (a product of the 1972 Byrd Amendment that Congress had passed to prevent the United States from boycotting "strategic" Rhodesian minerals).[41] Typical of his diplomacy, Kissinger got Ian Smith's white minority Rhodesian government to begin a transition to majority rule by threatening pressure against South Africa, which controlled land access into Rhodesia. In turn, the secretary secured South Africa's cooperation by promising to be more patient about allowing Pretoria to resolve its own racial destiny.[42] Yet even with South Africa, Kissinger stepped up public pressure, denouncing apartheid in his General Assembly speech of September 1976 and permitting Scranton to join the UN majority in condemning the white government's massacre of African protestors in Soweto.

In Southwest Africa, too, the Americans supported the black African majority. Kissinger knew that the handwriting was on the wall, especially after Portugal granted independence to its remaining colonies. Only South African control of Southwest Africa remained as a vestige of colonialism, and the secretary of state's General Assembly speech proposed a conference to prepare the territory for formal independence. With no strategic interests there and South Africa's presence helping to justify Marxist and Soviet policies in the entire region, America's most prominent geopolitician found himself standing on the General Assembly dais as a new recruit into the politics of human rights.[43]

Kissinger's transformation into an occasional spokesman for human rights may have had more substance than this chapter has previously suggested. Nonetheless, his transformation also says much about how much the world had changed in the eight years since Nixon's inauguration. Notwithstanding the secretary's differences with Moynihan, by the time Kissinger left the State Department in 1977 he granted the UN a much more visible role in American policy making. President Ford almost surely had something to do with this. It was Ford who insisted, over Kissinger's reservations, that first Moynihan and then the highly respected Scranton represent the United States in New York. The new president had more regard for the UN than had either Nixon or

Kissinger, and in his modest way he too shaped the course of American internationalism during his short term in office.

By the presidential campaign of 1976, however, Republican conservatives were already criticizing both the administration's human rights orientation and détente. These conservatives would line up behind the presidential candidacy of California's governor, Ronald Reagan. Although neither the Ford nor Reagan forces prevailed in November when a moderate Democrat, former Georgia governor Jimmy Carter, became president, the conservatives made it increasingly difficult for any Republicans to support the UN during the next decade. Despite Carter, American foreign policy would gradually shift rightward.

chapter 7

GUNS AND BUTTER

In the decades following the San Francisco Conference, the general public came to understand that collective security was the heart and soul of UN affairs. Terms like *cease-fire, negotiation, recognition, security, territorial integrity,* and *peacekeeping* became the UN's common language, supplemented by the vocabulary of anticolonialism after the mid-1950s. Nor surprisingly, the press and public ignored other kinds of UN-related issues of equal (perhaps greater) importance, issues that reporters often considered overly technical, numbingly arcane, or unnewsworthy because they posed less immediate threats than war or revolution.

This chapter will focus on two of those other issues: disarmament, which achieved occasional successes amid long-term failures; and economic development, which became the province of a number of unsexy UN economic bureaus rather than the more well-known UN agencies.

DISARMAMENT

Like the U.S. Constitution, the Charter proved itself open to change and interpretation that expanded the modest language of Article 11 authorizing UN activity to promote disarmament. The confusing array of disarmament conferences during the 1950s, many under UN auspices, testifies to the amount of attention given the subject. It says less, however, about the degree of seriousness with which officials approached disarmament. In the United States, for example, members of the Eisenhower administration differed sharply about the subject, especially as it pertained to nuclear weapons. Eisenhower himself was more sympathetic to arms control than his secretary of state, who came to see nuclear weapons as the centerpiece of Washington's strategy of deterrence. Eisenhower's influence was most vividly displayed in

The UN Monetary and Financial Conference, Bretton Woods, N.H.,
where the IMF was established. July 1, 1944.
(UN/DPI Photo)

his efforts to create the IAEA and his endorsement of a treaty banning military exploitation of Antarctica; it was less evident in U.S. approval of the
General Assembly's 1959 resolution calling for "general and complete disarmament," a vote that says more about propaganda warfare than about nuclear
warfare.

The Kennedy administration, which had capitalized on an imaginary missile gap during the presidential campaign of 1960, initially committed itself to
building arms, not reducing them. Conflict with the Soviets and the Cubans
did little to moderate a climate that quieted American arms-control advocates. But that same conflict raised the specter of a war that, as Khrushchev
warned, would leave the living envious of the dead. Increasingly aware of what
Dean Rusk termed the "irrelevance" of atomic weapons to decision making
the administration backed away from Eisenhower's strategy of massive retaliation.[1] It also established an Arms Control and Disarmament Agency under
the eye of the secretary of state though independent of both the State and
Defense Departments. The ACDA provided the first genuinely effective coordination of U.S. efforts in this area.

Successful arms control needed more than coordination. It needed private
advocacy and public acceptance. The latter emerged after 1961 when the

Soviets resumed nuclear testing following the three-year moratorium. The UN had become involved in this issue when it sponsored in 1958 the Special Geneva Conference on the Discontinuance of Nuclear Weapons Tests. This group met over 350 times, but achieved virtually nothing. In October 1961, three months before the Special Conference ended its labors, the Soviets advertised its futility by announcing that Moscow would detonate a 58-megaton hydrogen bomb. Even atomic enthusiasts in Washington shivered. By an overwhelming margin (87–11–1), the General Assembly pleaded with Moscow to desist, to no avail.[2] Although the Kennedy administration responded with a resumption of U.S. tests in the midst of a bomb-shelter craze at home, it did so with little enthusiasm.

The end of the testing moratorium may have made the public more receptive to a permanent test ban, but it was Adlai Stevenson, a supporter of a test ban since 1956, who did more than anyone else to persuade the administration to take the issue seriously. In the wake of Hammarskjold's death, Stevenson in late 1961 successfully lobbied the president to use the UN to call for "a truce to [nuclear] terror." He further advocated using the Eighteen Nation Disarmament Committee talks at Geneva for a final attempt at a comprehensive test ban.[3]

Although the Soviets rejected the American proposal in the spring of 1962, the administration, together with Great Britain, continued to propose variations of the ban. These proposals, too, might have gone nowhere but for the Cuban Missile Crisis, which changed everything. A week after the crisis ended, the General Assembly again overwhelmingly called for an end to testing.[4] As shaken by the Cuban crisis as their adversaries, the Soviets this time accepted the American proposal as a basis for further discussion.

On issues of substance, the United States and the Soviets have often ignored the UN. Such was the case with the test ban, where the final few months of negotiations were carried out directly between American and Soviet emissaries in Moscow. Once the two governments resolved some difficult problems concerning inspection and detection, they concluded one of the era's most noteworthy agreements: it banned nuclear tests in the atmosphere, under the sea, and in space. The agreement, however, did not ban underground tests, an omission that would preoccupy the UN for another 30 years. In the meantime, the UN became the forum in which the limited test ban treaty was offered to the rest of the international community for approval. One hundred and ten nations signed it; China and France did not. The test ban took effect on October 10, 1963.

It should be noted that American and Soviet officials would never have signed the treaty had it included a ban on underground tests. The superpowers hoped an atmospheric ban would inhibit nuclear development among the then nonnuclear countries (early program development virtually required atmospheric tests) while permitting continued underground testing for the more mature nuclear programs. In this way, the partial test-ban treaty was also designed to serve the purposes of nonproliferation.

During the next decade, the UN would continue to play an active role in the arms control arena with the blessing of the American government. As early as 1959, the General Assembly had created the 24-member Committee on Peaceful Uses of Outer Space. That committee made little headway until the limited test-ban treaty opened the way for the General Assembly to approve a December 1963 resolution prohibiting all weapons in outer space. Three years later, in part to prove its peaceful intentions to an international community increasingly critical of its conduct in Vietnam, the Johnson administration joined most members of the General Assembly to prohibit by treaty the "national appropriation" of outer space. This prohibition became part of international law four years to the day after the test-ban treaty went into effect, followed in 1971 by a convention establishing ground rules for liability from damage caused by falling space objects.[5]

Nuclear Nonproliferation Treaty

Of greater immediate importance was the nuclear nonproliferation treaty. Its origins, too, predated the test-ban treaty of 1963. In 1961, the Swedish government introduced a resolution inquiring about the willingness of nonnuclear states to refrain from manufacturing or acquiring weapons of mass destruction. Although Washington was hardly enthusiastic about proliferation, it worried about the effect of nonproliferation on NATO and joined with 11 other states—mostly NATO allies—in voting no. A few days later, however, it joined a unanimous General Assembly in supporting an Irish proposal to prevent the dissemination of weapons from nuclear states to as yet nonnuclear states.[6] A resolution, of course, was a far cry from a treaty, and the assembly asked the Eighteen Nation Disarmament Committee to produce a workable draft.

Washington's oddly incompatible votes on the Swedish and Irish resolutions of 1961 exposed the degree to which officials such as Rusk, and even Kennedy, had simply not thought through what they wanted in the area of nuclear defense. The administration's support for a Multi-Lateral Force (called the MLF, which involved sharing nuclear weapons with America's NATO allies) clashed with increasing pressure to declare central Europe a nuclear-free zone. Similar pressure already existed on other continents. Moreover, Soviet opposition to the MLF (Moscow worried that an MLF would permit West Germany to acquire nuclear weapons) initially blocked any serious progress on nonproliferation. But by the middle of the decade, the logjam began to break up. The test-ban treaty revealed not only that cooperation was possible, but that it conferred considerable political benefits. Tensions stemming from the Vietnam War ironically made cooperation in other areas more attractive to both superpowers. And China's first atomic test in 1964 reminded worried strategists in Washington and Moscow just how destabilizing proliferation could be. The result was that in November 1965, the General

Assembly, with only five abstentions, approved the principles of a nonprolif-eration treaty.[7]

It took another two years to resolve the remaining problems. Some, like inspection and verification, mainly involved negotiations between the super-powers that took place outside the UN. The Johnson administration had wanted the European atomic agency (EURATOM), not the UN's IAEA, to tackle the job, but eventually it conceded authority to the IAEA, which evolved into one of the UN's most effective agencies.

Other problems involved negotiations with the nonnuclear powers. Here the UN proved much more pivotal in advancing the final treaty. Every gov-ernment understood that a nonnuclear state favoring nonproliferation would be voluntarily accepting second-class nuclear citizenship. Most nonnuclear UN members seemed willing to do this; in turn, they wanted security guaran-tees that neither the Soviets nor the Americans were initially willing to pro-vide.[8] This hurdle was overcome in June 1968 when the General Assembly, with only four dissenting votes, approved the nonproliferation treaty. One week later, the United States, USSR, and United Kingdom fulfilled their part of the bargain when they pledged to defend any nonnuclear state threatened by nuclear aggression. The Security Council then endorsed this arrangement, with France and four other states abstaining. The treaty went into effect on March 5, 1970.

Three other noteworthy arms-limitation agreements emerged during this period: the 1967 Treaty of Tlatelolco, which developed out of earlier UN res-olutions designed to make Latin America a nuclear-free zone; the Sea Bed Treaty of 1970, which paralleled the Outer Space Treaty; and the Threshold Test Ban Treaty of 1974, which limited underground tests to 150 kilotons, 10 times the power of the Hiroshima bomb.[9] None of these treaties seriously compromised important U.S. interests. One, the Tlatelolco Treaty, positively aided U.S. policy by fusing sphere-of-influence diplomacy with apparent ide-alism.

Collectively, these agreements increased the zeal of General Assembly dis-armament advocates who eventually passed more than one thousand resolu-tions calling for limited or general disarmament. Most of these resolutions, it should be added, aimed at abolishing or limiting nuclear weapons. Too many words; too little meaning. The torrent of resolutions during the 1970s and 1980s ironically devalued the constructive disarmament activity of the 1960s, a process that bears on the larger issue of American use of the UN.

Nonaligned Countries Push for UN Authority

The 1963 test-ban treaty and the 1968 nonproliferation treaty were products of both bilateral superpower diplomacy and General Assembly activity. As the increase in UN membership altered the character of the organization by 1970, so did it affect the way the UN approached disarmament. For one thing, the nonaligned countries who came to dominate the General Assembly sought to limit the authority of those agencies, such as the Eighteen Nation Disarmament Committee (ENDC), that were unconnected to the UN and often reflected the interests of the superpowers. Naturally, both the United States and the Soviets resisted this development, leading to a deterioration in relations between the UN and the ENDC (renamed, as it expanded, the Committee on the Conference on Disarmament [CCD]; it would be renamed twice more between 1978 and 1986). In addition, the Nixon administration's commitment to the Strategic Arms Limitations talks, which led to the successful SALT I treaty in 1972, left U.S. officials increasingly intolerant of what they viewed as General Assembly interference.

There was more to this issue of "General Assembly interference" than was at first apparent, however. The nonaligned countries who wanted to protect UN authority in the disarmament field were motivated by two things that left them at odds with both superpowers. First, they wanted to democratize the UN—that is, they wanted to diminish the influence of the Great Powers at the same time that they would elevate their own influence. Second, they wanted to define disarmament as not only a military issue but an economic issue, integral to a worldwide redistribution of wealth. Their plan would be called the New International Economic Order, and it aroused *very* little sympathy in Washington. Its proponents argued that a reduction in arms expenditures would permit the industrial North to invest more in the less developed South. To the extent that the nonaligned majority identified its power with the authority of the UN, it vigorously fought anything that would diminish the UN. And because the United States and USSR used the CCD to steer arms-limitation issues away from the General Assembly (and also from the Disarmament Committee, composed of all UN members), the disarmament consensus of the 1960s was bound to shatter.

These developments in turn led to a number of others. To deflect criticism of their disarmament record, in 1976 the superpowers did produce a treaty limiting environmental modification, a very modest accomplishment that came out of the CCD, not the General Assembly. The nonaligned countries also proposed a World Disarmament Conference as a means to spotlight what they viewed as the inadequacy of the CCD. Both superpowers strongly opposed the proposal for exactly the same reasons they favored CCD consideration of disarmament in the first place.

Frustrated in their attempts to call a world conference, the nonaligned majority called a special General Assembly session on disarmament for 1978. Not since the World Disarmament Conference of the 1930s had so many governments directed so much attention to the subject. Washington, which had no more sympathy for the session than for the world conference proposal, had little choice but to attend and watch as the authority of the CCD was significantly reduced. Neither Washington nor Moscow was prepared to defy the wrath of the international community, and the result was a 112-point document, called the First Document, that incorporated the majority's disarmament agenda. It subordinated disarmament to economic reform, and it emphasized the General Assembly's "central role" in disarmament matters. It also called for a comprehensive test-ban treaty, the eventual end of nuclear weapons, and a system of general and complete disarmament.[10] In theory, it revolutionized the whole process of disarmament. In practice, it failed.

Why the failure? Because détente was dying. Indeed, it was dead by the end of the decade. Soviet and Cuban troops in Africa, the Soviet invasion of Afghanistan, the Carter human rights campaign in the USSR and in Eastern Europe, the USSR-U.S. recognition of China, the Carter administration's beefed up arms program including development of the MX missile, and the Senate's refusal to ratify the SALT II treaty all contributed to growing superpower tensions. The sense of impotence experienced by Americans during the Iran hostage crisis further undermined the confidence needed for arms limitations. The 1980 election of President Ronald Reagan, who doubled the U.S. defense budget while he quadrupled the national debt, ended any real prospect of UN-sponsored disarmament. By the mid-1980s, not one iota of the First Document had been fulfilled. Later, when President Reagan and his Soviet counterparts did in fact achieve real progress in arms limitation through the Strategic Arms Reduction Talks (START) and the 1987 Intermediate Nuclear Forces Treaty, they did so without reference to the UN. Certainly special General Assembly sessions on disarmament in 1984 and 1988 went nowhere. Their failure prompted the Reagan administration to announce publicly that the First Document had produced no "historic consensus."[11]

Not until the end of the Cold War did any kind of consensus again permit the UN to become productively involved in arms limitation. The UN's most recent disarmament activity has contained a degree of modesty that undoubtedly stemmed from the organization's disarmament failures during the previous few decades. Instead of demanding complete disarmament, the General Assembly since 1989 has lowered its sights. In 1995, it endorsed a treaty unconditionally prohibiting the spread of nuclear arms and technology, and in 1996 it backed overwhelmingly a comprehensive test ban that only India and two nonnuclear powers opposed. This latter agreement emerged from the original Eighteen (now 61) Member Disarmament Committee in Geneva. Following what the New York Times described as a "low key" debate at the UN, the State Department strongly supported this newest test ban.[12] The reduction of American and Soviet nuclear arsenals after 1991, compounded by complicated issues ranging from radioactive waste disposal to budgetary relief, reinforced a growing conviction in Washington that further testing carried more risks (including proliferation) than benefits. Because the treaty omitted reference to the use of computer simulations to assess nuclear testing and mandated no further reductions in America's nuclear stockpile, the Clinton administration gave it unambiguous support.

ECONOMIC DEVELOPMENT

Unlike the League of Nations Covenant, the UN Charter prominently addressed economic and social matters. Article 55 called for international "conditions of stability and well-being which are necessary for peaceful and friendly relations among nations." It sought "higher standards of living, full employment, and conditions of economic and social progress and development," as well as "solutions of economic, social, health, and related problems." To promote the kind of economic and social conditions that would make war less likely, the founders established the 24-member Economic and Social Council (ECOSOC), along with a number of specialized agencies including the Food and Agricultural Organization (FAO); International Labour Organization (ILO); International Refugee Organization (IRO), which continued the work of the late Relief and Rehabilitation Administration (UNRRA); UN Educational, Scientific, and Cultural Organization (UNESCO); and the UN International Children's Fund (UNICEF). The founders also established formal links to the International Monetary Fund (IMF), and the International Bank for Reconstruction and Development (IBRD). As with the UN proper, the Americans had originally expected to fund—and to control—this economic activity. They saw little incompatibility between their political objectives, which included stability and peace, and their economic objectives, including the restoration of international trade and the maintenance of post-Depression prosperity. They could not imagine in 1945 a UN in which the United States would hold only minority power.

Nor did American officials in 1945 anticipate that the UN would become a vehicle to redistribute global wealth. The rich countries after World War II did not feel very rich. They faced the prospect of inflation, the fear of another depression, and the costs of reconversion and reconstruction. ECOSOC seemed a fine idea in principle, but it had little success. Initially, the U.S. representative to ECOSOC was the assistant secretary of state for economic affairs, an official based in Washington whose work at the UN held low priority. After 1949, the State Department approved the appointment of a special representative to ECOSOC, Isador Lubin, who reported directly to Warren Austin at the U.S. Mission. Economic policy at the UN, therefore, became more clearly an adjunct of America's overall UN policy.[13]

ECOSOC, of course, was not the only economic agency at the UN; indeed, within 10 years, it had become the least important. Some of the other important agencies predated 1945. The FAO had been founded with strong American support at Hot Springs, Virginia, in 1943, and the UNRRA came into existence the next year, focusing on relief and refugee issues in war-ravaged Europe. At the Bretton Woods Conference in 1944, American and European delegates established two key economic instruments: the IMF to stabilize and regulate the postwar currency and monetary exchange system, and the International Bank for Reconstruction and Development (the World Bank) to provide loans for capital reconstruction. Although the IRO replaced UNRRA, which ended its brief existence in 1946, the IMF and World Bank soon operated very much at odds with what the UN majority would demand by the 1960s. Both focused almost exclusively on European, not Third World, development. Even so they were underfunded, with the World Bank only loaning about $300,000,000 annually during the late 1940s.[14] The $17 billion Marshall Plan would put this paltry sum in perspective.

The American relationship with these agencies came in for criticism almost from the beginning. Washington initially funded 40 percent of ECOSOC's budget and about the same percentage for the World Bank and the IMF. As foreign economies recovered, the United States reduced its contribution to approximately one-third. Few governments complained about these proportions, but non-Europeans increasingly criticized the degree to which the Americans dominated the work of these institutions, targeting mainly European industrial economies with loans and other forms of aid. Moreover, a weighted voting formula gave Washington and its allies a much larger voice in the bank and the IMF than in ECOSOC, which utilized a single-vote system. Indeed, American dissatisfaction with—and neglect of—ECOSOC stemmed in part from the voting formula.

There was another problem. American policy makers hardly understood during the early postwar period the huge appetite that the nonindustrialized world would have for aid, nor did they sufficiently understand the need for long-term aid. U.S. officials believed that the UN and its agencies would provide short-term relief, after which private investment and commerce would make up the difference. Their willingness to permit UNRRA to disappear in 1946 was perfectly consistent with this belief. But, of course, the war had created mountainous problems, and the Marshall Plan, which operated outside of the UN umbrella, would do what no UN agency was even remotely prepared to do. Although the Marshall Plan was directed toward Europe, it raised hopes elsewhere for economic assistance that might be channeled through UN agencies. ECOSOC had created regional economic bureaus that were already in place before Congress ever funded the plan. These bureaus did not entirely please U.S. officials who, for political reasons, muted their opposition. U.S. officials were also dismayed by the demand for Marshall-style aid by non-European delegates in these newly formed bureaus.

The fact of the matter is that Washington's economic use of the UN was drifting aimlessly by the late 1940s. Perhaps nothing better illustrates this than the fate of the International Trade Organization (ITO), favored by the Truman administration to realize Wilson's and Hull's dream of an international community made prosperous by free trade. American officials had helped design the ITO as a specialized agency with a closer connection to the UN than either the World Bank or the IMF. The dream notwithstanding, the ITO was stillborn. In part, it fell victim to Cold War tension during the late

1940s, following the Czechoslovakia coup and the Berlin Blockade. But it also suffered when U.S. groups like the Chamber of Commerce denounced it as a threat to the "free enterprise system by giving priority to centralized national governmental planning of foreign trade."[15] Paradoxically, ITO opponents denounced more than just the threat to free enterprise; ostensibly in the name of free trade, they denounced free trade itself. The Truman administration, fearing defeat, never even submitted the ITO charter to the Senate for ratification. Economic nationalism was making a comeback.

Perhaps the Truman administration was willing to see the ITO stillborn because the General Agreement on Tariff and Trade (GATT), founded in 1947 by the ITO's preparatory commission and approved by the Truman administration via executive agreement, created a parallel mechanism for bilateral and multilateral tariff reductions. Unlike the ITO, GATT stood apart from the UN, becoming a formal international agency in the mid-1950s when participating governments created an office to administer it. Had the ITO come into existence, it is doubtful that GATT would have survived. Ironically, some UN members would eventually see GATT as a threat to their own economies, a belief shared by protectionist Americans by the 1990s.

Truman administration support for economic development also involved technical assistance to non-European countries. The administration's Point Four program offering "scientific progress and technical assistance" became the basis for the UN's Expanded Program of Technical Assistance (EPTA), a 1950 initiative based on American recognition that the underdeveloped world (later to be called the "less developed" and still later the "developing" world) would become increasingly important within the Cold War context. The EPTA sought to coordinate the work of a number of UN specialized agencies, its price tag modest by later standards.

It was during the Eisenhower administration that the UN's economic activity became less attractive from Washington's perspective. U.S. policy makers tolerated expensive programs aiding Europe and inexpensive programs aiding the Third World, but they surely did not relish what the nonindustrial nations most needed: generous funding for capital development. American officials greeted frostily the Special UN Fund for Economic Development (SUNFED), a project that evolved between 1953 and 1957 into one of the UN's most ambitious initiatives. Ironically, the SUNFED idea had American origins; early in his first term President Eisenhower had proposed reallocating monies saved from disarmament for global economic development. Those savings never materialized, and the United States and its industrialized allies found themselves on the defensive in the UN's Second Committee (composed of all UN members), which spearheaded the SUNFED proposal.

Yet American opposition to SUNFED is too easily generalized as opposition to all economic aid. The story is more complex, involving a serious quarrel within the Eisenhower administration between advocates of aid led by Henry Cabot Lodge Jr. and opponents led by Treasury Secretary George

Humphrey. The more cosmopolitan Lodge came to believe that the United States could not compete in the Cold War unless it extended economic assistance to the Third World. But rather than embrace the SUNFED plan, which, by 1956, had been seriously discredited by American conservatives, he offered a variation of the plan, which, he argued, would involve three safeguards: no outright U.S. grants but only matching funds in convertible currencies; spending (about $75,000,000) only out of funds already allocated by Congress for foreign aid (i.e. no additional monies); and indirect U.S. control of the program by requiring all expenditures to be approved by the U.S.-dominated World Bank. Lodge even claimed to have gotten Hammarskjold's approval for an American administrator of the program. To Humphrey's assertion that such programs become never-ending, Lodge noted that even the much larger Marshall Plan "*did* come to an end, having magnificently achieved its objective."[16]

Despite Eisenhower's sympathies for the program, the chaotic year of 1956 turned out to be a bad time to gain administrative acceptance. Even a "Baby SUNFED" could muster no American support. What did materialize the following year was a scaled-down compromise called the Special Fund. It involved no capital spending, but rather provided grants for "preinvestment" assistance—surveys and training programs that would undergird capital projects. It would work in tandem with EPTA and, according to Maxwell Finger, who helped to author the scheme, owed its success in Washington to conservative Republican Walter Judd, a congressional delegate to the UN who originally opposed all UN aid projects.[17] Soviet opposition to the program led to increased U.S. support. The General Assembly finally approved the Special Fund in 1959 with the United States contributing 40 percent of the budget.

Many governments supported the Special Fund not as a substitute for SUNFED, but as a supplementary program. Compared to the 1950s, the 1960s would be more friendly to multilateral economic aid. In 1960, the General Assembly approved in principle a redraft of SUNFED, renamed the UN Capital Development Program (the word "capital" would soon be dropped). Five years later, praised by U.S. officials, it became an official UN agency, merging the Special Fund and the old EPTA. U.S. officials such as Rusk, Stevenson, and Assistant Secretary of State for African Affairs G. Mennen Williams, were certainly much more sympathetic to the economic needs of the nonindustrialized world than their Eisenhower administration predecessors, but by 1965 Congress had its hands full with Southeast Asia and the Mideast. Nor was the problem just America's ungenerous contributions; other industrial governments appropriated even less. The program never lived up to its original promise.

The American government during the 1960s did spend billions on foreign aid, but precious little ever went through the UN. The Cold War made foreign aid an important part of American foreign policy as the Agency for International Development occupied an increasingly important corner of the American foreign policy bureaucracy. Nevertheless, about 85 percent of all foreign aid was military aid, and even much of the so-called economic aid was actually camouflaged military aid. Of the genuinely economic aid, most was allocated bilaterally, often with strings attached, as part of the Cold War competition for Third World support. Less than one percent of U.S. foreign aid went through UN agencies.[18]

Why so little? The usual reasons: the United States preferred organs it could control rather than the General Assembly, which, during the 1960s, seemed less and less reliable; Communist support for UN aid programs made such programs automatically suspect; and the anticolonialist/socialist cast of the General Assembly gave Washington's hard-headed Realists a permanent trump card to play against its fuzzy idealists (of whom the Stevenson crew were cast as prime examples). Even American leadership of the Development Fund—it was headed by the innovative former Marshall Plan administrator Paul Hoffman, who deeply believed in economic solutions to political problems—carried little weight in the White House or the capitol.

The modest commitment to UN economic aid contrasts sharply to the lip service given such aid. In 1961 President Kennedy called for a UN Development Decade, though his Treasury Department, like Eisenhower's with SUN-FED, feared that it might mean spending real money. It did not, though the General Assembly, in adopting the Development Decade proposal, insisted on a 5 percent per year growth rate over U.S. objections. Still, despite the wide gap between promise and performance, U.S. contributions to the UN Development Program, and to associated bodies such as the FAO's Food Program, expanded steadily.

UN Conference on Trade and Development

Perhaps of greater importance was the appearance in 1964 of the UN Conference on Trade and Development (UNCTAD). Originally designed as a temporary program, it grew into one of the UN's most important units. Technically subordinate to the General Assembly, it subsequently came to have a large secretariat of its own and a permanence that even its founders had not foreseen. Maxwell Finger notes that the Kennedy and Johnson administrations did not favor its establishment, but judged the political risks of opposing it greater than the damage it might do.[19]

In general, since UNCTAD's establishment the United States and its allies have favored using GATT and the World Bank to tackle trade-related problems, while the nonindustrial world has preferred UNCTAD, where a majority vote is not offset by weighted formulas. Indeed, the Group of 77 originally emerged not from the General Assembly, but from UNCTAD, mirroring the nonaligned flavor of the organization.

Focusing on issues related to marketing, finance, and commodity stabilization, UNCTAD has sought, with some success, to engage the industrial nations rather than denounce them (as so often occurred in the Decolonization Committee). For this reason, even the skeptical Americans usually cooperate with UNCTAD. But UNCTAD has not had much success dealing with its greatest challenge: building a floor for commodity prices among the developing countries while placing price ceilings on goods coming from the industrialized nations. UNCTAD's most ambitious project—a so-called Common Fund to finance the "management of stockpiles" in order to guarantee price stabilization—received early support from the State Department, but not from either the Reagan administration or Congress, which scrapped the idea in 1985.[20] Rejection of the Common Fund reflected a fundamental disagreement between the industrial North, which typically wishes to sell the greatest number of goods to the developing South at the highest possible price, and the need among developing countries not only to reduce competition from more efficient producers in the industrialized world but also to buy goods from the industrialized North at the lowest possible price. Severe economic dislocations during the trade depression of the early 1980s made clear to both sides just how difficult it would be to resolve this dilemma. It hardly needs emphasis that the free-market orientation of the Reagan administration made the UN even less sympathetic to UNCTAD's economic radicalism than had been the case earlier.

Hostility to the Common Fund and to international economic aid in general reflected the same kind of ambivalence that characterized the American approach to the UN on political issues. Washington may have supported the vague principles of the UN's First Development Decade, but it was much less enthused about UN attempts to implement these goals after the General Assembly declared the 1970s the Second Development Decade. In 1961, not even conservative Republicans objected in principle to raising the standard of living for the poor nations; by 1970, not only conservative Republicans, but many moderates and liberals, too, objected to achieving this goal by taxing the richer nations. When the UN's Second Committee adopted a strategy document urging the industrialized nations to allocate one percent of their GNP to the poor by 1972 (in no case after 1975), American officials insisted on reservations making such a goal little more attainable than the goal of perpetual peace. They did the same with the sections dealing with tariff reduction and technology transfers, some with target dates barely more than a year away.[21] Unfortunately, the stagflation of the 1970s made such wealth transfers unlikely; even voluntary American contributions to UNICEF suffered during this period.

The handwriting was on the wall. Few U.S. officials were willing to endorse even a modest redistribution of wealth from North to South. And as American relations with the UN majority soured over colonial and Mideast problems, the blurring of lines between political and economic issues made a confrontation inevitable. It arrived when radical Third World leaders embraced the New International Economic Order (NIEO).

New International Economic Order

The NIEO had many roots, among them America's crumbling defense in Vietnam, the U.S. decision in 1971 to jettison the fixed gold standard, Libya's unilateral success during 1970 in raising oil prices, and the Arab (OPEC) oil boycott of 1973. Most important, perhaps, was UNCTAD's call for redressing economic wrongs, especially Mexican President Luis Echeverria's ringing call in 1972 to substitute the rights of states for those of individuals. As UN observer Rosemary Righter says, Echeverria did not so much extend the 1948 Declaration of Human Rights as break with it. The Third World, building on the dependency theory of Argentine economist and diplomat Rene Plebisch, did not politely critique the liberal international order established at Bretton Woods; rather it assaulted it. There was demand for a system of fixed commodity and trade relations to protect Third World producers from the hazards of price competition while forcing the rich to guarantee markets, reduce tariffs, set floors for commodity prices, and even accept the nationalization of foreign companies without regard for treaty protections.[22] The NIEO viewed international law as little more than window dressing to help the rich plunder the poor.

The Group of 77 formalized this radical program into declarations at Georgetown (Guiana) and Algiers during 1972 and 1973. In Righter's words, the Third World had "claimed its political kingdom," trivializing private property and converting wealth transfers into "reparations."[23] Washington nearly revolted. In his most memorable moment at the UN, US Ambassador John Scali—this was *before* Moynihan—denounced the NIEO as the "tyranny of the majority." The feel-good attitude about economic development that had prevailed during the Kennedy years now seemed like ancient history.

Nevertheless, the NIEO proposal, even when reinforced by the Group of 77's shrill antiwestern and anticolonialist rhetoric, did not spell the end of American cooperation with the UN's social and economic efforts. The Americans willingly joined in sponsoring the UN's global environmental conference in Stockholm during 1972. They also backed efforts in a number of other areas, including population control, antidrug interdiction, and use of the sea. On the other hand, the Nixon administration fought a running battle with Third World delegates who sought to link such activity with the NIEO. For instance, when the UN's Second Committee considered a statement mandating that population efforts should be considered in a way that would "contribute to the implementation" of the NIEO, the Americans abstained while 131 other countries approved the document.[24] Similarly, in 1976, the United States twice cast the sole negative vote against General Assembly resolutions reaffirming development formulas spelled out in the NIEO.

U.S. policy toward the UN, therefore, remained uneven. Congressional pressure led the Nixon administration, in 1972, to negotiate a reduction in America's proportion of UN dues from 31.5 percent to 25 percent of the UN's budget; contributions from new UN members Japan and West Germany cushioned the effect of the U.S. cutback on the organization. It is worth noting that the General Assembly approved this new financial formula based on expectations that the Americans would actually *increase* their contributions to the affiliated economic agencies. While some of these monies materialized—the United States, for instance, funded up to half of the UN's population control efforts during the 1970s—American contributions to other programs such as the UN Development Fund actually decreased by nearly 25 percent, a result of stagflation at home as well as pique over the NIEO.

In a sense, the General Assembly and UNCTAD majorities were playing an aid game that, at least in financial terms, they could not win. During the 1950s, the less developed countries (LDC's) welcomed economic aid from the industrial nations as charity; 20 years later, charity had been transformed into reparations. With few exceptions, the industrial countries disdainfully rejected these demands on their pocketbooks while questioning not only the legitimacy of certain programs, but the way in which the UN administered them. For instance, Righter describes stinging American criticism in 1984 of UNCTAD's "management, the quality of its research, its interpretation of its mandate, and the manner in which it conducted business." UNCTAD shot back that American criticism was politically motivated and that the West was merely obscuring its unwillingness to do enough for the Third World.[25]

The issue here was not really bureaucratic inefficiency. Righter correctly notes that it was a fundamental difference over global economic ideology, pitting what one State Department official called "paternalistic statism" against the Reagan administration's faith in free markets. By the mid-1980s, the atmosphere had become toxic, a condition that increased rather than decreased the stridency of the Group of 77. In the short run, all this hardly contributed to economic comity. It froze America's willingness to entertain requests for multilateral aid and even soured the relations between the United States and its European allies. A tariff-reduction demand by the United States is instructive. When Washington denounced high tariffs in some of the more prosperous developing countries like Malaysia and Korea, it encountered opposition not only by those it criticized, but in some unexpected places. Many poorer states who would have benefitted by the reductions lined up against the Americans (in the name of Third World solidarity), as did the wealthy Europeans who feared the loss of their own pet tariffs.

What was left of cooperation might easily have disappeared. That did not happen. Instead, cool heads in both Washington and the UN recognized that extreme reactions might become self-defeating. In the words of a former State Department official, "creeping moderation" replaced the reflexive anti-United-States reaction of many UNCTAD and ECOSOC officials. Buoyed perhaps by a thaw in U.S.-Soviet relations and a recognition that American complaints about the bloated and inefficient UN bureaucracy had validity, UNCTAD officers began the slow process of reform. It was enough, said one

U.S. official, to make it "impossible for us to go ahead with getting the organization scrapped."[26]

So UNCTAD survived. So did moderation. Yet significant levels of aid did not follow. At the beginning of the 1980s, one aid expert criticized "the failure of the U.S. to increase economic assistance to black Africa in any meaningful sense. . . ." He could have included most other Third World countries. The story had not changed at all by 1990. The Reagan administration had more than doubled spending for foreign aid between 1981 and 1989, but the entire increase had gone into military programs; indeed, nonmilitary aid had *declined* by nearly one-fifth. At the time of his inauguration, slightly over one-half of all U.S. foreign aid went into military projects; by the summer of 1987, that number had risen to 66 percent. Even a plan named after James A. Baker, Reagan's treasury secretary, to increase foreign assistance to the South by coordinating the efforts of the World Bank, the IMF, and the large banks disappointed its advocates. Stressing economic growth rather than austerity, the Baker Plan met with the reluctance of all three institutions to loan money during a decade in which many countries were struggling with the debt crisis. As governments like those in Mexico and Argentina flirted with bankruptcy, risk-averse bankers became less and less willing to extend loans to those who most needed them.[27]

Nor was this all. The administration's continued emphasis on free-market reforms in Third World economies, coupled with a domestic backlash against increased government spending as Reagan-era budgets tripled the national debt, contributed to the anti-aid mentality. Even the IMF and the World Bank reduced their activity. Relying almost exclusively on free-market strategies, both institutions exhibited signs of "disarray" by 1990, actually collecting more payments *from* Third World countries than lending *to* them.[28] Increasingly, the Americans resorted to negotiating trade and commodity agreements outside the framework of UN and other multinational agencies—as for instance, when Reagan's trade negotiator, William Brock, persuaded the Japanese voluntarily to curtail automobile exports to the United States.

By the end of the 1980s, the prospect for UN-sponsored economic cooperation was no more promising than it had appeared when Reagan became president. Occasional food relief undoubtedly reduced pockets of malnutrition, but UN-sponsored economic assistance to the most needy countries offered more hope than reality.[29] The UN might build a $65,000,000 branch headquarters in Nairobi, but abject poverty loomed in its shadow. In 1980, economist Barbara Ward had written that "wherever the place, whatever the context, whoever the parties," the outcome of the countless UN meetings dealing with the subject of Third World aid "has been virtually the same. . . . It has been nothing."[30] She could have penned the same thing a decade later.

The situation would not improve markedly during the Bush and first Clinton administrations. If anything, domestic budgetary pressures, combined with anti-UN sentiment among Republicans who controlled Congress during the

1995–96 session, made funding UN economic initiatives virtually impossible. By the mid-1990s, the Americans were in arrears to the UN for over a billion dollars in regular dues and peacekeeping assessments. Consequently, authorizing additional funds for economic aid stood very low on the priority list for both administrations. Washington would use the UN's failure to create a director-general for economic affairs, an economic "czar" to make sense of the many overlapping programs in this area, to justify its refusal to cooperate. No matter that the United States had actually opposed such coordination when, for instance, a proposal to create a Sustainable Development Commission sought to coordinate the activity of the UN Environmental Program and the Development Program (the Americans reversed course in 1992 and voted to create this new commission when they thought that it might actually *replace* ECOSOC).[31] The economic stalemate characterizing relations between the industrial North and the developing South that had taken hold by 1985 showed few signs of ending by the time the UN celebrated its 50th anniversary. Yet less than three years later, an economic crisis that threatened to engulf most of Asia, and that U.S. officials feared might not be confined to Asia, led to more IMF activity than had been seen since the Mexican collapse of the 1980s. President Clinton's treasury secretary, Robert Rubin, led in rounding up international support for IMF aid to countries standing on the brink of financial catastrophe, such as Thailand, South Korea, and Indonesia. Once again, the Americans welcomed the use of UN-affiliated agencies to aid foreign financial institutions that American bankers found too risky to rescue on their own.

chapter 8

CARTER

Ambassador Daniel Moynihan viewed himself as a friend of international cooperation, but his assault on the General Assembly majority gave aid and comfort to would-be isolationists that lingered for two decades. His successor at the UN, William Scranton, softened American criticism of the organization, but it was not until 1977 when Jimmy Carter became president that Washington seriously resolved to undo the Moynihan legacy.

Carter, a moderate Democrat who had been governor of Georgia, arrived in the White House with little foreign policy experience. Initially supporting continued dialogue with the Soviet Union, he did not challenge the fundamental shape of the Ford/Kissinger policy. His own course, however, lacked clarity. Alternating between an emphasis on morality and a reliance upon increasing American power, U.S. policy under Carter often appeared inconsistent and idiosyncratic. His insistence on damning Soviet human rights violations undermined détente at the same time that he failed to articulate a coherent strategy elsewhere in Europe and toward the Third World. Even at the UN, where Carter's representatives made a very favorable impression, the administration never formulated a clear policy.

The fault was not entirely Carter's. As during Nixon's first term, rivalry between the State Department and the NSC contributed to administrative inconsistency. Cyrus Vance, Carter's first secretary of state, had been appointed to propose broad lines of policy more than specific policy directions. The president, working closely with his national security adviser, fully expected to decide among policy alternatives; the State Department would then implement these decisions.[1] The new secretary of state was a thoughtful internationalist who had previously headed the policy studies section of the United States Association of the United Nations, the country's leading private pro-

U.S. ambassador Andrew Young (left), Mustafa Sam, Assistant Executive Secretary of the Organization of African Unity (center), and Mfanafuthi Johnstone Makatini, of the African National Congress of South Africa (right). October 26, 1977.
(UN/DPI Photo by Saw Lwin)

UN group. Vance turned out to be an excellent negotiator, but he proved unable to limit the influence of Zbigniew Brzezinski, a Polish emigre and academic strategist who, as Carter's NSC chief, moved more easily through the thicket of geopolitical strategy and placed a much higher priority on European and Middle Eastern issues than Third World problems. The rivalry between the two men—and therefore between the State Department and the NSC—grew intense as the foreign policy stakes increased. By the time that Maine senator Edmund Muskie, who had less direct foreign experience than Vance, became the new secretary of state in 1980, the NSC's primacy had become clear.

The story of the UN during the Carter years also involves perhaps the least orthodox foreign policy maker in the administration. Permanent representative Andrew Young came to his post with no previous diplomatic record, having been a civil rights activist closely associated with the Reverend Martin Luther King Jr. Following King's assassination, Young won election to the House of Representatives, where he served until Carter's presidential victory in 1976.

Young, like Moynihan before him, would place his imprint on the world organization to a degree that far outstripped his actual influence on policy. A preacher, a moralist, and a defender of the rights of those whom he viewed as powerless, he, like the new president, rooted his moralism deeply in Christianity. Unlike many of his colleagues in the State Department, Young rejected the persona of the cautious, gray diplomat. His superiors would view him as "irrepressibly outspoken."[2] The first African-American to represent the United States at the UN, Young developed a sympathetic relationship with many Third World delegates that stood in sharp contrast to Moynihan. But he ultimately proved no more capable of energizing the UN or revolutionizing North-South relations than had his predecessors. If he made a difference, it was a small one.

Certainly Young had the support of one of the more important officials to serve as assistant secretary of IO since World War II. Charles Maynes had been a foreign service officer who, after leaving government service in 1970, directed international organization affairs at the Carnegie Endowment until his return to the State Department in 1977. He had great respect for Vance, Young, and the UN, and his work at IO helped to repair a relationship between the State Department and USUN that had often been strained. Maynes's respect for his superiors did not extend to many others in official Washington: "I was distressed at how hostile [toward the UN] they were, at how difficult they were."[3] This attitude among officials, he implies, helped to explain some of the administration's failures at the organization. He viewed the 1960s, not the late 1970s, as the golden age of U.S.-UN relations.

In later years, Maynes would defend Andy Young's service, fully aware that the story of U.S.-UN relations during the Carter administration was often affected by Young's controversial statements. Young often spoke truth, but not always wisely. At various times he averred that American jails held thousands of political prisoners, that America's English and Swedish allies were racist, that Cuban soldiers in Angola served as a stabilizing force in southern Africa, and that PLO representatives at the UN served as a moderating influence on Mideast events. The validity of these comments was less important than the domestic political storm they caused when—depending on the comment— nationalist, conservative, anti-UN, and Jewish groups protested strongly. These protests took their toll, especially after the Israelis disclosed in 1979 that Young had held an unauthorized meeting with a PLO representative that was kept secret even from his superiors in Washington. To complicate things, he then misled the State Department once the meeting became known.[4] The meeting occurred during a period when U.S. officials assiduously avoided any public connection to the PLO. Worse, the Americans had promised Jerusalem that no such meetings would ever occur. Carter had little choice but to ask for Young's resignation.[5] The episode contributed to a sense of disarray within the administration and must have been painful to Carter, who not only had enormous respect for his ambassador, but was personally close to him. It need hardly be said that Young's untimely departure weakened Carter's support within the black community at home.

Yet Young's foot-in-mouth diplomacy was only a part—and not the most important part—of Carter administration contact with the UN. It was during Carter's presidency that the United States sent its first full-time representative to the UN's Human Rights Commission, complementing the administration's newly created office of assistant secretary of state for human rights affairs. President Carter also threw his support behind UN efforts to resolve the Rhodesian and Namibian situations. Both Presidents Ford and Carter supported repeal of the 1972 Byrd Amendment that had *required* American manufacturers to ignore UN sanctions designed to prevent Rhodesia from finding foreign markets for its chromium. Additionally, in May 1977 the State Department ended its more general antisanctions policy when it joined a unanimous Security Council to tighten the diplomatic screws against the Smith government in Salisbury, Rhodesia's capital. For the next two years, the department, with strong support from both Vance and Young, collaborated with London to pressure Smith into accepting a formula allowing for majority rule and nullifying Rhodesia's unilateral 1965 declaration of independence. That formula included an end to sanctions and a return to British rule until new elections, based on the one-man one-vote principle, could be held.

There is no doubt that Young's credibility with Rhodesia's African neighbors facilitated a final settlement. African mistrust of U.S. policy had escalated during the Kissinger/Moynihan years, and Young did more than any other single person to restore a basis for trust. Furthermore, in what might be called innocence by association, Young's unorthodox diplomacy aided British policy. Young's growing stature also reinforced (and was reinforced by) Washington's support both for UN sanctions and repeal of the Byrd amendment.

It has often been said that economic sanctions are ineffective in the international arena. This was not the case in Rhodesia, whose economy was heavily dependent on foreign trade. Nor was Rhodesia the only African country vulnerable to sanctions. South African officials, too, feared sanctions, and the Americans hinted at their possible use in order to pressure Pretoria to support UN policy toward Salisbury. Unstated by the Americans was that both Carter and Vance knew that Great Britain would likely veto sanctions against South Africa because of extensive British economic interests there. Consequently, the U.S. approach to South Africa contained a large element of bluff. In his memoirs, Vance wrote that the "greatest utility of the UN sanctions power was in the threat of its application rather than in its actual use."[6] The Americans brandished that threat continually. And successfully.

It took another year for a final settlement to emerge. British foreign secretary Lord Carrington led the effort to fashion a compromise with the Smith regime involving majority rule and protections for the white minority. Needing American support, Carrington implored his American partners not to outline *specific* conditions that would result in the lifting of sanctions; otherwise, he feared, the Smith regime would skillfully maneuver to end sanctions without meeting all of the UN's terms. While President Carter and his NSC chief initially opposed Carrington's tactics, Vance and Young argued in favor of unambiguous support for their British ally. Carter finally agreed, even though everyone understood that any delay in ending sanctions carried domestic political risks at a time when Congress was sharply divided over this issue.[7] With Carrington now speaking clearly for both Washington and London in support of UN policy, the Smith regime accepted the inevitable in December 1979.

THE NAMIBIAN DISPUTE

It took much longer to resolve the Namibian (Southwest African) dispute. Here the apartheid South African government proved to be even less accommodating than over Rhodesia, even though Portuguese withdrawal from neighboring Angola rendered Pretoria's semicolonial control of Southwest Africa very vulnerable to guerilla activity. Until 1977, the General Assembly had taken the lead on this matter, with the United States, along with some of its European allies, generally abstaining on formal resolutions. The 1974 revolution in Portugal and the subsequent deployment of Cuban troops and Soviet equipment into Angola brought an end to the luxury of abstention. Even before Young went to the UN, Kissinger had shifted American policy to achieve a quick South African withdrawal from its former mandate, fearful that delay would lead to more extensive Soviet involvement in the region. Brzezinski agreed, viewing politics in southern Africa as an extension of the Cold War. He believed that the United States had "underestimated the Eastern bloc connection in the region, and that Andy and Cy, along with most of those at State, took an excessively benign view of Soviet penetration of Africa, underestimating its strategic implications."[8]

This kind of thinking was vintage Brzezinski, who otherwise cared little about the Namibian puzzle. Vance and Young, who viewed the situation in both global and local terms, were much more involved in finding a solution that, to their dismay, eluded them. Still, they attacked the problem with a seriousness that Brzezinski typically directed only to European and Mideast affairs, and they placed the UN near the center of their efforts.

Underlying American efforts to remove South Africa from Namibia was a widely shared belief that only a Namibian settlement could lay the basis for the removal of Cuban troops from Angola. This settlement would be no easy task. Namibians distrusted the South Africans, who in turn distrusted the Cubans and their Namibian guerrilla allies, the Southwest African Peoples Organization (SWAPO). SWAPO's support was partly Marxist; it was also tribal. The intricacies of these relationships made a settlement difficult to reach. At the least, the South Africans sought to work with anti-SWAPO Namibians while the UN—and the Americans—increasingly saw no likely settlement without SWAPO. Indeed, Andy Young's success with Angola and other neighboring governments to persuade SWAPO to accept a compromise made a settlement more likely.

It was not the General Assembly, however, that shaped that settlement. Once the Americans became serious about Namibia, they turned to the less radical Security Council where the veto would protect American and British interests. During a special session devoted to Namibia during 1978, the council approved a number of resolutions that resembled the framework laid down in Resolution 385, passed in 1976. Calling for free elections and the withdrawal of South Africa, 385 framed the politics of the next four years.[9] Moreover, the administration resolved to support the UN's position via a "contact group" composed of five western nations in consultation with the "front-line" neighbors of Namibia. Donald McHenry, USUN's number three man during Young's tenure, took the lead in cobbling together a plan that moved South Africa quite close to a final settlement. By threatening sanctions against South Africa and by providing for a limited South African army presence of 1,500 troops in southern Namibia, the contact group offered enough of a carrot-and-stick approach to capture Pretoria's attention.

Unfortunately, the very things that attracted South African officials created distrust within SWAPO. Further complicating matters, South African leadership changes highlighted disagreements over a number of issues, including control of Namibia's only deep-water port (Walvis Bay), the size of a UN truce supervisory group (UNTAG), the location of SWAPO and South African units, and the relative authority of a South African administrator versus the UNTAG commander.

But the key dispute revolved around the issue of control, addressed in Security Council Resolution 435. Approved in September 1978, Resolution 435 authorized the UN to implement elections for a transition government and therefore threatened South Africa's hopes of sponsoring its own elections in Namibia.[10] With the African states demanding sanctions if Pretoria ignored 435, the Carter administration found itself in a pickle. Failure to support the resolution, warned Vance's advisors, would imperil reconstruction of the U.S. position in black Africa, while approving the sanctions would alienate not just Pretoria, but London. Led by McHenry, the contact group again tried to find room for compromise. There was little, and when the Security Council voted on sanctions in November 1978, the United States and its European allies got cold feet. They abstained, not only once again undermining their standing with the African states, but giving South Africa reason to believe that foot-dragging might accomplish more than cooperation.[11]

Faced with black African ire and South Africa's refusal to adopt the UN plan, both Carter and Vance warned that sanctions would follow any failure by Pretoria to call the elections mandated by Resolution 435. This threat led to more promises by the South Africans to hold UN-sponsored elections, but it did not lead to elections. It led only to excuses to postpone elections. The

South Africans understood that U.S. policy makers had other things on their minds by the fall of 1979. The Soviet invasion of Afghanistan, the Iranian crisis, and the deferral of the SALT II treaty had moved to center stage, weakening President Carter both domestically and internationally. Meanwhile, Namibia burned.

By the time it became clear to Vance that the Namibian situation had become an embarrassing stalemate, Young had resigned, to be replaced by the second deputy representative at USUN, Donald McHenry. McHenry was a consummate professional, similar in both temperament and conduct to Charles Yost. After resigning from the Foreign Service in 1973, he had served with the Carnegie Endowment for International Peace, where he specialized in multilateral issues.[12] Soft-spoken, unflappable, and cautious, he differed from Young in much the same way that the even-tempered Scranton had differed from Moynihan. In two ways, however, McHenry closely resembled Young: he had a firm sense of right and wrong tempered by an equally strong pragmatic core, and, as an African-American, he had a domestic constituency that gave him more influence than most career officers ever enjoy. He never pandered to that constituency or to any other. Like Yost and, later, Thomas Pickering, he set a standard of excellence that few other permanent representatives ever matched.

MIDEAST AGREEMENTS

Except for Rhodesia and Namibia, the Carter administration addressed most diplomatic issues outside of the UN. Some of these issues, however, affected Washington's standing at the world organization. For instance, President Carter's successful negotiation of a 1978 treaty turning over control of the Panama Canal to Panama increased U.S. influence among Latin American countries at the UN. Ironically, however, the president's best-known achievement, the Israeli-Egyptian agreements signed at Camp David in 1978, may have undermined American influence at the world body. The Camp David accords, which ended the 31-year state of war between Egypt and Israel, resulted primarily from two things: Israel's new sense of military vulnerability following the Yom Kippur War, and Egypt's desperate need for economic relief from military expenditures. Of the many agreements at Camp David, the most basic called for Israeli return of the Sinai peninsula to Egypt in return for Cairo's recognition of Israel and the negotiation of a peace treaty. These terms were clear. Other agreements were less clear. According to U.S. and Egyptian officials, the Israelis had also agreed to stop building settlements on the occupied West Bank. The Israelis disputed this. When the right-wing Likud government of Menachem Begin continued its popular settlements program, President Carter acquiesced because, he believed, he could not stop it. The administration's passivity damaged American credibility at the UN. The Camp David accords had been attacked by most other Mideast governments before the settlement issue became public. Now, said Young's number two man at USUN, "The secret supporters of Camp David at the UN all said, 'No more. That's it.' From then on it was all downhill."[13]

If the accords doomed any real support for Washington's Mideast diplomacy at the UN, the Carter administration had already come away with one modest achievement: the establishment of a peacekeeping force to police southern Lebanon. Israeli military retaliation south of Lebanon's Litani River in March 1978 had followed PLO terrorist attacks, raising the specter not only of Israeli-Lebanese conflict, but the prospect of a civil war in Lebanon (which occurred anyway) and Syrian-Israeli conflict (which did not). A Security Council resolution calling for Israeli withdrawal also created the United Nations Force in Lebanon (UNFIL), a peacekeeping contingent fated to be brushed aside during a subsequent Israeli attack.[14] Sponsored by the Americans and tolerated by the Soviets, UNFIL stood as a small reminder of the fragile peace in that region.

Mideast strategy as it pertained to the UN occasionally led to disagreements within the administration. For instance, with no real progress on the key issues of security and settlements, in March 1978 Vance proposed using the UN to convene a conference of all parties with an interest in the region, including the Soviets and the PLO. Brzezinski sharply disagreed, wishing to do nothing that would again open the door to Soviet involvement in the area.[15] The president agreed with his NSC chief. When new talks finally materialized, they were held at Camp David with no UN connection.

An even more troublesome situation occurred during early 1980. Secretary Vance finally authorized Donald McHenry, who had replaced Young, to support a General Assembly resolution condemning Jerusalem's settlement policy in the West Bank. Vance warned, however, that any resolution must not mention the thorny issue of Jerusalem, which the Israelis considered their capital and which the Arabs refused to view as part of Israel. Then came a serious foul-up. USUN informed Washington that the resolution had been cleansed of its "objectionable" features. This turned out to be incorrect, for, as Brzezinski puts it, the final version of the resolution was "replete" with references to Jerusalem and even called for the dismantling of existing West Bank settlements.[16] When the Americans cast their "yes" vote, the Israelis and their American supporters went apoplectic. The administration's special envoy on the Mideast, Robert Strauss, along with Vice President Walter Mondale and other political advisers, insisted that the United States repudiate its support for the resolution. These men were undoubtedly more concerned with the upcoming presidential primaries than with U.S. credibility at the UN. Brzezinski, on the other hand, although having little sympathy for the resolution, argued that repudiating McHenry would make the administration look "silly" and the president "weak." The political advisers prevailed. Brzezinski later wrote that the reversal proved "shattering" to Secretary of State Vance.[17] The Arabs were as incensed after the reversal as the Israelis had been at Washington's initial support for the resolution. The Camp David spirit had been dealt a serious blow, a factor that contributed to Vance's resignation two months later.

AFGHANISTAN AND IRAN

The limited American use of the UN on Mideast issues was duplicated in two other trouble spots during the Carter years: Afghanistan and Iran. Disorder in Afghanistan developed after a coup d'état brought into power a pro-Soviet government led by Barbrak Kahmal, a Marxist who summarily executed his (Marxist) predecessor in 1978 and asked for Soviet military assistance to suppress a fundamentalist Islamic uprising. Moscow complied, ordering 85,000 troops into the country in December 1979. Perhaps the Soviets really believed that Afghanistan was a strategic asset. Certainly Carter and Brzezinski believed that it had strategic importance. With the American position in Iran collapsing and with turmoil in other areas of the Mideast, including Pakistan and Saudi Arabia, both men viewed the Soviet action as a grave danger to the "rich oil fields of the Persian Gulf area and to the crucial waterways which so much of the world's energy supplies had to pass."[18] In retaliation, the United States suspended grain and high-technology exports to the USSR, then called for a special session of the Security Council.

The council meeting, held in January 1980, introduced an unambiguous resolution "deploring" the intervention and calling for Soviet withdrawal from Afghanistan. The assembly would pass a similar resolution in November.[19] No one had to remind Ambassador McHenry that the Soviets enjoyed the veto power. Nevertheless, the near unanimous support that both resolutions received proved that the anti-American sentiment so often evident in the General Assembly did not automatically carry over to the council. Indeed, even the assembly, using authority granted by the 1951 Uniting for Peace resolution, voted 111–22–12 to demand a Soviet withdrawal from Afghanistan.[20] This resolution, too, the Soviets ignored until they finally tired of Afghanistan 10 years later. The UN had proved no more able to resolve this matter than it had been able to bring peace to Vietnam.

Nor could the UN do much to end the Iranian crisis that began in 1978 and developed into a major dispute a month before the Soviet occupation of Afghanistan. In Iran, the stakes for the U.S. government were much higher than in Afghanistan where, despite Brzezinski's overwrought warnings, Americans had few concrete interests. Over the course of the previous quarter century, Washington had not just funneled billions in military equipment to Iran but it had gotten the shah's blessing to build two highly valuable listening posts to intercept Soviet communications. Furthermore, Iran's vast oil resources fueled European and American factories and transport, and its royal family had long moderated anti-Israeli policy in the Persian Gulf. So vital did the United States consider Iran that the White House would shortly enunciate the Carter Doctrine, which warned that any attempt by an "outside force" to gain control of the gulf region would be considered an assault on American vital interests and would be "repelled by any means necessary, including military force."[21]

American officials, therefore, viewed the 1979 overthrow of the shah by Islamic fundamentalists led by the Ayatollah Khomeini as a serious strategic challenge. Unfortunately for Carter, his administration was handicapped by deep-seated divisions concerning a response to the developing crisis. The NSC, under Brzezinski, repeatedly considered the possible use of military measures to support the shah, while Vance's State Department, preoccupied with Arab-Israeli affairs, remained dead set against the use of force. Neither the department nor the NSC understood the depth of anti-shah, antiwestern, and anti-American sentiment in Iran, nor the intense support for its theocratic leaders outside of a westernized middle class. Consequently, administration officials failed to grasp fully the nature of the crisis that transformed American foreign policy after pro-Khomenei radicals stormed the American embassy in Teheran and took more than 60 hostages on November 4, 1979.

Although no evidence suggests that the Iranian government instigated the hostage affair, the ayatollah backed it. He threatened to hold criminal trials and possibly to execute the hostages if the United States did not return the shah to Iran in order to stand trial for various "crimes." Within days, the hostage affair transformed a strategic issue into a profound cultural and political crisis in both countries.

Although American officials had much to learn about Iran, they understood that the episode might have serious repercussions on the president's electoral campaign, and some feared that it would undermine their entire foreign program. Ruling out a military response that might kill those whom it was intended to rescue, the administration had few resources in dealing with a government that rejected the usual rules of diplomacy. Nevertheless, it pursued a diplomatic rather than a military track, at least until April 1980 when it authorized a commando raid to rescue the hostages. That diplomatic track occasionally involved the United Nations, to which the Americans turned less out of hope than an absence of other alternatives.

Neither the White House nor the State Department expected much from the UN, but both hoped that the organization could, at a minimum, help maintain communications with Teheran. Carter actually used a number of UN channels simultaneously, including an appeal to the World Court. The court acted with surprising speed, issuing a provisional demand on December 15, 1979, for release of the hostages and restoration of the embassy to U.S. hands. Three months later, the court heard formal arguments on the case. On May 24, 1980, it unanimously held in favor of the United States, directing Iran to "terminate the unlawful detention" of the Americans and free them from the threat of criminal trial.[22] Iran ignored the court's judgment, just as the Americans five years later would ignore a court opinion declaring illegal a U.S. effort to mine the harbors of Nicaragua.

The State Department also instructed Ambassador McHenry to appeal directly to the Security Council. He did this five days after the hostage-taking. The council met repeatedly during the next two months, including a November 25 meeting called by Waldheim under the Charter's Article 99. With Iran's contempt for international law making almost every member of the UN—regardless of ideology—sensitive to the safety of its diplomats, the Security Council on December 4 approved Resolution 457, which asked the secretary general to use his good offices to resolve the problem.[23] Iran's inaction led to passage of a December 31 resolution calling for consideration of economic sanctions; the USSR abstained. Two weeks later, frustrated by the lack of any progress, the Americans demanded that the council authorize economic sanctions. McHenry called this a "temperate response to Iranian intemperance."[24] This time, Moscow cast its veto and the request failed.

Washington's call for sanctions reflected its inconsistent approach to the use of force. With the NSC generally arguing in favor of economic and even military measures, and with Vance and McHenry generally opposed, the administration had first ruled sanctions out, and then began to shift toward a harder line. It was never a smooth transition. After a particularly uncompromising speech by the ayatollah on November 20, Carter publicly referred to the Charter's force provisions as options. The Americans ordered aircraft carriers into the Persian Gulf to advertise to the Iranians—and to the Soviets— the vital importance of U.S. interests in the area.

Yet Vance's opposition to military measures, combined with the reservations of America's allies and the lingering hope that the Iranians were less radical than their rhetoric, led Carter to postpone serious consideration of the sanctions alternative. With the Afghanistan situation complicating the diplomatic puzzle, a UN-sponsored peaceful solution looked all the more attractive. Consequently, the Americans encouraged Waldheim to use his good offices to broker a settlement. This resulted in two initiatives: a risky and unsuccessful trip by Waldheim to Terehan on January 4, 1980, and an agreement approved by both the United States and Iran to appoint a UN commission to consider Iranian grievances. The Americans had approved the commission only on the grounds that commission members would first meet with the hostages to evaluate their condition (the United States had reluctantly conceded that the hostages would not be freed before the commission began its work).[25]

Failure now tumbled over failure. Khomeini broke the agreement's ground rules by insisting that the commission issue a report denouncing U.S. conduct even before permitting its members to visit the hostages. He also broke his promise to transfer control of the hostages from the militants to the Iranian government. In response, by March 11 the Americans gave up on the commission. Each failure made the use of force more likely. By April, Vance had become the last holdout in Washington against an armed rescue to free the hostages. Two days after the rescue effort failed, Vance resigned (he had tendered his letter a few days earlier) and UN efforts ended.[26]

The rescue fiasco did not worsen Iranian-American relations. It just signified how bad the relationship had become. Even before the rescue mission, the Carter administration on April 8 had finally broken relations with Iran, expelled all remaining Iranian officials from the United States, confiscated some of Iran's frozen assets to pay outstanding debts, and imposed a stiff embargo. The Americans, in other words, unilaterally took the very kind of action that the Soviets had earlier vetoed at the UN.[27] Nine months later, with the UN sitting on the sidelines and a new administration taking over in Washington, Iran released the hostages.

For all that officials like Vance, Maynes, Young, and McHenry valued the UN, the reality is that the UN had been no more central to U.S. policy making during their tenure than during that of the previous administration. Only the Rhodesian and Namibian disputes involved the UN in more than a marginal fashion. Yet the UN still generated more talk than action. For instance, regarding Cambodia (Kampuchea), the UN in September 1979 was faced with seating a delegation from either Pol Pot's murderous Khmer Rouge regime backed by the PRC, or a puppet government under Heng Samrin, who had recently been installed by a powerful Vietnam with Soviet backing. Both rivals were communist, and both were thoroughly objectionable to Americans who still recoiled from the bitter aftertaste of Vietnam.

To Vance, having to choose either faction was "wrenching."[28] Like Young and McHenry at the UN, he approached human rights issues with sincerity and intelligence. Yet he instructed Andrew Young to support Pol Pot for the UN seat without regard to the issue of human rights. The Khmer Rouge, he conceded, stood among the most barbaric regimes in world history, but it was supported by a number of countries—including all of Washington's Asian allies—that wanted to limit the influence of both Moscow and Hanoi in that region. "We made the only decision consistent with our overall national interest," Vance later wrote.[29] The *only* decision? He might have ordered an abstention.

In isolation, the Cambodian issue was a small matter. In context, together with the kind of criticism that Moynihan and his allies had leveled against the UN for the previous five years, it chipped away at the foundation of U.S. support for the organization. The erosion of U.S. support was especially evident in Congress. For example, in 1979, New York's junior senator, Daniel Moynihan, introduced a measure to forbid the United States to finance its share of any UN project supporting a liberation movement like the PLO. In the dicey political climate of 1979, neither the president nor his foreign policy advisers made a fuss. Called the Kemp-Moynihan amendment, it is not even mentioned in the memoirs of Carter, Vance, or Brzezinski. Yet the amendment was a sign of things to come: whatever the merits of the liberation movements, the Kemp-Moynihan amendment quickened the process of undermining U.S. financial support for the UN. The history of U.S.-UN relations during the next administration would illustrate exactly how real that financial threat had become.

chapter 9

REAGAN

No newspaper considered it front-page news in 1982 when President Ronald Reagan replaced Elliot Abrams with Gregory Newell as his assistant secretary of state for international affairs. The 32-year-old Newell was bright and eager. He was also unqualified. His only foreign affairs experience came from his work as a Mormon missionary in Western Europe. In the words of McHenry's former deputy at the UN, "He knows nothing about the UN."[1] And that was just fine with the new secretary of state, Alexander Haig, and the new UN ambassador, Jeane Kirkpatrick.

Reagan's election changed more than just the faces of America's chief foreign policy makers. As the most conservative president since Herbert Hoover, the new president spoke for a movement, not just a political party. Aiming to strengthen America, that movement would reassert nationalism and individualism at the expense of internationalism and collective action. Where Carter had begun his presidency by elevating the importance of human rights in both the developed and developing world, his successor subordinated human rights in the name of anticommunism and Realism. "Morning in America," Reagan called his presidency. The morning's new look in foreign policy meant not the UN, but NATO; not arms control but arms programs; not a recognition of the limits of power as taught by Vietnam, but a recognition of the possibilities of power. Right or wrong, Reagan officials believed the crisis in Iran, which destroyed the Carter presidency, had been brought on by timidity and weakness. They vowed not to make the same mistake.

The new president, whose only public office had been as California's governor, had no direct foreign policy experience. Those he appointed to run the State Department and the NSC had various levels of experience. Secretary Haig had most recently been commander of NATO forces, having previously

U.S. ambassador Jeane Kirkpatrick addresses the General Assembly.
November 11, 1982.
(UN/DPI Photo by Saw Lwin)

served under Henry Kissinger in Nixon's NSC and then as White House chief of staff. He had more sympathy for détente than many of his associates, but no more regard for the UN than had Kissinger. He was neither a serious thinker nor a strategist. He spent his time less concerned with day-to-day policy than with shoring up his own authority against colleagues seeking to diminish it. Bureaucratic infighting led to his ouster after 18 months.

The president's national security adviser, Richard V. Allen, was equally unsympathetic to the UN. Allen, too, had served under Kissinger in the NSC. As Reagan's chief White House foreign affairs adviser, he shared the president's nationalistic worldview but was not overly rigid in ideological terms. He had promised not to compete with Haig for influence (at least that is what he told Haig); rather, said Allen, he would mainly help to coordinate policy, more or less serving as a staff man.[2]

The most ideological member of the president's foreign policy team was Jeane Kirkpatrick, who served at the UN under Reagan until her resignation in 1985. No less strong willed than Haig, she had given a lot of thought to global issues during her years at Georgetown University's School of International Affairs. She had written widely on the subject, and had become well-known (notorious, said her adversaries) in academic circles for an article in which she argued that the United States could befriend noncommunist dictatorships but not totalitarian communist governments. "Only intellectual fashion and the tyranny of Left/Right thinking," she claimed, "prevents intelligent men of good will from perceiving the *fact* that traditional authoritarian governments are less repressive than revolutionary autocracies, that they are more susceptible of liberalization, and that they are more compatible with U.S. interests."[3] Her approach to the world paradoxically combined hardheaded realism and excessive moralism. By appointing her to the UN job, Reagan gave her a visibility that few other jobs could match.

An ambassador like Adlai Stevenson or Andrew Young brought prestige to the post. Kirkpatrick drew prestige from the UN, and she made the most of it. Outspoken and tough-minded, she reverted back to a style of UN diplomacy that had disappeared when Moynihan departed six years earlier. She was confrontational and acerbic, blunt and quietly angry. If the most effective UN ambassadors helped to create majorities, Kirkpatrick little worried about being a minority of one. Reagan-style nationalists loved her, though she alienated many other UN delegates as well as members of the State Department.

"I do not expect to be making policy in New York," Kirkpartick told a reporter before assuming her UN work.[4] Empty words. Few permanent representatives ever matched her efforts to formulate policy. As a member of both the cabinet and the NSC, she formally considered herself subordinate only in the most technical sense to the secretary of state, and certainly not to IO. Her relations with IO were mainly administrative, not political. When she had to follow orders that she personally found objectionable, she did so ungraciously. For instance, in June 1981 following a preventative Israeli air attack on Iraq's Osirak nuclear reactor, Kirkpatrick reluctantly joined a unanimous Security Council in condemning Jerusalem's "violation of the Charter . . . and the norms of international conduct."[5] She made no secret of her belief that Israel had acted in justifiable self-defense; at least she had the satisfaction of striking the word "aggression" from the resolution.[6] Still, she found the episode distasteful.

She felt much the same about the issue of PLO representation at the UN. Although the United States did not recognize the PLO, the UN Headquarters Agreement of 1945 gave any organization accredited by the UN the right to send representatives to New York. When the UN asked the State Department to provide visas for additional PLO envoys, Kirkpatrick, who consistently supported Israel, strongly objected, directly petitioning the secretary of state to reject the request. She had appealed to the wrong man. Haig, a former army commander who bristled when subordinates sidestepped his formal chain of command, allowed her appeal to inch its way through an unsympathetic bureaucracy before unceremoniously denying it. Kirkpatrick's ego rivalled Haig's. Not only did she resent the denial; she felt that Haig had not treated her as an equal. She was right. Haig rarely treated anyone as an equal.

For both Haig and Kirkpatrick, the bureaucratic pecking order had become the real issue, not PLO representation at the UN. Haig resisted his envoy's independence, while she, according to one of her assistants, "vowed that her right to correspond directly with the Secretary of State would never be compromised again by State Department 'clearance' procedures."[7] And while Haig's resignation the following year eased the tension between Washington and New York, the Haig-Kirkpatrick rivalry in part reflected a larger problem: the long-term competition for authority between the State Department and USUN that harked back to the days of Henry Cabot Lodge.

On substantive matters, Haig and Kirkpatrick had less disagreement. Haig did not exhibit what Kirkpatrick viewed as a troubling pro-Arab bias within the department on Mideast issues, and like Kirkpatrick, he shared a Kissingerian skepticism about the UN. It was during his term as secretary of state that the Americans accelerated their financial and ideological attack on the organization—"accelerated," because even before Reagan became president, the United States had temporarily severed its connection with one important UN agency, the ILO.

WITHDRAWAL FROM THE ILO

Moynihan's criticism of the UN during the mid-1970s had focused on General Assembly activity, but it reflected American dismay at the course of Third World behavior in many UN bodies. At the ILO, American conservatives, led by the Chamber of Commerce, had become disenchanted even before the labor organization acquired a Third World majority. One measure of American displeasure could be seen in congressional activity (or inactivity): as early as 1957, Congress had only ratified seven of 106 conventions approved by the ILO. McCarthy-style charges that the organization was "communist dominated" often put ILO supporters on the defensive. Still, strong support for the ILO by the American Federation of Labor provided a degree of protection that the ILO would lose by the seventies.[8]

Another warning sounded in 1971 when Congress refused to appropriate the annual dues payment to the ILO. Cold War rivalry, reinforced by dissension over Vietnam (the hawkish American labor movement became more and more hostile to Third World radicalism in general), contributed to this development. It was not Vietnam, however, but Mideast issues that finally led to the break. When the ILO's General Conference in 1974 condemned Israeli occupation of the West Bank and accused Israel of human rights violations— without investigating the charges or considering Israel's response—the State

Department protested. A year later, the ILO copied the UN by granting observer status to the PLO. This led Secretary of State Kissinger to caution that the United States would withdraw from the ILO following a two-year waiting period unless the labor organization changed its conduct.

Other issues had also contributed to Kissinger's warning, including the resignation in 1970 of American ILO director-general David Morse, and AFL-CIO anger over the appointment of a Soviet assistant director.[9] With the ILO standing firm, and with the AFL-CIO providing key support for Jimmy Carter's 1976 presidential campaign, the new president converted Kissinger's threat into reality. Carter withdrew the United States from the ILO in 1977. The Americans stayed away for three years.

It was not labor-related issues as much as the "politicalization" of the ILO that angered Americans; had the ILO not joined the attempt to delegitimize Israel, the Americans would surely not have left. In addition, the withdrawal debate in Washington made for some strange bedfellows and highlighted unpredictable rivalries. AFL-CIO head George Meany, aided by his allies in the Departments of Labor and Commerce, not to mention the White House, triumphed over opponents of withdrawal including Secretary of State Vance, Ambassador Andy Young, and National Security Adviser (and frequent Vance rival) Zbigniew Brzezinski. A number of craft-union leaders within the AFL-CIO opposed Meany on this issue, while Israeli labor leaders who generally favored ILO membership disagreed with American Jewish leaders who demanded withdrawal.[10]

American withdrawal hurt the ILO badly, not least because the ILO could barely balance its budget without American contributions. But Carter's decision also forced the organization to do a lot of soul-searching that eventually facilitated Washington's return. Satisfied by promises to reform the ILO and no longer badgered by Meany, who died shortly after the decision to withdraw, the United States returned to the organization before the end of Carter's presidency.

Nevertheless, the withdrawal precedent would be applied to other UN agencies during the next administration. Under Reagan, the Americans would suspend their IAEA membership for nearly six months, and their UNESCO involvement for years. The IAEA situation resembled that of the ILO. Angered by Israel's 1981 destruction of Iraq's Osirak nuclear reactor, the IAEA rejected Israel's credentials the following year, which in turn precipitated an American boycott (not as extreme as withdrawal nor requiring an end to the U.S. budgetary contribution).[11] Only when the IAEA director, Hans Blix, promised Israel full standing did the Americans return in February 1983. Critics faulted Washington for inconsistency: defending Israel on grounds of universality but not other countries, like South Africa and Cambodia, that had been expelled earlier.[12] Nevertheless, the State Department had acted decisively; no UN agency would again vote to banish Israel. It is worth noting that despite the ostensible reason for the IAEA's expulsion of

Israel—the attack on the Osirak reactor—the controversy over Israel that led to the American boycott really had little to do with nuclear policy. The Americans rightly complained that the agency's expulsion of Israel carried the IAEA into the swamp of politicalization, sidetracking the organization from its real mission. In this sense, the IAEA case was similar to that of the ILO.

The Reagan administration's withdrawal from UNESCO at the end of 1984 was more ideological. As with the ILO, anti-Israel sentiment within the organization had already resulted in a temporary American cutoff of funds during the mid-1970s. By the early 1980s, UNESCO censured Israel for conducting archeological and educational activity on the West Bank. Again the Americans protested, claiming that UNESCO's condemnation of Israel reflected a political position that should have been handled in the General Assembly or Security Council, not in a functional agency. By this time, however, U.S. dissatisfaction with UNESCO extended far beyond the Third World's obsession with Israel. American officials had come to detest the director-general of UNESCO, Kenya's Amadau-Mahtar M'Bow, whom they considered corrupt, inefficient, and anti-western. More importantly, American news organizations protested mightily when UNESCO resurrected a 1978 plan for a New World Information Order that would require government licensing of journalists and authorize official censorship of news reports. Reflecting Third World unhappiness at the way the western press reported on non-western cultures, the plan was an informational equivalent of the NIEO. It would subordinate the press values of North America and Europe to the political, economic, and cultural needs of the South.

Smart leaders know not to challenge those who buy ink by the barrel. By attacking the western press, UNESCO ignored such wisdom and therefore handed its enemies a powerful weapon. IO chief Greg Newell and his allies in the Reagan administration, who resented UNESCO's cultural internationalism, now attacked the organization with zest. UNESCO had left itself open to damaging criticism, not only because of its information proposal, but because of mismanagement, M'Bow's arrogance, and 1970s-style politicalization regarding Israel and other unpopular governments like South Africa and Portuguese Angola. Newell's proposed reforms for UNESCO merely camouflaged his contempt for the organization. The Reagan administration vented its ire on the politically vulnerable agency, ignoring other UN organs that had greater domestic support. According to political scientist Mark Imber, withdrawal from UNESCO was the product of "an ideologically motivated campaign to achieve the punitive humiliation of a major UN agency."[13] In short, the purpose was punishment, not reform.

The Reagan administration had concluded that it was not advisable to attack the UN directly. Even the anti-UN Heritage Foundation, along with the anticommunists, neoisolationists, and nationalists who might have preferred to see the United States out of the UN, had other things to worry about: funding the Strategic Defense initiative, for instance, or backing rebels in

Nicaragua while opposing insurgents in El Salvador. Few Americans gave opposition to the UN a high priority.

Even as a low priority, however, the U.S. relationship with the UN was guaranteed some attention, especially by the administration and Congress. Unable or unwilling to attack the organization directly, the administration resorted to economic skirmishing. In 1981 and 1982, Congress had already made it clear that expulsion of Israel from the UN would result in a cut-off of U.S. funds to the organization (which would mean not only a financial crisis, but also the probable end of some UN peacekeeping operations such as UNIFIL, and refugee aid through UNRWA). Then in 1983, American diplomats joined their Soviet counterparts to limit spending for agencies ranging from the UN Disaster Relief Organization to the UN Institute for Training and Research. These cuts may have affected the targeted programs, but they failed in their larger purpose: to persuade the Secretariat to limit or reduce UN expenses from 1982 levels. When the 1983 UN budget called for increased expenditures, an angry Congress quickly approved the Kassenbaum amendment. Introduced by Nancy Kassenbaum, a Kansas senator who sought genuine reform—not punishment—of the UN, Congress cut the American contribution to a number of UN agencies from 25 percent to 20 percent, totalling one-half billion dollars over four years.[14]

Although the Reagan administration initially protested this congressional initiative, preferring that UN policy remain an executive prerogative, the administration soon went beyond the Kassenbaum amendment by mandating further reductions based on the Gramm-Rudman Budget Balancing Act that Congress passed in 1985. By 1986, U.S. payments to the UN fell to less than 50 percent of the mandated assessment. Although the State Department's legal office worried about the implications, UN skeptics in the administration—and they were legion—applauded.

Were these cuts legal? International experts disagreed. Congressional and administration critics of the UN admitted that the World Court in 1962 had clearly obligated states to pay their assessments. They argued, however, that when the General Assembly refused to abrogate the USSR's right to vote during the Article 19 crisis in 1964, the UN effectively voided the World Court's opinion.

By the time Kassenbaum introduced her amendment, over 50 countries were in arrears on their payments to the UN. Then, to make matters worse from the U.S. perspective, the Group of 77 persuaded the General Assembly to change the assessment formula. The assembly lowered a member's minimum contribution from .04 percent to .01 percent of the UN budget, and also recalculated the base income of members to benefit newly rich countries like Malaysia, Brazil, and Iraq, but *not* the first-world states.[15]

For pro-UN groups in the United States, these changes could hardly have occurred at a worse time. Even members of Congress sympathetic to the UN had a hard time explaining why a majority of UN members collectively paid less than one percent of the organization's expenses. Nor was this the end of the matter. Congressional conservatives nearly succeeded in cutting off all UN funding until satisfied that Soviet espionage at the UN had ended. To the extent that the Reagan administration increasingly linked American contributions to UN reform, the Secretariat indeed got the message. Reforms, however, rarely occur overnight. By the time Reagan left the White House, the United States owed the UN nearly $520 million. With very little domestic pressure obliging either Congress or the White House to pay America's UN bill, nonpayment became an addiction by the 1990s. Even reform would no longer suffice to persuade Washington to ante up.[16]

THE FALKLANDS

The odd thing was that this economic skirmishing was only loosely related to the political activity of the Security Council, where American activity fell into the business-as-usual category. Washington's inconsistent approach to the council continued during the Reagan administration and was most evident over three controversies: the United Kingdom-Argentine dispute over the Falkland Islands during 1982, the U.S. invasion of Grenada in 1983 when the American military expelled a Marxist government, and American condemnation of the USSR, also in 1983, after the Soviets shot down a Korean Airlines passenger plane.

The Falklands crisis forced the Americans to choose between a NATO ally and an important Latin American friend. When Argentina's military government declared the British-controlled Falklands (Malvinas) to be Argentinean and ordered the British out in March 1982, London prepared for war. A conservative government under Margaret Thatcher resolved to defend itself against what it viewed as Argentinean aggression. The Argentineans, in turn, wrapped themselves in the mantle of anticolonialism. The Americans found themselves in the uncomfortable middle, observing their old allies in a quarrel that had no Cold War ramifications (and therefore would not likely attract a Soviet veto).

The whole episode frayed U.S. nerves. Haig, the former NATO commander, argued in favor of strong support for London once Argentina ordered a surprise landing on April 2, while Kirkpatrick argued equally forcefully that the United States for too long had ignored the needs of Latin America. For Haig, the Atlantic alliance was at risk; for Kirkpatrick, at risk was Third World support for U.S. policy. Moreover, neither Haig nor Kirkpatrick would surrender an ounce of authority to the other. When Haig embarked on a week of shuttle diplomacy to resolve the dispute, Kirkpatrick, unbeknownst to him, conducted talks with Argentine officials in New York and Washington. Both agreed that preventing war was priority number one, but that was all they agreed on. Certainly Haig refused to tolerate the concessions that Kirkpatrick would allow Argentina.

The formal UN role in the crisis began when Britain appealed to the Security Council one day after Argentinean troops landed on the islands. Following the usual appeal for restraint and negotiation, the UN stepped aside while Haig unsuccessfully rode his shuttle searching for a formula to avoid hostilities.[17] When Haig gave up, Secretary-General Perez de Cuellar of Peru attempted to bring the two sides together. An imaginative proposal to fly three flags over the islands (the third would be a UN flag) met with an enthusiastic response from Kirkpatrick, but not from the belligerents. With both sides backed into public positions that would not allow for real compromise, and with Britain confident of a naval victory eight thousand miles from her home ports, the war began in earnest on May 2.

The passage of time had placed the United States in a vulnerable position. Initially, few UN members defined the issue in conventional anticolonialist terms. By the time hostilities commenced, almost all did. London's hard line alienated even her other NATO allies—all, that is, but the Americans. With British forces grinding the Argentineans down, efforts to prevent war evolved into a Latin American resolution for a cease-fire that could not save Argentina's battered military, but might save its face. Yet Britain, anticipating victory, refused to permit even this. Flushed with the cockiness of victory, the British offered no concessions. Kirkpatrick desperately sought to avoid a vote that, should it be tallied, would find a lonely United States joining the United Kingdom in vetoing the cease-fire. In other words, given Haig's pro-British sympathies, the United States would publicly surrender any last pretense of neutrality. From Kirkpatrick's perspective, this would almost certainly alienate most of Washington's Western Hemisphere neighbors.

Haig did exactly what Kirkpatrick feared. Accompanied by both Reagan and Thatcher at a Paris conference, he ordered Kirkpatrick to support the United Kingdom by voting against the cease-fire. Kirkpatrick pleaded to abstain. Even France would abstain, she told him. Haig would not temporize. Perhaps viewing himself as half MacArthur, half Kissinger, he dug in his heels, leaving Kirkpatrick no choice but to join London in vetoing the resolution.

From the perspective of the U.S. delegates in New York, the veto was bad enough. What happened next was worse, for Haig would prove himself to be neither MacArthur nor Kissinger, but a Keystone cop. Minutes after the vote, Kirkpatrick *did* receive a message from Haig ordering her to abstain on the resolution. When she told him that it was too late, that the vote had already been cast, he ordered her to demand a revote so that she could support the cease-fire. From a secretary of state with a control-fixation, this was farcical. In any event, council procedures prevented a revote, and a furious Kirkpatrick told Haig that she would not reverse her position even if the rules permitted it. The farce continued when Haig ordered her into the council to announce that the United States would abstain *if* the vote *could* be retaken. The British were stunned. The disarray reminded some observers of the Truman administration's chaotic policy concerning Palestine's partition in 1948. The Americans had embarrassed themselves while doing nothing to aid the UN in its peacemaking efforts. Kirkpatrick took it all quite personally, coming to believe that the imperious Haig had deliberately tried to humiliate her.[18] Their poisonous relationship had reached its breaking point. Three weeks later, Reagan dismissed Haig.[19]

Ironically, U.S. support for Britain during the Falklands dispute was not reciprocated one year later when President Reagan ordered American troops to overthrow the government of Grenada. A radical government on that Caribbean island had recently deposed a slightly less radical government, summarily executing three of its leaders. Ostensibly to protect U.S. citizens on the island, but actually to limit what the Americans feared would become greater Soviet and Cuban influence, the United States in October 1993 launched a joint military operation with some Lilliputian-like Caribbean allies. Grenada would not become another Cuba.

Washington was playing Goliath. When Nicaragua and Guyana called for a meeting of the Security Council, the Americans found themselves nearly isolated. With most Latin American states repaying the United States for its pro-British stance during the Falklands war, with the British looking for redemption in Latin America, and with almost all of America's closest allies embarrassed by Washington's neo-Dollar Diplomacy, Ambassador Kirkpatrick stood almost alone defending the indefensible. When the Security Council "deplored" the attack as "violating international law and Grenada's independence," she cast the sole veto.[20] Even in the General Assembly, the United States got support only from Israel and those Caribbean allies that were part of the joint invasion force. In an odd twist, State Department officials tied Kirkpatrick's hands. She planned to justify the invasion in terms of the Charter's self-defense language. The department feared, however, that other states might appropriate an "expanded" definition of self-defense for their own purposes.[21] In other words, the department wanted to prevent the erosion of the very Charter principle that it was eroding. Kirkpatrick was reduced to defending U.S. action by asserting what everyone knew was false: that Reagan had ordered the invasion to protect American medical students from the new leftist government. Like Dulles's defense of the Guatemalan operation in 1954, it was a crass performance. Understanding the UN's limitations and perhaps remembering that 1954 precedent, Secretary-General Perez de Cuellar maintained a discreet silence.

CIVIL WAR IN LEBANON

During the waning days of the Falklands dispute, the Israelis launched a military offensive into Lebanon to eliminate the armed PLO presence in that country. At first masking the scope of the operation, Israel advanced to the outskirts of Beirut, angering even some of its American allies when the operation threatened to lead to a wider war with Syria. Also alarming to Israel's western allies was the length of the operation; days turned into weeks filled with TV images of terrified Beruit residents. Most damaging to Israel, however, was an appalling massacre of Palestinian civilians after Israeli authorities permitted the entry of anti-PLO Maronites (Israel's Lebanese allies) into Palestinian refugee camps. In the west, popular support for Israel plummeted.[22]

Israel's offensive raised more than moral issues. It threatened to complicate the U.S. role in the Mideast by snapping the fragile Israeli-Egyptian accord that had followed Israel's return of the Sinai to Egypt in the aftermath of Camp David. Although the United States initially welcomed the invasion, the State Department and Kirkpatrick, too, quickly came to see it as another threat to stability in the region. U.S. policy became a delicate balancing act, especially after Israeli forces laid siege to Beirut in an attempt to destroy the PLO once and for all.

As with previous Israeli military operations, Israel's enemies at the UN quickly called for condemnation and sanctions. The early signs of Israeli mobilization led Jordan to call for an emergency meeting of the Security Council. Despite this warning, the scope of the assault that began on June 6 caught the Americans off guard, leaving them to react defensively and fitfully. An Irish resolution linking a cease-fire with an end to "cross-border attacks" led the Soviets to demand a separation of these goals; Moscow also demanded an "unconditional" Israeli withdrawal.[23] The Americans objected, claiming this would obscure Israel's justification for the operation. By riveting attention on the demand for withdrawal rather than on PLO guerilla attacks, the Soviet amendment would place the United States in an awkward position: either veto the resolution, or join what Washington and USUN viewed as ganging up on Jerusalem. Fearing a wider war, Haig sent Kirkpatrick a simple instruction: join the majority. Kirkpatrick's response was not so simple: she ordered her deputy to explain to the council that although the United States would support the demand for unconditional withdrawal, in fact the United States favored linking withdrawal to the end of PLO raids against Israel. An "inextricable linkage" connected the two. In other words, the United States did *not* favor "unconditional" withdrawal.[24]

When Spain proposed yet another resolution demanding the immediate and total withdrawal of Israeli forces as a foundation for implementing the other UN resolutions, the United States vetoed it.[25] Increasingly, the Americans clarified their own goals, the most important being to weaken if not completely eliminate the PLO in Lebanon. Believing that even Syria had quietly come to see the PLO as an unwelcome rival in Lebanon, American policy makers had few inhibitions about standing alone at the UN.

Yet the Americans did not want a Syrian-Israeli war, which became more likely after Israeli pilots shot down two dozen Syrian planes on June 9. Consequently, Washington held back. With American policy makers divided—Haig and Kirkpatrick detested the PLO, while Vice President George Bush,

Secretary of Defense Casper Weinberger, and the Near East Bureau at the State Department would maintain favor with Egypt by accommodating the PLO—the United States stood near the sidelines. The situation in Lebanon deteriorated as the Israeli army advanced toward Beirut. By the end of June the Americans began to take a more active role once again. No longer content to merely veto resolutions, USUN began to formulate a strategy to resolve the crisis. Linking an Israeli withdrawal to a PLO departure from Lebanon, the American plan resurrected the concept of an "inextricable linkage." But whereas in early June neither the Syrians nor the PLO would take such an idea seriously, Israeli arms narrowed their options by July. The Syrians increasingly feared a direct confrontation with Israel as they came to understand that the Soviets would not bail them out. The PLO was in more dire straits. Facing strangulation, not even its propaganda victories concerning civilian casualties could obscure its military weakness.

The real story, therefore, was written on the battlefield, not in UN chambers. Yet USUN did become central to one final diplomatic drama when the French government with Egypt's assistance introduced a Security Council resolution calling for PLO withdrawal in return for a cease-fire. It demanded Israel's recognition of the "legitimate rights of the Palestinian people," including self-determination—long a code for creating a Palestinian state.[26] To Kirkpatrick, and eventually to the State Department, this formula undermined the basic framework of U.S. policy, which rested on Security Council resolutions 242 and 338. Therefore, the Americans again promised a veto. When the French unexpectedly announced that they would not ask for a vote on their resolution, however, and instead only offer it as a basis for discussion, the UN's role in this crisis effectively ended.[27] Diplomatic attention shifted entirely to American negotiator Philip Habib's efforts to work out the details of moving the PLO from Lebanon to Tunisia. With the PLO increasingly fearful not only of military annihilation, but Syrian control, Yassar Arafat accepted the plan on August 13.

Ironically, the State Department, which had resented Kirkpatrick's independence and tried to limit her role, ultimately benefited from her efforts to keep the French plan (which the Americans disliked) under consideration. Why? Because UN discussion of the plan allowed time for Habib to succeed in his own efforts. Nevertheless, USUN's role during this episode reveals some odd twists. Haig and Kirkpatrick had come to detest each other, yet they agreed enough on policy to cooperate in ways that preserved U.S. influence with both Egypt and Israel. After Reagan fired Haig in the midst of the Lebanon crisis, Kirkpatrick went out of her way to let Haig's successor, George Shultz, know that she would be a team player. She muted her criticism of State Department policy, especially policy from the Bureau of Near East Affairs that she considered too sympathetic to the PLO (just as the bureau believed she was too pro-Israel). In fact, Shultz and Kirkpatrick did not always agree: Shultz accepted the bureau's view—not USUN's view—of the PLO. But by the time

Shultz got his diplomatic feet on the ground, the PLO had lost its voice, allowing the new secretary to overlook the divisions between U.S. officials in Washington and New York.

KOREAN AIRLINES TRAGEDY

If resolution of the Lebanon crisis kept the Americans focusing on diplomatic activity outside the UN, the USSR's downing of a Korean airliner on September 1, 1983, enabled the Reagan administration to use the UN as a stage for an international morality play in much the way that Kennedy had used it during the missile crisis. The bare facts of the matter were quite clear: Soviet fighter planes had fired air-to-air missiles at a Korean civilian airliner that for two hours had flown off course over Soviet airspace. Two minutes later, the Boeing 747 plunged into the Sea of Japan, killing 269 passengers and crew members, many of them American. After initially condemning the Soviet action, Reagan administration officials learned that both American and Japanese intelligence had monitored the conversation among the Soviet pilots. Tapes of these conversations proved that the airliner received no warning and that the Russians fired their missiles deliberately.[28]

Although the tapes did not prove that the Russian pilots knew KAL 007 was a civilian aircraft, the State Department anticipated a sweet propaganda victory. The department prepared a dog and pony show to rival what Stevenson had done with the photos of Soviet missiles in 1962. Shultz immediately recalled Kirkpatrick from Morocco, then permitted her chief deputy to denounce the Soviets in unusually undiplomatic language. But the main event would await Kirkpatrick. With the Soviet UN representative denying that Russia downed the plane, Kirkpatrick ostentatiously unveiled the tapes at a Security Council meeting. They left little to the imagination.

Skeptics would later float a number of theories as to why the airliner flew over Soviet territory. Some theorized that the Americans or Koreans wanted to locate Soviet radar defenses; others surmised that the plane was photographing Soviet military installations. Nothing could be proven, and the most authoritative study of the incident suggests pilot error.[29] Regardless of these theories, the Soviets, who inexplicably denied responsibility even after the tapes had been produced, looked like liars, not merely bunglers or outlaws. By denying responsibility, the Soviets enabled the Americans to marshall a Security Council majority to denounce the destruction of the airliner in an unambiguous resolution. "Violence and lies are regular instruments of Soviet policy," Kirkpatrick told her international audience; the Soviet state is based on "the dual principles of callousness and mendacity."[30]

The Soviets, of course, vetoed the resolution. Rather than resolving a conflict, the Security Council stage show worsened U.S.-Soviet relations. The White House in 1983 had no interest in reducing friction. Even the nonaligned states who usually avoided direct denunciation of the USSR obliged the United States. For good or ill, both sides—the United States by its rigid damning of Soviet behavior, the Soviets by their inept and preposterous defense—used the UN in ways that once again proved the organization's inability to beat Cold War swords into plowshares.

The secretary-general had been unable to head off the misuse of the UN over KAL 007. Javier Perez de Cuellar had been elected to his post in 1981 when China saved the UN from embarrassment by vetoing Kurt Waldheim's hopes for a third term. As had often occurred before, the new secretary-general was no one's first choice. By threatening a veto, the Americans paid back the early favorite for the secretary-general's post, Salim Ahmed Salim of Tanzania, for his anti-American celebration following China's admission to the UN. A half dozen other candidates soon canceled each other out. That left Perez de Cuellar, a quiet and intellectual Peruvian diplomat, who had served as Lima's ambassador in Moscow and earned a Soviet abstention (the Soviets traditionally threatened to veto candidates from the Western Hemisphere). Perez de Cuellar would exceed the expectations of many critics, although he lacked the forcefulness of Sweden's Hammarskjold, who set the standard for the office. The Peruvian's failures to prevent violence in the Falklands and Lebanon represented an inauspicious start. His subsequent direction of the UN resulted in some genuine successes, most notably in Cambodia and El Salvador, and also in prodding the UN bureaucracy toward U.S.-inspired reform. In hotspots like Afghanistan, his influence proved slight; in the Iran-Iraq war, which lasted for eight years, his considerable efforts eventually paid real dividends.

THE IRAN-IRAQ WAR

The UN has tackled some long-term disputes during its history: Cyprus, for instance, where UN peacekeepers have patrolled for decades, and the Mideast, where UN observers have come and gone since the late 1940s. Measured in these terms, the Iran-Iraq war of the 1980s was brief. To the new secretary-general, however, it was his longest lasting headache.

Iraq launched the war in September 1980 to gain control of oil-rich territory in Iran, to weaken the Shiite influence of the Iranian revolutionaries (an important minority of Iraq is Shiite), and to expand its own influence in the region. With Iran undergoing revolutionary turmoil and isolated by its role in the hostage dispute, the Iraqi leader, Saddam Hussein, gambled on a quick victory. He failed. After initial Iraqi victories, the Iranians counterattacked in early 1981 and, despite huge manpower losses, expelled Iraqi troops from Iranian territory. By 1982 the conflict increasingly looked like a stalemate. Neither Iraq's superior military equipment nor its use of poison gas could overcome the effects of Iran's larger army and revolutionary zeal.

Historians of the Cold War have long argued that although the UN has been impotent in disputes involving the Great Powers, it has had plenty of success dealing with smaller countries that have no permanent veto. Unfortunately, success eluded the organization during the Iran-Iraq conflict, where the UN remained impotent for years. What seems odd is that UN ineffectiveness persisted despite the fact that neither superpower had much sympathy with the belligerents. Both Washington and Moscow desired a regional power balance in the oil-rich area, and both favored free navigation through the Persian Gulf. Their mutual interests might have led them to advocate strong UN action to preserve peace; instead, preoccupied with their own rivalry from Afghanistan to Nicaragua, they sat on their hands, thus neutralizing the UN in the Persian Gulf until the late 1980s.

Within days of the initial Iraqi attack, then-Secretary-General Waldheim had asked both powers to settle the problem peacefully and offered his own good offices; he also asked for "consultation" among the members of the Security Council. Little materialized. Not only did the Security Council elect an Iraqi president at this critical moment, but the first resolution passed by the council referred only to a "situation"—no mention then of a dispute much less a conflict.[31] With both superpowers declaring their neutrality, it appeared that all parties hoped for a quick victory and a return to the pre-war balance.

These were empty hopes. A number of desultory council meetings followed. By mid-October, Iran adopted a policy it would hold for the next few years: it would not permit a cease fire until Iraqi troops had been repulsed, and Iraq vanquished and punished. The Iranian representative declared, "The decision of the Council, whatever it may be, will not change anything for us."[32]

Other than the failed mission of former Swedish prime minister Olaf Palme to mediate the dispute (he travelled to the region five times as a representative of the secretary-general), the conflict temporarily dropped off the UN's horizon. Not until 1982 did it reappear, and then only sporadically. With the resurgence of Iranian military fortunes, Baghdad, which had foolishly started the war, looked for a way out. It encouraged UN intervention as enthusiastically as the Iranians resisted it. Iran's reasons for rejecting UN diplomacy ranged from the strategic to the theological, but the country's revolutionary (Americans often said pathological) hostility toward the United States must be placed near the top of the list. This hostility remained intact during the long conflict. During 1985 and 1986, for instance, the American government clearly tilted toward Iraq, sending arms to Baghdad and even removing Iraq from the list of states suspected of sponsoring terrorism. The Iranians scoffed at American protestations of neutrality.

Nevertheless, aided powerfully by the belligerents' mutual exhaustion, the UN did eventually help to end the war. Cameron Hume, a former U.S. diplomat who worked closely with USUN during the decade, argues that Perez de Cuellar transformed the Security Council into a meaningful instrument of peace by initiating informal meetings among the five permanent powers. For the first time, according to Hume, Soviet and Chinese delegates actively cooperated with their western counterparts to line up support for an end to the conflict. At the same time, the State Department announced its support for an arms embargo against Iran and, in the event that Iran refused to accept a cease-fire, economic sanctions. This kind of rhetoric might have been dismissed two years earlier. By 1987, however, the council was travelling on a much more cooperative track. Moreover, Washington backed up its diplomatic language with military pressure, warning Iran against initiating naval action against neutral shipping in the Persian Gulf and reflagging Kuwaiti tankers under American registry.

Out of all this came Resolution 598 calling for an "immediate cease-fire," and a mutual withdrawal of military forces to "the internationally recognized borders without delay."[33] Iran predictably denounced the resolution as "a vicious American diplomatic manoeuver." Careful observers noticed, however, that Teheran, which had only recently begun talking to the UN again, did not completely reject 598. A conversation began that ended a year later when Iran finally accepted the cease-fire demand.

That conversation was not an easy one. Before it finally ended, the United States had initiated air attacks on Iranian gunboats threatening the reflagged tankers, and apologized when the USS *Vincennes* mistakenly shot down an Iranian civilian airliner carrying 290 passengers and crew. The Americans also failed to persuade the Soviets and Chinese to implement economic sanctions against Iran before Teheran accepted the cease-fire. While the Soviets remained skeptical of U.S. aims in the Persian Gulf, China protested U.S. efforts to prevent American allies from purchasing Chinese arms (some of which might be redirected to Iran) and denounced Iraqi use of poison gas and the USS *Vincennes*'s action. Perhaps sanctions would have stiffened Iran's resistance rather than weakened it. Perhaps, too, the Iranians were as influenced by domestic politics as international developments. Almost certainly, the Iranians were swayed by recent Iraqi military victories on Iranian soil. But with Saddam Hussein now agreeing that his troops would not remain in Iran, the government in Teheran accepted the terms of 598 almost one year to the day after passage of the original resolution.

Secretary of State Shultz would later write that President Reagan's "resolve" and "persistence" had been key to this settlement.[34] The secretary was being modest. Certainly Reagan supported Shultz against the NSC when it came to applying American military pressure in the Persian Gulf. But it was the State Department, not the White House, that made and coordinated U.S. policy leading to the UN-sponsored cease-fire; and it was Shultz and Ambassador Vernon Walters, Kirkpatrick's 1985 replacement at USUN, who deserve the credit. Shultz resisted the temptation to humiliate Iran. Walters, unlike his predecessor, was a pragmatist and conciliator. Aided by the exhaustion of both belligerents, the two men skillfully promoted Perez de Cuellar's mediation efforts.

LATIN AMERICA

The Reagan administration promoted no one's mediation efforts in Latin America. Among the most troublesome problems for American policy makers during the 1990s were El Salvador, where the United States supported a right-wing government against leftist guerrillas, and Nicaragua, where Washington aided right-wing rebels against the leftist Sandinista government of Daniel Ortega. As with Grenada, the State Department did not welcome UN involvement in a region that Reagan administration officials continued to consider an American sphere of influence. Secretariat officials fully understood that a U.S. veto would loom over any anti-American resolution proposed in the Security Council. Nevertheless, America's influence by no means ended UN activity in Latin America. The General Assembly's decision in 1982 to seat Nicaragua on the Security Council signaled continuing resentment at the U.S. role during the Falklands war. This virtually guaranteed, from Washington's perspective, unwelcome criticism during debates concerning Grenada and Central America.

It was not in the Security Council, however, that U.S. policy regarding Nicaragua was most dramatically—and literally—put on trial. It was in the International Court of Justice (World Court), where the 15-member tribunal ruled provisionally against the United States on May 10, 1984 (and formally on June 27, 1986), in a case brought by Nicaragua accusing the United States of violating international law by aiding the "contra" rebels opposing the Managua government. Then in November 1984, the court rejected a similar claim by El Salvador charging that Nicaragua's assistance to guerrillas fighting the pro-American regime in El Salvador violated international law.[35]

On the face of things, these rulings created a legal double standard. The court had reasoned that Nicaragua's aid to the Salvadorean rebels had not exceeded a threshold of volume so large as to become illegal. In contrast, the court ruled that U.S. aid to the contras, including the mining of Managua harbor, did exceed that threshold.[36] But the whole affair was more than a legal disaster from Washington's perspective. By the time the court issued its opinion, the case had already become a public relations disaster. Alerted to the likely political nature of the ruling shortly before the case was formally argued, the Americans outraged internationalists by withdrawing their 1946 acceptance of the court's compulsory jurisdiction in cases affecting American interests (unless specific treaties guaranteed the court such jurisdiction, which was not the case in this instance). Although few countries unreservedly accepted the court's compulsory jurisdiction, domestic critics of the administration's Nicaraguan policy damned the administration for what Daniel Moynihan described as "a combination of ineptitude and arrogance." The former permanent representative, whose reverence for law equaled his anger at the General Assembly's double standard, noted that it was as if his own government "had suffered a massive stroke and all memory of a vital and fundamental [legal] tradition had vanished."[37]

The administration had stumbled into a no-win situation: be hammered for repudiating the court's compulsory jurisdiction, or be hammered for acting illegally in Nicaragua. In this case, it was hammered for both. State Department policy had been poorly coordinated throughout the affair, first rejecting the court's authority, then reversing the rejection, and then reversing the reversal. Washington and USUN had offered up another textbook case of policy confusion. Reagan conservatives, who for the past decade had criticized the General Assembly majority for breaking the law, now found themselves repudiating the one international organ that most clearly stood for the rule of law. A few argued that the episode exposed as myth the World Court's impartiality. It was time, wrote Kirkpatrick's legal adviser, to recognize the court as "part and parcel of the UN system and its politics."[38]

The Reagan administration's clumsy rejection of the court's jurisdiction reflected the general weakening of internationalism. Likewise did reductions in the U.S. financial contribution to the UN. So too did congressional measures in the mid-1980s requiring the president and secretary of state to inform Congress about the votes of every UN member on matters of interest to the United States.[39] Designed to connect Washington's multilateral and bilateral diplomacy, these measures permitted American diplomats to better evaluate whether a particular country deserved U.S. support for, say, Security Council membership or higher levels of American aid. The spirit of Moynihan's proposal for diplomatic rewards and penalties was alive and well.

"The Twilight of Internationalism" was how Carnegie Endowment for Peace president Thomas L. Hughes titled the most important article on the subject of U.S. multilateral diplomacy during the Reagan years. Hughes argued that a number of factors combined to weaken the commitment to international cooperation that had stood unchallenged since the years of Woodrow Wilson. The marriage of conservative anticommunism and Wilsonian liberalism had, according to Hughes, produced postwar internationalism: the 1980s witnessed their divorce. A resurgence of populist and evangelical nationalism, fear of U.S. decline in a complex and international economy, cultural shock over Vietnam, military impotence in places like Iran and Afghanistan, the loss of U.S. influence in the UN and of U.S. ideological innocence all contributed, said Hughes, to the loss of internationalist faith. Sudden changes of direction, such as Nixon's turn toward China—he might also have mentioned Reagan's retreat from Lebanon after the 1983 bombing of the U.S. Marine barracks—led to cynicism about further international involvement. "The Reaganites sleep better at night knowing that the UN's 40th anniversary was a wake," wrote Hughes.[40]

But what Hughes, and many other so-called experts, had not yet foreseen was the dramatic change in U.S.-Soviet relations that characterized the last three years of the Reagan administration. It injected new vigor into internationalism. Battered by the Iran-Contra affair and mellowed by admiration for

Soviet Premier Mikhail Gorbachev, President Reagan and Secretary of State George Shultz had joined their Soviet counterparts to engineer what would soon look like a diplomatic revolution. Internationalism may have been wounded, but it was far from dead. In New York, the cooperation between the United States and the USSR that had helped to end the Iran-Iraq war became routine by the conclusion of Reagan's presidency. The beneficiaries were soldiers and civilians trapped in civil wars that had raged for a decade or more, most notably in Angola, Namibia, Nicaragua, and El Salvador.

The Latin American settlements would occur during the next administration, but the southern African accord was signed while Reagan and Shultz still held office. The discord in Angola and Namibia went back decades. The efforts of Donald McHenry and his colleagues in the UN "contact group" of the late 1970s had nearly brought the Namibian dispute to resolution, but South Africa had held out for a degree of control that Namibian rebels would not accept. Reagan administration policy during the early 1980s had shifted American sympathies even closer to the South Africans, with the United States vetoing UN sanctions against Pretoria in 1982.

"Constructive engagement,"[41] Reagan called his policy; critics called it unconstructive appeasement. But the administration's sympathy for South Africa may have been more apparent than real. In Angola, for example, where a Marxist government tolerated Cuban troops and aided the rebels in Namibia, State Department denunciation of Soviet and Cuban involvement stood in contrast with U.S. approval of Export/Import Bank loans and increasing business and diplomatic contact.[42] Especially under Shultz and his chief African deputy, Chester Crocker, American policy was much more pragmatic than its anticommunist rhetoric implied.

Such pragmatism made the final Angolan-Namibian agreement possible. The pro-South African group in the administration was led by ideological hardliners such as CIA Director William Casey and NSC adviser Admiral John Poindexter. After 1986, their influence declined precipitously as a result of the Iran-Contra scandal (Casey soon died). With Congress showing less sympathy for Pretoria and with American firms leaving South Africa, the influence of Shultz and Crocker soared. And when in early 1988 the Cubans, themselves subject to a reduction of Soviet support, evinced a willingness to withdraw their units from Angola, the Cold War implications of the Angolan-Namibian-South African situation faded away. With the British pressuring the South Africans and the Soviets pressuring the Angolans and Cubans, Crocker concluded a package deal that finally ended the dispute. It included the implementation of Resolution 435, resulting in a cease-fire, Namibian independence, free elections, and the formal withdrawal of all Cuban and South African troops. Although the UN had not brokered the arrangement, two decades of UN diplomacy served as its foundation. Secretary Shultz recognized the UN's contribution by traveling to New York for the signing of the peace agreement. He looked forward, he said, to "a new usefulness to the United Nations."[43]

He would not have to wait long. What is noteworthy is that his praise of—and hopes for—a revived UN role grew out of the work of an administration that in 1981 had expressed something between indifference and contempt for the organization. While the Soviet-American role had changed dramatically, the U.S.-UN relationship had changed subtly. To the degree that Washington proved willing to approach the UN pragmatically and not ideologically during Shultz's tenure at the State Department, internationalism's "twilight" would remain on hold.

chapter 10

BUSH

When Thomas Hughes offered his gloomy prognosis for the UN in his 1985 article "The Twilight of Internationalism," he could hardly have known that the next president of the United States would be the only White House occupant who had previously served as a permanent representative to the UN. Nor could even the most optimistic UN proponent dream that the organization was about to enjoy its most promising chapter in decades.

George W. Bush had the good fortune to move into the White House just months before the Berlin Wall came tumbling down. Although he campaigned as a Republican conservative, his foreign policy views reflected little sympathy with the neoisolationism espoused by many members of the coalition that elected him to office. Having been director of the CIA and, later, vice president under Reagan, Bush was a pragmatist whose views were much closer to those of George Shultz than to those of the cold warriors whose real commitment to international cooperation extended only as deep as their anti-communism. Bush would be the last president who had grown to maturity during World War II. Supportive of Reagan's efforts in the areas of arms limitation and lowering trade barriers, Bush saw the UN not as a panacea for the world's problems, but surely as a palliative.

Bush's secretary of state also prided himself on his nonideological approach to foreign affairs. James A. Baker had only limited influence in the foreign policy arena, but he was smart, tough-minded, and agile. As Reagan's secretary of the treasury, he had helped broker currency agreements to make American commerce more competitive at a time when the United States was running huge trade deficits, and when the global primacy of the American economy could no longer be taken for granted. Baker, who had long outgrown his idealism, had no special affection for the UN, but he recognized its usefulness as a means to simplify diplomatic communications and cooperation.[1] He believed that it might, if used carefully, help to stabilize a fractious international system both politically and economically.

Baker was an instinctively political being (he titled his memoirs *The Politics of Diplomacy*). His fear of the factionalism that at times had crippled Reagan's presidency led him to support Brent Scowcroft as National Security Adviser. Scowcroft, a former Kissinger deputy, who had already headed the NSC under President Ford, was loyal and level-headed. He lacked Baker's will to power, and he detested bureaucratic rivalries. In other ways, though, he was a quieter version of Baker, a calming influence during a turbulent four years. At a time when the end of the Cold War made ideology more a burden than a help, the Bush foreign policy team was able to travel light. None of them had a well thought out vision of the future, but all three understood that it would not look like the past. They were good negotiators, and they appreciated the UN as the premier palace of negotiation.

As a result, they knew they needed a good negotiator at the UN. Bush selected Thomas Pickering, a career diplomat in the mold of Charles Yost and Donald McHenry. Like Vernon Walters before him, Pickering lacked the cabinet status and personal connection to the president that had elevated the stature of many predecessors at USUN, but he understood the diplomatic game as well as any of his contemporaries and commanded the loyalty and respect of his staff. During his four years in New York, the UN reestablished a high profile. With the White House offering strong support, the U.S. Mission in New York could afford a skillful technician rather than a well-known personality.

There were few signs at the time of Bush's inauguration that the UN's importance would inflate during the next four years, but UN insiders knew two things. First, the cooperation of Gorbachev and Reagan had already reinvigorated the Security Council; witness the Iran-Iraq armistice and the Namibian settlement. Second, the last years of the Reagan administration witnessed the creation of the first UN peacekeeping operations in over a decade, including UNGOMAP, established to oversee the withdrawal of Soviet troops in Afghanistan and Pakistan, and UNIIMOG, established to supervise the Iran-Iraq armistice. The United States supported both operations in order to secure settlements that Washington had favored for nearly a decade.

These were just the beginning. The fading Cold War meant that settlements in other trouble spots became possible, leading to a veritable explosion of peacekeeping operations. By the end of January 1989, UN peacekeeping had been authorized for both Namibia (UNTAG) and Angola (UNAVEM), part of the UN-brokered comprehensive settlement in southern Africa that ended European colonialism on that continent. During the next five years, Washington and the other permanent members of the Security Council would authorize an additional 18 peacekeeping operations, a number that exceeded *all* the peacekeeping missions of the UN's first 45 years. Unfortunately for the organization, this new activity coincided with the refusal of the United States and some other members to pay their UN debts. Peacekeeping came at a high price, contributing to a sour irony: the financial crisis that threatened to destroy the UN by the mid-1990s was in part a product of the international community's new confidence in the organization. (This will be discussed in greater detail in chapter 11.)

PEACE IN CENTRAL AMERICA

Washington's enthusiasm for peacekeeping during the Bush administration was hardly uniform. The State Department and the White House supported some missions—such as El Salvador (ONUSAL) and Nicaragua (ONU-CA)—much more enthusiastically than others, such as the 1994 rescue operation in Rwanda (UNAMIR). Where it offered strong support, the Bush administration almost invariably favored the UN doing collectively what the United States could (or would) not do alone. The Nicaragua mission was quite modest. Factors extraneous to the UN had led to a settlement there: Soviets and Americans had grown weary of the conflict; economic pressures and the palpable benefits of a rapprochement with the United States led Soviet leaders to curtail their aid (and by extension, Cuban aid) to the Sandinistas. On the American side, the Iran-Contra affair alerted U.S. policy makers to the huge political risks that Nicaragua represented. These factors, combined with the exhaustion of the combatants, produced an agreement in February 1989 to implement a 1987 arrangement calling for a cease-fire and elections, to end the most vexing conflict in the Western Hemisphere since 1945, or at least since the Cuban crisis. The Security Council limited the UN role to supervising the February 1990 elections, though UN observers remained for another two years. The UN had proved to be a minor convenience, not a major factor, in the restoration of peace.

In El Salvador, the UN role turned out to be much more significant. Here the United States had protected a repressive and often brutal rightist regime against a popular insurgency aided by influential elements of the Catholic hierarchy. Reagan officials had viewed this conflict through ideological blinders that they had already abandoned in other areas, such as Angola and Cambodia. Peace became possible when the Bush administration, in the words of the secretary of state, decided to get both Nicaragua and El Salvador "off the domestic political agenda," and therefore backed a UN mediation role that lasted from 1989 to 1991.[2] With both the Americans and Soviets no longer willing to fight proxy wars in the area, with the Nicaraguan election guaranteeing that Managua's aid to the rebels would end, and with Castro less able to intervene as Soviet support to Havana diminished, mediation brought about a compromise agreement. It not only produced a cease-fire but allowed for human rights investigations supervised by a UN observer mission. Even the conservative president of El Salvador later admitted that there could not have been peace without the UN's intervention.[3]

Secretary Baker offered solace for congressional conservatives who hated to compromise with Marxist groups, but he often ended with "but we don't have the votes."[4] His solace may or may not have been genuine, but he fully understood that the Bush administration did not have enough congressional support to reject the need to compromise in Central America. He also believed that the UN, despite isolationist and conservative objections, could facilitate political compromise better than any other international agency. Such views were shared by Bernard Aronson, a Democrat who served as his assistant secretary for inter-American affairs. Like the secretary of state, Aronson played a critical role in both the Nicaraguan and El Salvadoran settlements. Indeed, during the Bush administration, the regional divisions headed by assistant secretaries such as Aronson played a much more important role in policy making than the assistant secretary for international organization. This was true even of matters that centrally involved the UN, such as the most important Asian issue before the organization—Cambodia.

THE CAMBODIAN CIVIL WAR

Like the Central American disputes, the civil war in Cambodia was more than just an internal conflict, and the anguish that Secretary of State Vance had experienced when he ordered Ambassador McHenry to support Pol Pot's application for a UN seat was merely one small moment in a continuing tragedy. For more than 15 years, the Cambodian conflict pitted a genocidal faction—the Khmer Rouge—against a faction supported by neighboring Vietnam and led by Hun Sen. The war had become a fratricidal struggle between ideological bedfellows. During its early phase when genocide peaked, the UN had ignored the conflict entirely. With China backing the Khmer Rouge and the Soviets supporting the Vietnamese-backed government in Phnom Penh, the permanent veto guaranteed UN inaction.

After the fall of South Vietnam, American officials no longer claimed that Washington had vital interests in Cambodia. For the next 15 years, however, they continued to support their Asian allies in seeking a Cambodian settlement, expecting that peace would confer political, economic, and humanitarian benefits. With the end of the Cold War signaling that the struggle in Cambodia no longer served the interests of any outside country, with the Vietnamese announcing that they would withdraw their troops from Cambodia (raising the possibility of another Khmer Rouge-sponsored genocide), with the Chinese government seeking international respectability after the Tiananmen Square massacre, and with the Bush administration refusing to ostracize China on humanitarian grounds, the UN augmented separate negotiations already being conducted at the 1991 International Paris Conference on Cambodia to settle the conflict. Calling for elections and a cease-fire, the Security Council's Resolution 718 of October 31, 1991, approved a plan negotiated at the Paris conference. A decade earlier, it would have been stymied by the now obsolete U.S.-USSR-PRC rivalry.[5]

The plan was ambitious. During 1992 and 1993, the UN sent 22,000 peacekeeping troops in two separate forces (UNAMIC, a small advance team; and UNTAC, the main force) to maintain the cease-fire and oversee elections. When Pol Pot's Khmer Rouge denounced the elections, the UN rejected a military confrontation. Instead, UNTAC isolated the Khmer Rouge, with UN peacekeepers helping to curtail the sporadic fighting that had so long divided the warring parties. Had it enlisted more peacekeepers, UNTAC might have taken control of the political process; with its limited numbers (large by UN standards, but not enough to pacify or disarm the disputants), it tailored its role to electoral supervision, humanitarian protection, and "quick impact" civic action projects related to infrastructure repair and economic reform.[6]

In all of this, the Americans played a secondary role. Having discovered after Vietnam exactly how unvital the area was, U.S. officials never again gave a high priority to Cambodia. No U.S. troops served in UNTAC. But neither did the Americans hinder the UN, recognizing that a UN settlement would keep Vietnam out of Cambodian affairs, which in turn would lessen the risk of Chinese involvement. To damn the UN for inaction during the genocidal 1970s, as some critics do, is to miss the point; until the Great Powers were willing to cooperate in the Security Council, as they did after 1991, there could be no Cambodian peace.[7]

UN officials learned much about peacekeeping during the early 1990s, about its potential for both success and failure. The achievements of the UN in Cambodia and El Salvador rested on the exhaustion of the warring parties, their mutual willingness to tolerate outside intervention (more in El Salvador than Cambodia), and a clear UN mandate. Success also required the financial resources necessary to do the job, along with a well-defined UN command and adequate training.[8] The mixed record of UN peacekeeping owed much to the degree to which some, but usually not all, of these conditions were present. The most notable failures—Somalia and Bosnia—would later illustrate what happens when these ingredients are absent.

THE GULF WAR

But the UN during Bush's presidency did more than peacekeeping. Saddam Hussein's invasion of Kuwait in August 1990 would trigger the most important UN military operation since Korea. "Peace enforcement," UN officials called it. Operating under Chapter 7 of the Charter, a military coalition gave internationalists reason to believe that the collective-security machinery designed in 1945 just might guarantee what President Bush and NSC chief Brent Scowcroft repeatedly described as a "new world order."

Burning oil wells in Kuwait three weeks after the Gulf War ended.
March 25, 1991.
(UN/DPI photo by J. Isaac)

Iraq had never reconciled itself to an independent Kuwait, but Iraqi preoccupation with its war against Iran had left the medieval oil barons of Kuwait
quite secure during the 1980s. The end of the Iran-Iraq war in 1988 finally
gave Saddam Hussein the freedom he needed to prepare for an assault on his
vulnerable neighbor. Nor had the West unambiguously warned him against
such a plan. Fearing an expansionist Iran, the United States and its Western
European allies offered Hussein economic and military support, including
agricultural credits that he diverted to the purchase of war materials. Such aid

may well have persuaded him that he could attack Kuwait with impunity. Just days before the attack, the U.S. ambassador in Baghdad, April C. Glaspie, apparently failed to convey a clear warning about Iraqi expansion.[9] Mixed messages—from the State Department to Glaspie and from Glaspie to Saddam Hussein and the Iraqi foreign minister—reflected policy confusion, perhaps even an intelligence failure. In Washington, photo intelligence about Iraqi troops movements on the Kuwait frontier had not been taken seriously enough. No country—not even Israel—believed that an attack was imminent at the end of July.

Nevertheless, the American government was as committed to guaranteeing its access to Middle Eastern oil in 1990 as it was when Jimmy Carter proclaimed the Carter Doctrine a decade earlier. When, therefore, reports reached the White House on August 1 (Washington time) that Iraqi troops were storming into Kuwait, the Bush administration reacted swiftly. The State Department ordered Ambassador Pickering to call for a special meeting of the Security Council, and the United States cosponsored Resolution 660 condemning the attack and calling for Iraqi withdrawal. Even Cuba supported it.[10]

By basing the resolution on the Charter's Chapter 7, the Americans reserved the option to employ UN economic or military sanctions against Iraq if Baghdad refused to withdraw. Four days after 660 passed, the Security Council approved an arms embargo and broad economic sanctions against Iraq.[11] With the Soviets supporting these resolutions, American policy makers were rescued from needing to act unilaterally. Multilateral diplomacy, believed Secretary Baker, was much preferable to operating as a "Lone Ranger." UN cooperation would offer a "breadth of support," enough, hoped Baker, to convince Hussein that he confronted the "entire civilized world, not just a single superpower he might be able to demonize."[12]

Less than three years earlier, *New Republic* columnist Charles Krauthammer had called for U.S. withdrawal from the UN.[13] He had spoken for a growing number of conservatives and neoliberals, including some who served in the Reagan administration. After the Iraqi invasion, the success of Bush and Baker in using the UN to protect what millions of Americans believed to be a vital Mideast oil interest silenced this kind of criticism. Somalia would later revive it, but for the time being, Bush secured more support for the organization than it had enjoyed for decades.

Critical to that support were the efforts of Pickering. One journalist claimed that Pickering "dominated the Security Council in a way that no American ambassador, not even Adlai Stevenson, had ever done before": cajoling, persuading, threatening, compromising.[14] His low-key but exceedingly skillful diplomacy resulted in a small cascade of resolutions that converted the supposedly anti-American UN into a bureau of the State Department. Virtually all these resolutions were authored in Washington. Pickering deserves credit for getting the Security Council to pass most of them unanimously. Of course he did not do this alone. By 1990, the Berlin Wall had fallen and the Soviets (and, to a lesser extent, even the Chinese) had lost their interest in supporting former Cold War clients who offered more trouble than help. To the extent that Gorbachev had come to value Washington's friendship more than Baghdad's, the Soviet leader backed Bush and Britain's Margaret Thatcher, who took an uncompromisingly hard line against Saddam Hussein. True, the Soviets had misgivings about seeing U.S. troops massing in Saudi Arabia for a possible assault on Iraq, but they kept their reservations out of the Security Council.

Resolutions 661, which included an oil embargo, and 670, which the Security Council passed at the ministerial level to add a total air embargo to the earlier trade restrictions, should have signaled to the Iraqis just how serious the UN was.[15] Recalling the disruption following Iran's 1979 decision to cut off oil exports, the Americans in1990—along with their European and Asian allies—faced an even greater oil deficit with the loss of shipments from Iraq and Kuwait. In 1990, however, they would not be caught by surprise. Assurances that Saudi Arabian exports would fill the gap muffled potential discontent at home. During subsequent weeks, additional resolutions further isolated Iraq, culminating in Resolution 678, which authorized the "use of all necessary means" to expel Saddam Hussein's army from Kuwait by January 15, 1991.[16] Secretary Baker pulled no punches. When Yemen denounced U.S. policy before joining lonely Cuba in voting against 678, he scribbled to an aide that "Yemen's permanent rep. just enjoyed about $200 to $250 million worth of applause for that speech."[17] As council president that month, Baker carefully orchestrated the debate. He even arranged to have foreign ministers, rather than permanent representatives, sitting at the council table, only the fourth time this had occurred since the UN's birth.

So the pendulum had swung back to multilateral diplomacy. Baker's memoirs make clear that American policy makers—and Margaret Thatcher, too— believed that the United States *could* take unilateral action under the Charter's self-defense Article 51. But where Thatcher believed that the United States *should* act unilaterally, the White House and State Department agreed that "as a practical matter the United States had no choice but to try the coalition approach. . . ."[18]

Nevertheless, multilateralism had its limits. *Without* consulting the UN, President Bush had announced his decision to send U.S. troops to Saudi Arabia. *Without* seeking UN authorization, the United States initially resolved to intercept Iraqi ships headed to their home ports, although a Security Council resolution did, in fact, eventually provide this authority. When Soviet Foreign Minister Eduard Shevardnadze proposed reviving the UN's military staff committee to coordinate possible armed measures against Iraq, the suggestion, according to Baker, "went nowhere" with a White House that wanted to minimize Soviet influence in the peacekeeping field.[19] Even so, Baker won his own battle within the foreign policy apparatus when, against the opposition of

UNSCOM officials at Jabel Hamraym, site of an Iraqi supergun that had been under construction when the Gulf War started. August 11, 1991. (UN/DPI Photo by H. Arvidsson)

the Defense Department and the Joint Chiefs, he won presidential approval to invite the Soviets to be part of the military coalition (they refused).

The issue of using military force against Saddam Hussein became especially serious in early October 1990 when American policy makers concluded that economic sanctions would not dislodge the Iraqi army from Kuwait. From then on, the Americans pursued a dual strategy: one offered verbal support for economic sanctions, the other prepared for war. Even before passage of Resolution 678, the Defense Department had resolved to double the number of U.S. troops in Saudi Arabia, at the same time urging America's coalition partners to increase their military presence in the area. To marshall political support from the Security Council and military support from potential allies, the State Department promised much: credits to some, cancellation of debts to others, a curtailing of human rights complaints to still others. Two hundred thousand troops in October grew to more than 600,000 by January 1991. The military buildup known as Desert Shield would soon become Desert Storm. When neither Saddam Hussein nor George Bush encouraged compromise, and when Secretary-General Perez de Cuellar failed to interest the Iraqi leader in a peaceful settlement after a last minute visit to Baghdad, the UN operation entered its military phase.[20]

But was it really a UN operation? The Bush administration said yes, a hundred times yes. The United States used UN cover as a glue to keep the coalition together—a coalition that included such unlikely partners as Israel and Syria. Would the Arab members of the coalition pull out if Israel attacked Iraq? Would they tolerate the bombing of Iraq? Would they be willing to fight under American command? Baker needed assurance on all these questions, and he could only get it if the operation appeared to serve UN—not strictly American—purposes.[21] "History has now given us another chance," he would soon tell his Security Council colleagues. "We must not let the United Nations go the way of the League of Nations. . . . We have the chance to make this Security Council and this United Nations true instruments for peace and justice around the globe."[22]

The president probably took this rhetoric more seriously than the secretary of state. Not everyone else did. When asked if he would permit the coalition to fight under the UN flag as had occurred during the Korean War, Secretary-General Perez de Cuellar said no. He viewed the coalition not as a UN force, but as a U.S.-led operation patched together with Security Council tape.[23] There was no military staff committee, no UN command to decide when to initiate or end the fighting. A crusade to save the UN? Careful observers knew very well that the Security Council had not authorized sanctions in respect to a half dozen other recent instances of armed assault (the Chinese in Tibet, the Russians in Afghanistan, Iraq in Iran, the United States in Grenada); it acted now mainly because the United States and Great Britain saw their own interests so threatened as to warrant military measures. The end of the Cold War, of course, secured the Americans against use of the veto, therefore making UN action possible. Had Kuwait been filled with soybeans instead of oil, it is unlikely that Baker would have bothered to resurrect memories of the old League of Nations.

The end of the fighting on February 28, 1991, did not end the Security Council's role in the conflict. Again led by the United States, the council passed Resolutions 686 and 687 establishing the terms of the cease-fire and keeping the economic embargo in place until Saddam Hussein agreed to strict conditions limiting his military power.[24] The United States continued to savor its UN cover, but when U.S. officials reasoned that they did not need that cover, they proved quite willing to act alone. The administration did not seek council approval to establish no-fly zones in northern and southern Iraq to protect the Iraqi Kurds and Shiites. Nor did NSC deputy Robert Gates notify the Council when he announced that sanctions would remain in place until Saddam Hussein had been removed from power, a requirement that had not found its way into Resolution 687. Stanley Meisler is correct to note that the Gulf War strengthened the UN and gave the Security Council an "exciting confidence"; he is equally correct to note that it also had a negative effect on the UN, especially because it convinced many Americans "that the UN was their UN."[25] When the UN subsequently acted in ways that did not conform to the American view of reality, the internationalist zeal of 1990 and 1991 evaporated.

SOMALIA

The UN's mission in Somalia during 1992 and 1993 would be a case in point. Somalia, an exceedingly poor country on the Horn of Africa, had endured 21 years of dictatorship under Mohamed Said Barré, best known for machine-gunning protestors who jeered him. For most of this period, Somalia had been a client of either the United States or the USSR, both of which supplied Barré with weapons in order to shore up their regional influence (and to limit their rival's influence). When the Cold War ended, Somalia's importance to both superpowers vanished. The result was that Somalia more or less dropped out of sight. To complicate matters, Barré's fall in 1989 led to freedom that looked increasingly like anarchy. During the next two years, the country slipped into civil war. Warlord-led clans and subclans armed teenagers, destroyed the communications and food distribution systems, and pillaged a people who already were suffering from widespread famine. Only after the western press rediscovered Somalia did advocates of humanitarian aid call for help.

One official who noticed was the new secretary-general, Boutros Boutros-Ghali, an independent-minded Egyptian Christian who in 1992 became Africa's first UN chief. Boutros-Ghali had taught political science and later served in the Egyptian foreign ministry. He had no international constituency when his own country proposed him for the UN post. With the Americans supporting former Canadian prime minister Brian Mulroney, whom most Third World delegates rejected, Boutros-Ghali secured support less because of his own reputation than the general belief that Africa's time had come. French-speaking and acceptable to the Russians, Boutros-Ghali was a nonobjectionable second choice to the State Department. Few in Washington imagined that he would become the most forceful secretary-general since Hammarskjold.

More than any other individual, the new secretary-general turned international attention to Somalia. Why, he asked in 1992, should the UN devote its main attention to the carnage in the former Yugoslavia at a time when Somalia was in no better shape? Was it because the Great Powers cared more for white (Bosnian) Moslems than black (Somalian) Moslems? By April of that year, the Bush administration, without any particular passion, supported Security Council Resolution 751, the latest of many resolutions dealing with the Somalia famine.[26] It authorized the first peacekeepers into that unhappy land as part of the United Nations Operation in Somalia (UNOSOM). They arrived lightly armed in September, shortly after President Bush ordered an American airlift of food and other supplies. Bush may have been motivated primarily by humanitarian concerns; he may have been responding to Democrat presidential nominee Bill Clinton's criticism that the White House was ignoring a preventable tragedy. For the next six months, U.S. planes delivered thousands of tons of supplies. The rescue effort failed to achieve its objectives, however, for much of the aid was hijacked or stolen by the armed thugs who served the various warlords. UNOSOM did not have enough force to stop the pillage. Indeed, the Americans joined with their Security Council allies to pass yet another resolution—775—increasing the number of peacekeepers, but without coordinating this effort with the units already in Somalia or with Somali clan leaders, like Mohamed Fared Aideed, who had the ability to undermine the UN goals.[27] Consequently, the UN peacekeepers, even with their expanded numbers, could not contain the violence.

It would not be until after the U.S. presidential election that George Bush really turned his attention to the crisis. Assistant Secretary of State Frank Wisner and the chairman of the Joint Chiefs of Staff, Colin Powell, recognized the humanitarian tragedy and did the spadework that resulted in a new plan of action. The lame-duck president, stung by criticism that his administration was not doing enough, approved Powell's proposal for a military rescue effort that would bring nearly 25,000 American troops to famine-stricken Somalia. Boutros Boutros-Ghali, who had conferred repeatedly with Wisner, happily obliged the U.S. plan. The goal of the mission was expressed in Security Council Resolution 794. Passed unanimously in early December, it authorized a new force called the United Nations Unified Task Force (UNITAF). With 36,000 troops, two-thirds of them American, Resolution 794 sought to "establish a secure environment for humanitarian relief operations. . . ."[28]

What did not appear in the resolution were the means by which the troops would guarantee the peace. Was this really peacekeeping, or that newer and more risky activity known as peace enforcement or peacemaking? The secretary-general argued for the latter, claiming that the troops must disarm the Somalians if the rescue effort were to succeed. The Americans interpreted the resolution more narrowly, seeking to avoid an armed clash with the warlords. The dispute over this resolution would be the first serious disagreement between Boutros-Ghali and the White House. It would not be the last.

The arrival of the Americans shortly before President Bush left office was great theater. U.S. Marines in full battle gear arrived on the beaches of Mogadishu in the glare of TV klieg lights illuminating the dark. Rescue workers literally cried in happiness as the troops finally insured the safe arrival of food and medical supplies. As in the Gulf War, internationalism had another good day.

But, of course, things were more complicated than they appeared. UNITAF, only loosely coexisting with UNOSOM, was not really a traditional UN peacekeeping force.[29] As they had during the recent Gulf War, the Americans arrived under their own command and their own flag. The Security Council endorsed their mission, but it neither created it nor controlled it. Moreover, the connection between this U.S. force and the formal UN peacekeeping operation that would likely follow was unclear. General Powell had envisaged that a larger UN operation, to be called UNOSOM II, would replace most of the U.S. troops, while Boutros-Ghali strongly favored the retention of U.S. units, which he believed would be much better equipped to guarantee a lasting peace. He favored nothing less than what President Bush's special envoy to Somalia would call "a full-scale, total disarmament program over the entire country, using whatever force might be required."[30] The American commanders were much less ambitious. There was mutual buck-passing here: Boutros-Ghali hoped the Americans, not the UN, would enforce the peace; the Americans had already recommended a more ambitious UN program to take effect *after* the United States would withdraw. The new Clinton administration inherited this disagreement on January 20, 1993.

THE BALKANS

Uncertainty and irresolution also characterized the UN's involvement in the remnants of Yugoslavia during the last year of Bush's administration. Just as the Americans had dragged their feet in making a commitment in Somalia, so too did they hold back in the Balkans. It was there that the post-Cold War disintegration of Yugoslavia led a number of states in the old Yugoslavian federation to declare their independence, in turn touching off a nasty and uncivil war where, as one author says, "madness is a permanent mood."[31] Serbian tanks first rolled into Slovenia in July 1991, then into Croatia and Bosnia. Lurid propaganda, bitter recriminations, and human rights violations had already fomented enough hatred to turn Yugoslavia into a thunderstorm of nationalisms. When in December 1991 Germany recognized Slovenia and its old ally, Croatia, the storm could no longer be contained. First, the Serbs expelled Croatians from the Krahina region of Croatia, a situation not reversed until 1995. Then multiethnic Bosnia-Herzegovnia declared its own independence, leading to Serbian attacks on Bosnia, and Bosnian Serb assaults on Moslems within Bosnia. The memories ("ghosts," says Robert Kaplan) of a half millennium of hatred fueled these conflicts, stirring a nasty brew of nationalistic, ethnic, and religious poison.[32] The mixture produced the shelling of historic cities, sickening sieges, population expulsions ("ethnic cleansing"), and large-scale massacres, most initiated by the Serbs. Not since World War II had Europe witnessed such violence.

The Balkans, of course, were not Somalia. The motives for UN and U.S. involvement in Somalia were overwhelmingly humanitarian. No U.S. official after 1991 suggested that Washington had strategic interests in that land. Not so with Yugoslavia, where the interests of the Great Powers had once fueled the outbreak of World War I, and where the clash of Catholic (Croatia), Orthodox (Serbia), and Moslem (Bosnia) passions threatened to widen a regional struggle. For the NATO allies, Yugoslavia was, geographically, just too close for comfort. But proximity fueled fear of becoming involved in the conflict as well as the urgency to end it. The buck-passing that had occurred with Somalia, therefore, would be repeated in the Balkans. While the Europeans awaited U.S. leadership, Secretary Baker would claim that the Americans were "comfortable with the [Europeans] taking responsibility for the war in the Balkans."[33] Baker was more than just "comfortable." He would not have it any other way.

The major powers also tried to pass the buck to the UN. Only Paris called for action; the other governments found plenty of reason not to lead as countless cease-fires failed to end the fighting. Between September 1991 (when the first resolution passed) and January 1993 (when President Bush left office), with Serbian armies destroying cities such as historic Dubrovnik and Vukovar, and laying siege to Sarajevo, where thousands of civilians died from gunfire, starvation, and shortages of medicine, the European Union (EU) and the United States supported literally scores of toothless Security Council resolutions to preserve lives and end the fighting.

The Americans did not approach this UN activity with enthusiasm. Secretary of State Baker admits that he feared "involving the United Nations in what had been an exclusive [European Community] negotiating process."[34] However, he could not really prevent the Europeans from handing the crisis over to the UN. Therefore, with the United States hiding behind the Europeans, and the Europeans hiding behind the UN, the Security Council approved a blitz of resolutions dealing with the crisis. Resolution 713 embargoed arms to all disputing parties. Resolution 721 called for the "possible establishment" of a UN force to keep the peace. Resolution 743 created the UN Protection Force in Yugoslavia (UNPROFOR) for Croatia, Bosnia, and Macedonia (with no U.S. participants) and authorized former Carter secretary of state Cyrus Vance, together with Britain's David Owen, representing the European Community, to draft a plan to end hostilities.[35]

Washington approved all these resolutions. The alternative, feared the State Department, was risky military intervention. For all his rhetoric about a new world order, President Bush had told reporters at the time Yugoslavia threatened to explode that "We're not the world's policemen."[36] Europeans and Americans alike had come to see the Balkans as much more akin to Vietnam than to Iraq. Getting in would be easy; not so getting out. After Germany precipitated the heaviest fighting by granting recognition to some of the disputants, even the European community was divided, a factor that increased American reluctance to step into the mess.

Secretary Baker may have initially feared UN involvement, but he realized that the UN might protect the United States against the kind of efforts (establishing safe havens for civilians, sending arms to the victims of Serbian brutality) that newspaper columnists like William Safire and Anthony Lewis were demanding. Significantly, it was not only Baker and Bush who had come to see Bosnia as the face of the new world disorder. So too had Secretary-General Boutros-Ghali, who better than most observers knew that the refusal of the West to send troops to Bosnia made the UN's peacekeeping task well-nigh impossible. Lacking a western commitment, Boutros-Ghali opposed UN involvement, but the Security Council brushed aside his concerns. The next two years would prove just how right he was.

chapter 11

CLINTON

During the presidential campaign of 1992, candidate Bill Clinton had criticized his opponent for inaction in both Somalia and Bosnia. His election victory would provide him an opportunity to make his own mistakes. Clinton, who had served as governor of Arkansas, brought into the White House much less international experience than had George Bush. Nevertheless, Clinton appointed a foreign policy team of considerable talent. Reflecting his own nonideological approach to the subject, he selected Warren Christopher to be his secretary of state and Anthony Lake to head the NSC.

Christopher, formerly Carter's deputy secretary of state, had negotiated an end to the Iranian hostage crisis during 1980 and 1981. He was a soft-spoken diplomat better known as a skillful negotiator than as a maker of grand strategy. A team player of uncommon patience, Christopher thoroughly rejected the neoisolationism and anti-UN sentiment of the Republican Party's right wing, often expressed by North Carolina senator Jesse Helms, the ranking Republican on the Senate's Committee on Foreign Relations (Helms would become chairman of that committee in 1995). Christopher would chart few new directions, but he sought—often unsuccessfully—to impose more consistency in the area of foreign affairs and to reconcile executive and congressional interests in light of "mutually accepted commitments and mutually reinforcing restraints."[1]

NSC adviser Anthony Lake complemented the secretary. Reflective and smart, Lake, a former marine, had once resigned from Kissinger's foreign policy staff to protest the Nixon administration's position on Vietnam War policy. He later served in Jimmy Carter's NSC before moving to Amherst College, where he taught international relations. As someone with as much interest in the policy making process as in the policy itself, he advocated minimizing

U.S. ambassador Madeleine Albright, President of the Security Council.
February 29, 1996.
(UN/DPI Photo by Evan Schneider)

potential disputes between the State Department and the White House as
well as subordinating partisan differences in pursuit of the broad national
interest. Like Christopher, Lake sought to align the country's goals with the
means to attain them, and, even more than Brent Scowcroft during the previous four years, he viewed the UN as part of those means.

The positive view of the UN held by both Christopher and Lake coexisted
with growing anti-UN sentiment in Congress and among the public. By 1993,
American relations with the UN looked increasingly equivocal. The adrena-
line pumped into the organization by the Gulf War had dissipated. Although
the new president had not criticized the UN during the recent campaign, his
choice of the little-known Madeleine Albright to be UN permanent representative did not promise much in the way of highlighting UN issues or the
UN's role in the making of U.S. foreign policy.

Albright, however, surprised both pro- and anti-UN observers. Although
her academic resume was longer than her diplomatic record, she did not lack
confidence, soon proving herself to be the country's most outspoken UN
envoy since Kirkpatrick. While she was more liberal and less ideological than
Kirkpatrick, she was no less assertive. Perhaps the most important difference
from Kirkpatrick was that, from day one, she forged a much more harmonious
relationship with her superiors in Washington and a less harmonious relation-

ship with the Secretariat. When Christopher insisted that she clear her speeches with the State Department, she cleared her speeches. Indeed, her own hard-hitting comments about foreign affairs allowed Christopher to speak softly. She, not he, would publicly question the sanity of Russia's nationalist leader, Vladimir Zhirinovsky, and the manhood of Cuban leaders who ordered the shootdown of an anti-Castro plane in international waters. While running political interference for the secretary of state, she was able to get so much visibility at the UN that Clinton would nominate her to become Christopher's successor in 1997.

Albright never viewed the UN as "a dangerous place," but she did express enough differences with Boutros-Ghali to undermine the secretary-general's chances to serve a second term. Moreso than many of his predecessors, Boutros-Ghali understood both the necessity of the UN and its fragile foundations. In his 1992 treatise *An Agenda for Peace*, written in the wake of UN successes in the Persian Gulf, southern Africa, and Central America, but before the failures in Somalia and Bosnia, he spelled out his concept of UN authority, especially as it related to peacekeeping and enforcement.[2] An ambitious document, it called for rapid deployment of troops during international emergencies, a beefed up conception of peace enforcement, and new sources of revenue (including a UN Endowment fund) in order to pay for the UN's increased responsibilities. The coming months would leave American policy makers increasingly unhappy with his approach, once again illustrating U.S. unwillingness to entertain rival authority.

FAILURE IN SOMALIA

The UN's most highly publicized failure since the Congo—if failure it was— occurred in Somalia, where UNITAF troops, most of them American marines and mountain troops, had more or less superseded UNOSOM in December 1992. Having sent American forces to maintain what increasingly looked like a very shaky peace, President Bush had refused to authorize, as Boutros-Ghali urged, the one thing that might have made the peace less shaky—the disarming of the subclan militias, an action that would risk unwelcome casualties. UNITAF did confiscate what the American chief in Somalia, Robert Oakley, called "visible weapons," but did not attempt "comprehensive disarmament."[3] Indeed, because UNITAF patrolled only the southern section of the country anyway, Oakley and UNITAF commander, Lt. General Robert Johnson, believed comprehensive disarmament was "out of the question." Oakley would later claim that UNITAF's effort was intentionally modest, a kind of "embryonic" process to restore stability to Somalia. Although it did achieve some genuine early successes in towns like Baidoa and Merca, it lacked a mandate for long-term pacification.

Clinton was sworn into office on January 20, 1993, and his administration inherited this limited conception of U.S. responsibility. At roughly the same

Secretary-General Boutros Boutros-Ghali and French commander
Maurice Quadri at orphanage in Baidoa, Somalia. October 1993.
(UN/DPI Photo by Fabrice Ribère)

time, Boutros-Ghali, at an airline stopover in Mogadishu, confronted an angry
demonstration by General Aideed's supporters protesting the UN presence.
The scene turned ugly, leaving many UN staffers deeply shaken and contributing to a serious deterioration in the UN's relationship with Aideed.
However much Boutros-Ghali and Aideed came to detest each other, their
hostility reflected more than a personal feud. It also reinforced UN reservations about American plans to turn UNITAF over to the UN.

It was at this point that the seeds were irrevocably sown for the UN's failure in Somalia. According to Oakley, U.S. and UN conceptions of the mission differed markedly. Bush had already announced that once the environment had been stabilized, U.S. troops would withdraw in favor of a UN
peacekeeping force (UNOSOM II) that would undertake nothing more than
a "limited and specific" plan to disarm the Somali clans and subclans. The
secretary-general, on the other hand, favored a disarmament approach that
would require a much larger UN force, and would encompass the entire country, not just areas occupied by UNITAF. Washington viewed Boutros-Ghali's
plan as impractical. According to Oakley, "The UNITAF command felt
strongly that it was vital to avoid serving as a police force. . . ." The acting secretary of state, Lawrence Eagleburger, agreed. Policing, the Americans argued,
must be done by the Somalis themselves.

Boutros-Ghali never accepted this idea. He viewed the Somalis as prisoners of disorder, not agents of order. Unable to agree that the United States should scale back its responsibilities, he postponed the kind of planning that might have allowed UNOSOM to achieve its objectives. Consequently, observed Oakley, the UN "never drew up a plan for disarmament, demobilization, and the reintegration of Somali militias into civilian life, even though it had prepared such plans for Namibia, El Salvador, and other peacekeeping operations. . . ."[4]

Boutros-Ghali's rigidity and American timidity had placed the UN in a difficult position. The secretary-general and his staff could not walk away from Somalia without doing great injury to the UN itself, yet could not muster the assistance it needed. In March 1993, under strong American pressure, the Security Council approved Resolution 814 setting up UNOSOM II and requesting (not demanding) "humanitarian *and other assistance* to the people of Somalia in rehabilitating their political institutions and economy and promoting political settlement and national reconciliation "[5] (my italics). Both UNOSOM I and UNITAF had been somewhat traditional peacekeeping operations; the much more ambitious mandate incorporated into Resolution 814 turned the UN toward a kind of "nation-building" that involved considerably greater risks.

After the first UNOSOM troops arrived in May, replacing most of the U.S. troops in UNITAF, UN officials found themselves plagued not only with having a force too small to accomplish its main purposes but also by a breakdown in coordination between those who focused on humanitarian efforts and those who demanded a political settlement. Although the 5,000 U.S. troops in UNOSOM II nominally served under UN command, the actual command structure was American, with officers recommended by the United States to the UN. Both the UN and the United States advertised joint decision making for UNOSOM II. In practice, joint decision making faded quickly, one more way in which the Somalia mission disappointed its designers.[6]

The failure of joint decision making foreshadowed trouble. With the withdrawal of the U.S. troops in UNITAF leaving a much smaller American contingent in UNOSOM II, UN units would face an impossible task. Aideed and other clan leaders, emboldened by the American withdrawal, now launched aggressive operations against the less-well-equipped UN units. After Aideed's militia ambushed 24 Pakistani troops who were inspecting weapons storage depots on June 5, French and Italian contingents in UNOSOM II joined U.S. units in substituting orders from their own governments for those from UN command. More killings followed: 10 Moroccan soldiers died on June 17, up to 70 Somalis died when the U.S.-led quick reaction force attacked Aideed's headquarters on July 12, and four journalists were slain in retaliation for that attack.

Until August 8, few U.S. soldiers had been targeted. On that day, four perished when a remote-control bomb blew up their vehicle. But it was the October 3 deaths of 18 U.S. soldiers after a failed attempt to capture Aideed that led to a general reassessment of the U.S. role in Somalia. Staggered by public revulsion at films of a dead American soldier dragged through the streets of Mogadishu, President Clinton had enough. Conceding that the goals of the mission had changed from humanitarian to political and charging that the UN had "personalized" the issue, the president announced that the United States would no longer seek to capture Aideed. For the short run, he approved reinforcing the U.S. troops in UNOSOM II; but he then informed the Secretariat that he would pull all U.S. personnel out of Somalia within six months.

Boutros-Ghali accepted the inevitable. Seeing the American core of UNOSOM II preparing to depart and understanding that it would be impossible to convince other governments to commit troops when Washington was leaving, he recommended scaling back UNOSOM's mission, reemphasizing the importance of humanitarian objectives while promoting "Somali initiatives."[7] But he did not accept the change in U.S. policy gracefully, and his relationship with Clinton administration officials, including Albright, never recovered. Nor did the UN role in Somalia recover. The gradual withdrawal of UN units exposed those who remained to violence and pillage. By the time the last UN troops had left in the spring of 1995, the American public had lost interest. Somalia had become a bad memory and, to many Americans, a symbol of UN incompetence and inefficiency.

No peacekeeping operation in UN history had so sharply revealed the UN's limitations. Poor coordination among the UN bureaus responsible for peacekeeping had exacerbated the failures of communication and cooperation between the U.S. command and the UN. As for Clinton, lacking both a clear mandate and the means to achieve his cloudy objectives in Somalia, he became an easy target for anti-UN critics in Congress and the press. Instead of admitting the degree to which his administration shared responsibility for the mess in Somalia, he did what most politicians do: he ducked accountability and implied that UN leadership was to blame.

There was some truth to his charge. Boutros-Ghali and his subordinates had been as remiss as the White House in pursuing an ill-defined mission. Might the mission have been handled differently? Yes, especially if the Secretariat and the Security Council had applied "preventative diplomacy" during 1991 and 1992. The UN's sharpest critic, Robert Patman, concluded in an assessment of the mission that "The UN's negligence toward Somalia during 1991 was almost criminal."[8] Perhaps so, but Patman forgot what Clinton hoped he would forget: the UN—and especially the Security Council—could do no more than what its member states would permit it to do. What got lost amid all the finger-pointing was the fact that the UN deserved credit as well as censure: by the time the last UN units departed, the Somali famine had ended and the most violent clan warfare had (at least temporarily) subsided.

FRUSTRATION OVER BOSNIA

Despite their best efforts, Clinton and his secretary of state, Warren Christopher, had failed to bring clarity to U.S. policy in Somalia. They did no better with policy in Bosnia, where the UN had established UNPROFOR in 1992 but had otherwise mainly substituted resolutions for serious efforts to bring about peace. Indeed, the UN's ineffectiveness in Bosnia was in part a response to the ripple effect of the UN's trouble in Somalia. Washington and its allies were even more fearful of being sucked into a whirlpool of guerrilla activity in the Balkans than in Africa.

Conventional wisdom at the UN long held that peacekeeping could not succeed unless all parties to a dispute accepted in advance the UN presence. In the Balkans, such acceptance did not exist where it was most needed. In some areas, such as Slovenia and Macedonia, where the UN stationed relatively few peacekeepers, UNPROFOR admirably met its objectives. In Bosnia, it did not. UN attempts to disarm Serbian irregulars in Bosnia met with stiff resistance, while UN efforts to carve out six urban "safe areas" for Bosnian Moslems met with even less success. UN troops could guarantee neither free passage for food and medicines into the safe areas, nor passage out. The atrocities of 1991 and 1992 extended into the first months of the Clinton administration.

The State Department vacillated. Sympathetic to cries for humanitarian assistance amplified by reporter Christiane Amanpour's CNN coverage of Bosnian suffering, yet see-sawing over Bosnia's importance and acutely conscious of the conflict's deep historical roots, the department substituted words for soldiers.[9] Many appeared in UN resolutions. When Christopher supported Security Council Resolution 844 in June 1993, which authorized 7,600 peacekeepers to protect the safe areas, he volunteered no American troops.[10] When the UN deployed only a fraction of those 7,600 troops, he issued no protests.

Making matters even worse, the United States undermined support for the imaginative Vance-Owen plan. Authored by the former secretary of state under Carter, who in 1993 became an emissary for the Security Council, and a former British foreign minister, who spoke for the EU, the plan's main offense was that, like most compromises, it satisfied no one completely. Looking to partition Bosnia among Moslems, Croats, and Serbs in a manner roughly consistent with their populations, the plan would have used western troops, including U.S. units, to guarantee the end of atrocities after requiring the Bosnian Serbs to withdraw from much of the territory they occupied in early 1993. Perhaps scared off not only by predictable Serb denunciations of the plan, but by initial Bosnian Moslem criticisms (the Moslems eventually accepted it), Clinton and Christopher offered Vance-Owen the kind of silence that A. M. Rosenthal in the *New York Times* called "death through lockjaw." As Lord Owen himself put it, the administration had decided that "the price of putting U.S. troops on the ground to reverse ethnic cleansing was too high." The fighting continued.[11]

With no serious effort to impose a settlement, UN efforts began to unravel. Lacking U.S. support for Vance-Owen, the Bosnian Serbs soon rejected it (they might have done this anyway). The safe areas had become dreadfully unsafe; UNPROFOR proved unable to protect even shipments of food sent by the UN High Commissioner for Refugees (UNHCR) to the besieged cities. The UN official in charge of Bosnian operations, Japan's Yasushi Akashi, charged that Somalia had made the Americans "somewhat reticent, somewhat afraid, timid, tentative." He was right, of course, but so were American complaints about European—and UN—timidity. This backbiting did not facilitate the making of effective policy, especially after Madeleine Albright reminded UN officials not to criticize the powers who paid their salaries.[12]

For the duration of 1993 and for most of 1994, the Bosnian story remained a record of ambiguity, self-justification, and buck-passing. Washington continued to argue that Europe must take the lead, while the Europeans claimed that American involvement was a sine qua non for a genuine resolution of the fighting. The fact is that Bosnian Serb strength persuaded both U.S. and European capitals that the Bosnian Moslems would eventually surrender regardless of the aid given them, therefore making intervention useless.[13]

Yet complete inaction was politically unacceptable for American policy makers. Led by Kansas Senator Robert Dole, some Republicans charged Clinton with weakness, an accusation echoed in Clinton's own party and among influential columnists like A. M. Rosenthal and Anthony Lewis. The administration, therefore, resorted to half measures. With no officials going so far as to advocate committing ground troops to Bosnia, the president in January 1994 endorsed air strikes against the Bosnian Serbs while selectively lifting the UN arms embargo in order to aid the Moslems.

Now it was the Europeans who balked, especially the United Kingdom and France, who feared that bombing might place their own troops in UNPRO-FOR—about 20,000 of them—in jeopardy. They understood what the Americans could afford to ignore: if the Serbs retaliated against UNPROFOR, only the Europeans would be at risk. For the same reason, they were unenthusiastic about lifting the arms embargo against the Serbs and Bosnians.

So both the United States and the Europeans had reason to distrust one another. It all made for delay and recrimination while Bosnians died. Eventually, the Clinton administration won its argument. NATO agreed to conduct air strikes against Bosnian Serb positions, but for months even these were generally ineffective. Disputes between NATO commanders and UN officials led to deadly delays, advance warning of attacks to the Serbs, and the scaling back of air activity. Even when NATO air operations increased after the Serbs killed scores of civilians in a Sarajevo market during February 1994, disputes between UN and NATO officials prevented the kind of sustained air campaign that might have forced the Serbs to retreat. The Serbs, as it turned out, were aided not only by the restraint shown by NATO commanders, but by the way UN officials, especially Ashaki, limited air assaults.

The Serbs also countered the air strikes by taking hundreds of UN peace-keepers as hostages, thereby advertising the UN's vulnerability. Bombing had indeed hurt the Serbs, but it would not end the war by itself, and it came with a price higher than the United States or the UN was willing to pay. It was the UN's economic sanctions against what remained of Yugoslavia, combined with the air assaults on Bosnian Serb positions, that finally led to a truce. Once President Milosovic of Yugoslavia concluded that the war must end, his Serb allies in Bosnia had little choice but to accept a settlement. Negotiated from November 2 to November 21, 1994, in Dayton, Ohio, the agreement ended the war on American-proposed terms not much different from those that Vance and Owen had drafted almost three years earlier.

With NATO having already replaced the UN as the international military arm in Bosnia, American troops joined IFOR, NATO's successor to UNPRO-FOR. The latter did not leave entirely; UNPROFOR units remained in Mace-donia as preventative peacekeepers, a reminder of the secretary-general's *Agenda for Peace* advice. Some peacekeeping troops, known as Blue Helmets, also remained to work as adjuncts to local police units. The main UN role, however, had petered out after NATO air attacks became more frequent in 1994. As with Somalia, the UN's failure in Bosnia had ironically weakened the organization just three years after its heyday in Iraq.

HAITI

The most traditional UN peacekeeping missions have involved separating two warring parties who *agreed* to be separated. The three largest UN operations— Cambodia, Somalia, and Bosnia—had *not* fallen into that category, which is what defined them more as peace enforcement operations than peacekeeping missions. Haiti, the most successful of the UN missions with which the Clin-ton administration associated itself, also fell into the peace enforcement cate-gory.

Haiti, the poorest nation in the Western Hemisphere, had less a history of revolution than of violent, unstable reaction. Misgoverned by a corrupt gov-ernment for years, Haiti's fortunes looked to change when a democratically elected government under the populist and mildly anti-American Father Jean-Bertrand Aristide took power in December 1990, four years after the overthrow of the Duvalier family's 29-year despotism. Optimism died, how-ever, after a military coup returned Haiti to dictatorship in 1991. American officials might have tolerated this situation as they had tolerated political repression in Haiti for decades, but 1992 was an election year that followed the end of the Cold War; "democracy" had again become fashionable. Secre-tary of State Baker had already announced that Aristide's overthrow "cannot and will not be allowed to stand," while candidate Bill Clinton, not to be outflanked, stated that "no national security issue is more urgent than securing democracy's triumph around the world."[14]

Trapped by such rhetoric, Clinton's White House continued a crippling OAS-initiated economic embargo against Haiti that had begun shortly after the October 1991 coup. The embargo was aimed at the military junta in Haiti but mainly hurt the already poor population.[15] Facing renewed political repression and deep economic distress, thousands of Haitians were fleeing to the United States. At a time when immigration was becoming an increasingly divisive issue in the United States, the Clinton administration eventually concluded that the most effective way to resolve the problem was to eliminate the political conditions in Haiti that produced the emigration (and the embargo) in the first place.

"Assertive multilateralism," Madeleine Albright had called the administration's approach to the UN; a slogan without a definition. Albright seemed to suggest that American policy should be proactive, using the UN to shield the United States from the burdens of military intervention. But "assertive multilateralism" also presumed something uncommon in UN peacekeeping—that U.S. troops would fully participate, as Washington was about to demonstrate in Somalia. The problem was that Somalia nearly killed the concept by reminding Americans of peacekeeping's complexity and risk.

Nearly killed it, but not entirely. When Washington decided in July 1994 to "restore democracy" in Haiti, it did so under at least a pretense of UN and OAS authority. Not only did U.S. officials remember that the last strictly unilateral intervention in Haiti had lasted an agonizing 15 years, they also recalled that President Bush's 1989 invasion of Panama had revealed just how unpopular the United States could be in Latin America when pursuing unilateral ventures. Clinton's team, therefore, preferred the multilateral route. They called in their legal experts to justify such action under a UN Charter that was terribly ambiguous about violations of state sovereignty. Conditions in Haiti, claimed these experts with a straight face, threatened "international peace and security."[16]

In fact, the Americans had advocated multilateral action in Haiti ever since the 1991 coup. USUN under both Pickering and Albright welcomed UN and OAS support for the economic embargo. The State Department endorsed a General Assembly denunciation of the coup and Security Council creation in 1993 of two separate missions: the UN Mission in Haiti (UNMIH), which would assist in training and modernizing the Haitian police and army, and the International Civilian Mission in Haiti (MICIVIH), a companion operation sponsored jointly with the OAS to monitor legal and human rights compliance.[17] If multilateral measures helped to resolve the problem, fine. If not, then Washington need not face failure alone.

Assertive multilateralism? Hardly. These two missions were modest. A more serious American effort was made unilaterally when Washington brokered the July 1993 Governors Island Agreement, with UN endorsement an afterthought. By threatening Haiti's military rulers with stronger economic sanctions, the State Department forced them to agree to restore constitutional procedures and to transfer authority back to Aristide and the civilian parliament. In return for signing the agreement, the United States would grant the junta amnesty and the Security Council would suspend the economic sanctions that had been authorized in June 1993 by Resolution 841.[18]

These inducements—along with the agreement's silence about human rights issues—may have sent the wrong message, for the military government proceeded ostentatiously to ignore its pledges to restore constitutional government. In an action that seriously embarrassed the U.S. Navy, the junta even prevented the USS *Harlan County* from landing UNMIH officials in Port au Prince. Had the Haitians similarly humiliated the United States a few years earlier, Washington undoubtedly would have responded in Teddy Roosevelt fashion. By the fall of 1993, however, Somalia and Bosnia had turned Clinton more into Hamlet than TR. The administration temporized, going no further than to ask the Security Council to reimpose economic sanctions suspended by the Governors Island Agreement. Washington increasingly used the UN to cover its timidity and uncertainty. Nor did Boutros-Ghali protest. He, too, had been weakened by the Somali debacle and had no desire to upstage the Americans in their Caribbean backyard.

It would not be until the late spring of 1994 that the Clinton administration again formulated a clear policy toward Haiti. Until then, the administration could not even settle upon whether it favored a stronger or weaker embargo, finally joining the Security Council majority on May 6 in calling for stiffened sanctions.[19] From this point, it was not the abstract demands of democracy, but the exigencies of domestic politics, that prompted change. With Clinton under attack by both conservative Republicans and liberal Democrats for vacillating over Haiti, and with more and more Haitians fleeing from junta repression and the embargo's economic effects, the administration finally settled on a policy of armed intervention. On this subject, the Americans initially had few international friends; as late as May, only Argentina among the Western Hemisphere countries offered strong support for an American-led invasion. Even at home, public opinion polls reflected strong opposition to using military force to unseat the junta.[20]

Despite his legendary sensitivity to public opinion, Clinton ignored those polls during the summer of 1994. Fearing the political risks of inaction more than the military risks of facing Haiti's tiny army, he finally approved an invasion scheduled for September 19. He called it off at the last minute when, with planes already in the air, the junta accepted American demands for Aristide's return. Yet even at this late date, Clinton paid a price, allowing the junta to pry important concessions out of Washington, including a role for the hated police and amnesty for junta leaders. For the next five months, 20,000 American troops protected Aristide. There was something incongruous about the populist president of Haiti restored to power by a government that had never really trusted him. Clinton wistfully described "lasting democracy" as a goal of the occupation. During the next year and a half, the Americans would spend over $2 billion sowing their version of democracy in Haiti's undemocratic soil.[21]

As with Cuba in 1962 and the Falklands in 1982, the UN had played a strictly secondary role in resolving yet another Western Hemisphere crisis. The organization initially provided little more than legal window dressing; eventually it supplied troops. Once Washington resolved to use military force, the State Department persuaded the Security Council to approve Resolution 940 authorizing "all necessary measures" to carry out the terms of the Governors Island Agreement.[22] Sixteen countries assisted the United States in what the State Department kept emphasizing was a multilateral operation.

Multilateral, yes, but only marginally UN. Greater UN involvement would come in January 1995, however, when the Security Council authorized a peacekeeping force of 6,900 to replace the Americans in order to maintain order and train the Haitian police. But overall command remained American, as did nearly one-third of this force (the last American troops would leave Haiti in 1997). Suffering almost no casualties and sharply limiting its role to avoid turning Haiti into Somalia, the UN's Haitian peacekeeping operation offered both U.S. and UN officials a welcome contrast to the UN's recent failures.

RWANDA

Much less welcome to the Americans was UN activity in Rwanda, a former German and, after 1919, Belgian colony. Rwanda was troubled by bitter tribal rivalry that pitted the majority Hutus against the minority Tutsis, who controlled the armed forces. When in April 1994 the country's Tutsi president, Juvenal Habryarimana, died in a plane crash, most likely caused by a missile, internal stability gave way to one of the few instances of twentieth-century savagery other than the Holocaust truly deserving the name genocide. The world watched in horror as CNN broadcast scenes of rivers filled with bloated bodies and churches turned into human abattoirs. As casualties exceeded 200,000 dead, a number that would eventually reach more than one-half million, the secretary-general called for international action to halt the slaughter. Like Somalia, the violence had no obviously international roots. And like Somalia, the violence occurred in distant Africa where the major powers, including the United States, no longer had vital interests.

Political scientist John Ruggie observed in 1985: "One is struck by the inability of the United States to define and maintain a kind of strategic orientation toward the United Nations."[23] At no time was his observation proven more true than in the wake of Somalia, which had an even greater effect on American policy toward Rwanda than it did on policy toward Haiti. Most Americans had never heard of Hutus or Tutsis before 1994; few could locate

Rwanda on a map. Any moral outrage members of the State Department may have felt was offset by fear that U.S. involvement would be futile or dangerous or both, and that Congress and the public would never back a UN mission to Rwanda in light of the Somalian debacle.

The truth is that just as political considerations had prompted the Clinton administration to intervene in Haiti, political considerations deterred the administration from intervening in Rwanda. By May 1, 1994, nonintervention in Rwanda had become policy. Yet the administration feared ignoring the slaughter altogether, and therefore pledged to help organize a joint force from among Rwanda's neighbors. Even this promise, however, illustrated the administration's fecklessness. First the State Department sought to scale down the size of the force, then it reversed itself at the urging of angry African delegates and the secretary-general himself, and then it reverted yet again to the smaller force plan.[24] Supported by nervous Europeans in the Security Council, USUN contributed to what the secretary-general undoubtedly interpreted as a sharp rebuke.

It was not just domestic politics that motivated the Clinton administration. The State Department genuinely feared, said Madeleine Albright, that a mission lacking sufficient numbers of troops would be "folly." Even the normally pro-UN New York Times agreed, editorializing on May 18 that "It is simple prudence for the U.N. not to leap into an empty swimming pool."[25]

The hundreds of thousands who died in that empty pool would have disagreed. The French government, which persuaded the Security Council to endorse sending 2,500 French troops to Rwanda the following month, also demurred. Of course, it was too little and too late. Perhaps Albright was correct: unless the Americans and their allies were prepared to mount a major operation (which they were not), peacekeeping in Rwanda would fail. If the episode proved anything, it was that Boutros-Ghali, who chafed at seeing the West preoccupied by the Balkans while ignoring bloodshed in Africa, would lose what little support he still enjoyed in Washington. And, of course, Rwanda also proved John Ruggie correct in judging American policy toward the UN to be no real policy at all.

DECLINING U.S. SUPPORT FOR UN OPERATIONS

The United States has not had a defined policy toward the UN in recent years, just some political tendencies. Until Clinton's presidency, the State Department had never reviewed Washington's UN orientation in a comprehensive fashion. Even the Reagan administration had no systematic approach to the UN; Reagan continued to offer the UN public support while his subordinates often undermined it or ignored it. "When human rights progress is made, the United Nations grows stronger," said the president in his General Assembly address of 1988, "and the United States is glad of it."[26] Reagan had not been glad enough to pressure Congress to pay its outstanding UN debts, however. The UN's rejuvenation after the Gulf War, followed by plunging support after Somalia and Bosnia, led the State Department, in May 1994, to publish a sweeping reappraisal of U.S. policy toward UN peacekeeping. Known as PDD 25, its authors, working under the direction of Albright and IO chief Douglas J. Bennet, reflected the new skepticism about multilateral commitments to use force.

The heart of PDD 25 was its recommendation that several questions must be considered before the United States would contribute to UN peacekeeping activity. Are American interests threatened? Are adequate funds available? Does the mission have clear objectives? Will it have congressional support and a reasonable chance of success? Unless the answers were affirmative, concluded PDD 25, Washington would no longer support peacekeeping. As Albright told the New York Times, the UN had been asked to do "too much."[27] Noble ambitions must be reined in by a sense of the possible, and the limitations of UN activity must be recognized.

Of course there was more here than met the eye. For one, PDD 25 abruptly reversed Clinton's own 1992 campaign rhetoric calling for more American support for UN operations. The death of the 18 U.S. Marines killed in Somalia had reinforced conservative opposition at home both to a standing UN army and to placing U.S. troops under "foreign" (meaning UN) command. PDD 25 formalized the conservative objections on both counts. Although the document called for a more selective approach to peacekeeping, some who applauded it, like the ranking Republican on the Senate Foreign Relations Committee, Jesse Helms of North Carolina, hoped to end U.S. peacekeeping contributions altogether. Others who applauded it, like the internationalist editors of the New York Times, argued that "there should be a shift back toward more limited objectives like policing cease-fires."[28]

PDD 25, then, reflected disillusionment, frustration, and even exhaustion with peacekeeping during a period when such operations exhibited explosive growth. Under such circumstances, even a president without Bill Clinton's highly sensitive political antennae would likely have pulled in his internationalist horns. The UN had developed a hearty peacekeeping appetite; policy makers like Christopher and Albright felt it was time for digestion rather than expanding that appetite even further. Between 1945 and 1988, the organization had been involved in 11 separate disputes; by the time PDD 25 appeared, that number had reached 28. The five peacekeeping operations of 1988 had grown to 17 by 1994. Fewer than 10,000 UN troops from 26 countries relied on a peacekeeping budget of $230 million in 1988; by 1994, the UN sponsored nearly 74,000 troops from 76 countries at a cost of over $3.6 billion.

With the Americans paying 31.7 percent of the peacekeeping budget, a reaction in Washington became inevitable. The House of Representatives, in February 1995, passed a bill that would not only reduce the U.S. contribution to 20 percent but would deduct from U.S. peacekeeping contributions the

Pentagon's share of primarily American operations having UN endorsement (such as U.S. troop activity in Haiti). Although the Senate did not pass this measure, misleadingly dubbed the National Security Revitalization Act, Senate majority leader Bob Dole's charge that UN peacekeeping was "out of control" served notice on the administration that Congress might impose even more restrictions than PDD 25.[29]

In areas unrelated to peacekeeping, Congress did impose more restrictions. In December 1995, for instance, the United States withdrew entirely from the UN Industrial Development Organization amid charges of UN inefficiency.[30] Neither Boutros-Ghali's sharp cuts in UN personnel nor the appointment of an American, Joseph E. Connor, to the new post of undersecretary-general for administration and development could stem American criticism. By the end of 1995, the secretary-general had cut roughly one-third of all higher ranking jobs in the Secretariat, and the UN Development Program announced that it would eliminate up to 30 percent of its staff.[31]

These cutbacks undoubtedly resulted in part from the effect of U.S. non-payment of dues since the Reagan years and, of course, the threat of even more reductions. But the refusal of other states to pay their UN assessments also contributed to the organization's financial crisis. The $1.1 billion owed by the United States by mid-1995 was matched by a nearly equal amount owed (collectively) by others, most importantly Russia and Ukraine. Nor was the charge of inefficiency made exclusively by Americans. When the chief Australian delegate to the UN charged that the bureaucracy was "designed in hell," many of his colleagues murmured amen.[32]

The Clinton administration, therefore, found itself in a quandary. By leading the fight against UN inefficiency, it stirred the pot of isolationist opposition to the UN. Yet it could not carry the crusade against inefficiency too far for fear of creating still more problems. For instance, the State Department was well aware that the Trusteeship Council had lost its raison d'être after virtually all of the old trust territories had become independent. But to eliminate the council meant revising the Charter, and Charter revision would open up a Pandora's box. The first revision, everyone feared, would likely aim not at bureaucratic reform but the elimination (or expansion) of the Security Council's permanent veto. Publicly, the United States supported permanent seats for Germany and Japan. Privately, Washington and Moscow (and perhaps Paris and London and Beijing) viewed tampering with the veto as an anathema. The administration therefore walked a fine line. "Does the UN need to be reformed?" the president asked in October 1995. "Has a lot of our money and everybody else's money been wasted? Does there need to be greater oversight? Of course there does. Is that an argument against taking a dive at the United Nations? No."[33]

The fall of 1995, consequently, was a momentous time for the UN. The UN's 50th anniversary commemoration brought over 140 heads of state to speak at the General Assembly when it convened in New York during October. The pomp belied anxiety.[34] If some observers feared that the birthday party might soon be followed by a wake, others viewed it as an opportunity. Historian Paul Kennedy and political scientist Bruce Russett, coordinating the most important of a number of reform commissions, proposed expansion of the Security Council's permanent membership, restricting the veto to issues of enforcement and peacekeeping, integrating more effectively (and splitting bureaucratically) the economic and social activity of the UN, and establishing independent sources of financing to free the UN from relying so heavily on its most wealthy and powerful members.[35] Swedish Prime Minister Ingvar Carlsson would cover similar ground in his influential *Foreign Policy* article, "The U.N. at 50: A Time to Reform."[36] The U.S. government remained unenthused.

WORKING WITH NGOS

But change could not be bottled up. The UN had already curtailed its peacekeeping responsibilities by the time of the 50th anniversary celebration. Nongovernmental organizations (NGOs) were playing an increasingly important role in the organization; even the National Rifle Association would be accredited to the UN by 1997, along with another 1,800 groups from around the globe. Moreover, the UN's scope of interest continued to expand. The 1972 UN Stockholm Conference on the Human Environment had trumpeted the idea of a world without boundaries. Attended by 113 countries, the conference had initiated the first sustained international examination of environmental decay, producing a widely acclaimed Declaration and an Action Plan containing 109 recommendations. The conference had also laid the groundwork for the United Nations Environmental Program (UNEP). This Nairobi-based organization, the first UN agency to be headquartered in the Third World, was slated to coordinate and encourage scientific and informational activity rather than to formulate policy. It did not work as expected. The UNEP increasingly reflected the clash of interests between the industrial North, focusing on issues of soil erosion, air and water pollution, and species extinction, and the developing South, which feared the negative effect of environmental regulation on economic development. With Third World countries demanding relief from World Bank debt that, many believed, could only be paid off by pursuing economic programs that further degraded the environment, U.S. policy makers grew increasingly unsympathetic to the UNEP's thinking. Stockholm's Action Plan would end up in the inaction file.

The need to reconsider the Action Plan, which really meant the need to reconcile North-South environmental interests, led to a second environmental conference—called the Earth Summit—in Rio de Janiero. Held in 1992, officials in both the North and the South recognized that environmental degradation was accelerating, not slowing down. The dumping of industrial and nuclear waste, the destruction of rain forests, and the thinning of the ozone layer reinforced Stockholm's lesson that environmental threats rarely respected national boundaries. The Earth Summit provided ample evidence of how routine global thinking about the environment had become, but it did *not* reconcile the North-South differences. Ten thousand delegates from 178 countries, led by 120 heads of state (hence, the name Summit), could hardly resolve the clash of interests that pitted the rich against those who wanted to become rich. The conference succeeded in publicizing problems ranging from the need to stabilize prices of raw minerals in order to render over-exploitation unnecessary, to the hugely expensive cost of detoxifying the environment. It even produced an 800-page supplement to the Action Plan called Agenda 21, along with two important conventions, one on biodiversity, the other on climate change and the "greenhouse effect" (a third convention, on forestry, never made it out of Rio).

Unfortunately, the Earth Summit had no more success committing governments to solve these problems than did its predecessor in 1972. By the 1990s, with some rare exceptions such as a treaty to protect the earth's ozone layer and proposed conventions to protect fresh water and to prevent the importation of the most hazardous chemicals, few reasons existed to believe that either North or South would sacrifice fundamental economic interests in pursuit of environmental objectives. Nothing illustrated this better than the refusal of the Bush administration to sign the biodiversity treaty for fear that American corporations would be required to share with Third World countries profits from U.S.-developed biotechnology. "We cannot permit the extreme in the environmental movement to shut down the United States," said Bush.[37] A year later, Bush's successor quietly signed the treaty, but Congress never ratified it, reemphasizing the Bush administration's economic point.

Nor did the last major UN-sponsored environmental conference of the decade, the UN Conference on Climate Change held in Kyoto, Japan, during December 1997, prove any more encouraging. Called to address the problem of global warming, the participants signed a convention to reduce carbon dioxide emissions among the industrial countries to 1990 levels. Business opponents of the convention, focusing on the convention's failure to apply restrictive standards to Third World countries, argued that the United States would be placed at a serious competitive disadvantage. The Clinton administration therefore compromised at Kyoto, agreeing to slow the pace by which it—and other industrial countries—would restrict emissions, knowing full well that the Republican majority in Congress warned that even a watered down convention stood no chance of being ratified without the kind of changes likely to be rejected by the other signatories.

Perhaps the most important accomplishment of both the Rio and the Kyoto meetings was to provide evidence that governments and NGOs could work in tandem. The 1995 Beijing World's Conference on Women would highlight this cooperative approach. As George Bush's appearance in Rio de Janiero provided a stamp of American legitimacy to the environmental work of the UN, so Hillary Rodham Clinton's appearance in Beijing did the same for women's rights. "It is no longer acceptable to discuss women's rights as separate from human rights," Mrs. Clinton proclaimed in a country not known for respecting either human or women's rights.[38] More importantly, the Beijing conference resembled Rio by exposing deep divisions between the North and South, and even by publicizing splits within these regions (the abortion controversy may have been the most visible, but it was by no means the only one). American delegates to Beijing focused on protecting women from violence, especially violence resulting from domestic abuse, genital mutilation, and rape in wars like the civil conflict in the former Yugoslavia. The American delegates also demanded that women have rights guaranteeing work and education; such rights, the Americans argued, would result in smaller families, which American delegates believed to be necessary to guarantee women personal freedom of choice.

As at Rio, Third World delegates in Beijing focused more on development issues that would presumably improve women's lives by increasing the standard of living for all people. Once again, such demands raised the issue of wealth transfers that would get little sympathy in Washington. To deflect attention away from such unresolvable questions, delegates eventually focused on a less contentious agenda, including the demand for compliance with the UN-sponsored 1981 Convention Against All Forms of Discrimination Against Women. Yet even that convention had pulled its punches by taking account of different cultural and social conditions. The torrent of talk over this issue in Beijing threatened to lead nowhere, and the universal good feeling that followed the meeting failed to take into account the degree to which the conference's "Platform for Action" contained no binding resolutions, no treaties, no governmental commitments. The conference's quiet compromises papered over some deep disagreements; the Vatican, for instance, dropped its opposition to the use of condoms to prevent disease, while Clinton administration spokespersons said little about their support for abortion rights. Beijing may have been a climax to UN efforts reaching back to ECOSOC's 1946 Commission on the Status of Women and the numerous conferences held during the International Women's Decade from 1976 to 1985, but it was certainly no conclusion to that work.

Rio, Beijing, and Kyoto received the most attention, but they were not the only nonpolitical conferences to kindle the attention of American internationalists. The Clinton administration would also send delegates to noteworthy conferences on human rights in Vienna (1993); population and development in Cairo (1994), a conference that set the stage for much of the work at Beijing; and social and urban issues at Habitat II in Istanbul (1996). All these meetings encountered the same challenges that bedeviled the North-South dialogue since the 1970s, weighing demands to protect human rights in a world of violence and repression, against demands to promote economic and social justice requiring investment by the rich in the geography of the poor. With the triumph of free-market economics widening the gap between the haves and have-nots during the 1990s, such debates at UN-sponsored conferences had become a staple of international life.

However difficult it might be to resolve such problems, the Clinton administration offered more support to the UN's (ostensibly) nonpolitical activity than it did to peacekeeping. Unlike peacekeeping, all these conferences committed Washington to little. They provided directions, not commitments to action. In the economic arena, the administration proved more willing to take risks than it did in the field of peacekeeping after 1994. Perhaps the outstanding example of economic cooperation was the administration's campaign for the GATT treaty that was signed in Morocco during 1994. The president and his treasury secretary managed to marshal just enough support among both liberals and conservatives to ratify a treaty that capped four decades of effort to facilitate international trade. The treaty not only maintained prohibitions against higher tariffs; it also provided mechanisms to resolve disputes over issues as diverse as environmental controls and government subsidies that threatened to undermine the system of free (or low-tariff) commerce. The GATT was itself transformed into a new World Trade Organization (WTO) that, tellingly, was not made a part of the UN system.[39] Nevertheless, the treaty was a striking example of economic internationalism. Such cooperation might not have been so surprising in 1965. By 1995, recommending such a treaty to the Senate took at least a small amount of political courage. Why? Because global economic developments, such as the rise of low-wage manufacturing in East Asia, Brazil, and Mexico, threatened the jobs of enough Americans to discredit economic internationalism and inject the treaty issue into the presidential campaign of 1996.

In the field of human rights, the Clinton administration also offered the UN some reasonable support. The administration never made human rights issues as central as Jimmy Carter's White House did, even though Madeleine Albright gave the subject more attention than any UN representative since Andrew Young. It was also true, however, that in trouble spots like Bosnia and Iraq, the administration fell far short of its goals, failing to appreciate the contradictions between its humanitarian policy and the ways military action might undermine that policy.

However seriously the Clinton administration addressed human rights, the president's efforts should not obscure the support that his predecessor, George Bush, gave to the UN in creating a UN Department of Humanitarian Affairs. The effectiveness of this new office, seeking to coordinate the work of many UN agencies, including those dealing with development, refugees, disaster relief, and peacekeeping, remains an open question. This is in part because, as in so many other areas, American human rights policy remains uneven. For instance, the Clinton administration has been moderately supportive of efforts to bring war criminals in Bosnia and Rwanda to justice under UN auspices, but has strongly opposed UN efforts to tie development aid together with human rights. "As long as Northern governments pursue only condemnations and sanctions as the method of enhancing human rights, their commitment to human rights will continue to be seen as reaching no further than saving themselves money," wrote one critic of U.S. policy. Her opinion—widely shared outside the United States—is that human rights necessitates investment. Little has been forthcoming from the United States, underscored in 1997 whan a private citizen, CNN founder Ted Turner, pledged a stunning $1 billion gift for UN humanitarian programs.[40]

As with so many of its predecessors, the Clinton administration has used the UN consistently when and where the UN has been able to serve U.S. interests. An example can be seen in the UN's role in Iraq. Here the United States has led in demanding IAEA inspections of Iraqi nuclear facilities, and has pressured the Security Council to maintain the 1991 economic embargo against the Iraqis in order to squelch any renewal of Saddam Hussein's political or military ambitions.[41] By February 1998 this policy led the U.S. to the brink of war against Iraq in order to maintain the integrity of the UN's inspection authority. Only a last minute agreement negotiated in Baghdad by Secretary General Kofi Annan prevented conflict. Annan persuaded the Iraqis to permit UN inspection teams unimpeded access to all nuclear, chemical, and biological warfare facilities.

The terms of the agreement became part of the Security Council Resolution 1154, but not before some hard bargaining among the former Gulf War allies. France, for economic reasons, and Russia, resenting the expansion of NATO, joined the PRC in opposing any use of force against Saddam Hussein. Washington, on the other hand, wanted the resolution to sanction the use of force without ambiguity should Iraq violate the new agreement. When Secretary of State Albright dubiously claimed that Resolution 687 (1991) already gave council members permission to bomb Iraq without the need for additional authorization, the Security Council compromised. Resolution 1154, approved on March 2, 1998, omitted explicit language authorizing force against Iraq, but did threaten "the severest consequences" should Baghdad violate the resolution.

So the UN—not quite unambiguously—has again served U.S. interests. Where the UN is less clearly able to serve U.S. interests (and, with the exception of Haiti, this means almost everywhere else), the administration's UN record has been mixed, as in the peacekeeping operations and human rights.

Ironically, the administration's inconsistent approach to the UN resulted in one of its few consistent themes: namely, its hostility to Boutros Boutros-Ghali, at least after mid-1994. Boutros-Ghali's sin was to expose—and occasionally to denounce—that inconsistency. He would pay dearly for his candor. The administration came to resent a strong secretary-general in much the same way that the Soviets rejected a strong Hammarskjold in 1960. Additionally, the administration found itself at odds with the secretary-general over the

UN's most controversial missions, including Somalia, Bosnia, and Rwanda. Added to legitimate disagreement, however, was the degree to which Boutros-Ghali served the Clinton administration during the presidential campaign of 1996 as a convenient punching bag. The administration tried to appease conservative critics at home by arguing that Boutros-Ghali's considerable reform efforts were never enough.

Boutros-Ghali's American-educated successor, Kofi Annan from Ghana, who became secretary-general in January 1997, has proved much more compliant in respect to U.S. demands for reform. His cooperation, together with Secretary of State Albright's careful courting of the chairman of the Senate Foreign Relation's Committee, Jesse Helms, persuaded the Republican-controlled committee in October 1997 to support a bill to pay a substantial portion of the U.S. debt to the UN. Yet even this was to no avail, as the Senate majority rejected the agreement by tying it to domestic abortion politics, thus guaranteeing a presidential veto.

If the Clinton administration does manage to pay the UN debt, much credit will undoubtedly go to Albright. She may have been as outspoken as Jeane Kirkpatrick, but she proved to be a much more skillful conciliator. More uncertain is the effectiveness of Clinton's choice to replace Madeleine Albright at the UN, former New Mexico Democratic representative Bill Richardson. He has restated the administration's support for "assertive multilateralism," but Washington's inability during 1997 and 1998 to secure allied cooperation in dealing with Iraq suggests that Richardson may be facing a life of many frustrations. Richardson, who had even less direct foreign experience than Albright when she took the job, and much less stature than ambassadors like Lodge, Stevenson, and Goldberg, brought to his post little more than a reputation as a skillful negotiator. With former UN ambassador Albright as his department head, it is unclear if he will have as much impact on UN policy as did his predecessor. But lack of foreign experience does not necessarily render an envoy impotent: remember, Richardson might point out to his critics, the career of the last member of Congress to serve the UN, Andy Young.

chapter 12

CONCLUSION

On the day that I began this final chapter, a C-Span interviewer was asked: "Why did Clinton give Yellowstone Park to the UN?"

In 1996, a young American soldier serving with UN peacekeepers in Macedonia refused to wear a UN insignia; threatened with a court martial, he became a minor hero to anti-UN groups throughout the United States.

Just months before former secretary-general Boutros Boutros-Ghali left his post, he ruefully told an American reporter that he was happy to end his summer vacation so he could get back to work flying his black helicopters, imposing world taxes, lowering his staff's morale, and blocking meaningful reform. Some Americans probably believed him.

Yet by the late 1990s it was not clear that the general public had turned against the organization. One pollster told the *New York Times* that Congress tended to exaggerate popular hostility to the UN. The polls, he claimed, actually revealed that the public wanted more, not less, involvement in peacekeeping, even more spending on foreign aid.[1] Perhaps. Surely a public that believed 10 percent of the federal budget was spent on foreign aid (as most Americans did) would react to questions about international cooperation differently from a public that believed 1.4 percent of the budget (the actual figure) funded foreign aid.

One thing had become indisputable: The pro-UN consensus of the 1940s had long ago disappeared. Even the UN's proponents recognized that the UN system needed reform and that ignoring reform might endanger the organization. When *Foreign Affairs*, the nation's most prominent internationalist journal, featured an article by Senate Foreign Relations chairman Jesse Helms flatly asserting that "as it currently operates, the United Nations does not deserve

The Secretariat building at the UN's 50th anniversary. December 21, 1994.
(UN/DPI Photo by E. Schneider)

continued American support," even the United States Association for the United Nations had to listen.[2]

The real issue had become less the UN than internationalism, however, and what Harvard's Stanley Hoffman considered internationalism's "crisis." Hoffman feared that the inconsistencies of both UN activity and U.S. policy (as discussed in the previous chapters) had led to "a discrediting of international organizations comparable to [that which] submerged the League of Nations in the 1930s. . . ."[3] The liberal, humane, democratic, and peaceful intentions of the Charter, all fundamentally Wilsonian in spirit, found themselves challenged by two global developments: the nationalism of the Cold War and the self-determination movements of the 1960s and 1970s that turned the UN toward a much more interventionist and illiberal direction. If American internationalists of the Cold War period such as Moynihan and Kirkpatrick had warmly applauded anticolonialism and human rights, they could hardly applaud the authoritarian regimes that populated the Third World nor the Third World assault on liberal values. Most American liberals, neo or not, joined conservatives to condemn the Third World's promotion of NIEO (which damned the free market), NWICO (which disdained press and speech freedoms), and the double standard (which condemned western or Israeli repression while ignoring human rights abuses among the Group of 77).

Moreover, the Americans had never reconciled themselves to the use of force by the UN except when U.S. interests were directly affected. Hoffman observes that Wilsonian internationalism legitimized the collective use of force only as a last resort: for self-defense or to prevent aggression. But just as proponents of the old League of Nations hoped that real force would only have to be threatened but never used, so too did American proponents of the UN find themselves more comfortable using peacekeeping to prevent wars—Cyprus, Lebanon in 1958 (but not 1982), UNEF I and II—than to restore peace, as in Somalia and Bosnia. Washington's preference for prevention over intervention has persisted even when the price of *not* using force has meant tolerating human rights atrocities (Bosnia, Rwanda), which in turn has damaged the UN's reputation.

George Bush's New World Order, Hoffman rightly noted, really was just another name for the hopes of liberal internationalists from Wilson to Truman.[4] Seeking to reconcile the requirements of international order with individual freedom, the New World Order proved messy and, to many Americans, even menacing in a world that appeared dauntingly complex. The Cold War gave the United States a sense of purpose in an international arena that seemed understandable even if threatening. By the late 1990s little seemed understandable. U.S. willingness to sacrifice its soldiers where American interests were not clearly at risk had disappeared. To make matters worse, fear about the nation's economic future affected UN policy. Huge trade deficits and a weakening dollar led Congress to lessen its support for UN economic institutions like the World Bank and the IMF that had stabilized the Wilsonian world for the past half century. Always proclaiming the value of human rights, Americans often appeared inconsistent, ignoring the abuses of friends as they damned others at the UN for maintaining a double standard.

Such behavior took its toll on American support for the UN. By the 1990s, a fractious global community of 185 nations seemed much less definable than the smaller though not necessarily more comfortable world of 1945. The colossal American influence that followed V-J Day had disappeared, and few Americans 50 years later believed it could be restored. Most reconciled themselves to this new state of affairs; some did not, retreating into xenophobia or isolationism.

Yet those Americans who continued to embrace internationalism did so with a better understanding of its limits. The 1945 vision of collective security, with each state automatically committing itself to the defense of all upon orders of the Security Council, had proved mythical. The permanent veto crippled genuine collective security, while the stillbirth of Article 43's Military Staff Committee guaranteed the UN's military impotence. Writing for an American audience, former Israeli foreign minister Abba Eban spoke for many so-called Realists by ridiculing the idea that states would commit their troops to fight where their national interests were not at risk, or would ever be able to define "aggression," or would be willing to impose sanctions against their closest allies. The Charter, he observed, called on states "suddenly to behave in a way that states had never behaved in the whole of human history."[5]

Eban was partly right, though he undervalued the degree to which countries from Canada to Fiji routinely committed their troops to remote peacekeeping operations. Still, he accurately described, if not explained, the vacillations of the major powers at the UN, including the United States. Some of this inconsistency could be laid at the feet of the Secretariat. The UN had indeed asked its members to provide more than they could reasonably be expected to contribute in order to guarantee collective security; even Boutros-Ghali in 1996 admitted that "the secretary-general must insist that mandates given to the United Nations itself be clear, realistic, and backed by the human and material resources required to complete the assigned task successfully."[6]

Some of this inconsistency also stemmed from conditions at the UN. Secretaries-general might occasionally be overly ambitious (this was rare), or imprudent (rarer still). More commonly, UN bureaus worked at cross purposes. More ominously, they sometimes failed to coordinate UN policies with those of member governments (witness Somalia). But much of the inconsistency that bedeviled the UN came not from the Secretariat, but from the UN's membership. And no state was less consistent than the United States.

Had the Americans been minor partners in the UN's work, U.S. inconsistency would have been of little consequence. Unfortunately for the UN, there was nothing trivial about the U.S. role. American political, economic, and military resources played a critical part in shoring up the organization, and Washington's withdrawal from agencies like the ILO and UNESCO brought this truth home to every official in the Secretariat who might otherwise have liked to ignore it. The UN, in fact, had been overly dependent on the Americans from the day of its birth, which proved healthy for neither the UN nor the United States.

Surely, some observers might remind us, the United States was not the only country to pursue an inconsistent UN policy. The Soviets, for instance, blew hot and cold regarding the UN, boycotting it at some moments, viewing it as an important feature of their foreign policy at others (think of Khrushchev using the UN to call for general disarmament). During years when Moscow was in the minority, the Soviets demanded that all decisions—including funding budgets for peacekeeping—be approved by the Security Council to allow for a Soviet veto; when the General Assembly turned against Moscow's rivals in North America and Western Europe, the USSR downplayed the importance of the council in favor of the larger assembly.

Other countries, too, acted inconsistently, most notably France; during President DeGaulle's tenure, for instance, the French refused to cooperate with UN efforts to quell the Congo fighting. Third World countries tended to value the UN more consistently than their first world counterparts. Only in the post Cold War period, when the UN might be expected to restrain the behavior of these smaller countries should international conflict become more common, have Third World countries approached the UN as erratically as has the United States.

Still, the story of Washington's inconsistency needs more than description. It needs explanation, for its roots were many.

For one thing, American goals often stood in conflict with one another. American policy makers often veered between ideals (such as the defense of human rights in Cambodia and Bosnia) and realities (such as the difficulty of persuading the Cambodian factions or the Bosnian Serbs and Moslems to lay down their arms). At other times, the Cold War produced its own inconsistencies, as when, seeking to end the Yom Kippur War in 1973, American policy makers considered convening an international conference at the same time that they wanted to exclude the Soviets from a diplomatic role in the area.

There was also conceptual inconsistency. The commitment of American internationalists to a postwar community of cooperation and collective action frequently clashed with Washington's promotion of a brand of free-market individualism that undermined the UN's work. For instance, although the Americans in theory supported UN environmental efforts and helped organize the Stockholm, Rio, and Kyoto conferences, they quietly subverted UN environmental efforts that clashed with American economic objectives. For example, they rejected the Law of the Sea Treaty and the biodiversity treaty of 1992. Similarly, American support for UN-sponsored economic development mobilized the energies of the IMF and World Bank, but not the UNDP, which relied less on western banks and sought trade concessions that western corporations found unappealing. And, of course, the Americans utterly rejected the Group of 77's efforts to create the NIEO.

The American political system contributed to policy inconsistency as well. Between 1945 and 1998, 10 U.S. presidents appointed 21 secretaries of state, who in turn selected 21 different chiefs of the IO division. The mission in New York fared no better, where 21 permanent representatives, some with cabinet rank, all struggling for political influence, served on average only slightly more than two and one-half years each. A nation, as Jefferson said, may have permanent interests, but those officials—mostly men, mostly professionals—hardly agreed on what those interests were or how to use the UN to advance them. To further complicate matters, the rivalries between secretaries of state and their national security advisers (for example, Rogers versus Kissinger, Vance versus Brzezinski) repeatedly sabotaged any hope for policy consistency.

Nevertheless, some consistency does emerge from the U.S.-UN story. First, Washington's lip service to the organization never wavered, not even during the tenure of anti-UN officials like Secretary of State Dean Acheson or President Ronald Reagan. For instance, when Acheson, who disdained the UN, promoted NATO as the country's first line of collective defense, he covered his internationalist flanks by saying that "[NATO] is designed to fit precisely into the framework of the United Nations . . . in harmony with the Charter."[7] Even ardent UN-proponents like Eleanor Roosevelt could hardly object to such statements, though they had good reason not to believe him. Ironically, this kind of deference, expressed repeatedly over 50 years, imparted a legitimacy to the UN that could not be ignored even by the UN's enemies. When Senator Helms in 1995 attacked the organization, he could only demand its "fixing," not its destruction.

Second, Washington continued to use the UN as an instrument of American diplomacy throughout the Cold War. From Korea to the Congo to the downing of Korean Airlines 007, American officials lost few opportunities to castigate their enemies in UN forums. The sharp attacks of Henry Cabot Lodge on Soviet and Chinese policy during the mid-1950s, the eloquent rhetoric of Adlai Stevenson during the Cuban crisis, and Andrew Young's sympathetic airing of Third World concerns during the 1970s were all designed to minimize Communist influence. As long as the Americans had an automatic majority at the UN, they could utilize UN forums effortlessly. Once the nonaligned nations came to dominate the General Assembly during the 1960s, Washington's UN diplomacy required more finesse, and, beginning in the early 1970s, occasional vetoes. This more careful approach to the UN remained necessary whether American officials were highly sympathetic to the organization (Harlan Cleveland and Vance), indifferent to it (Kissinger and Brzezinski), or hostile (Acheson and Reagan). The UN would do for Washington collectively what the Americans preferred not to do unilaterally. The UN was a means to an end, and the end was to prevail in the superpower competition. Did such Realpolitik strike these officials as cynical? No, for to the extent that they viewed the defense of freedom and resistance to totalitarianism as the foundation of America's Cold War diplomacy, they saw no conflict between their means and their ends.

Third, no administration ever placed the welfare of the UN over U.S. interests. Where the organization could serve these interests, Washington had even gone so far as to place its troops—as in Korea—under a UN flag (though it should be remembered that President Truman resolved to defend South Korea *before* he brought the issue to the UN). If the UN might prove to be an impediment to U.S. interests, as in Guatemala only a year after the Korean armistice, then the State Department would ignore the Charter. Some officials did this with impunity, such as Lodge with Guatemala and Kirkpatrick with Grenada. Others, may have had an uneasy conscience, such as Vance, Young, and McHenry, who ignored the UN during the Camp David negotiations and used the UN mainly to score debating points after the Soviets invaded Afghanistan., Still others, such as Dulles and Rusk, who had strongly supported the UN before moving to the State Department, self-righteously rationalized their Realism when they rejected a role for the world organization in Central America and Vietnam.

Fourth, with the exception of the Uniting for Peace Resolution that the United States used during the 1950s in Korea, Suez, Hungary, and Lebanon, Washington jealously protected the authority of the Security Council at the expense of the General Assembly. The tension between the Idealist view of international organization, first articulated by Cordell Hull, and the more Realist view of the UN favored by FDR, continued throughout the next half century. The Idealists never really had a chance. When the nonaligned majority took control of the General Assembly during the 1960s, even U.S. officials who had never used the veto understood that they might cast a few in their future (and that future arrived soon enough: from 1971 to the end of the Cold War, Washington cast almost three times more vetoes than Moscow). Although U.S. officials supported the enlargement of the Security Council from 11 to 15 members in 1966, they consistently rejected proposals to modify the veto. Indeed, they sought to *increase* their influence in the other UN bodies by various weighted voting formulae. No U.S. president or secretary of state ever seriously considered diminishing American influence on the council after the Yalta Conference in 1945.

Fifth, never did the United States favor the election of a strong secretary-general. American officials may have underestimated the strength and character of some candidates, but they certainly did not encourage the kind of independence that Hammarskjold so dramatically displayed within a year of moving to the 38th floor. Neither did they welcome use of the Charter's Article 99 permitting the secretary-general on his own authority to bring issues to the Security Council.[8] In those few instances when a secretary-general had the temerity to publicly criticize American behavior, he almost certainly signed his professional death warrant as both U Thant and Boutros Boutros-Ghali painfully discovered.

Sixth, the U.S. government treated the specialized agencies no more consistently than it treated the parent UN. The World Court, for instance, found itself generally ignored by the United States (and by others) for most of its post-1945 history. When the State Department believed that the court might serve American political interests, however (for example, during the Iranian hostage crisis), the court found new life, only to see the United States reverse course when the Nicaraguan government used the court to embarrass Washington. Other UN agencies fared similarly. The *least* political agencies enjoyed the most sustained U.S. aid—including the World Health Organization and the refugee agencies. The more political agencies were not so lucky.

Seventh, the Americans, like their counterparts elsewhere, subordinated human rights issues at the UN to political considerations. Even the legacy of Eleanor Roosevelt was not enough to move Washington to criticize American allies, such as Turkey and the Shah's Iran, for the kind of human rights abuses that Washington routinely denounced elsewhere. Ironically, the most discomfiting UN moment regarding human rights occurred during the term of Jimmy Carter, the president *most* committed to right these wrongs: it happened when Ambassador McHenry voted to seat Pol Pot's representative in the General Assembly. It is fair, therefore, to charge the United States with applying a double standard. Of course, the Group of 77 applied an even more egregious double standard, inviting Moynihan's and Kirkpatrick's barbs. Only NGO's like Amnesty International had the courage to condemn human rights abuses in a genuinely impartial manner. Governments tended to be much more circumspect.

Finally, after 1945 the U.S. government quickly learned to use the UN to do what it simply could or would not do alone. Without the UN, the United States could not have created the coalition to fight North Korea in 1950 or Iraq in 1991; it could not have tiptoed through scores of political minefields such as the 1949 quarrel between Indonesia and The Netherlands. The very fact of the UN's presence allowed Washington to avoid a choice that might otherwise have alienated either the awakening anticolonial world or America's NATO partners. Such dilemmas appeared with frequency during the life of the UN.

For all the inconsistency and even hypocrisy, a steady hum of pragmatism has guided U.S. activity at the UN. Washington's decision not to veto the admission of scores of small and potentially hostile new states testifies to this pragmatism. So has Washington's willingness to use the UN to pressure friendly governments, like South Africa or the NATO allies, in respect to decolonization; unilateral measures would have been awkward at best, impossible at worst. Research by David Armstrong reminds us that, even when the United States seemed most isolated at the UN during the years when the Group of 77 dominated the General Assembly, things were not always what they seemed. Yes, he notes, in 1982 the United States found itself on the losing side of 133 out of 157 votes on General Assembly resolutions (even Israel abandoned the United States 19 times). But, he adds, the United States found itself, during the 1970s and 1980s, voting more frequently on the side of Poland than Mexico, successfully using the UN to condemn the Soviets in Afghanistan, blocking consideration of Cuba's demand for Puerto Rico's independence, and censuring Vietnam for occupying Cambodia.[9]

Armstrong suggests an important dimension of UN life that has been too often neglected: voting patterns may well have reflected the Cold War rivalry, but they also reflected a North-South split. If Jeane Kirkpatrick failed to adjust to these polarities, most American officials at the UN did. That is why not even President Reagan called for U.S. withdrawal from the organization.

The future of the UN is not likely to be a future without American membership. President Clinton's January 1997 pledge to repay America's debt to the organization occurred on the same day that Madeleine Albright became the new secretary of state. There is no reason to think that the Clinton administration wants a more independent UN than past administrations, but, equally, there is no reason to believe that Albright, with her intimate knowledge from her ambassadorial years, will neglect the UN. The United States at the end of the twentieth century understands the limits of its own power better than it did one-half century earlier. The UN, too, better understands its limits. Caution and understanding may not make for a torrid love affair, but they may well strengthen a marriage.

CHRONOLOGY

1939   September 1: World War II begins.

1941   August 14: FDR and Churchill sign Atlantic Charter princi-
                ples.

                December 7: Japanese attack Pearl Harbor.

1942   January 1: FDR and Churchill issue Declaration of the United
                Nations based on Atlantic Charter principles.

1943   October 30: Moscow Declaration commits Big Four to join a
                United Nations.

1944   August 21: Dumbarton Oaks meeting convenes; agreement
                to establish an organization signed on October 9. The Chinese
                phase of the meeting begins on September 29.

1945   February 4: Yalta Conference opens.

                April 25: San Francisco Conference opens.

                May 8: Germany surrenders.

                June 26: UN Charter signed.

June 27: First meeting of UN Preparatory Commission.

August 15: Japan surrenders.

October 24: Charter formally comes into force.

December 20: Congress adopts United Nations Participation Act giving the president authority to conduct relations with the UN.

1946   January 10: First meeting of General Assembly. Security Council meets one week later.

January 19: Iran appeals to Security Council concerning Soviet troops in Northern Iran.

January 21: USSR brings civil war in Greece to the Security Council; Ukraine asks Council to condemn Dutch conduct in Indonesia.

February 1: Trygve Lie becomes secretary-general.

February 4: Military Staff Committee meets for first time.

February 14: General Assembly chooses New York as UN temporary headquarters. Made permanent headquarters on December 14.

March 28: Acheson-Lilienthal report on sharing atomic secrets released.

April 8–18: UN formally dissolves old League of Nations.

June 14: Baruch Plan proposed in General Assembly.

1947   February 10: UN's Commission on the Status of Women meets.

February 14: Britain unilaterally announces end of its Palestine mandate. On April 2, asks UN to consider the issue.

March 12: Truman announces his "Doctrine" in message to Congress.

August 1: Security Council calls for cease-fire in Indonesia/ Netherlands dispute.

August 31: UN Committee on Palestine recommends partition. Approved by General Assembly on November 29.

October 30: GATT final act signed in Geneva.

November 15: IMF and World Bank become formally connected to UN.

1948   May 14: U.S. recognizes independent Israel. War begins between new state and Arab neighbors the next day. Soviets initiate Berlin Blockade.

September 17: Count Folke Bernadotte assassinated while mediating Arab-Israeli dispute.

December 9: General Assembly approves Genocide Convention. Approves Human Rights Declaration the next day.

December 12: General Assembly creates Commission on Korea and recognizes South Korea (Republic of Korea).

1949   May 12: End of Berlin Blockade.

December 27: The Netherlands relinquishes control of Indonesia except for West Irian.

1950   January 12: Dean Acheson delivers Perimeter speech.

January 3: Soviets walk out of UN.

June 25: North Korea attacks South Korea. Security Council calls for withdrawal. Two days later, the council authorizes aid to South Korea.

July 7: Security Council authorizes unified UN command for Korea under U.S. lead.

October 7: General Assembly endorses decision to cross 38th parallel in Korea.

October 12: USSR vetoes Lie's reappointment.

November 3: General Assembly approves Uniting for Peace Resolution.

1951	February 1: PRC labeled "aggressor" by General Assembly. On May 18, General Assembly approves economic sanctions against PRC and North Korea.
1952	November 1: U.S. detonates hydrogen bomb.
1953	January 20: Bricker Amendment introduced into Congress to limit executive treaty making power. Defeated in 1954 by one vote in Senate.
	March 31: Dag Hammarskjold appointed secretary-general.
	July 27: Armistice in Korea.
	December 8: Eisenhower delivers "Atoms for Peace" speech before General Assembly.
1954	June 19: Guatemala asks Security Council to condemn U.S.-sponsored revolution.
	December 4: International Atomic Energy Agency (IAEA) approved by General Assembly. Formally begins on July 29, 1957.
1955	January 5–10: Dag Hammarskjold travels to PRC to discuss downed airmen held as prisoners.
	February 3: PRC refuses Security Council invitation to discuss offshore islands dispute.
	August 1: PRC releases American airmen.
	December 13–14: China and USSR veto package deal for membership of 16 new states, including Mongolia.
	December 16: General Assembly endorses President Eisenhower's "open skies" proposal.
1956	July 26: Gamel Abdel Nasser nationalizes Suez Canal.
	October 22: Hungarian Revolution begins; placed before Security Council on October 28.

October 29: Israel invades Egypt; France and Great Britain attack the next day. UN debate continues for next 12 days. UNEF approved on November 5.

December 22: United Kingdom and France complete withdrawal from Suez.

1957   December 14: SUNFED established.

1958   June 11: UNIGOL (UN Observer Group in Lebanon) created.

July 15: U.S. sends troops into Lebanon. Last troops leave on November 10, and UNIGOL ceases operation on December 9.

1959   September 18: USSR proposes general and complete disarmament in General Assembly.

1960   May 1: U-2 plane shot down; USSR breaks up Paris summit meeting 16 days later.

July 1: Belgium Congo granted independence. Disorder leads to UN debate 12 days later, resulting in creation of ONUC.

September 22: Premier Khrushchev proposes "troika" to replace secretary-general. Attacks Hammarskjold.

1961   February 12: Patrice Lumumba assassinated in Congo.

April 17: Bay of Pigs invasion of Cuba begins.

September 1: USSR resumes nuclear testing; detonates 58-megaton bomb on October 30.

September 13: Without authorization, Hammarskjold deputy orders troops to crush Katangan insurrection, discrediting ONUC.

September 18: Dag Hammarskjold killed in plane crash trying to resolve Congo crisis. U Thant becomes his replacement on November 3.

December 17: India attacks Goa. Adlai Stevenson denounces India in UN the next day.

1962	January 22: ONUC reunifies Congo as Katangan secession ends.
	April 25: U.S. resumes atmospheric testing of nuclear weapons.
	October 23–30: Cuban crisis is debated at the UN, with secretary-general playing active role in settling the conflict.
1963	August 5: Limited atomic test ban treaty signed. Endorsed by General Assembly on November 27.
	November 6: General Assembly passes resolution requesting superpowers to suspend nuclear tests.
	December 17: General Assembly proposes to enlarge Security Council from 11 to 15 members, and ECOSOC from 18 to 25 members.
1964	March 4: U.S. supports Security Council creation of Cyprus peacekeeping force (UNICYP).
	June 30: ONUC operations in Congo end.
	December 1–23: Article 19 dispute over Soviet payments results in no votes being taken in General Assembly.
1965	February 18: General Assembly defeats Albanian attempt to force a vote on Article 19.
	February 24: U Thant publicly criticizes U.S. government for not pursuing UN proposal for a settlement of the Vietnam War.
	May 14: Security Council calls for cease-fire in Dominican Republic.
	August 16: U.S. drops Article 19 demand to deprive USSR of vote in the UN.
	December 21: General Assembly approves Convention on the Elimination of All Forms of Racism.
1966	December 15: Security Council votes economic sanctions against Southern Rhodesia.

1967   May 16: Egypt's President Nasser demands withdrawal of UNEF peacekeepers from Sinai Desert. U Thant accedes to request, and Nasser closes Straits of Tiran to Israeli shipping on May 22.

            June 5: Six-Day War in Mideast begins; Security Council calls for cease-fire.

            November 22: Security Council adopts Resolution 242, setting framework for Mideast negotiations during next 30 years.

            December 5: General Assembly approves Tlatelolco Treaty to keep Latin America nuclear-free.

1968   June 12: Non-Proliferation Treaty approved by General Assembly.

1969   July 14–August 2: West Irian dispute settled.

1970   March 17: U.S. casts first Security Council veto, barring economic sanctions against Southern Rhodesia.

            December 7: General Assembly recommends Sea-Bed Treaty Prohibiting Nuclear Weapons.

1971   October 6: Congress passes Byrd Amendment, barring U.S. from joining UN sanctions against importation of Rhodesian chrome. Reaffirmed on May 31, 1972.

            October 25: General Assembly approves PRC to fill the Chinese seat at UN.

1972   June 5–16: Stockholm Conference on the Human Environment.

            December 13: General Assembly amends dues formula, reducing US share of UN budget from 31.6 percent to 25 percent.

            December 15: General Assembly establishes UNEP.

1973   September 9: Algiers Summit issues demand for a New International Economic Order (NIEO).

            October 6–23: Yom Kippur War. Security Council Resolution 338 calls for implementation of Resolution 242. Resolution 340 creates UNEF II.

1974 June 20–25: U.S. and USSR agree to sign Threshold Treaty limiting nuclear tests to 150 kilotons. U.S. never ratifies the agreement.

November 13: Yassar Arafat addresses General Assembly.

December 12: General Assembly formally endorses NIEO in its Charter on the Economic Rights and Duties of States.

1975 November 10: General Assembly Resolution 3379 labels Zionism as Racism, and invites PLO to all UN meetings dealing with Mideast. The Zionism-Is-Racism resolution is repealed in 1991.

1976 July 14: Security Council resolution condemning Israel for rescue of hostages at Entebbe airport, vetoed by United Kingdom.

1977 September 7: U.S. signs Panama Canal treaty.

November 4: Security Council votes economic sanctions against South Africa.

November 5: Carter administration terminates U.S. membership in ILO. Resumes membership in April 1980.

1978 March 19: Security Council calls for Israeli withdrawal from Lebanon and establishes UNIFIL.

September 5–17: President Carter meets with Menachem Begin and Anwar Sadat at Camp David.

September 29: Security Council passes Resolution 435 setting the terms for a Namibian settlement.

1979 August 15: U.S. Ambassador Andrew Young dismissed after holding unauthorized meeting with PLO representative.

November 4: Iranian radicals take hostages at U.S. embassy in Teheran.

December 27: USSR invades Afghanistan. UN calls for withdrawal.

1980   March 1: Controversial U.S. vote in Security Council supports dismantling of new Israeli settlements, including in Jerusalem.

May 24: World Court condemns Iran in hostage case.

September 22: Iraq invades Iran, beginning eight-year conflict.

1981   June 19: Security Council condemns Israeli attack on Osirak nuclear reactor in Iraq.

October 13: U.S. joins majority at UN to seat Pol Pot's faction in Cambodia.

October 26: U.S. vetoes candidacy of Salim Ahmed Salim of Tanzania to be secretary-general.

1982   April 3: Security Council calls for Argentina to end invasion of Falklands (Malvinas) Islands. On June 4, the U.S. and UK veto call for immediate cease-fire over Ambassador Jeane Kirkpatrick's objections.

June 5: Security Council calls for cease-fire in Lebanon as Israeli troops cross Litani River. On September 19, Security Council condemns massacre of Palestinian civilians in refugee camps.

September 24: U.S. suspends membership in IAEA for nearly five months.

1983   September 1: Soviet pilots shoot down Korean airliner. On September 12, USSR vetoes U.S.-sponsored resolution of condemnation in Security Council.

October 20: Senate approves Kassenbaum amendment, reducing U.S. contributions to UN agencies by 20 to 25 percent.

October 28: U.S. vetoes resolution deploring armed invasion of Grenada. Vetoes a second resolution on November 2.

1984   April 4–6: U.S. vetoes Security Council resolution condemning mining of Managua harbor, then suspends U.S. acceptance of the World Court's compulsory jurisdiction as Nicaragua appeals to the court. The court issues a preliminary ruling against the U.S. action on May 10.

November 26: World Court rules that it has jurisdiction in the Nicaraguan complaint against the U.S..

December 9: Law of the Sea Treaty signed by 159 states, but not the U.S..

December 31: U.S. officially withdraws from UNESCO.

1985	January 18: U.S. informs World Court that it will no longer participate in proceedings relating to Nicaragua.
1986	March 3: World Jewish Congress links former secretary-general Kurt Waldheim to Nazi atrocities during World War II.
	June 27: World Court condemns U.S. activity against Nicaragua as a violation of international law. U.S. vetoes Security Council resolution calling for full compliance with court's judgment.
1987	July 20: Security Council Resolution 598 calls for cease-fire, leading to settlement of Iran-Iraq War.
1988	August 20: Truce goes into effect between Iran and Iraq.
	September 29: UN "Blue Helmets" receive Nobel Peace Prize.
	December 22: Protocol for Namibian independence signed at UN.
1989	January 16: Security Council authorizes formation of UNTAG to supervise Namibian truce.
	November 9: Symbolic end to Cold War as Berlin Wall comes down.
1990	August 1–2: Iraq invades Kuwait.
	August 6: Security Council imposes economic sanctions against Iraq with passage of Resolution 661. On November 29, the Security Council authorizes use of "all necessary means" to expel Iraq (Resolution 678).

1991 January 17: Gulf War begins. Ends on February 27. Resolution 687, passed on April 3, continues economic sanctions until Saddam Hussein complies with all earlier resolutions.

 October 31: UN approves October 23 Paris Accords, including establishment of UNTAC to reestablish order in Cambodia.

 December 16: General Assembly revokes Zionism-Is-Racism resolution.

 December 31: UN accords ending civil war in El Salvador signed at UN.

1992 February 21: Security Council Resolution 713 creates UNPROFOR to maintain order in former Yugoslavia. UNPROFOR enlarged on April 7.

 June 3–14: Earth Summit in Rio de Janiero.

 June 17: Secretary of State Boutros Boutros-Ghali issues his *Agenda for Peace.*

 December 3: Security Council passes Resolution 794 authorizing the use of force to reestablish order in Somalia.

1993 March 26: Security Council Resolution 814 expands UNOSOM II in Somalia.

 May: Clinton administration retreats from support of Vance-Owen peace plan in former Yugoslavia.

 October 3: Somalia attack kills 18 American soldiers.

1994 January 10: NATO endorses air strikes in Bosnia to protect UN forces.

 May 5: Clinton administration issues PDD 25, scaling back UN commitments.

 September 19: U.S. troops occupy Haiti under UN auspices, using authority of Resolution 940 (passed on July 31) to support terms of July Governors Island Agreement.

1995 September 4–15: Beijing Conference on Women.

November 2–21: Dayton, Ohio conference leads to truce in Bosnia.

1996   June 19: U.S. rejects a second term for Secretary-General Boutros-Ghali.

1997   January 2: Kofi Annan replaces Boutros Boutros-Ghali as secretary-general.

October–December: President Saddam Hussein of Iraq challenges UN inspection of facilities that produce chemical and biological weapons. President Clinton fails to persuade Security Council to impose new sanctions on October 22, but council does expand travel restrictions regarding Iraq on November 12.

December 1–11: UN Conference on Climate Change (global warming) held in Kyoto, Japan.

1998   February 22: Kofi Annan averts war by persuading Iraqi leaders to comply fully with UN inspection teams as mandated in Resolution 687 (1991). Agreement incorporated into S.C. Resolution 1154, approved on March 2.

APPENDIX A
ASSISTANT SECRETARIES OF STATE
FOR INTERNATIONAL ORGANIZATION

Note: Until 1949, International Organization (IO) was a bureau or department called Special Political Affairs.

Alger Hiss 1945–1947

Dean Rusk 1947–1949

John D. Hickerson 1949–1953

Robert D. Murphy 1953

David McKey 1953–1955

Francis O. Wilcox 1955–1961

Harlan Cleveland 1961–1965

Joseph J. Sisco 1965–1968

Samuel De Palma 1969–1973

David H. Popper 1973

William B. Buffum 1974–1975

Samuel Lewis 1975–1977

Charles W. Maynes 1977–1980

Richard L. McCall 1980–1981

Elliot Abrams 1981

Gregory J. Newell 1982–1985

Alan Lee Keyes 1985–1987

Richard Williamson 1988

John R. Bolton 1989–1992

Douglas Bennet Jr. 1993–1995

Princeton M. Lyman 1997–

APPENDIX B
U.S. PERMANENT REPRESENTATIVES
TO THE UNITED NATIONS

Edward R. Stettinius Jr. 1946

Hershel V. Johnson (acting) 1946

Warren Austin 1947–1953

Henry Cabot Lodge 1953–1960

James J. Wadsworth 1960–1961

Adlai Stevenson 1961–1965

Arthur J. Goldberg 1965–1968

George W. Ball 1968

James Russell Wiggins 1968–1969

Charles W. Yost 1969–1971

George W. Bush 1971–1973

John A. Scali 1973–1975

Daniel P. Moynihan 1975–1976

William W. Scranton 1976–1977

Andrew Young 1977–1979

Donald McHenry 1979–1981

Jeane J. Kirkpatrick 1981–1985

Vernon A. Walters 1985–1989

Thomas R. Pickering 1989–1993

Madeleine Albright 1993–1997

William Richardson 1997–

APPENDIX C
UN OBSERVER AND PEACEKEEPING OPERATIONS
(AS OF JANUARY 1998)

UNTSO   Jerusalem 1948–

UNMOGIP   Pakistan 1949–

UNEF I   Suez 1956–1957

UNOGIL   Lebanon 1958

ONUC   Congo 1960–1964

UNSF   West Irian 1962–1963

UNYOM   Yemen 1962–1964

UNFICYP   Cyprus 1964–

DOMREP   Dominican Republic 1965–1966

UNIPOM   India/Pakistan 1956–1966

UNEF II   Suez 1973–1979

UNDOF   Golan Heights 1974–

UNIFIL   Lebanon 1978–

UNGOMAP   Afghanistan/Pakistan 1988–1990

UNIIMOG   Iran/Iraq 1988–1991

UNAVEM I   Angola 1989–1991

UNTAG   Namibia 1989–1990

ONUCA   Central America 1989–1992

UNAVEM II   Angola 1991–1995

ONUSAL   El Salvador 1991–

UNIKOM   Iraq/Kuwait 1991–

MINURSO   Western Sahara 1991–

UNAMIC   Cambodia 1991–1992

UNPROFOR   Former Yugoslavia 1992–1995

UNTAC   Cambodia 1992–

UNOSOM I   Somalia 1992–1993

ONUMOZ   Mozambique 1992–1994

UNOSOM II   Somalia 1993–1995

UNOMUR   Uganda/Rwanda 1993–1994

UNOMIG   Georgia 1993–

UNOMIL   Liberia 1993–1997

UNTMIH   Haiti 1993–1997

UNAMIR   Rwanda 1993–1996

UNASOG   Chad/Libya 1994

MINUGUA   Guatemala 1994–1997

UNMOT   Tajikstan 1994–

UNCRO   Croatia 1993–

UNAVEM III   Angola 1995–1997

UNPREDEP   Macedonia 1995–

UNMIBH   Bosnia-Herzogovia 1995–

UNSMIH   Haiti 1996–1997

UNMOP   Prevlaka (Croatia) 1996–

UNTAES   Eastern Slavonia, Baranja, Western Sirmium (Croatia) 1996–

UNMOP   Croatia 1996–

MIPONUA   Haiti 1997–

NOTES AND REFERENCES

1. ROOSEVELT

1. For the story of the League's shaky World War II existence, see Frank P. Walters, *A History of the League of Nations*, vol. 2 (New York and Toronto: Oxford University Press, 1952), chap. 66, 801–10.

2. See my own *Collective Insecurity: The United States and the League of Nations during the Early Thirties* (Lewisburg, Pa.: Bucknell University Press, 1979), 41.

3. The group was originally called the Committee for the Study of the Organization of Peace. Its early history is covered in Clark M. Eichelberger, *Organizing for Peace: A Personal History of the Founding of the United Nations* (New York: Harper & Row, 1977), 111–18.

4. Ibid. 115-16.

5. Robert A. Divine, *Second Chance: The Triumph of Internationalism in America during World War II* (New York: Atheneum, 1971), 36. The results of numerous public opinion polls can be found in William A. Scott and Stephen B. Withey, *The United States and the United Nations: The Public View, 1945–1955* (New York: Manhattan Publishing Company, 1958), 9–15.

6. Divine, 52–57.

7. Townsend Hoopes and Douglas Brinkley, *FDR and the Creation of the U.N.* (New Haven: Yale University Press, 1997), 38–39 (page proofs).

8. Clarence K. Streit, *Union Now: The Proposal for an Inter-Democratic Federal Union* (New York: Harper & Brothers, 1940); Divine, 36–39.

9. Divine, 41–42. See also Sumner Welles, *The World of the Four Freedoms* (New York, Harper & Brothers, 1943), and the discussion of interwar planning in his book *The Time for Decision* (New York and London: Harper & Brothers, 1944).

10. Eichelberger, 190.

11. Divine, 55–56.

12. Cordell Hull, *Memoirs of Cordell Hull* (New York: Macmillan Company, 1948), 2:1735.

13. Hull offers a very comprehensive discussion of the debate between the regionalists and the universalists in his *Memoirs*, 2:1639–48. On the other issue, the international air force, Hull and his colleagues were not terribly consistent. The Americans favored it by the time of Dumbarton Oaks, then backed away before the conference ended.

14. Hull, 2:1638–39. The bureaucratic politics of international organization preoccupied Hull from mid-1942 until July 1943 (Divine, 81–83, 113–16).

15. Wilkie's public pronouncements greatly irritated President Roosevelt, who feared that his own freedom of action might be limited by the activity of his opponent in the 1940 election. The activity of Wallace and Wilkie is found in Divine, 62–72.

16. The Advisory Committee had been designed by Hull to be nonpartisan and broadly representative. It was really too large to be meaningful, and its work of "advising" the president increasingly became the task of Welles's Subcommittee on Political Problems. Hull, 2:1638

17. Divine, 92–97.

18. Divine, 110–12. A good discussion of the isolationist position on the resolution is found in Wayne S. Cole, *Roosevelt and the Isolationists, 1932–45* (Lincoln and London: University of Nebraska Press, 1983), 522–24, and Eugene Brown, *J. William Fulbright: Advice and Dissent* (Iowa City: University of Iowa Press, 1985), 17.

19. Public opinion remained an elusive subject; support or opposition for international organization had much to do with the way that questions were phrased. "Do you favor the use of international force to keep the peace?" might bring a substantially different response from "Do you think it a good idea for the United States to join a postwar union of nations?" To the latter question, at least, 81 percent of those polled responded in the affirmative in September 1943 (Divine, 134).

20. Hull, 2:1227–30.

21. Hoopes and Brinkley, 78–82, offer the best account of the attack on Welles, including a description of the intrigue orchestrated by FDR's former ambassador to Vichy, William Bullitt.

22. The text of many important wartime documents relating to the United Nations, including the Moscow Declaration, is found in *Dumbarton Oaks*, compiled by Robert E. Summers (New York: H. W. Wilson Company, 1945). The Moscow agreement was signed on October 30, 1943.

23. Divine, 150–53. The text can be found in Summers, 99.

24. Hoopes and Brinkley, 102.

25. Many historians have addressed the degree to which FDR took the "spheres of influence" concept seriously. It is noteworthy that he never consciously embraced the idea. Adam Ulam is most likely correct when he writes that FDR thought of the Four Policemen as acting not selfishly but "selflessly and on behalf of law"; he is also correct to note that to most other people, this idea was reminiscent of a "spheres of influence" approach. See Ulam's *The Rivals: America and Russia Since World War II* (New York: Viking Press, 1971), 36–37.

26. Spykman's most influential work is *America's Strategy in the World Politics* (New York: Harcourt, Brace & Company, 1942). Lippmann deals with these themes in

U.S. Foreign Policy: Shield of the Republic (Boston: Little Brown & Company, 1943), chap. 10, in which he proposes a "nuclear alliance" among the Great Powers in order to maintain a liberal peace. See also Hull, 1642–48.

27. See, for instance, Frederick W. Marks, *Wind over Sand: The Diplomacy of Franklin D. Roosevelt* (Athens, Ga., and London: University of Georgia Press, 1988), 283–84. Even some friendly historians accept the view of a divide-and-conquer style of administration. See Robert C. Hilderbrand, *Dumbarton Oaks: The Origins of the United Nations and the Search for Postwar Security* (Chapel Hill: University of North Carolina Press, 1990), 24; Robert Dallek, *Franklin D. Roosevelt and American Foreign Policy, 1933–1945* (New York: Oxford University Press, 1979), 421.

28. It is not clear whether Roosevelt himself believed this. There is evidence, according to Hull, that FDR favored "entirely separate functional agencies." But the State Department, says Hull, saw formation of the FAO and UNRRA as a "rehearsal" for the UN conference (Hull, 2:1643, 1654).

29. Arthur Vandenberg, ed., *The Private Papers of Senator Vandenberg* (Boston: Houghton Mifflin Company, 1952), 70. Divine, 116–19, 156–57. This episode clearly reminded Hull about the dangers of ignoring Congress. It is not so certain that FDR got the message. In February 1944, an impatient president suggested to one State Department official that the new United Nations be created immediately; he ignored Congress altogether in outlining this proposal (Divine, 192).

30. Welles's book *The Time for Decision* became an immediate best-seller. The organizational structure proposed by Welles is found on pp. 374–77 of his text.

31. Divine, 184–85.

32. Vandenberg, 95–96. See also Hoopes and Brinkley, 125.

33. Richard N. Smith, *Thomas E. Dewey and His Times* (New York: Simon & Schuster, 1982), 412–15; Hull, 2:1689–95; Divine, 216–20.

34. Even FDR, despite the wartime conferences, had rarely discussed the subject before June 1944. His voluminous published correspondence with Churchill contains only one letter dealing with international organization before that month. See *Roosevelt and Churchill: Their Secret Wartime Correspondence*, eds. Francis L. Loewenheim, Harold D. Langley, and Manfred Jonas (New York: Saturday Review Press/E. P. Dutton, 1975), 310.

35. Hilderbrand, 44.

36. Hilderbrand, 39.

37. Evan Luard, *A History of the United Nations: The Years of Western Domination, 1945–1955* (New York: St. Martin's Press, 1982), 1:25.

38. Hilderbrand, 75–79; Hoopes and Brinkley, 133–36.

39. *The Diaries of Edward R. Stettinius, Jr., 1943–1946*, eds. Thomas M. Campbell and George C. Herring (New York: New Viewpoints, 1975), 110–14.

40. Hilderbrand, 123–27; Stettinius, *Diaries*, 1–13, 118.

41. Stettinius's published diaries, one of our most important sources on Dumbarton Oaks, do not even mention the Chinese phase of the conference.

42. Stettinius, *Diaries*, 252–53. According to Diane Shaver Clemens in *Yalta* (New York: Oxford University Press, 1970), 232–33, members of the American delegation held the British responsible for caving in to the Soviet demand.

43. Stettinius, *Diaries*, 284–85.

44. Hilderbrand, 249.

2. SAN FRANCISCO

1. Harry S. Truman, *Memoirs: The Year of Decisions* (Garden City, N.Y.: Doubleday and Company, 1955), 1:22–23.

2. FDR may have appointed him, rather than more seasoned officials like Byrnes, for both of these reasons. See Stettinius, *Diaries*, xxiv.

3. Some elements of this campaign are included in Divine, 283–85, Eichelberger, 255–57, and Porter McKeever, *Adlai Stevenson: His Life and Legacy* (New York: William Morrow and Company, 1989), 94–96.

4. Vandenberg, 215.

5. Divine, 291–92.

6. Truman, 1:279.

7. Among the historians who emphasize the shift away from internationalism and a forthright commitment to the UN are Thomas M. Campbell in *Masquerade Peace: America's UN Policy, 1944–1945* (Tallahassee: Florida State University Press, 1973) and Hilderbrand in *Dumbarton Oaks*. In *A Preponderance of Power: National Security, the Truman Administration, and the Cold War* (Stanford, Calif.: Stanford University Press, 1992), Melvin P. Leffler has produced a monumental study of American policy during these years; his text may become the standard work on the subject of Cold War diplomacy. Tellingly, he barely mentions the San Francisco Conference. Competition, not cooperation, is his theme. Leffler argues that in 1945 the United States acted on an "impulse to compete and contain the Soviet Union," not the impulse to "maintain Allied solidarity" (26).

8. See memorandum and minutes, March 29 and 30, 1945, Department of State, *Foreign Relations of the United States* (hereafter *FRUS*), 1945, United Nations (Washington, D.C.: Government Printing Office, 1972), 1:166–70; Truman, 1:73.

9. The presidency controversy even goes unmentioned in Eden's memoirs, *The Memoirs of Anthony Eden, Earl of Avon, The Reckoning* (Boston: Houghton Mifflin Company, 1965) and in the section on San Francisco in Eden's main biography, by Robert Rhodes James, *Anthony Eden* (London: Weidenfeld & Nicholson, 1986), 292–94. It is worth noting that tension between the Soviets and the West predated the conference. Eden, for instance, wrote to Prime Minister Churchill a month before the conference: "The Russians are behaving so abominably that I hope you will not mind my suggesting that it might be well that you should cut down your personal messages to Marshal Stalin to a minimum." Churchill agreed (James, 293).

10. Minutes of meeting, May 26, 1945, *FRUS*, 1945, 1:930. A series of memoranda contained in *FRUS* includes the entirety of these debates over the veto.

11. Vandenberg, 203–4.

12. Article 21 stipulated that nothing in the Covenant should inhibit "engagements" such as the Monroe Doctrine from securing the peace.

13. Many documents cover this subject, but the minutes of the 9 A.M. meeting of the American delegation on May 9, 1945, provide the best overview of the debate (*FRUS*, 1945, 1:617–26, 627–28). Also, meeting of 6:18 P.M. of May 7 (*FRUS*, 1945, 1:631–40).

14. Luard, 1:54.

15. Minutes of 23rd Five Power meeting, June 16, 1945, 6 P.M., FRUS, 1945, 1:1131–38. Vandenberg, 210–11.

16. Article 10: "The General Assembly may discuss any questions or any matters within the scope of the present Charter or relating to the powers and functions of any organs provided for in the present Charter. . . . "

17. Article 23 required League members to "endeavor to secure and maintain fair and humane conditions of labour," to establish the necessary international organizations for this purpose, and to supervise agreements in a number of related areas from the traffic in women and children to the drug trade.

18. See Articles 62 and 68 of the Charter.

19. Nor were many other powers, big or small. Article 2, section 7 specifically prohibits the UN from intervening in matters "essentially within the domestic jurisdiction" of a member state. The subject of domestic jurisdiction was discussed at some length at San Francisco. See, for instance, *FRUS*, 1945, 1:582–84, 599.

20. Minutes of 26th meeting of U.S. Delegation, May 2, 1945, 5:30 P.M., *FRUS*, 1945, 1:532–35.

21. On the critical subject as to which colonies would become trust territories, the Charter stipulated former mandates, colonies of the former enemy states, and those which UN members would *voluntarily* place under trusteeship. Article 77.

22. Minutes of the 45th meeting of the U.S. Delegation, May 18, 1945, 9 A.M., *FRUS*, 1945, 1:792–98; 959–62. Leland M. Goodrich and Edvard Hambro, *Charter of the United Nations: Commentary and Documents* (Boston: World Peace Foundation, 1946), 233–36. The italics are mine.

23. Minutes of 23rd meeting of the U.S. delegation, April 30, 1945, 9:30A.M., *FRUS*, 1945, 1:491–95.

3. TRUMAN

1. Near-unanimous but not unanimous. The Truman Library contains a surprising number of angry letters by Americans who were as opposed to the UN as to the old League.

2. Trygve Lie, *In the Cause of Peace: Seven Years with the United Nations* (New York: Macmillan Company, 1954), 55–63. Stettinius had been the main U.S. proponent of an American site for the UN: "Any move to leave this country," he wrote in 1946, would . . . have serious repercussions upon the United Nations and would seriously damage the prestige and influence of the United States." Letter to president, May 13, 1946, found in Truman Library.

3. A useful account of this affair is found in Lie, chapter 1. A cable from Adlai Stevenson, U.S. representative to the Preparatory Commission, looked to Lie as a compromise candidate for General Assembly president as early as December 1945. See *FRUS*, 1945, 1:1509. The most provocative account of this issue is found in James Barros, *Trygve Lie and the Cold War: The UN Secretary-General Pursues Peace, 1946–53* (Dekalb: Northern Illinois University Press, 1989), chapter 1. Barros suggests that the Soviets had always favored Lie, that their support for Simic was a cover for their support for Lie, that they subtly maneuvered Stettinius into supporting Lie for the assembly presidency, and that they supported a North American site for the UN precisely because they understood that it would undermine support for Pearson—or any other North American candidate—as secretary-general.

4. Barros, 20, 26.

5. The best short description of this article appears in Goodrich and Hambro, 170–72.

6. See Articles 39, 42, and 43 of the UN Charter.

7. See the MSC's report on General Principles, found in *Yearbook of the United Nations 1946–1947* (New York: UN Department of Public Information, 1947; hereafter cited as *UN Yearbook*), 424–443, especially chapter 4 called "Contribution of Armed Forces by Member Nations."

8. The MSC continues in a strictly formal sense. Military representatives of the permanent members of the Security Council meet biweekly to do nothing other than set the date of their next meeting. The American mission to the UN contains a number of high-level military officials who comprise its MSC delegation (Seymour Maxwell Finger, *American Ambassadors at the UN: People, Politics, and Bureaucracy in Making Foreign Policy* [New York and London: Holmes & Meier, 1988], 17).

9. Jonathan Soffer, "All for One and One for All: The UN Military Staff Committee and the Contradictions within American Internationalism," *Diplomatic History* 21 (Winter 1997), 63–65; D. W. Bowett, *United Nations Forces* (London: Stevens & Sons, 1964), chapter 2; Ralph M. Goldman, *Is It Time to Revive the UN Military Staff Committee?* (Los Angeles: Center for the Study of Armament and Disarmament, 1990), 7–9.

10. Soffer, 68. The author does not mention it, but he is apparently referring to PDD 25, covered in chapter 11.

11. Truman, 290; *FRUS*, 1946, (Washington, D.C.: Government Printing Office, 1972), 1:1167; *The Truman Administration: Its Principles and Practice*, ed. Louis W. Koenig (New York: New York University Press, 1956), 267.

12. Vandenberg, 223.

13. Acheson's views are outlined by David Lilienthal, found in Bert Cochran, *Harry Truman and the Crisis Presidency* (New York: Funk & Wagnalls, 1973), 279. Byrnes's defense is found in James F. Byrnes, *Speaking Frankly* (New York: Harpers & Brothers, 1947), 267–73.

14. See Brynes, 270; Cochran, 281. Lilienthal was often feeling sick. See David McCullough, *Truman* (New York: Simon & Schuster, 1992), 349 and 389 about Lilienthal's feelings regarding Truman as president in 1945.

15. Truman to Charlie Ross, January 22, 1950, found in PSF-Personal: Political v.p. nomination 1944, Box 321, Truman Library.

16. Jordan Schwarz, *The Speculator: Bernard M. Baruch in Washington, 1917–1965* (Chapel Hill: University of North Carolina Press, 1981), 498. Baruch's rivalry with Acheson and Lilienthal is suggested by Baruch's failure to even mention their names in his autobiography. Bernard M. Baruch, *My Own Story* (New York: Henry Holt & Company, 1957).

17. One historian claims that Austin's refusal to resign should be viewed as a sign of strength, not weakness. See George T. Mazuzan's article about Austin in *Biographical Dictionary of Internationalists*, ed. Warren F. Kuehl (Westport, Conn.: Greenwood Press, 1983), 37.

18. The confusing changes in State Department bureaucracy are partly covered in Warren I. Cohen, "Dean Rusk," in *American Secretaries of State and Their Diplomacy*, ed. Robert H. Ferrell (Totowa, N.J.: Cooper Square Publishers, 1980), 31–35.

19. *UN Yearbook 1946–47*, 327–36.

20. Leffler, 80.

21. Randall B. Woods and Howard Jones, *Dawning of the Cold War: The United States Quest for Order* (Chicago: Ivan L. Dee, 1994), 102.

22. Truman, 1:551–52.

23. James A. Bill, *The Eagle and the Lion: The Tragedy of American-Iranian Relations* (New York and London: Yale University Press, 1988), 35.

24. Woods and Jones, 103–4.

25. Paul Porter, an American official ordered by the Truman administration to investigate the situation, said that the Greek government was hardly a government "in the western sense." He called the civil service a "depressing farce," and believed it was riddled with corruption. Quoted in H. W. Brands, *The Devil We Knew: Americans and the Cold War* (New York and Oxford: Oxford University Press, 1993), 19.

26. See, for instance, *UN Yearbook 1946–1947*, 336–38.

27. *UN Yearbook 1946–1947*, 361–62, *UN Yearbook 1947–1948*, 68. The story of UNSCOB is especially well told in Amikam Nachmani, *International Intervention in the Greek Civil War: The United Nations Special Committee on the Balkans, 1947–52* (New York: Praeger, 1990), 36–43.

28. Even historians sympathetic to the UN accept this view. See, for instance, Luard, 1:125–26.

29. Mazuzan, 71–72.

30. Among the best sources on this subject are Michael J. Cohen, *Palestine and the Great Powers* (Princeton: Princeton University Press, 1982); and the same author's *Truman and Israel* (Berkeley, Los Angeles, and Oxford: Oxford University Press, 1990), 143–49.

31. Truman, 1:140.

32. Bruce J. Evensen, *Truman, Palestine, and the Press: Shaping Conventional Wisdom at the Beginning of the Cold War* (New York; Westport, Conn.; and London: Greenwood Press, 1992), 136–37.

33. The best discussion of the use of American troops appears in W. Cohen, 20–24. Rusk was among the few high-level Department officials who favored the use of troops, believing that the UN had a moral obligation to support its policy. Secretary of War Robert Lovett, too, believed that troops must be used if U.S. policy was to be taken seriously, but Navy Secretary Forrestal demurred, and the White House did not challenge Forrestal's judgment.

34. Roy Jenkins, *Truman* (New York: Harper & Row Publishers, 1986), 120. Eleanor Roosevelt was so incensed at the change of position that she nearly resigned from her UN post. Her anger may have been reinforced by her disappointment with U.S.-Soviet relations and her belief that the United States was not giving the UN enough support (Letter to George Marshall, March 13, 1948, PSF personal file, ER folder 2, Box 321, Harry S. Truman Papers, Truman Library). Nine days later, she wrote to Marshall that "I feel that . . . we have more or less buried the UN." This letter included an offer to resign from the Human Rights Commission. (Letter to Marshall of March 22, 1948, same folder).

35. Luard, 1:84–89.

36. In his memoirs, Lie implies that his position, which he does not call "pro-Jewish," was influenced by the willingness of the Jewish Agency (speaking for the Jews) to cooperate with UNSCOP and the subsequent Palestine Commission, while the Arabs mainly hurled threats. Found in Lie, 165.

37. Clark Clifford, *Counsel to the President* (New York: Random House, 1991), 22.

38. This last point has been highly controversial for decades. As late as 1991, Clark Clifford's memoirs argued that domestic political considerations had no effect on Truman's policies. However, publication of Michael Cohen's *Truman and Israel* should end this argument; Cohen shows (conclusively, I believe) that Truman's political calculations were at least partly responsible for the decision to recognize Israel.

39. Leffler, 242–43.

40. Leffler, 243–45.

41. Avi Shlaim, *The United States and the Berlin Blockade, 1948–1949: A Study in Crisis Decision-Making* (Berkeley and Los Angeles: University of California Press, 1983), 346–68, 376–82.

42. To get a flavor of the time see a fine memoir by a UNESCO employee who was eventually cleared: Julian Behrstok, *The Eighth Case: Troubled Times at the United Nations* (New York, Lanham, and London: University Press of America, 1987).

43. Lie, 396–401. Lie's account is instructive. His great affection for Feller, whom he calls "liberal in politics, conservative in his lawyerlike respect for due process," is evident. It is also self-justifying, for many UN officials, including by his own account many Europeans, denounced the treatment of those who were fired after UN "due process."

44. Shirley Hazzard, "Breaking Faith," *New Yorker*, September 25, 1989, 64–68. Hazzard's charge against Price is not corroborated by documentation; she might have been writing metaphorically. Hazzard covers this whole story with less detail in her highly critical account of the UN: *Defeat of an Ideal: A Study of the Self Destruction of the United Nations* (Boston: Little, Brown & Company, 1973). In the book, she claims that the investigations "made a mockery" of the UN (20). The best single account of the loyalty issue appears in Barros, 311–20. Barros does not affirm Hazzard's accusation against Price and is much more sympathetic to Lie, arguing that the secretary-general's conduct was understandable—though not honorable—in light of the anticommunist hysteria in the U.S. Congress. Barros stresses that a genuinely nonpolitical secretariat is just not possible in the real world.

45. Hazzard ("Breaking Faith," 75) claims that only the completion of the FBI's work led to closure of the office. In fact, Hammarskjold closed the office after FBI Director J. Edgar Hoover complained to a Senate committee that the bureau was hampered when investigating international agencies by the principle of extraterritoriality. Brian Urquhart, *Hammarskjold* (New York: Harper Colophon Books, 1972), 63–64. The phrase about witch hunters appears in Urquhart's *A Life in Peace and War* (New York: Harper & Row, 1987), 123.

46. *UN Yearbook 1947–48*, 88.

47. *FRUS, 1947* (Washington, D.C.: Government Printing Office, 1973), 1:776. Résumé of World Situation, produced by the State Department's Policy Planning Staff, November 6, 1947.

48. NSC 68. *FRUS, 1950* (Washington, D.C.: Government Printing Office, 1977), 1:235–92.

49. The best discussion of this memo remains John L. Gaddis, *Strategies of Containment: A Critical Appraisal of Postwar American National Security Policy* (New York and Oxford: Oxford University Press, 1982), 91.

50. Linda Fasulo, *Representing America: Experiences of U.S. Diplomats at the U.N.* (New York: Facts on File Publications, 1984), 45, quotes Ernest Gross, a deputy U.S. representative at the UN, when he told Acheson that he wished assignment to the international organization. He "thought that I was a little bit silly." But Gross claims that while Acheson had little interest in the UN, he did give it support.

51. Dean Acheson, *Present at the Creation* (New York: W. W. Norton, 1969), 354.

52. Not all historians agree about this. Peter Lowe (*The Origins of the Korean War* [London and New York: Longman, 1986], 160–61) suggests that Stalin did not relish the presence of Mao's China on the Security Council. Bruce Cumings (*The Origins of the Korean War*, 2 vols. [Princeton: Princeton University Press, 1981, 1990], 2:636–37) says that the boycott was "ostensibly" about Chinese representation, and that Stalin deliberately kept his delegates away after the North Korean attack because he may have wanted to suck the United States into a remote war, or because he wanted to prove that the UN was merely a U.S. tool.

53. Cumings, 2:625.

54. Fasulo, 40.

55. Cumings, 2:629, quotes Senator Robert Taft as calling Acheson's decision "a complete usurpation by the President of the authority to use armed forces." See also Barros, 275–76.

56. Acheson, *The Korean War* (New York: W. W. Norton & Company, 1971), 19, contains the text of the resolution. See also *UN Yearbook 1950* (New York: Columbia University Press, 1951), 222–24.

57. Barros, *Trygve Lie*, 259.

58. *UN Yearbook 1950*, 230.

59. *UN Yearbook 1950*, 264–66.

60. The text of the resolution is found in *UN Yearbook 1950*, 193–95. The U.S.-Soviet debate over the resolution is found on pp. 180–93.

61. Luard, 1:95.

62. Text of resolution, *FRUS*, 1951 (Washington, D.C.: Government Printing Office, 1983), 7:150–51. In *A Substitute for Victory: The Politics of Peacemaking at the Korean Armistice Talks* (Ithaca and London: Cornell University Press, 1990), 32–33, Rosemary Foot notes that both houses of Congress had already applied pressure to the administration by branding China the aggressor in separate resolutions.

63. *UN Yearbook 1951* (New York: Columbia University Press, 1952), 228.

64. Luard, 1:243.

65. Foot, 152–57.

66. Letter, Marshall to Roosevelt, March 24, 1948, PSF—Personal. E. Roosevelt folder 2, Box 231, Truman Library.

67. William Korey, "Genocide Treaty Ratification: Ending an American Embarrassment," in *America Unbound: World War II and the Making of a Superpower,*" ed. Warren F. Kimball (New York: St. Martin's Press, 1992), 165–66.

4. EISENHOWER

1. Oral history, David Wainhouse, OH-278, Dwight D. Eisenhower Presidential Library.

2.   Oral history, Francis O. Wilcox, OH-246, Eisenhower Library, 185. See, too, Wainhouse Oral History, 14–15. But Lodge was not always a good soldier, and Robert Murphy's memoirs describe how he continued to maintain great independence when he wanted it (*Diplomat Among Warriors* [New York: Praeger, 1968]; 367). Lodge's memoir, *As It Was: An Inside View of Politics and Power in the '50s and '60s* (New York: W. W. Norton & Company, 1976) is silent about this situation. In fact, the memoir is very superficial and of only limited value to historians.

3.   Dwight D. Eisenhower, *Mandate for Change, 1953–56* (Garden City, N.Y.: Doubleday, 1963), 8.

4.   Ibid.

5.   Even Taft had demanded the resignation of Acheson for the so-called loss of China. The Ohio senator might have opposed McCarthy on some issues, such as firing communist professors when their politics did not influence their teaching, or by giving lukewarm support to Eisenhower's diplomatic appointees (e.g., Charles Bohlen as ambassador to Moscow), but Taft frequently parroted the McCarthy line on foreign policy questions. See James T. Patterson, *Mr. Republican: A Biography of Robert A. Taft* (Boston: Houghton Mifflin, 1972), 591–96.

6.   Jeff Broadwater, *Eisenhower and the Anticommunist Crusade* (Chapel Hill: University of North Carolina Press), 131.

7.   Frederick W. Marks III, *Power and Peace: The Diplomacy of John Foster Dulles* (Westport, Conn.: Praeger, 1993), 92–94.

8.   Barros, 272. What adds complexity to this issue is that the Charter never specified how long the secretary-general would serve, nor did the Security Council's initial recommendation to appoint Lee include a stated term of service. The term—and the criteria for reappointment—would be settled by later agreement between the Security Council and the General Assembly, understanding that any appointment was subject to a Great Power veto. E-mail by Sam Daws, New College, Oxford University (November 21, 1996, ACUNS-IO: American Council of United Nations Studies).

9.   The Russians were themselves on weak legal ground. The Security Council's 1946 recommendation to the General Assembly never specified the length of the secretary-general's term. After the Lie episode, the Security Council always set a renewable five-year limit. Sam Daws, E-mail, November 21, 1996, to American Council of the United Nations Studies (ACUNS-IO).

10.   Barros, 329, 333–40. Lie had few supporters in Washington, but the United States could not admit this publicly.

11.   See, for instance, the speech of Senator Pat McCarran, January 29, 1954, 83rd Cong., 2nd sess., *Congressional Record*, C, pt. 1:934–37.

12.   Herbert Brownell, *Advising Ike: The Memoirs of Attorney General Herbert Brownell* (Lawrence: University Press of Kansas, 1993), 265–66. Senators like Jenner and Bricker were not intellectual heavyweights. Reporter John Gunther described Bricker as "intellectually ... like interstellar space—a vast vacuum occasionally crossed by homeless, wandering cliches." Quoted in Arthur M. Schlesinger, Jr., "A Man From Mars," *Atlantic Monthly*, 279 (April 1997): 115.

13.   William Korey, "Genocide Treaty Ratification: Ending an American Embarrassment," in *America Unbound: World War II and the Making of a Superpower*, ed. Warren F. Kimball (New York: St. Martin's Press, 1992), 176–77.

14.   Anthony Clark Arend, *Pursuing a Just and Durable Peace: John Foster Dulles and International Organization* (New York: Greenwood Press, 1988), 201–3 is more gen-

erous to Dulles than my own interpretation. The long story of delay in ratifying the genocide treaty is found in Korey, 160–79.

15. Brands, 30.

16. Norman A. Graebner, "Eisenhower and Communism," in Richard A. Melanson and David Mayers, eds., *Reevaluating Eisenhower: American Foreign Policy in the 1950s* (Urbana and Chicago: University of Illinois Press, 1987), 68–69.

17. Nancy Bernkopf Tucker, "John Foster Dulles and the Roots of the 'Two Chinas' Policy,' " in *John Foster Dulles and the Diplomacy of the Cold War*, ed Richard H. Immerman (Princeton: Princeton University Press, 1990), 255; Gordon H. Chang, *Friends and Enemies: The United States, China, and the Soviet Union, 1948–1974* (Stanford: Stanford University Press, 1990), 146–47.

18. *UN Yearbook 1954*, (New York: Columbia University Press, 1955), 40–42.

19. *UN Yearbook 1954*, 43.

20. Urquhart, *Hammarskjold*, 114.

21. Chang, 126.

22. Richard H. Immerman, *The CIA in Guatemala: The Diplomacy of Intervention* (Austin: University of Texas Press, 1982), 11.

23. Dulles's speech of June 30, 1954, Department of State, *Bulletin* 31 (July 12, 1954): 43.

24. *UN Yearbook 1954*, 96.

25. *UN Yearbook 1954*, 97–99.

26. Immerman, 171–72; Blanche Wiesen Cook, *The Declassified Eisenhower* (Garden City, N.Y.: Doubleday & Company, 1981), 280–81. Lodge may have thought the whole Guatemalan episode of little importance; he ignores it in his memoirs, *As It Was*.

27. Luard, 1:300.

28. Urquhart, *Hammarskjold*, 92–94. Article 103 states: "In the event of a conflict between the obligations of the Members of the United Nations under the present Charter and their obligations under any other international agreement, the obligations under the present Charter shall prevail."

29. The Chinese Nationalists vetoed membership for Outer Mongolia and the USSR vetoed Japan's application. On December 14, 1955, 16 other states were admitted including Albania, Austria, Bulgaria, Ireland, Portugal, Cambodia, Spain, and Laos.

30. Robert L. Branyan and Lawrence H. Larsen, eds., *The Eisenhower Administration: A Documentary History, 1953–1961* (New York: Random House, 1971), 200.

31. Eisenhower, 1:254–55.

32. Urquhart, *Hammarskjold*, 323.

33. *UN Yearbook 1955* (New York: Columbia University Press, 1956), 12–13; see also the unanimous General Assembly vote on February 14, 1957, in *UN Yearbook 1957* (New York: Columbia University Press, 1958), 103–4.

34. *New York Times*, January 24, 1956, 1.

35. *UN Yearbook 1956* (New York: Columbia University Press, 1957), 4–7.

36. Robert Rhodes James, *Anthony Eden* (London: Weidenfeld & Nicolson, 1986), 446–50. James implies not only that the Americans worried about a Russian role in financing the dam, but that some U.S. officials like Assistant Secretary of State

Herbert Hoover Jr. and Treasury Secretary George Humphrey also distrusted the British.

37. Anthony Eden, *Full Circle: The Memoirs of Anthony Eden* (Boston: Houghton Mifflin Company, 1960), 481.

38. Most early accounts suggest that a moralistic Dulles, not Eisenhower, led the campaign to prevent the use of force. Today, however, it is generally agreed that the opposition to military measures came from the president, not the secretary of state. See, for instance, Herbert S. Parmet, *Eisenhower and the American Crusades* (New York: Macmillan Company, 1972), 485. Marks (*Power and Peace*, 29) says that "Ike was leading with Dulles's chin." See also James, 476–77. William Roger Louis says in "Dulles, Suez, and the British" (in *John Foster Dulles and the Diplomacy of the Cold War*, ed. Richard H. Immerman, 134–35), that Dulles was just the "stalking horse" of Eisenhower.

39. Herman Finer, *Dulles Over Suez: The Theory and Practice of His Diplomacy* (Chicago: Quadrangle Books, 1964), 395.

40. *UN Yearbook 1956*, 28, 34–35.

41. Luard, 2:43.

42. The United States played tough by withholding IMF loans that London needed to stabilize the pound. This story is told brilliantly by Diane Kunz in *The Economic Diplomacy of the Suez Crisis* (Chapel Hill and London: University of North Carolina Press, 1991), 143–52. Kunz considers American economic sanctions against Britain to be "one of the most successful examples of this kind of pressure" in recent history (193).

43. Memo of conversation, December 28, 1956. *FRUS, 1955–57* (Washington, D.C.: Government Printing Office, 1990), 16:1342.

44. Ibid, 48.

45. Article 34 permitted the Security Council to investigate a situation that might lead to a dispute "in order to determine whether [it] is likely to endanger the maintenance of international peace and security."

46. *UN Yearbook 1956*, 84–85.

47. Dwight D. Eisenhower, *Waging Peace 1956–61*, (New York: Doubleday, 1965), 2:89.

48. Eden, 609. Urquhart, *Hammarskjold*, 238, 242.

49. *UN Yearbook 1958* (New York: Columbia University Press, 1959), 41–43.

50. Ibid., 45–47.

51. Ibid., 45.

52. Ibid., 46, 50.

53. Luard, 2:154.

54. Luard, 1:322.

55. *UN Yearbook 1946–47*, 64–66.

56. Michael A. Guhin, *John Foster Dulles: A Statesman for His Times* (New York: Columbia University Press, 1972), 228–29.

57. Quoted in Robert A. Strong, "Eisenhower and Arms Control," in *Reevaluating Eisenhower*, 258.

58. Mark A. Zacher, *Dag Hammarskjold's United Nations* (New York and London: Columbia University Press), 201–2. Inaugurating the Ten-Power Committee, the Great Powers said "the setting up of the . . . Committee in no way diminishes or

encroaches upon U.N. responsibilities in this field." But, of course, this is exactly what it did. The joint announcement is found in Keesing's Research Report, *Disarmament: Negotiations and Treaties, 1946–1971* (New York: Chas. Scribner's Sons, 1972), 204.

59. Robert Divine, *Blowing in the Wind: The Nuclear Test-Ban Debate, 1954–60* (New York: Oxford University Press, 1978), chaps. 9–11.

60. *UN Yearbook 1960* (New York: Columbia University Press, 1961), 44.

61. The text of the resolution appears in *UN Yearbook 1960*, 49–50.

62. The cheering delegate was Mary Lord. The other delegate was Oregon's senator Wayne Morse, quoted in Max Harrelson, *Fires around the Horizon: The U.N.'s Uphill Battle to Preserve the Peace* (New York: Praeger, 1989), 115. The resolution is found in *UN Yearbook 1960*, 49–50.

63. Memorandum of phone conversation between Christian Herter and Lodge, July 14, 1960, *FRUS, 1958–60* (Washington, D.C.: Government Printing Office, 1992), 14:306–7.

64. Press notes, September 7, 1960, Ann Whitman files, DDE diaries, Staff notes, Box 53, Eisenhower Library.

65. Memo of conversation between Secretary of State Christian Herter and Lumumba, July 27, 1960, *FRUS, 1958–1960*, 14:359–66. See also Ernest W. Lefever, *Uncertain Mandate: Politics of the U.N. Congo Operation* (Baltimore: Johns Hopkins University Press, 1967), 78. On the question of Lumumba as a communist, U.S. officials in the Congo clearly stated that the prime minister was *not* a communist. See, for instance, McIlvaine to State Department, July 26, 1960, *FRUS, 1960*, 14:356.

66. *New York Times*, September 9, 1960, 7.

67. Urquhart, *Hammarskjold*, 459–60.

68. Urquhart, *Hammarskjold*, 463–64.

69. Memorandum, September 27, 1960 11:30 A.M. (UN), and memorandum, October 11, 1960, Ann Whitman files, DDE series, staff notes, Box 53. Eisenhower Library.

5. KENNEDY AND JOHNSON

1. Following the election, Stevenson had told a friend that he did *not* want to be the UN ambassador. See John Bartlow Martin, *Adlai Stevenson and the World* (Garden City, N.Y.: Doubleday & Company, 1977), 558; and Porter McKeever, *Adlai Stevenson: His Life and Legacy* (New York: William Morrow and Company, 1989), 473. Kennedy's refusal to appoint Stevenson as secretary of state resulted from political resentments. Stevenson had refused to select Kennedy as the vice presidential candidate in 1956, and had refused to place Kennedy's name in nomination for president in 1960, when the former Illinois governor hoped to prolong his own candidacy. Also, Kennedy believed Stevenson to be too soft and indecisive. Dean Acheson, one of Kennedy's advisers, said Stevenson's tenure as secretary of state would be "disastrous" (J. Martin, 552).

2. McKeever, 475–76; Jeff Broadwater, *Adlai Stevenson and American Politics: The Odyssey of an American Liberal* (New York: Twayne Publishers, 1994), 194.

3. The best account of this relationship remains Arnold Beichman, *The "Other" State Department: The United States Mission to the United Nations—Its Role in the Making of Foreign Policy* (New York: Basic Books, 1967).

4.   Statement of Charles Yost, in McKeever, 490.

5.   Dean Rusk, *As I Saw it*, as told to Richard Rusk, ed. Daniel S. Papp (New York and London: W. W. Norton & Company, 1990), 197.

6.   Rusk's main biographer shares this view. See W. Cohen, *Dean Rusk*, 83–84.

7.   Cleveland memorandum to the secretary, March 5, 1965. National Security files, Lyndon B. Johnson Library.

8.   Harlan Cleveland, *The Obligations of Power: American Diplomacy in the Search for Peace* (New York and London: Harper & Row Publishers, 1966), 14.

9.   Luard, 2:261–65.

10.   Though UN authorities had refused to arrest Lumumba during the fall of 1960, they placed him under guard, which he left (without UN opposition) for Stanleyville, only to be captured by Congolese troops who eventually shipped him to Katanga for "safekeeping." There he was murdered. Luard, 2:250–51; *Public Papers of the Secretaries-General of the United Nations, Dag Hammarskjold, 1960–1961*, ed. Andrew W. Cordier and Wilder Foote, vol. 5 (New York and London: Columbia University Press, 1975). The United States undersecretary of state believed the CIA *did* have its hand in the assassination. See James A. Bill, *George Ball: Behind the Scenes in U.S. Foreign Policy* (New Haven, Conn. and London: Yale University Press, 1997), 138.

11.   In *The Congo Cables: The Cold War in Africa from Eisenhower to Kennedy* (New York: Macmillan Publishing Company, 1982), 128–39, Madeleine G. Kalb includes an excellent account of U.S. policy in regard to Lumumba. The United States was not responsible for Lumumba's arrest or assassination, but Kalb offers good evidence that American officials had unsuccessfully tried to murder him, and that the U.S. ambassador to the Congo, Clair Timberlake, had subsequently encouraged both the UN and Leopoldville to arrest him. Indeed, Timberlake was highly critical of UN officials, believing that the UN was partial to Lumumba. He was wrong.

12.   The reformulated U.S. policy is best defined in a memorandum from Rusk to the president dated February 1, 1961, *FRUS*, 1961–63 (Washington, D.C.: Government Printing Office, 1994), 20:40–45.

13.   *Public Papers of the Secretaries-General of the United Nations: Dag Hammarskjold, 1960–61*, vol. 2, eds. Andrew W. Cordier and Wilder Foote (New York and London: Columbia University Press, 1975), 342.

14.   Memorandum, Rusk to the president, February 1, 1961, *FRUS*, 1961–63, 20:45.

15.   Text is found in *FRUS*, 1961–63, 20:34.

16.   Stanley Meisler, *United Nations: The First Fifty Years* (New York: Atlantic Monthly Press, 1995), 123–24.

17.   A good overview of the American position is found in two memoranda: Rusk to president, August 3, 1961, and "memorandum of conversation," August 7, 1961, *FRUS*, 1961–63, 20:184–85, 186–87.

18.   Conor Cruise O'Brien, *To Katanga and Back: A UN Case History* (New York: Simon & Schuster, 1962), 121.

19.   As said by Urquhart, *A Life in Peace and War*, 174. O'Brien's remark is reported in O'Brien, 256.

20.   Telegram, September 15, 1961, 10:47 P.M., *FRUS*, 1961–63, 20:220.

21.   Quoted in Urquhart, *Ralph Bunche: An American Life* (New York and London: W. W. Norton, 1993), 343.

22. See, for instance, Kennedy's memorandum of a phone conversation with British Prime Minister Harold Macmillan, December 13, 1961, *FRUS*, 1961–63, 20:310–11.

23. *UN Yearbook 1960*, 157–58.

24. J. Martin, 633–34.

25. The quotation is found in Michael R. Beschloss, *The Crisis Years: Kennedy and Khrushchev, 1960–1963* (New York: Edward Burlingame Books, 1991), 506.

26. *UN Yearbook 1960*, 160. (The 1961 Bay of Pigs controversy appears in the 1960 yearbook.) See also Luard, 2:387.

27. Any assessment of motives must take into account publication of *Cuba on the Brink: Castro, the Missile Crisis, and the Soviet Collapse*, James G. Blight, Bruce J. Allyn, and David A. Welch (New York: Pantheon Books, 1993). The debate over motives—strategic balance versus defense of Cuba—existed even within Soviet circles (7–8).

28. J. Martin, 719.

29. Charles Bartlett and Joseph Alsop so charged in *The Saturday Evening Post*. The best discussion of this subject appears in J. Martin, 741–43. Stevenson said during the crisis: " . . . perhaps we need a coward in the room when we are talking about nuclear war." Historian Donald Kagan compares this to British diplomat Alexander Cadogan who said in 1938: "*How* much courage is needed to be a coward?" Found in Kagan, *On the Origins of War and the Preservation of Peace* (New York: Doubleday, 1995), 514.

30. Barton Bernstein, "Reconsidering the Missile Crisis: Dealing with the Problems of the American Jupiters in Turkey," in *The Cuban Missile Crisis Revisited*, ed. James A. Nathan (New York: St. Martin's Press, 1992), 100.

31. The text of the speech, and of the U.S. resolution as well as the OAS resolution, is found in volume 8 of *The Papers of Adlai E. Stevenson: 1961–65*, ed. Walter Johnson, (Boston and Toronto: Little Brown & Company, 1979), 309–25.

32. *Papers of Adlai E. Stevenson*, 8:331–32.

33. Abram Chayes, *The Cuban Missile Crisis: International Crises and the Role of Law* (New York and London: Oxford University Press, 1974), 83.

34. J. Martin, 729–31; Ramses Nassif, *U Thant in New York, 1961–71* (New York: St. Martin's Press, 1988), 28–31.

35. J. Martin, 739–40.

36. Luard, 2:168.

37. James A. Stegenga, *The United Nations Force in Cyprus* (Columbus: Ohio State University Press, 1968), 192–93; see also Luard, 2:432–33.

38. J. Martin, 685–86.

39. Luard, 2:336.

40. In fact, Stevenson's published papers contain no documents about this issue, and even his most conscientious biographer, John Bartlow Martin, devotes less than a page to it (J. Martin, 663).

41. See, for instance, Rusk, 411.

42. McKeever, 502. Kalb, 299–301.

43. Quoted in J. Martin, 748.

44. Luard, 2:447–49.

45. Susan R. Mills, "The Financing of UN Peacekeeping Operations: The Need for a Sound Financial Basis," in *The United Nations and Peacekeeping: Results, Limitations, and Prospects—The Lessons of 40 Years of Experience*, ed. Indar Jit Rik Lye al

Kjell Skjeslback (New York: St. Martin's Press, 1991): 96; Luard, 2:449; the "extremely stubborn" comment appears in J. Martin, 788.

46. A good example of State Department thinking appears in a memorandum from William B. Buffum to Harlan Cleveland, February 5, 1965, Country file, UN, Box 289, National Security files, Lyndon B. Johnson Library.

47. See, for instance, memorandum from Sam Belk to Mr. Bundy, December 22, 1964, Country file, UN, Box 289, National Security files, LBJ Library.

48. *Papers of Adlai Stevenson*, 8:646. After initial resistance, Stevenson's superiors accepted his proposal. Publicly, they downplayed the change in American policy.

49. Luard, 2:459–62.

50. It is worth noting that an important subtheme in State Department and National Security Council memoranda addressed exactly this point. As NSC staffer Gordon Chase put it, permitting the Soviets to get away without paying would establish a precedent for voluntary contributions; he called this a "silver lining". Not only did Chase argue that such a precedent would make it easier for the UN to approve such operations, but it would "allow us to avoid paying for a UN operation to which we fundamentally object." See Chase memorandum to Mr. Bundy, February 12, 1965, Country file, UN, Box 289, National Security files, LBJ Library.

51. Johnson, as quoted in Luard, 2:493.

52. Jerome Slater, *Intervention and Negotiation: The United States and the Dominican Revolution* (New York: Harper & Row, 1970), 103–6; General Bruce Palmer Jr., *Intervention in the Caribbean: The Dominican Crisis of 1965* (Lexington: University Press of Kentucky, 1989), 63.

53. Luard, 2:510–11.

54. The best account of this incident is by Walter Johnson in "The U Thant-Stevenson Peace Initiatives in Vietnam, 1964–65," *Diplomatic History* 3 (Summer 1977): 285, 95; and in his commentary in *The Papers of Adlai Stevenson*, 8:661–67. Fredrik A. Logevall shows conclusively that the Johnson administration did not want a negotiated settlement with Hanoi in 1964 and 1965. Of the U Thant issue, he says that the United States' response in fact "precluded the possibility of any such negotiations by insisting that the continued existence of a separate, non-communist South Vietnam was non-negotiable" (*Choosing War: The Year 1964 and the Last Chance for Peace in Vietnam* [Berkeley: University of California Press, forthcoming], chap. 8).

55. Rusk, 463.

56. Ibid.

57. Rusk memorandum, found in *Papers of Adlai Stevenson*, 8:664.

58. Oral history of Benjamin Read, 1969–1970, LBJ Library.

59. Cleveland memorandum, March 17, 1965, Central Files, UN, Box 6, National Security files, LBJ Library.

60. The Goldberg proposal is found in Memorandum to President Johnson, June 23, 1965, Ex19/CO312, Box 216, LBJ Library; the Morse letter is dated June 22, 1965, IT 47, Box 9, White House Central files, LBJ Library. Seventy-five congressmen asked for UN consideration in a letter of January 21, 1966, Ex19/CO312, Box 220, LBJ Library. The quotation is in a telegram, U.S. Mission to Department of State, July 11, 1965, Public Statements, Central Files, UN Box 5, National Security files, LBJ Library.

61. CIA memorandum, September 25, 1964, Memos miscellaneous, vol. 7, November 1963–64, Central files, UN, Box 5, National Security files, LBJ Library.

62. Abba Eban, *An Autobiography* (New York: Random House, 1977), 320–21.

63. In 1967, Egypt and Syria comprised the United Arab Republic (UAR).

64. Rusk, 384. Lyndon B. Johnson, *The Vantage Point: Perspectives on the Presidency, 1963–1969* (New York: Holt, Rhinehart, & Winston, 1971), 290.

65. Quoted in John G. Stroessinger, *The United Nations and the Superpowers: China, Russia, and America*, 3d ed. (New York: Random House, 1973), 85.

66. Urquhart, *A Life in Peace and War*, 212–13. Meisler, 174. No one has better argued that Thant could have played for more time than Michael B. Friedland in "The United Nations Emergency Force and American Foreign Policy in the Egyptian-Israeli Conflict, 1956–1967" (master's thesis, Pennsylvania State University, 1987), 144–65. Friedland perceptively notes that Cairo hinted at a partial withdrawal. Rusk later claimed that Nasser more than hinted at this, but Thant demanded an all or nothing response. A partial withdrawal might have been beneficial in two important ways: delaying a final break, and leaving the UN with at least some influence. Friedland quotes the British foreign secretary, George Brown, who admitted that although U Thant was legally correct, "wise men, faced with big events whose consequences are immeasurable, shouldn't in my view act as though they were working in a solicitor's office conveyancing property." (Found in Michael Brecher, *Decisions in Israel's Foreign Policy* [New Haven: Yale University Press, 1974], 365).

67. See the comment about Friedland's master's thesis in the previous footnote.

68. In *Ralph Bunche* (411–12), Urquhart demolishes the myth that Nasser did not want UNEF to be removed from the Strait of Tiran.

69. Johnson, 294. In his memoirs, Rusk claims that the Israeli president, Levi Eshkol, hinted at delaying hostilities for as long as two weeks, but Eban, in his own memoirs, notes that Rusk had said on June 1, when asked about U.S. plans to slow down the road to war, "I don't think it is our business to restrain anyone." Eban took Rusk at his word. See Rusk, 386; Eban, *Autobiography*, 385.

70. *United Nations Yearbook 1967* (New York: UN Office of Public Information, 1969), 174–84.

71. Finger, *American Ambassadors*, 182.

72. Rusk would complain that the Israelis had turned the United States "into a twenty-year liar." Rusk, 388.

73. Anatoly Dobrynin, *In Confidence: Moscow's Ambassador to America's Six Cold War Presidents, 1962–1986* (New York: Times Books, 1995), 160.

74. *UN Yearbook 1967*, 258. Finger, "Lord Caradon," in *The New World Balance and Peace in the Middle East*, ed. Seymour Maxwell Finger (Cranbury, N.J.: Associated Universities Press, 1975), 221, 254.

6. NIXON AND FORD

1. Stephen E. Ambrose, *Nixon: The Triumph of a Politician, 1962–1972*, vol. 2 (New York: Simon & Schuster, 1989), 236.

2. Charles Yost, *The Conduct and Misconduct of Foreign Affairs* (New York: Random House, 1972), 191–92.

3. Charles H. Malik, "The United Nations as an Ideological Battleground," in *The United Nations in Perspective*, ed. E. Berkeley Tompkins (Stanford, Calif.: Hoover Institution Press, 1972), 14–28.

4. Finger, *American Ambassadors*, 212.

5. Finger, *American Ambassadors*, 213–14; *UN Yearbook 1970* (New York: UN Office of Public Information, 1972), 186–94, 733–58.

6. Finger, *American Ambassadors*, 211.

7. Mark Tessler, *A History of the Israeli-Palestinian Conflict* (Bloomington and Indianapolis: Indiana University Press, 1994), 420.

8. The so-called Rogers Plan, the secretary of state's proposal to resolve the differences based on Israeli territorial concessions, never had Kissinger's support, while Nixon—who had no confidence that it would succeed—gave it only inconsistent backing. See David Schoenbaum, *The United States and the State of Israel* (New York: Oxford University Press, 1993), 173; and Burton I. Kaufman, *The Arab Middle East and the United States: Interarab Rivalry and Superpower Diplomacy* (New York: Twayne Publishers, 1996, 71–73.

9. *UN Yearbook 1973* (New York: UN Office of Public Information, 1976), 196–200, 213.

10. *UN Yearbook, 1973*, 200–202, 213.

11. *UN Yearbook, 1973*, 198.

12. W. Cohen, 164–67.

13. Richard Nixon, "Asia After Vietnam," *Foreign Affairs* 46 (October, 1967): 122–23.

14. *UN Yearbook 1971* (New York: UN Office of Public Information, 1974), 126–32, 135–37.

15. Quoted by Deputy Permanent Representative Christopher Phillips, found in Fasulo, 148.

16. Rosemary Righter, *Utopia Lost: The United Nations and World Order* (New York: Twentieth Century Fund Press, 1995), 270.

17. Urquhart, *A Life in Peace and War*, 228.

18. Robert E. Herzstein, "The Pending Reform of FOIA: A Researcher's Report," *SHAFR Newsletter* 27 (March 1996): 31.

19. Herzstein, 41. Arkady N. Schevchenko, the highest ranking Soviet citizen in the UN bureaucracy, notes that the Soviets routinely "sheltered" spies at the UN (Schevchenko, *Breaking with Moscow* [New York: Alfred A. Knopf, 1985], 293).

20. Quoted in Shirley Hazzard, "Breaking Faith," 74.

21. Hazzard, "Breaking Faith," 78.

22. If the Soviets did know about Waldheim's past and used it to influence him, they did so in odd ways. Gromyko, for instance, humiliated Waldheim in 1976 when he forced Waldheim to meet him in a corridor office, not in Waldheim's quarters on the 38th floor (Schevchenko, 291–92).

23. Daniel P. Moynihan, *A Dangerous Place* (Boston, Toronto: Little, Brown & Company, 1978), 3.

24. The statement comes from Helmut Sonnenfelt, in Moynihan, 3.

25. Moynihan, 11.

26. Ibid., 250, 30.

27. Ibid., 90–91.

28. Ibid., 105

29. *UN Yearbook 1975* (New York: UN Office of Public Information, 1978), 632–33, 650.

30. Quoted in Moynihan, 153–54.

31. *UN Yearbook 1975*, 590–93.

32. Finger, *American Ambassadors*, 240.

33. Meisler, 216. Uruqhart, *In Peace and War*, 264.

34. *UN Yearbook 1975*, 242–49.

35. Schoenbaum, 241. In his memoirs, Kissinger says very little about the PLO. See especially *Years of Upheaval* (Boston: Little, Brown and Company, 982), 1037. A former NSC member, William Quandt, argued that for all of Kissinger's brilliance as a strategist and negotiator, he had a "blind spot" in dealing with the Palestinian side of the Mideast puzzle (Quandt, *Peace Process: American Diplomacy and the Arab-Israeli Conflict since 1967* [Washington, D.C.: Brookings Institution, 1993], 251).

36. Finger, *American Ambassadors*, 250.

37. Kissinger, 1029–30.

38. Raymond L. Garthoff, *Detente and Confrontation: American Soviet Relations from Nixon to Reagan* (Washington, D.C.: Brookings Institution, 1985), 525. The italics are Kissinger's.

39. Walter Isaacson, *Kissinger: A Biography* (New York: Simon and Schuster, 1992), 682.

40. Ibid., 686.

41. *UN Yearbook 1976* (New York: UN Office of Public Information, 1979), 794–95, 803–4, 806.

42. Isaacson, 689.

43. *New York Times*, October 1, 1976, 1.

7. GUNS AND BUTTER

1. Rusk, 249.

2. *UN Yearbook 1961* (New York: Columbia University Press, 1963), 21, 23–24.

3. Richard J. Walton, *The Remnants of Power: The Tragic Last Years of Adlai Stevenson* (New York: Coward-McCann, 1968), 108.

4. *UN Yearbook 1962* (New York: Columbia University Press, 1964), 22–23, 24–25.

5. John G. Stoessinger, *The United Nations and the Superpowers: China, Russia, and America*, 3d ed. (New York: Random House, 1973), 151.

6. *UN Yearbook, 1961*, 17–18, 31.

7. *UN Yearbook 1965* (New York: UN Office of Public Information, 1967), 66–73.

8. Dimitris Bourantonis, *The United Nations and the Quest for Nuclear Armament* (Aldershot, U.K.: Dartmouth, 1993), 88.

9. Jozef Goldblatt, "The Role of the United Nations in International Peace and Security: An Assessment," in *The United Nations and the Maintenance of International Peace and Security* (Dordrecht, Neth.: Martinus Nijhoff Publishers, 1987), 373.

10. Its text is found in the appendix of Bourantonis.

11. Ibid., 160.

12. *New York Times*, September 10, 1996, A12.

13. Finger, *American Ambassadors*, 47.

14. Louie F. Hyde, *The United States and United Nations: Promoting the Public Welfare* (New York: Manhattan Publishing Company, 1960), 90.

15. Ibid., 103.

16. Lodge letter to the president, May 11, 1956, "UN Multilateral Aid," Ann Whitman File, Eisenhower Library.

17. Finger, *American Ambassadors*, 87.

18. John Stoessinger, *Might of Nations: World Politics in Our Time* (New York: Random House, 1969), 199.

19. Finger, *American Ambassadors*, 146.

20. Gamani Corea, "Creating a Framework to Strengthen and Stabilize International Commodity Markets," in *Negotiating World Order*, 169, 176. The author, a Sri Lankan economist, served as secretary-general of the United Nations Conference on Trade and Development (UNCTAD) from 1974 to 1986.

21. *UN Yearbook, 1970*, 306–8, 313–15.

22. Righter, 98–109.

23. Ibid., 107–8.

24. Finger, *American Ambassadors*, 234.

25. Righter, 228–29.

26. See Richard N. Gardner, "The Case for Practical Internationalism," *Foreign Affairs* 68 (Spring 1988): 827; Righter quotes Dennis Goodman, who headed the U.S. delegation to the 7th UNCTAD (230–31).

27. See David Ottaway, "Africa: U.S. Policy Eclipse," *Foreign Affairs* 58 (1980): 658; Christine A. Bogdanowicz, "World Debt: The United States Reconsiders," *Foreign Affairs* 64 (Winter 1985–1986): 269; and John W. Sewell and Christine Contec, "Foreign Aid and Gramm-Rudman," *Foreign Affairs* 66 (Summer 1987): 1010–21.

28. C. Michael Aho and Marc Levinson, "The Economy after Reagan," *Foreign Affairs* 67 (Winter 1988–1989): 19; and Ivan L. Head, "North-South Dangers," *Foreign Affairs* 68 (Summer 1989): 79.

29. James N. Schubert, "The Impact of Food Aid on World Malnutrition," *International Organization* 35 (Spring 1981): 350–52.

30. Barbara Ward, "Another Chance for the North?" *Foreign Affairs* 59 (Winter 1980–1981): 386.

31. Mark Imber, "Too Many Cooks? The Post Rio Reform of the United Nations," *International Affairs* 69 (January 1993): 55–56.

8. CARTER

1. The best general outline of these roles appears in Erwin C. Hargrove, *Jimmy Carter as President: Leadership and the Politics of the Public Good* (Baton Rouge: Louisiana State University Press, 1988), 113–16.

2. Zbigniew Brzezinski, *Power and Principle: Memoirs of the National Security Adviser, 1977–1981* (New York: Farrar, Strauss, & Giroux, 1983), 37.

3. Fasulo, 257.

4. An apologetic version of this episode appears in Bartlett C. Jones, *Flawed Triumphs: Andy Young at the United Nations* (New York: University Press of America, 1996), 139–47.

5. The president would later claim that Young had not violated American policy by speaking to the Palestinians, and that "a mountain was made out of a molehill" (Jimmy Carter, *Keeping Faith* [Toronto and New York: Bantam Books, 1982], 491).

6.   Cyrus Vance, *Hard Choices: Critical Years in America's Foreign Policy* (New York: Simon & Schuster, 1983), 271.

7.   Brzezinski, 140–43. Dissatisfied with the Anglo-American approach, Brzezinski claims that he even recommended turning the whole problem over to the UN.

8.   Brzezinski, 143.

9.   *UN Yearbook 1975*, 838–39; *UN Yearbook 1976*, 161–63; *UN Yearbook 1978* (New York: UN Office of Public Information, 1981), 228–29.

10.   *UN Yearbook 1978* ; the text is also found as appendix 4 in Vance's memoirs, *Hard Choices*.

11.   Vance, 309–11.

12.   The best account of McHenry's service is his own oral history account: by Charles Stuart Kennedy, Foreign Affairs Oral History Program, the Association for Diplomatic Studies and Training, (1993–94).

13.   From an interview with James F. Leonard, found in Fasulo, 240.

14.   *UN Yearbook 1978*, 303; Schoenbaum, 258. UNIFIL was "overrun or bypassed" by invading Israeli forces in 1982 (*UN Yearbook 1982* [New York: UN Department of Public Information, 1986], 489–90).

15.   Brzezinski, 245.

16.   Ibid., 441–42.

17.   Bzrezinski, 442. McHenry concurs (see McHenry oral history, 90–93).

18.   Carter, as quoted in Burton Kaufman, *The Presidency of James Earl Carter* (Lawrence: University Press of Kansas, 1993), 163.

19.   See *UN Yearbook 1980* (New York: UN Department of Public Information, 1983), 296–99, 304–6.

20.   Ibid., 304–6, 308–9.

21.   Bzrezinski, *Power and Principle, 426.*

22.   *UN Yearbook, 1980*, 1121–22.

23.   *UN Yearbook 1979* (NY: Department of Public Information, 1982), 309, 311–12.

24.   Report by the President, *United States Participation in the UN, 1979* (Washington, D.C.: Government Printing Office, 1980), 19–21. See also Yonah Alexander and Allan Nanes, eds., *The United States and Iran: A Documentary History* (Frederick, Md.: Altheia Books, 1980), 498.

25.   Vance, 401–6. See also Barry Rubin, *Paved with Good Intentions: The American Experience with Iran* (New York and Oxford: Oxford University Press, 1980), 318–20; Pierre Salinger, *America Held Hostage* (New York: Hill & Wang, 1981), 184–86.

26.   Vance, 411–12.

27.   Vance, *Hard Choices*, 407–8; Richard C. Thornton, *The Carter Years: Toward a New Global Order* (New York: Paragon House, 1991), 492–94.

28.   Vance, 124.

29.   Ibid., 127.

9. REAGAN

1.   The statement was made by William J. Vanden Huevel (Fasulo, 269).

2. Alexander M. Haig Jr., *Caveat: Realism, Reagan, and Foreign Policy* (New York: Macmillan & Company, 1984), 12.

3. Jeane Kirkpatrick, "Dictatorships and Double Standards," *Commentary* 68 (November 1979): 44.

4. *New York Times*, January 12, 1981, 3.

5. *UN Yearbook 1981* (New York: UN Department of Public Information, 1985), 282. When the General Assembly passed a similar resolution in November, the United States alone joined Israel in opposition.

6. Allan Gerson, *The Kirkpatrick Mission: Diplomacy without Apology, America at the United Nations, 1981–85* (New York: Free Press, 1991), 14.

7. Gerson, 43.

8. Mark F. Imber, *The USA, ILO, UNESCO, and IAEA: Politicalization and Withdrawal in the Specialized Agencies* (New York: St. Martin's Press, 1989), 50–51.

9. Wilfred Jenks of the United Kingdom, the new director-general, had promised that he would not appoint a Soviet candidate to the assistant director's post, then reversed himself within a month of succeeding Morse. Paul E. Masters, "The International Labor Organization: America's Withdrawal and Reentry," unpublished paper, Carter Presidential Library, 1997, 3–4.

10. Masters, 13–14.

11. In 1981, Congress by concurrent resolution had warned that if a UN agency suspended or expelled Israel or any other democratic state, the United States would suspend its own membership in that agency, as well as withhold its monetary contribution until the agency reversed its action. Imber, *The USA,* 33.

12. See, for instance, Imber, *The USA,* 85.

13. Imber, *The USA,* 119.

14. Thomas M. Franck, *Nation against Nation: What Happened to the U.N. Dream and What the U.S. Can Do about It* (New York: Oxford University Press, 1985), 264.

15. Franck, 257–58.

16. For instance, by 1997, Secretary-General Boutros Boutros-Ghali had cut the secretariat's workforce by 10 percent in response to U.S. demands, but the U.S. debt to the organization had grown to nearly $1.2 billion. In 1997 President Bill Clinton promised to repay the U.S. debt shortly after Kofi Annan replaced Boutros-Ghali, but congressional cooperation appeared doubtful. See chap. 11.

17. *UN Yearbook 1982*, 1321, 1347.

18. Gerson, 130–31.

19. Not surprisingly, Haig ignores this story in his memoirs. Haig, 294–95.

20. *UN Yearbook 1983* (New York: UN Department of Public Information, 1987), 211. The General Assembly would call it a "flagrant" violation (214).

21. Gerson, 226–27.

22. In *The US and the State of Israel*, Schoenbaum presents relevant polling data (291).

23. *UN Yearbook 1982*, 435–36, 450.

24. Gerson, 137–40.

25. But only after much confusion. According to Haig, Vice President George Bush, who headed the crisis management team dealing with Lebanon and who was much offended by the Israeli attack, persuaded Reagan to support the Spanish resolution. Though not initially consulted on this matter, Haig claims in his memoirs that he

managed to convince the president to reverse himself, leading to Kirkpatrick's veto. Haig, 338–40. See also Gerson, 141–42.

26. George Shultz, *Turmoil and Triumph: My Years as Secretary of State* (New York: Charles Scribner's Sons, 1993), 51. The French and Egyptian resolution is covered in *UN Yearbook 1982*, 448–49.

27. Gerson, 168.

28. Seymour M. Hersh, *The Target Is Destroyed: What Really Happened to Korean Airlines Flight 007 and What America Knew about It* (New York: Random House, 1986), 60–61.

29. Hersh, chap. 15.

30. Gerson, 211. In his study of the tragedy, Seymour Hersh concludes that the Soviets made a genuine mistake, believing—incorrectly—that the plane was military, not civilian (Hersh, chap. 17, esp. 232–39). But the Soviet pilot who shot down KAL 007 contradicts him. Gennadi Osipovich in 1996 said that he knew he was firing at a Boeing civilian craft, though he continued to believe that it was flying on a military mission and that it carried no civilian passengers (*New York Times*, December 9, 1996, A12).

31. *UN Yearbook 1982*, 313, 318–19.

32. Cameron Hume, *The United Nations, Iran, Iraq: How Diplomacy Changed* (Indianapolis: Indiana University Press, 1994), 41.

33. Quoted in Hume, 117. Resolution 598 is found in *UN Yearbook 1987* (Dordrecht, Neth.: Martinus Nijhoff Publishers, 1992), 223.

34. Shultz, 935.

35. *UN Yearbook 1984* (New York: UN Department of Public Information, 1988), 1084–85; *UN Yearbook 1986* (Dordrecht, Neth.: Martinus Nijhoff Publishers, 1990), 981–83.

36. The issue of mining harbors was only the subject of the 1984 ruling (*UN Yearbook 1984*, 1084–85).

37. Quoted by Anthony Lewis, *The New York Times*, May 28, 1984, 19.

38. Gerson, 273–75.

39. Ibid., 244.

40. Thomas L. Hughes, "The Twilight of Internationalism," *Foreign Policy* 61 (Winter 1985–1986): 31.

41. Chester A. Crocker, *High Noon in Southern Africa* (New York: W. W. Norton & Company, 1992), 75–82.

42. Donald Rothschild and John Ravenhill, "From Carter to Reagan: The Global Perspective on Africa Becomes Ascendant," in *Eagle Defiant: United States Foreign Policy in the 1980s*, ed. Kenneth A. Oye et al. (Boston: Little Brown & Company, 1983), 350–51.

43. Shultz, 1129. Crocker, 395.

10. BUSH

1. James A. Baker, *The Politics of Diplomacy: Revolution, War and Peace, 1989–92* (New York: G. P. Putnam's Sons, 1995), 45.

2. Baker, 49–50.

3. Meisler, 255.

4. See, for instance, his comments to Senator Jesse Helms and Congressman Duncan Hunter, found in Baker, 55, 58.

5. *UN Yearbook 1991* (Dordrecht, Neth.: Martinus Nijhoff Publishers, 1992), 154–56.

6. Jane E. Heninger, *Peacekeeping Transition: The United Nations in Cambodia* (New York: Twentieth Century Fund Press, 1994), 63–64, 88–90, 99–100.

7. See, for instance, the harsh judgment concerning UN passivity in Linda Melvern, *The Ultimate Crime: Who Betrayed the UN and Why* (London: Allison & Busby, 1995), 331–32.

8. Ibid., 334.

9. Many observers agree that Glaspie was made into a scapegoat for the United States's diplomatic failure. See, for instance, Elaine Sciolino, *The Outlaw State: Saddam Hussein's Quest for Power and the Gulf Crisis* (New York: John Wiley & Sons, 1991), 179–81; Jean Edward Smith, *George Bush's War* (New York: Henry Holt & Company, 1992), 55–58.

10. There is no *UN Yearbook* for 1990. The substance of the resolution is covered in Department of State, *United States Participation in the UN, 1990* (Washington, D.C.: Government Printing Office, 1991), 7.

11. *U.S. Participation 1990*, 7.

12. Baker, 279.

13. Charles Krauthammer, "Let It Sink: Why the United States Should Bail Out of the U.N.," *New Republic*, August 24, 1987, 18–23.

14. Meisler, 263.

15. *U.S. Participation 1990*, 10–12.

16. The text is found in J. Smith, *George Bush's War*, 258. See also *US Participation 1990*, 13–14.

17. Baker, 325–327. Baker later added that Yemen received only $70 million in U.S. aid, not $200 million.

18. Ibid., 279.

19. Ibid., 282.

20. Baker would later say that compromise had been out of the question, that "we should not and indeed *could* not negotiate down from the Security Council resolutions . . ." (Baker, 351 [italics in original]).

21. Ibid., 306.

22. Ibid., 326.

23. Melvern, 297–98.

24. *UN Yearbook 1991*, 170–76. Resolution 687, which maintained the embargo, would be modified in 1997 to permit Iraq to export oil in order to fund food and medical imports.

25. Meisler, 276–77.

26. *UN Yearbook 1992* (Dordrecht, Neth.: Martinus Nijhoff Publishers, 1993), 202–3.

27. Ibid., 207.

28. Ibid., 209–10.

29. Robert G. Patman, "The UN Operation in Somalia," in *A Crisis of Expectations: UN Peacekeeping in the 1990s*, ed. Ramesh Thakur and Carlyle A. Thayer (Boulder, Colo.: Westview Press, 1995), 93.

30. John L. Hirsch and Robert B. Oakley, *Somalia and Operation Restore Hope:Reflections on Peacemaking and Peacekeeping* (Washington, D.C.: US Institute of Peace, 1995), 42–47. Bush had appointed Oakley, who previously served as ambassador to Somalia, to be the U.S. special envoy during the crisis.

31. The quotation is from Misha Glenny, *The Fall of Yugoslavia: The Third Balkan War* (New York: Penguin Books, 1993), 128. Writes the author laconically, "The posthumous mutilation of Croatian policeman in Borovo Selo [in 1991] provided a most public announcement that the forthcoming war would be grisly" (121).

32. Robert D. Kaplan, *Balkan Ghosts: A Journey through History* (New York: St. Martin's Press, 1993).

33. Baker, 636.

34. Ibid., 638.

35. These resolutions are found in *UN Yearbook 1992*, 330–34. The *Yearbook* also contains the text of many companion debates and resolutions.

36. Quoted in Melvern, 309.

11. CLINTON

1. I. M. Destler, Leslie H. Gelb, and Anthony Lake, *Our Own Worst Enemy: The Unmaking of American Foreign Policy* (New York: Simon & Schuster, 1984), 276.

2. Boutros Boutros-Ghali, *An Agenda for Peace* (New York: United Nations, 1992); reprinted in Adam Roberts and Benedict Kingsbury, *United Nations, Divided World: The UN's Role in International Relations*, 2nd ed. (Oxford: Clarendon Press, 1994).

3. Hirsch and Oakley, 83.

4. Ibid., 105–6.

5. *UN Yearbook 1993* (Dordrecht, Neth.: Martinus Nijhoff Publishers, 1994), 290–92. Text of the resolution is also found in Hirsch and Oakley, 199–205. The Americans favored the resolution as a way of reducing U.S. responsibility while simultaneously beefing up the effort to "save" Somalia. The Clinton administration did consult Congress about this enormously important resolution. See John R. Bolton, "Wrong Turn in Somalia," *Foreign Affairs* 73 (January–February 1994): 62–63.

6. Patman, 96–98.

7. See Hirsch and Oakley, 141–42. Boutros-Ghali made his statement on January 4, 1994.

8. Patman, 102. See also the reflections on this mission in Hirsch and Oakley, 161–71.

9. In February, the new secretary of state had defined Bosnia as a vital interest; in June, he said the opposite. See David Owen, *Balkan Odyssey* (New York: Harcourt, Brace & Company, 1995), 184.

10. *UN Yearbook, 1993*, 459.

11. Owen quotes Rosenthal in *Balkan Odyssey*, 113.

12. Akashi's statement and Albright's comment appear in Meisler, 326.

13. Owen's memoir, *Balkan Odyssey*, is the best single account of this subject. Owen, more than I, believes the Europeans were more serious about using force to restrain the Bosnian Serbs. He therefore places most of the blame for failure on Washington (see chapters 3 and 4).

14. Bush is quoted in Pamela Constable, "Dateline Haiti: Stalemate Caribbean," *Foreign Policy* 89 (Winter 1992–1993): 182; and Clinton in Tony Smith, "In Defense of Intervention," *Foreign Affairs* 73 (October–November 1994), 40.

15. Ironically, the Bush administration had undercut the political impact of the embargo by allowing numerous exemptions for American firms. See Constable, 184.

16. *UN Yearbook, 1993,* 343.

17. Ibid., 335, 348–49.

18. Ian Martin, "Haiti: Mangled Multilateralism," *Foreign Policy* 95 (Summer 1994): 80. The Security Council action appears in Resolution 861 (*UN Yearbook 1993,* 346).

19. Security Council Resolution 917, *New York Times,* May 7, 1994, A1.

20. *New York Times,* May 10, 1994, A1; *New York Times,* September 13, 1994, A13.

21. John Sweeney, "Stuck in Haiti," *Foreign Policy* 102 (Spring 1996): 143.

22. *New York Times,* July 31, 1994, A11.

23. John Ruggie, "The United States and the United Nations: Toward a New Realism," *International Organization* 39 (Spring 1985): 354.

24. *New York Times,* May 14, 1994, A1; May 18, A1.

25. *New York Times,* May 18, 1994, A1, A22.

26. Department of State, *United States Participation in the UN, 1988* (Washington, D.C.: Government Printing Office, 1989), 337.

27. *New York Times,* May 6, 1994, A1.

28. The *New York Times* editorial is found on January 12, 1995, A24. About Helms, see his recommendation that the UN should allow, as an option, peacekeeping "without U.S. funding or participation. If others in the world want to undertake nation-building operations, there is no reason the United States should discourage them—so long as American taxpayers do not have to pay for a third of it" (Jesse Helms, "Saving the U.N.," *Foreign Affairs* 75 [September–October 1996], 7.

29. *New York Times,* February 17, 1995, A1, editorial on A30.

30. *New York Times,* December 5, 1995, A4.

31. *New York Times,* October 22, 1995, A1.

32. *New York Times,* June 23, 1995, A1.

33. *New York Times,* October 7, 1995, A1.

34. Former IO chief Charles Maynes, in 1995 the editor of the influential journal *Foreign Policy,* would title his own contribution to an issue devoted to the UN's 50th anniversary "The New Pessimism" (*Foreign Policy* 100 [Fall 1995]: 33–49).

35. Report of the Independent Working Group of the Future of the United Nations, *The United Nations: Its Second Half Century* (New York: Ford Foundation, 1995).

36. Found in *Foreign Policy* 100 (Fall 1995): 3–18.

37. Quoted in Geoff Simons, *United Nations,* 233. See also David J. Whittaker, *United Nations in Action* (Armonk, N.Y.: M. E. Sharpe, 1995), 241.

38. *New York Times,* September 6, 1995, A1.

39. Myriam Vander Stickele, "World Trade: Free for Whom? Fair for Whom?" in *Challenges to the United Nations,* ed. Erskine Childers (New York: St. Martins Press, 1994), 64.

40. Katarina Tomasevski, "Human Rights: Fundamental Freedoms for All," in *Challenges to the United Nations*, 105.

41. In 1997, the Americans agreed to modify economic sanctions in order to permit the export of Iraqi oil as a means to fund purchases of food and medicine.

12. CONCLUSION

1. Steven Kull of the University of Maryland's School of Public Affairs, quoted in the *New York Times*, September 23, 1996, A6. See also *New York Times* editorial, January 4, 1998, at www.nytimes.com on the Internet.

2. Helms, 2.

3. Stanley Hoffman, "The Crisis of Liberal Internationalism," *Foreign Policy* 98 (Spring 1995): 176.

4. Hoffman, 166–67.

5. Abba Eban, "The U.N. Idea Revisited," *Foreign Affairs* 74 (September–October 1995): 46–47,

6. Boutros Boutros-Ghali, "Global Leadership after the Cold War," *Foreign Affairs* 75 (March–April 1996): 95.

7. Quoted in Alan K. Henrikson, "The North Atlantic Alliance as a Form of World Order," *Negotiating World Order: The Artisanship and Architecture of Global Diplomacy*, ed. Alan K. Henrikson (Wilmington, Del.: Scholarly Resources, 1986), 117.

8. David Armstrong, Lorna Lloyd, and John Redmond, in *From Versailles to Maastricht: International Organization in the Twentieth Century* (New York: St. Martin's Press, 1996), argue that Article 99 was largely meaningless because states opposed to its use would refuse to cooperate anyhow. For example, witness Iran in 1980 after Waldheim invoked Article 99 over the hostage crisis (111).

9. Armstrong, 114–15.

BIBLIOGRAPHY

The body of literature about the UN is huge. So, too, is the number of books and articles about U.S. foreign policy in the post–World War II era. The following bibliography does not pretend to be exhaustive. It includes those works that proved most helpful in writing this account of U.S.-UN relations.

I researched in a number of presidential libraries: those of Truman, Eisenhower, Kennedy, Johnson, and Carter.

Official UN documents are found in the Dag Hammarskjold Library in New York and in a number of UN "depository" libraries. Rather than using the verbatim text of UN records, I chose to use annual volumes of the *Yearbook of the UN*, which includes the full text of all Security Council and General Assembly resolutions, along with summaries of debates and decisions of the International Court of Justice and other UN organs. With the exception of the complete record, it is the one indispensable source for information of this type. Coming close in importance is the Department of State's annual *United States Participation in the UN: Report by the President to the Congress*. Like the *Yearbook*, it includes a great variety of information, including speeches by the presidents and the secretaries of state at the UN. I also used the State Department's *Foreign Relations of the United States* series, covering UN-related matters through the mid-1960s, along with a number of other primary source collections listed below. A major source for the 1990s was the *New York Times*.

There are many bibliographies and fact books of UN affairs. The most helpful are Kumiko Matsuura, et. al, *Chronology and Factbook of the United Nations, 1941–1991* (Dobbs Ferry, N.Y.: Oceana, 1992); John E. Jessup, ed., *A*

Chronology of Conflict and Resolution, 1945–1985 (New York: Greenwood Press, 1989); Joseph Preston Baratta, ed., *Strengthening the United Nations: A Bibliography on U.N. Reform and World Federalism* (New York: Greenwood Press, 1987), and the same author's *United Nations System* (New Brunswick, N.J.: Transaction Publishers, 1995), with superb annotations; and Edmund Jan Osmanczyk, ed., *Encyclopedia of the United Nations and International Agreements* (Philadelphia: Taylor & Francis, 1985). The UN's Blue Book series, focusing on peacekeeping, proved very helpful.

BOOKS AND ARTICLES

PUBLISHED PRIMARY RESOURCES

Alexander, Yonah, and Allan Nanes, eds. *The United States and Iran: A Documentary History.* Washington, D.C.: Government Printing Office, 1980.

Branyan, Robert L., and Lawrence H. Larsen, eds. *The Eisenhower Administration: A Documentary History, 1953–1961.* New York: Random House, 1971.

Chang, Laurence, and Peter Kornbluh, eds. *The Cuban Missile Crisis, 1962.* New York: New Press, 1962.

Cordier, Andrew W., and Max Harrelson, eds. *Public Papers of the Secretaries-General of the United Nations.* New York: United Nations, various dates. An invaluable source of primary documents from the secretariat's 38th floor, with supplemental commentary.

Goodrich, Leland M., and Edvard Hambro. *Charter of the United Nations: Commentary and Documents.* Boston: World Peace Foundation, 1946.

Higgins, Rosalyn, ed. *United Nations Peacekeeping, 1946–67: Documents and Commentary.* New York: Oxford University Press, 1969.

Janello, Amy and Jones, Brennon, eds. *A Global Affair: An Inside Look at the United Nations.* (New York: Jones and Janello, 1995). Generally uncritical essays describing UN programs without blemishes.

Johnson, Walter, ed. *The Papers of Adlai E. Stevenson: 1961–1965.* Vol. 8. Boston: Little Brown & Company, 1979.

Lincoff, Daphne Doran, ed. *Annual Review of United Nations Affairs.* Dobbs Ferry, N.Y.: Oceana, annual volumes. Each volume contains numerous articles and documents.

Keesing's Research Report, *Disarmament: Negotiations and Treaties, 1946–1971.* New York: Charles Scribner's Sons, 1972.

Lowenheim, Francis L., et. al. *Roosevelt and Churchill: Their Secret Wartime Correspondence.* New York: E. P. Dutton/Saturday Review Press, 1975.

Perez de Cuellar, Javier. *Anarchy or Order: Annual Reports.* New York: United Nations, 1991.

MEMOIRS AND DIARIES

Acheson, Dean. *Present at the Creation.* New York: W. W. Norton, 1969.

Baker, James A., III. *The Politics of Diplomacy.* New York: Putnam, 1993.

Baruch, Bernard. *My Own Story*. New York: Henry Holt & Company, 1957. A superficial account that says little about Baruch's efforts in the atomic energy field.

Behrstock, Julian. *The Eighth Case: Troubled Times at the United Nations*. New York: University Press of America, 1987. A first-person account of the U.S. government's attempt to purge the UN of leftists during the 1950s.

Brownell, Herbert. *Advising Ike: The Memoirs of Attorney General Herbert Brownell*, Lawrence: University Press of Kansas, 1993.

Brzezinski, Zbigniew. *Power and Principle: Memoirs of the National Security Adviser, 1977–1981*. New York: Farrar, Straus, Giroux, 1983.

Buckley, William J. *United Nations Journal: A Delegate's Odyssey*. New York: Putnam, 1974. Acerbic comments about a one-year appointment.

Byrnes, Jimmy. *Speaking Frankly*. New York: Harper Brothers, 1947.

Carter, Jimmy. *Keeping Faith: Memoirs of a President*. New York: Bantam Books, 1982.

Crocker, Chester A. *High Noon in Southern Africa: Making Peace in a Rough Neighborhood*. W. W. Norton & Company, 1992. Half memoir, half narrative history, this is easily the best account of U.S. policy ("constructive engagement") and the resolution of conflict in Namibia, Angola, and South Africa, by the assistant secretary of state for African affairs during the Reagan administration.

Dobrynin, Anatoly. *In Confidence: Moscow's Ambassador to America's Six Cold War Presidents, 1962–1986*. New York: Times Books, 1995.

Eban, Abba. *Abba Eban: An Autobiography*. New York: Random House, 1977. Very critical of U Thant before the Six-Day War.

Eden, Anthony. *The Memoirs of Anthony Eden: Full Circle*. Boston: Houghton Mifflin, 1960.

———. *The Memoirs of Anthony Eden: The Reckoning*. Boston: Houghton Mifflin, 1965.

Eichelberger, Clark M. *Organizing for Peace: A Personal History of the Founding of the United Nations*. New York: Harper & Row, 1977.

Eisenhower, Dwight D. *The White House Years: Mandate for Change, 1953–1956*. New York: Doubleday, 1963.

———. *The White House Years: Waging Peace, 1956-61*. New York: Doubleday, 1965.

Haig, Alexander M. Jr. *Caveat: Realism, Reagan, and Foreign Policy*. New York: Macmillan & Company, 1984.

Jessup, Philip C. *The Birth of Nations*. New York: Columbia University Press, 1974. An episodic view of the UN's role going back to the League's efforts to deal with Japan's 1931 occupation of Manchuria.

Johnson, Lyndon Baines. *The Vantage Point: Perspectives of the Presidency, 1963–1969*. New York: Holt, Rinehart, Winston, 1971.

Kissinger, Henry. *White House Years*. Boston: Little Brown & Company, 1979.

———. *Years of Upheaval*. Boston: Little Brown and Company, 1982. Contains much more UN material than the *White House Years*, suggesting the higher priority the author gave to UN matters after 1973.

Lie, Trygve. *In the Cause of Peace*. New York: Macmillan & Company, 1954. Like Waldheim's, this memoir is more notable for what it does not contain than for what it does.

Lodge, Henry Cabot. *As It Was: An Insider's View of Politics during the 50s and 60s*. New York: W. W. Norton, 1976. Very little value.

Moynihan, Daniel P. *A Dangerous Place*. Boston: Atlantic, Little Brown, 1975. A riveting account of the author's two years as UN ambassador; captures his growing contempt for what he viewed as the UN's double standard.

Murphy, Robert. *Diplomat among Warriors*. New York: Praeger, 1968. Very useful account of the UN role in the Suez Crisis.

Owen, David. *Balkan Odyssey*. New York: Harcourt Brace & Company, 1995. Easily the best book on the Balkan Crisis of the 1990s; sharply critical of Clinton administration policy.

Nixon, Richard. *RN: The Memoirs of Richard Nixon*. New York: Grosset & Dunlap, 1978.

O'Brien, Conor Cruise. *To Katanga and Back*. New York: Simon & Schuster, 1962. A self-serving yet fascinating account of UN efforts to rejoin Katanga to the Congo during 1961.

Perez de Cuellar, Javier. *Anarchy or Order?* New York: United Nations, 1991. Essays.

———. *Pilgrimage for Peace: A Secretary-General's Memoirs*. New York: St. Martin's Press, 1997.

Rusk, Dean. *As I Saw It*. New York: W. W. Norton, 1990.

Shultz, George P. *Turmoil and Triumph: My Years as Secretary of State* New York: Charles Scribner's Sons, 1993. Among the better memoirs; the author pays back many of his detractors.

Stettinius, Edward R., Jr. *The Diaries of Edward R. Stettinius, 1943–46*. Edited by Thomas W. Campbell and George C. Herring Jr. New York: New Viewpoints, 1975. Useful for the San Francisco Conference.

Thant, U. *View from the UN.* (New York: Doubleday, 1978. An honest if not very colorful account of the secretary-general's term.

Truman, Harry S. *Memoirs: The Year of Decisions*. Garden City, N.Y.: Doubleday & Company, 1955.

Urquhart, Brian. *A Life in Peace and War*. London: Weidenfeld & Nicolson, 1987. The UN's undersecretary for political affairs reflects on his work, offering some pithy comments about the men he worked with.

Vance, Cyrus. *Hard Choices: Critical Years in America's Foreign Policy*. New York: Simon & Schuster, 1983. Vance's very sympathetic view of the UN—and of Andy Young—is evident throughout this volume.

Waldheim, Kurt. *In the Eye of the Storm*. Bethesda, Md.: Adler & Adler, 1986.

BIOGRAPHIES

Abramson, Rudy. *Spanning the Century: The Life of W. Averill Harriman, 1891–1986*. New York: William Morrow, 1992.

Ambrose, Stephen E. *Nixon, 1962–72*. Vols. 2 and 3. New York: Simon & Schuster, 1989, 1991. A tough and fair appraisal of Nixon's diplomacy.

Barros, James. *Trygve Lie and the Cold War: The UN Secretary-General Pursues Peace, 1946–53*. Dekalb: Northern Illinois University Press, 1989. A numbingly detailed but excellent account of a very flawed official.

Broadwater, Jeff. *Adlai Stevenson and American Politics: The Odyssey of a Cold War Liberal*. New York: Twayne, 1994.

Clifford, Clark. *Counsel to the President*. New York: Random House, 1991. Contains a detailed account of the decision to recognize Israel.

Cohen, Warren I. "Dean Rusk." In *American Secretaries of State and Their Diplomacy*. Totowa, N.J.: Cooper Square Publishers, 1980.

Donovan, Robert J. *Conflict and Crisis: The Presidency of Harry S. Truman, 1945–1948*. New York: W. W. Norton & Company, 1977.

————. *The Tumultuous Years: The Presidency of Harry S. Truman, 1949–53*. New York: W. W. Norton, 1982. This and the previously cited work are by a journalist whose deep admiration for Truman did not prevent him from being fair and often critical.

Guhin, Michael A. *John Foster Dulles: A Statesman for His Times*. New York: Columbia University Press, 1972. Dulles is seen as shaping and shaped by anticommunism.

Hamby, Alonzo. *A Man of the People: A Life of Harry S. Truman*. New York: Oxford University Press, 1995. More scholarly and less colorful than McCullough's biography.

Hersh, Seymour M. *The Price of Power: Kissinger in the Nixon White House*. New York: Summit Books, 1983. A highly critical account that contains little about the UN.

Hixon, Walter. *George F. Kennan: Cold War Iconoclast*. New York: Columbia University Press, 1989. Looks at how Kennan's internationalim suffered from serious contradictions.

Hoopes, Townsend. *The Devil and John Foster Dulles*. Boston: Atlantic Monthly Press, 1973. Emphasizes Dulles's moralism and ideological rigidity.

Isaacson, Walter. *Kissinger: A Biography*. New York: Simon and Schuster, 1992. The best biography of the secretary of state.

Isaacson, Walter and Evan Thomas. *The Wise Men: Six Friends and the World They Made—Acheson, Bohlen, Harriman, Kennan, Lovett, McCloy*. New York: Simon & Schuster, 1986. One of the most insightful accounts of the architects of the Cold War.

James, Robert Rhodes. *Anthony Eden*. London: Weidenfeld & Nicolson, 1986. Stresses the U.S. rivalry with Britain during the period leading up to the Suez crisis.

Jones, Bartlett C. *Flawed Triumphs: Andy Young at the United Nations*. New York: University Press of America, 1996. Uncritical and marred by serious errors of judgment, though containing factual material not easily available elsewhere.

Levantrosser, William F., ed. *Harry S. Truman: The Man from Independence*. New York: Greenwood Press, 1986. Essays; see especially the essay focusing on Truman's recognition of Israel, by George deVries Jr., and the one by Herbert Druks claiming that Jewish pressure is much too simple an explanation to understand the roots of administration policy concerning Israel.

McCoy, Donald. *The Presidency of Harry S. Truman*. Lawrence: The University Press of Kansas, 1984. An excellent general biography that views the departure of Byrnes as the end of real efforts to negotiate a postwar settlement with the USSR.

McCullough, David. *Truman* New York: Simon & Schuster, 1992. A superb biography that captures both Truman's idealism about the UN and his practical reasons for abandoning UN diplomacy.

McKeever, Peter. *Adlai Stevenson: His Life and Legacy*. New York: William Morrow & Company, 1989. Not much on the UN period, but the best account of Stevenson's entry to his UN post.

Marks, Frederick, III. *Power and Peace: The Diplomacy of John Foster Dulles*. Westport, Conn.: Praeger, 1993. A sympathetic though quirky account of Dulles that emphasizes his pragmatism, not his ideology.

Martin, John Bartlow. *Adlai Stevenson and the World*. Garden City, N.Y.: Doubleday, 1977. Very sympathetic, very useful.

Marton, Kati. *A Death in Jerusalem*. New York: Pantheon, 1994. A long over-due look at the assassination of Counte Folke Bernadotte.

Mazuzan, George T. *Warren Austin at the U.N., 1946–1953*. Kent, Ohio: Kent State University Press, 1977.

Miller, Richard Lawrence. *Truman: The Rise to Power*. New York: McGraw-Hill, 1986. Traces Truman's support for an "improved" League of Nations after Pearl Harbor that included an international police force to prevent war.

Nassif, Ramses. *U Thant in New York, 1961–71*. New York: St. Martin's Press, 1988. Brief and superficial; by one of Thant's chief aides.

Parmet, Herbert S. *Eisenhower and the American Crusades*. New York: Macmillan Company, 1972. A friendly account of Eisenhower foreign policy that effectively links domestic politics to foreign developments.

Patterson, James T. *Mr. Republican: A Biography of Robert A. Taft*. Boston: Houghton Mifflin, 1972.

Pearson, Geoffrey A. H. *Seize the Day: Lester B. Pearson and Crisis Diplomacy*. Ottowa, Ont.: Carleton University Press, 1992. Written by his son, with excellent coverage of Suez in 1956.

Pogue, Forrest C. *George C. Marshall: Statesman 1945–59*. New York: Viking Press, 1987. Views the secretary of state as a moderate on the issue of Israeli independence, arguing that the White House had become "in effect the Foreign Office of the state of Israel" during these years.

Robertson, David. *Sly and Able: A Political Biography of James F. Byrnes.* New York: W. W. Norton, 1994.

Schwarz, Jordan. *The Speculator: Bernard Baruch in Washington: 1917–1965.* Chapel Hill: University of North Carolina Press, 1981. Stresses Truman's misplaced faith in Baruch's atomic energy plan.

Smith, Richard N. *Thomas E. Dewey and His Times.* New York: Simon & Schuster, 1982.

Stebenne, David L. *Arthur J. Goldberg: New Deal Liberal.* New York: Oxford University Press, 1996. Gives Goldberg, not the State Department, the lion's share of credit for the diplomacy following the Six-Day War.

Stoler, Mark A. *George C. Marshall: Soldier-Statesman of the American Century.* Boston: Twayne, 1989. An insightful account that minimizes Marshall's policy-making role.

Truman, Margaret. *Harry S. Truman.* New York: William Morrow & Company, 1973. The president's daughter defends his decision to recognize Israel in opposition to a band of "conspirators" in the State Department.

Urquhart, Brian. *Hammarskjold.* New York: Harper & Row, 1972. The best book on its subject by a chief deputy to Hammarskjold. Very sympathetic though not uncritical.

———. *Ralph Bunche.* New York: W. W. Norton, 1993. The best study of Bunche's work in the Mideast, viewing Bunche as both pragmatist and idealist.

Welles, Benjamin. *Sumner Welles: FDR's Global Strategist.* New York: St. Martin's Press, 1997.

GENERAL HISTORIES OF THE UN AND OF U.S. INVOLVEMENT

Armstrong, David, Lorna Lloyd, and John Redmond. *From Versailles to Maastrict: International Organization in the Twentieth Century.* New York: St. Martin's Press, 1996. A highly useful survey of the League of Nations, the UN, and the European Union, along with some other organizations.

Finger, Seymour Maxwell. *American Ambassadors at the UN: People, Policy, and Bureaucracy in Making Foreign Policy.* New York: Holmes & Meier, 1988. An uneven but valuable account of U.S. representatives. The author was a member of the USUN staff for two decades.

Harrelson, Max. *Fires All Around the Horizon: The U.N.'s Uphill Battle to Preserve the Peace.* New York: Praeger, 1989. A highly episodic and respectful account of UN activity to maintain the peace by a reporter for the Associated Press.

Luard, Evan. *A History of the United Nations.* 2 vols. New York: St. Martin's Press, 1982, 1989. An excellent detailed history, but covering only the first 20 years of the UN's life, to 1965.

Meisler, Stanley. *United Nations: The First Fifty Years.* New York: Atlantic Monthly Press, 1995. A journalist's helpful overview of the UN's most notable episodes.

Melvern, Linda. *The Ultimate Crime: Who Betrayed the UN and Why.* London: Allison & Busby, 1995. The betrayer is the United States; the book is, in equal parts, informative and tendentious.

Riggs, Robert. *US/UN:Foreign Policy and International Organization.* New York: Appleton-Century-Crofts, 1971. The author focuses on the work of the political UN rather than the specialized agencies, with an emphasis on the way that Washington used the UN to legitimize U.S. objectives.

Simons, Geoff. *The United Nations: A Chronology of Conflict.* New York: St. Martin's Press, 1994. A highly selective account that damns the United States for subverting UN machinery to serve mainly American foreign objectives.

SECONDARY WORKS ON SPECIALIZED TOPICS

Accinelli, Robert. "Pro-U.N. Internationalists and the Early Cold War: The United States Association for the United Nations and U.S. Foreign Policy, 1947–52." *Diplomatic History* 9 (Fall 1985): 347–62. Traces how the AAUN stood to the left of Truman's Cold War consensus, adding geopolitical realism without surrendering its Wilsonianism.

Alston, Philip, ed. *The United Nations and Human Rights: A Critical Appraisal.* Oxford: Clarendon Press, 1992. A very valuable set of essays.

Anderson, Carol. "From Hope to Disillusion: African Americans, the United Nations, and the Struggle for Human Rights, 1944–1947." *Diplomatic History* 20 (Fall 1996): 531–64.

Arend, Anthony Clark. *Pursuing a Just and Durable Peace: John Foster Dulles and International Organization.* New York: Greenwood Press, 1988. Traces Dulles's support for international organization, as well as how his post-1949 anticommunism affected his view of the UN.

Ball, George. *The Discipline of Power.* Boston: Atlantic Monthly Press, 1968. Argues for a more equitable power relationship among the industrialized countries, and for more discipline and clarity regarding U.S. foreign policy objectives.

Bill, James A. *The Eagle and the Lion: The Tragedy of American-Iranian Relations.* New Haven, Conn.: Yale University Press, 1988. Provides excellent background to the hostage crisis.

Blight, James G., Bruce J. Allyn, and David A. Welch, eds. *On the Brink: Castro, The Missile Crisis, and the Soviet Collapse.* New York: Pantheon, 1993. A highly provocative view of the missile crisis using new evidence from Soviet sources as well from former U.S. officials.

Bogdanowicz-Bindert, Christine A. "World Debt: The United States Reconsiders." *Foreign Affairs* 64 (Winter 1985–1986): 259–73.

Bolton, John. "Wrong Turn in Somalia." *Foreign Affairs* 73 (January-February 1994): 56–66. The wrong turn was toward nation-building instead of humanitarian protection, says this former IO chief.

Bourantonis, Dimitris. *The United Nations and the Quest for Nuclear Disarmament*. Aldershot, U.K.: Dartmouth, 1993. Argues that the UN missed an opportunity by not including the League's sweeping provisions for disarmament; ends with a 129-item program for action in order to increase UN effectiveness in the field.

Bourantonis, Dimitris, and Jarrod Weiner, eds. *The United Nations in the New World Order*. New York: St. Martin's Press, 1995. Ten essays, with a useful analysis of U.S. leadership at the UN by Weiner, concluding that the future is up for grabs.

Boutros-Ghali, Boutros. "Global Leadership after the Cold War." *Foreign Affairs* 75 (March–April 1996): 86–98. Asserts the need to place international interests over national interests.

Brands, H. W. *The Devil We Knew: Americans and the Cold War*. New York: Oxford University Press, 1993. An irreverent view of U.S. diplomacy since 1945 that rejects a single overarching explanation for U.S. policy.

Broadwater, Jeff. *Eisenhower and the AntiCommunist Crusade*. Chapel Hill: University of North Carolina Press, 1992. The title offers the theme.

Brucken, Rowland. "The Shattering of Idealism: American Human Rights Policy, 1941–1945. Unpublished paper, 1994.

Campbell, Thomas M. *Masquerade Peace: America's UN Policy, 1944–1945*. Tallahassee: Florida State University Press, 1973.

Carlsson, Ingvar. "The U.N. at 50: A Time to Reform." *Foreign Policy* 100 (Fall 1995): 3–18.

Chang, Gordon H. *Friends and Enemies: The United States, China, and the Soviet Union, 1948–1972*. Stanford, Calif.: Stanford University Press, 1990. Views Dulles as favoring a two-China policy at the UN with expectations that UN Charter revision in 1955 would permit the change.

Childers, Erskine, ed. *Challenges to the United Nations*. New York: St. Martin's Press, 1995. Essays looking toward reform by a leading supporter of the UN.

Claude, Inis, Jr. *Swords into Plowshares: The Problems and Progress of International Organization*. 4th ed. New York: Random House, 1971. A classic about the theory and practice of IO.

Cleveland, Harlan. *The Obligations of Power*. New York: Harper & Row, 1966. Attempts to combine realism with a commitment to international order and the UN Charter by a former assistant secretary of state for international organization.

Coate, Roger A., ed. *U.S. Policy and the Future of the United Nations*. New York: Twentieth Century Fund Press, 1994. Excellent contemporary analysis, especially the essay by former UN deputy ambassador James Leonard on U.S. relations with the UN.

Cohen, Michael. *Palestine and the Great Powers*. Princeton, N.J.: Princeton University Press, 1982.

———. *Truman and Israel.* Berkeley: Oxford University Press, 1990. This source and the one previously cited are the best two sources on the diplomacy of Israel's independence.

Cohen, Warren I. "America in the Age of Soviet Power: 1945-1991." In *The Cambridge History of American Foreign Relations.* New York: Cambridge University Press, 1993.

Cook, Blanche Wiesen. *The Declassified Eisenhower.* Garden City, N.Y.: Doubleday & Company, 1981. A critical account of Eisenhower's diplomacy that emphasizes the hegemonic elements of UN policy.

Constable, Pamela. "Dateline Haiti: Stalemate Caribbean." *Foreign Policy* 89 (Winter 1992–1993): 175–90. Sees Bush administration policy as highly inconsistent.

Cumings, Bruce. *The Origins of the Korean War.* 2 vols. Princeton, N.J.: Princeton University Press, 1981, 1990. The Korean War is viewed as a product mainly of internal Korean class politics, not foreign aggression.

Dallin, Alexander. *The Soviet Union and the United Nations.* New York: Frederick A. Praeger, 1962.

Dayal, Rajeschwar. *Mission for Hammarskjold: The Congo Crisis.* New Delhi: Oxford University Press, 1976. The secretary-general's chief deputy in the Congo sees Hammarskjold's flaws, but judges his service "heroic and selfless."

Destler, I. M., et al. *Our Own Worst Enemy: The Unmaking of American Foreign Policy.* New York: Simon & Schuster, 1984. The title signals the authors' view of Reagan policy.

Divine, Robert A. *Second Chance: The Triumph of Internationalism in America During World War II.* New York: Atheneum, 1971. Much more detailed than the Brinkley-Hoopes volume, with less of an emphasis on the White House.

Divine, Robert A., ed. *The Johnson Years: LBJ at Home and Abroad.* 3 vols. Lawrence: University Press of Kansas, 1994. Essays by the leading scholars of the LBJ period.

Dumbrell, John. *The Carter Presidency: A Reappraisal.* New York: Manchester University Press, 1993. Sees Carter's foreign policy as insightful in respect to the "postliberal" dilemma, but unfulfilled.

Durch, William J., ed. *The Evolution of UN Peacekeeping: Case Studies and Comparative Analysis.* New York: St. Martin's Press, 1993. Twenty-four essays: concise and insightful.

Eban, Abba. *The New Diplomacy: International Affairs in the Modern Age.* New York: Random House, 1983. A brilliant analysis of the paradoxes of modern diplomacy (most importantly, the paradox of a world wedded to national sovereignty in an age of increasing multilateralism).

———. "The U.N. Idea Revisited." *Foreign Affairs* 74 (September-October 1995): 39–55. Views internationalism as a myth because states will retain a traditional view of their national interests.

Foot, Rosemary. *A Substitute for Victory: The Politics of Peacemaking at the Korean Armistice Talks.* Ithaca, N.Y.: Cornell University Press, 1990. Views U.S. policy as trapped by domestic pressures.

————. *The Practice of Power: U.S. Relations with China Since 1949.* Oxford: Clarendon Press, 1995. Sees U.S. rapprochement with China as a result of the erosion of both domestic and foreign support for nonrecognition of China. This book contains the best analysis of the 1971 vote to seat the PRC at the UN.

Forsythe, David P., ed. *The United Nations in the World Political Economy: Essays in Honor of Leon Gordenker.* New York: St. Martin's Press, 1989. Thirteen essays by leading UN scholars.

Franck, Thomas M. *Nation against Nation: What Happened to the U.N. Dream and What the U.S. Can Do about It.* New York: Oxford University Press, 1985. The author encourages scaling down expectations, but rejects grand illusions.

Fraser, T. G. *The USA and the Middle East Since World War 2.* New York: St. Martin's Press, 1989. A balanced and cautious account of U.S. policy and the degree to which it has been dominated by concerns over Israel.

Gaddis, John L. *Strategies of Containment: A Critical Appraisal of Postwar American National Security Power.* New York: Oxford University Press, 1982. Rivals Leffler as the best book on the subject of strategic thinking during the Truman administration.

Gardner, Lloyd C. *A Covenant with Power: America and World Order from Wilson to Reagan.* New York: Oxford University Press, 1984. A very sound historical survey. Focusing on world order, it oddly ignores the UN while viewing postwar diplomacy in terms of institutional requirements rather than personality.

Gardner, Richard N. "The Case for Practical Internationalism." *Foreign Affairs* 66 (Spring 1988): 827–45. The view of a former IO chief who detests knee-jerk anti-UN sentiment.

Garritsen de Vries, Margaret. *The IMF in a Changing World, 1945–85.* Washington, D.C.: International Monetary Fund, 1986. Gives special attention to the debt problem of the early 1980s.

Garthoff, Raymond L. *Detente and Confrontation: American Soviet Relations from Nixon to Reagan.* Washington, D.C.: Brookings Institution, 1985. Perhaps the best single account of American diplomacy written in the post-World War II era, offering a view of U.S. policy that highlights occasional ignorance, confusion, and contradiction.

Gerson, Allan. *The Kirkpatrick Mission: Diplomacy without Apology—America at the United Nations, 1981–1985.* New York: Free Press, 1991. A spirited defense of Kirkpatrick's UN diplomacy, written by her chief legal adviser.

Glenny, Misha. *The Fall of Yugoslavia: The Third Balkan War* (New York: Penguin Books, 1993. An authoritative and sad account stressing the irrationality of recent Balkan history.

Goldman, Ralph. *Is It Time to Revive the UN Military Staff Committee?* Los Angeles: Center for the Study of Armament and Disarmament, 1990. The author answers "yes" to the question posed in the title.

Gordenker, Leon, ed. *The United Nations in International Politics.* Princeton, N.J.: Princeton University Press, 1971. Essays, including a very useful piece by Stanley J. Michalak Jr. comparing U.S. policy at the UN with the old League of Nations.

Gordon, Wendell. *The United Nations at the Crossroad of Reform.* Armonk, N.Y.: M. E. Sharpe, 1994. A comprehensive and balanced approach to the subject of reform.

Gray, Colin S. *House of Cards: Why Arms Control Must Fail.* Ithaca, N.Y.: Cornell University Press, 1992. Helps explain the UN's many disarmament failures.

Greene, John Robert. *The Presidency of Gerald R. Ford.* Lawrence: University Press of Kansas, 1995.

Haftendorn, Helen, and Jakob Schissler, eds. *The Reagan Administration: A Reconstruction of American Strength?* New York: Walter de Gruyter, 1988. Essays with the theme that Reagan's foreign policy was driven not by ideology but a pragmatic recognition of the limits of power.

Hargrove, Erwin C. *Jimmy Carter as President: Leadership and the Politics of the Public Good.* Baton Rouge: Louisiana State University Press, 1988. Among the best analyses of how the Carter administration conducted its foreign policy, contrasting the way things were supposed to work with the way they actually worked.

Hatcher, Patrick Lloyd. *The Suicide of an Elite: American Internationalists and Vietnam.* Stanford, Calif.: Stanford University Press, 1990. Argues that Vietnam altered forever the naive faith that Americans had placed in internationalism as a means to avoid war or fight war.

Hazzard, Shirley. *Countenance of Truth.* New York: Viking, 1990. Hazzard writes as muckraker, damning UN passivity, which she ascribes to McCarthyism during the 1950s and Waldheim's betrayal of UN principles during the 1970s.

———. *Defeat of an Ideal: A Study of the Self-Destruction of the United Nations.* Boston: Atlantic Monthly Press Book, 1973. A passionate and angry account of what the author, a former member of the Secretariat, sees as U.S. subversion of the UN's ideals and machinery.

Head, Ivan L. "North-South Dangers." *Foreign Affairs* 68 (Summer 1989): 71–86.

Helms, Jesse. "Saving the U.N." *Foreign Affairs* 75 (September–October 1996): 2–7. The chairman of the Senate's Foreign Relations Committee calls for drastic reform or else departure from the UN.

Heninger, Janet E. *Peacekeeping in Transition: The United States in Cambodia.* New York: Twentieth Century Fund Press, 1994. Easily the best single study of the UN in Cambodia; views UN limited ambitions as the key to its success.

Henrikson, Alan K. *Negotiating World Order: The Artisanship and Architecture of Global Diplomacy.* Wilmington, Del.: Scholarly Resources, 1986. Some very important essays, especially those of Brian Urquhart and Gamani Corea.

Hersh, Seymour M. *The Target Is Destroyed: What Really Happened to Korean Airlines Flight 007 and What America Knew about It.* New York: Random House, 1986. Claims that the plane was not deliberately flying over Soviet territory and that the Soviet command was confused.

Herzstein, Robert E. "The Pending Reform of FOIA: A Researcher's Report." *SHAFR Newsletter* 27 (March 1996). Claims that the Americans and Soviets knew of Waldheim's Nazi past at the time Waldheim became secretary-general.

———. *Waldheim: The Missing Years.* New York: Paragon House, 1989. An evenhanded yet damning account of Waldheim's Nazi past.

Hilderbrand, Robert C. *Dumbarton Oaks: The Origins of the United Nations and the Search for Postwar Security.* Chapel Hill: University of North Carolina Press, 1990. Argues that the UN would be a combination of the old League and Roosevelt's Four Policemen: considering the state of the world, "it could hardly have been otherwise."

Hirsch, John L., and Robert B. Oakley. *Somalia and Operation Restore Hope: Reflections on Peacemaking and Peacekeeping.* Washington, D.C.: U.S. Institute for Peace, 1995. A fresh and hardheaded assessment of U.S.-UN mistakes by one of the principal U.S. military policy makers in Somalia.

Hoffman, Stanley. "The Crisis of Liberal Internationalism." *Foreign Policy* 98 (Spring 1995): 159–77. Sees American internationalism being eviscerated by its desire to maintain order without resorting to the use of force.

———. *Primacy or World Order: American Foreign Policy Since the Cold War.* New York: McGraw-Hill, 1978. A sober analysis of the need for internationalism.

Hoffman, Walter, ed. *A New World Order: Essays on Restructuring the United Nations.* Washington, D.C.: World Federalist Association, 1991. Many of the essays ask not just for changes in the UN's Charter, but for changes in the way that governments view the whole system of international relations.

Hughes, Thomas L. "The Twilight of Internationalism." *Foreign Policy* 61 (Winter 1985–1986): 25–48. Premature forecast, but excellent analysis of the reasons why internationalists found themselves on the defensive during the 1980s.

Hume, Cameron. *The United Nations, Iran, Iraq: How Diplomacy Changed.* Indianapolis: Indiana University Press, 1994. A former UN officer explains how the Security Council derived new importance during the 1980s.

Imber, Mark F. "Too Many Cooks: The Post Rio Reform of the United Nations." *International Affairs* 69 (January 1993): 55–70. Sees bureaucratic confusion slowing down prospects for real reform.

———. *The USA, ILO, UNESCO, and IAEA: Politicization and Withdrawal in the Specialized Agencies*. New York: St. Martin's Press, 1989. Argues that U.S. opposition to the politicization of the UN's specialized agencies was based on the false assumption that politics and technical work can be isolated.

Immerman, Richard H. *The CIA in Guatemala: The Diplomacy of Intervention*. Austin: University of Texas Press, 1982. A highly critical account of U.S. policy, stressing the degree to which policy makers saw Guatemala as an extension of the Cold War.

———, ed. *John Foster Dulles and the Diplomacy of the Cold War*. Princeton, N.J.: Princeton University Press, 1990. Essays.

Iriye, Akira. *The Globalizing of America, 1913–1945*. Cambridge History of American Foreign Relations. New York: Cambridge University Press, 1993. A survey that traces the growing international dimension of U.S. diplomacy.

Independent Working Group on the Future of the United Nations. *The United Nations in Its Second Half-Century*. New York: Ford Foundation, 1995. Chaired by Bruce Russett and Paul Kennedy, this is one of the most important UN reform proposals.

Kagan, Donald. *On the Origins of War and the Preservation of Peace*. New York: Anchor Books, 1995. Looks at war and peace from ancient period to the present, with an excellent analysis of the Cuban Crisis and the use of UN channels to maintain peace.

Kalb, Madeleine. *The Congo Cables*. New York: Macmillan, 1982. One of the best secondary accounts, offering a view of American policy contradicting the official story and arguing that although the CIA did not assassinate Lumumba, it was not for lack of trying.

Kaplan, Robert. *Balkan Ghosts: A Journey through History*. New York: St. Martin's Press, 1993. A pessimistic visit to the Balkans implying that angry myths will define the future.

Karns, Margaret, and Karen A. Mingst, eds. *The United States and Multilateral Institutions*. Boston: Unwin Hyman, 1990. Some excellent essays, especially David Forsythe on human rights.

Kaufman, Burton I. *The Arab Middle East and the United States: Interarab Rivalry and Superpower Diplomacy*. New York: Twayne, 1996. An excellent overview with an equally excellent chronology and bibliography.

Kennedy, Paul, and Bruce Russett. "Reforming the United Nations." *Foreign Affairs* 74 (September–October 1995): 56–71.

Keohane, Robert O., Joseph S. Nye, and Stanley Hoffman, eds.. *After the Cold War: International Institutions and State Strategies in Europe, 1989–91*. Cambridge, Mass.: Harvard University Press, 1993. Very little reference to the UN, which says much about the UN's irrelevance in relation to European security.

Kirkpatrick, Jeane J. "Dictatorships and Double Standards." *Commentary* 68 (November 1979): 34–49. Controversial article in which the future UN ambassador argues that noncommunist dictatorships have redeeming value to the United States.

Korey, William. "Genocide Treaty Ratification: Ending an American Embarrassment." In *America Unbound: World War II and the Making of Superpower*, ed. Warren F. Kimball. New York: St. Martin's Press, 1992. Argues that the Bricker Amendment led to inaction on the genocide treaty, and that an absence of strong domestic support kept it under wraps until the 1980s.

Kleinman, Robert. *Organizing for Peace: Neutrality, the Test Ban, and the Freeze.* Syracuse, N.Y.: Syracuse University Press, 1993. A good overview of the subject.

Krauthammer, Charles. "Let It Sink: Why the United States Should Bail Out of the U.N." *The New Republic*, August 24, 1987, 18–23. Reflects the author's petulant nationalism.

Kuehl, Warren, and Lynne K. Dunne. *Keeping the Covenent: American Internationalists and the League of Nations, 1920–1939.* Kent, Ohio: Kent State University Press, 1997.

Kunz, Diane B. *The Economic Diplomacy of the Suez Crisis.* Chapel Hill: University of North Carolina Press, 1991. A meticulous study concluding that U.S. economic sanctions against Great Britain were among the most successful examples of sanctions in recent history.

Kymlicka B. B., and Jean V. Matthews, eds. *The Reagan Revolution?* Chicago: Dorsey Press, 1988. Canadian diplomat John W. Holmes assesses Reagan's use of the UN in this volume.

LaFeber, Walter. *America, Russia, and the Cold War, 1945–1990.* 3d ed. New York: McGraw-Hill, 1991. Views Soviet policy as less aggressive than many more conventional accounts, and U.S. policy as assertive.

Lake, Anthony. *The "Tar Baby" Option: American Policy toward Southern Rhodesia.* New York: Columbia University Press, 1976. A fascinating tale of the way that the United States undermined UN sanctions during the Nixon administration.

Leffler, Melvin P. *A Preponderance of Power: National Security, the Truman Administration, and the Cold War.* Stanford, Calif.: Stanford University Press, 1992. Brilliantly uncovers the flawed assumptions and mixed strategic and economic motives that made U.S.-USSR competition, not cooperation, the hallmark of U.S. policy during the early Cold War.

Logevall, Fredrik A. *Choosing War: The Year 1964 and the Last Chance for Peace in Vietnam.* Berkeley: University of California Press, forthcoming. U.S. officials never seriously sought a peaceful solution in Vietnam.

Lundestad, Gar. *East, West, North, South: Major Developments in International Politics, 1945–1986*. Oslo: Norwegian University Press, 1988. Views the UN as accelerating the process of decolonization.

Lustick, Ian S., ed. *Arab-Israeli Relations in World Politics*. New York: Garland, 1994. Essays; most valuable is one by Nathan A. Pelcovits about UN peacekeeping.

————. *Unsettled States, Disputed Lands: Britain and Ireland, France and Algeria, Israel and the West Bank-Gaza*. Ithaca, N.Y.: Cornell University Press, 1993. The UN has a surprisingly small role in this analysis of territorial disputes.

Mackinlay, John. *The Peacekeepers: An Assessment of Peacekeeping Operations at the Arab-Israeli Interface*. London: Unwin Hyman, 1989. Argues that not the UN connection but the agreements that precede peacekeeping between two disputants explain the success or failure of peacekeeping.

Martin, Ian. "Mangled Multilateralism." *Foreign Policy* (Summer 1994): 72–89. Sees U.S. policy masquerading under the UN flag.

Maynes, Charles. "The New Pessimism." *Foreign Policy* 100 (Fall 1995): 33–49. The former IO chief offers a gloomy view of the prospects of U.S. commitment to multilateral efforts in the security field.

Maynes, Charles, and Richard S. Williamson, eds. *U.S. Foreign Policy and the United Nations System*. New York: W. W. Norton & Company, 1996. A collection of essays held together by a sense that the UN must be reformed to command U.S. support.

Melanson, Richard A., and David Mayers, eds. *Reevaluating Eisenhower: American Foreign Policy in the 1950s*. Urbana: University of Illinois Press, 1987. Essays.

Messer, Robert L. *The End of the Alliance: James F. Byrnes, Roosevelt, Truman, and the Origins of the Cold War*. Chapel Hill: University of North Carolina Press, 1982. Views Truman's use of Byrnes as a way to undermine Congressional opposition to the UN, and then traces Byrnes's evolution to a hard-line position in respect to the USSR.

Mingst, Karen A., and Margaret P. Karns. *The United Nations in the Post Cold-War Era*. Boulder, Colo.: Westview Press, 1995. To make the UN work, the authors assert that the United States needs to build both new coalitions within the UN and domestic support at home.

Moskos, Charles C., Jr. *Peace Soldiers: The Sociology of a United Nations Military Force*. Chicago: University of Chicago Press, 1976.

Moynihan, Daniel P. *On the Law of Nations*. Cambridge, Mass.: Harvard University Press, 1990. Shows the author's continuing commitment to legal and constitutional procedures in the anarchic international sphere.

Nathan, James A., ed. *The Cuban Missile Crisis Revisited*. New York: St. Martin's Press, 1992. Nine essays by prominent historians, though very little consideration of the UN role.

Nachman, Amikam. *International Intervention in the Greek Civil War, 1949–1952*. New York: Praeger, 1990.

Nixon, Richard. "Asia after Vietnam." *Foreign Affairs* 46 (October 1967): 111–25. Argues against isolating China.

O'Brien, Conor Cruise. *The United Nations: Sacred Drama*. New York: Simon & Schuster, 1968. A highly idiosyncratic book by a former UN official who views the organization in mythic terms.

Ostrower, Gary B. *The League of Nations from 1919 to 1929*. Garden City, N.Y.: Avery Publishing Group, 1996.

Ottaway, David. "Africa: U.S. Policy Eclipse." *Foreign Affairs* 58 (1980): 637–58.

Oye, Kenneth A., et al., *Eagle Defiant: United States Foreign Policy in the 1980s*. Boston: Little Brown & Company, 1983. Essays, with an especially good one on African policy by Donald Rothschild and John Ravenhill.

Palmer, Bruce, Jr. *Intervention in the Caribbean: The Dominican Crisis of 1965*. Lexington: University Press of Kentucky, 1989. Stresses American unhappiness with the UN role, yet views the UN as serving American policy.

Pines, Burton, ed. *A World Without a U.N.* Washington, D.C.: Heritage Foundation, 1992. There is no support for the UN in these essays.

Quandt, William B. *Peace Process: American Diplomacy and the Arab-Israeli Conflict since 1967*. Washington, D.C.: Brookings Institution, 1993. A superb, comprehensive study by a former member of the NSC.

Quinn, Dennis J., ed. *Peace Support Operations and the U.S. Military*. Washington, D.C.: National Defense University Press, 1994. Sixteen essays on how to make the U.S. role in peacekeeping more effective, including the need for the United States to accept risks that it has avoided after Somalia.

Righter, Rosemary. *Utopia Lost: The United Nations and World Order*. New York: Twentieth Century Fund Press, 1995. One of the few indispensable books about the UN, tracing the way that the UN's ponderous bureaucracy, the United States, and the Third World have, at various times, subverted the UN's original purpose.

Rikhye, Indar Jit, and Kjell Skjelsbaek, eds. *The United Nations and Peacekeeping: Results, Limitations, and Prospects—The Lessons of 40 Years of Experience*. New York: St. Martin's Press, 1991. Essays by participants in a 1988 Oslo Conference where Alan James argued that if U Thant had not removed the peacekeepers from Sinai in 1967, never again would countries have agreed to a peacekeeping presence on their own soil.

Roberts, Adam, and Benedict Kingsbury. *Presiding over a Divided World: Changing UN Roles, 1945–1993*. Boulder, Colo.: Lynne Reiner, 1994. Notes the withdrawal of the United States from UN peacekeeping and the way that this may cripple the UN in its basic function.

Rocha, Geisa Maria. *In Search of Namibian Independence: The Limitations of the United Nations*. Boulder, Colo.: Westview Press, 1984. The subtitle spells out the book's approach; written before the UN helped to successfully resolve the Namibian conflict.

Rochester, J. Martin. *Waiting for the Millennium: The United Nations and the Future of World Order*. Columbia: University of South Carolina Press, 1993. Examines both structural and theoretical impediments to a revitalized UN.

Rodman, Peter W. *More Precious Than Peace: The Cold War and the Struggle for the Third World*. New York: Charles Scribner's Sons, 1994. The former Reagan NSC staff member calls for a muscular internationalism.

Rosner, Gabriella. *The United Nations Emergency Force*. New York: Columbia University Press, 1963. Contains some very useful background to peacekeeping activity predating 1956.

Rostow, W. W. *Eisenhower, Kennedy, and Foreign Aid*. Austin: University of Texas Press, 1985. A former NSC chief during the 1960s sees the Kennedy approach to selective foreign aid as much more effective than that of the Eisenhower administration.

Rubin, Barry. *Paved with Good Intentions: The American Experience and Iran*. New York: Oxford University Press, 1980. Views the U.S.-Iran relationship in terms of tragedy from 1945 to the hostage crisis. Sees anti-Americanism in Iran as central, not peripheral, to Iranian ideology.

Rubinstein, Alvin Z., ed. *The Arab-Israeli Conflict: Perspectives*. New York: Praeger, 1984. Seven essays, with the editor claiming that the UN has "internationalized" the Mideast conflict.

Rubinstein, Alvin Z., and George Ginsburg, eds. *Soviet and American Policies in the United Nations: A Twenty-Five Year Perspective*. New York: New York University Press, 1971. Essays of varying quality focusing on UN efforts to manage force rather than to eliminate the weapons of war.

Ruggie, John. "The United States and the United Nations: Toward a New Realism." *International Organization* 39 (Spring 1985): 343–56. Argues that U.S. policy toward the UN has no definable shape.

Russell, Ruth B. *A History of the United Nations Charter: The Role of the United States*. Washington, D.C.: Brookings Institution, 1958. An indispensable source.

———. *The United Nations and United States Security Policy*. Washington, D.C.: Brookings Institution, 1968. A pessimistic appraisal of the prospects for U.S. use of the UN on security issues, written during the height of the Vietnam War.

Russett, Bruce, and James Sutterlin. "The U.N. in a New World Order." *Foreign Affairs* 70 (Spring 1991): 69–83. Reflects strong support for UN enforcement machinery.

Ryrie, William. *First World, Third World*. New York: St. Martin's Press, 1995. Begins with the premise that international economic aid is in crisis, but then claims that the World Bank and the International Finance Corporation (which the author headed) can solve the problem if they are sensible.

Salinger, Pierre. *America Held Hostage*. New York: Hill & Wang, 1981. Good discussion of the way that Iranian officials undermined the work of a UN commission seeking to resolve the hostage crisis.

Schlaim, Avi. *The United States and the Berlin Blockade: A Study in Crisis Decision-Making*. Berkeley: University of California Press, 1983.

Schlesinger, Arthur, Jr. "A Man from Mars." *The Atlantic Monthly* 279 (April 1997): 113–18. An article about reporter John Gunther with pithy observations about Republican ultracold warriors.

Schoenbaum, David. *The United States and the State of Israel*. New York: Oxford University Press, 1993. Traces the hesitancy in Nixon's Mideast policy after 1967 as the United States, preoccupied in Vietnam, feared difficult complications in the Mideast.

Schubert, James N. "The Impact of Food Aid on World Malnutrition." *International Organization* 35 (Spring 1981): 329–54. Argues that food aid has had little impact in reducing hunger.

Sciolino, Elaine. *The Outlaw State: Saddam Hussein's Quest for Power and the Gulf Crisis*. New York: John Wiley & Sons, 1991. A standard account, sympathetic to April Glaspie who, according to the author, merely followed State Department policy in dealing with the Iraqi president.

Sewell, John, and Christine Contec. "Foreign Aid and Gramm-Rudman." *Foreign Affairs* 66 (Summer 1987): 1015–36.

Shevchenko, Arkady. *Breaking with Moscow*. New York: Alfred A. Knopf, 1985. The highest-ranking Soviet on the UN staff, who spied for the United States, tells a story that confirms some U.S. suspicions about Soviet espionage at the UN.

Simons, Geoff. *UN Malaise: Power, Problems, and Realpolitik*. New York: St. Martin's Press, 1995. A broad-ranging critique of the UN and the need for reform; sees U.S. hegemony as the root of the problem.

Slater, Jerome. *Intervention and Negotiation: The United States and the Dominican Revolution*. New York: Harper & Row, 1970. Contains little on the UN role.

Smith, Gaddis. *Morality, Reason, and Power: American Diplomacy in the Carter Years*. New York: Hill & Wang, 1986. A judicious view of a diplomatic record that the author sees as a failure, in part because the president was inexperienced, moralistic, and unable to mediate between advisers who deeply disagreed about the world.

Smith, Jean Edward. *George Bush's War*. New York: Henry Holt & Company, 1992. Highly critical of what the author views as Bush's manipulation of the media and the policy making process.

Smith, Tony. "In Defense of Intervention." *Foreign Affairs* 73 (October–November 1994): 34–39. Supports U.S. action in Haiti.

Soffer, Jonathan. "All for One and One for All: The UN Military Staff Committee and the Contradictions within American Internationalism." *Diplomatic History* 21 (Winter 1997): 45–69. Internationalists want both peace and order, and cannot always have both.

Spiegel, Steven L. *The Other Arab-Israeli Conflict: Making America's Middle East Policy from Truman to Reagan.* Chicago: University of Chicago Press, 1985. Excellent discussion of the Rogers Plan, emphasizing the inconsistency of U.S. policy.

———, ed. *The Arab-Israeli Search for Peace.* Boulder, Colo.: Lynne Reiner, 1992. Essays, with little focus on UN machinery.

Stegenga, James A. *The United Nations Force in Cyprus.* Columbus: Ohio State University Press, 1968. Concludes that UNFICYP will likely be the model for future peacekeeping missions, although the author recognizes the limits on UN activity to solve deeply rooted problems.

Stoessinger, John G. *The United Nations and the Superpowers: China, Russia and America.* 3d ed. New York: Random House, 1973. Argues that the veto—or the threat of veto—is the key to understanding U.S. behavior at the UN.

Streit, Clarence. *Union Now: A Proposal for Inter-Democracy Federal Union.* New York: Harper & Brothers, 1940. A clarion call for world federalism.

Sweeney, John. "Stuck in Haiti." *Foreign Policy* 102 (Spring 1996): 143–51. American idealism is wrecked by Haitian realities.

Thakur, Ramesh, and Carlyle A. Thayer, eds. *A Crisis of Expectations: UN Peacekeeping in the 1990s.* Boulder, Colo.: Westview Press, 1995. Excellent essays on individual peacekeeping missions.

Tompkins, E. Berkeley, ed. *The United Nations in Perspective.* Stanford, Calif.: Stanford University Press, 1972. Contains an outstanding essay by Charles Malik viewing the UN as a clash of cultures.

United Nations. *The United Nations and Disarmament: 1945–1985.* New York: United Nations, 1985. Excellent summary of UN activity.

United Nations Institute for Training and Research (UNITAR). *The United Nations and the Maintenance of International Security.* Boston: Martinus Nijhoff Publishers, 1987. Particularly good essays by Brian Urquhart on security and Jozef Goldblatt on disarmament.

Van den Haag, Ernest, and John P. Conrad. *The U.N.: In or Out?* New York: Plenum Press, 1987. A debate, with van den Haag arguing the case for withdrawal.

Walker, Martin. *The Cold War: A History.* New York: Henry Holt & Company, 1993. Sees the Cold War as having a warped stability that shielded the world from a nuclear catastrophe.

Walton, Richard J. *The Remnants of Power: The Last Tragic Years of Adlai Stevenson.* New York: Coward-McCann, 1968. A sympathetic view of Stevenson at the UN by a historian who views Stevenson's loss of real influence as tragic.

Ward, Barbara. "Another Chance for the North?" *Foreign Affairs* 59 (Winter 1980–1981): 386–97. Damns UN inaction in feeding the Third World.

Welles, Sumner. *A Time for Decision*. New York: Harper & Brothers, 1944. A best-seller by FDR's former undersecretary.

White, N. D. *Keeping the Peace: The United Nations and the Maintenance of International Peace and Security*. Manchester, U.K.: Manchester University Press, 1993. A broad and competent overview of the many peacekeeping operations.

Whittaker, David J. *United Nations in Action*. Armonk, N.Y.: M. E. Sharpe, 1995. A sophisticated primer about the UN, with some excellent quick reference sections on such things as peacekeeping, environmental action, and womens' rights.

Wilcox, Francis O., and H. Field Haviland Jr. *The United Nations and the United States*. Baltimore: Johns Hopkins University Press, 1961. Essays by leading internationalists, including Harlan Cleveland, Ernest Gross, and Inis Claude Jr.

Wittner, Lawrence S. *Rebels against War: The American Peace Movement, 1941–1960*. New York: Columbia University Press, 1969. Describes peace advocates from many backgrounds.

———. *One World or None: A History of the World Nuclear Disarmament Movement through 1953*. Stanford, Calif.: Stanford University Press, 1993. A comprehensive study of the subject, illustrating the limited usefulness of the UN in arms limitation

Woods, Randall B. *Changing of the Guard: Anglo-American Relations, 1941–1946*. Chapel Hill: University of North Carolina Press, 1990.

Woods, Randall B., and Howard Jones. *Dawning of the Cold War: The United States Quest for Order*. Chicago: Ivan L. Dee, 1994.

Wooley, Wesley T. *Alternatives to Anarchy: American Supranationalism since World War II*. Bloomington: Indiana University Press, 1988. Traces the need for—and the failure of—international authority since the 1940s.

Yost, Charles. *The Insecurity of Nations*. New York: Frederick A. Praeger, 1968. Dedicated to Stevenson and Goldberg; the author sees strengthened UN peacekeeping as necessary to reduce insecurity among the superpowers that might lead to war.

———. *The Conduct and Misconduct of Foreign Affairs*. New York: Random House, 1972. A former UN ambassador offers generous and often shrewd judgments about U.S. leaders, seeing the UN as central to international stability.

Zacher, Mark W. *Dag Hammarskjold's United Nations*. New York: Columbia University Press, 1970. An admiring view of Hammarskjold, who offered internationalists a sense of expanded limits.

ORAL HISTORIES

I have read over 100 oral histories, of which a few are especially noteworthy: From the Truman Library: Dean Acheson, John D. Hickerson, David A.

Morse, Harold Stassen, and Francis O. Wilcox. From the Eisenhower Library: Robert R. Bowie, Luther Harris Evans, Gordon Gray, John W. Hanes Jr., Mary P. Lord, Robert D. Murphy, and David W. Wainhouse. From the Kennedy Library: Harry N. Howard, and Livingston Merchant. From the Johnson Library: Arthur Goldberg, and Dean Rusk. From the Carter Library: David Aaron, and Zbigniew Brzezinski. From the Yale/UN Project: Harlan Cleveland, Abba Eban, Ernest Gross, Gunnar Jarring, Jeane Kirkpatrick, Arthur Lall, Sture Linner, and Joseph Sisco. From the Association for Diplomatic Studies Foreign Affairs Oral History Program: Donald McHenry.

Also useful was Linda Fasulo, ed., *Representing America: Experiences of U.S. Diplomats at the U.N.* (New York: Facts on File Publications, 1984), containing partial transcripts of interviews.

CYBER SOURCES

For historians, UN-related material appears on many pages, including the UN's own web page (www.UN.org). Of special help to me has been: ACUNS-IO (American Council of the United Nations—International Organization); H-DIPLO (the diplomatic history list of History-Net); the website of the United Nations Association in Canada (www.ncf.carleton.ca); and Yale University's UN work site (www.library.yale.edu//UN/UNhome.htm).

INDEX

THE AUTHOR

Born shortly after World War II began, Gary B. Ostrower spent his childhood in Woodbridge, New Jersey. He attended Alfred University in upstate New York and received his doctorate from the University of Rochester. Ostrower has specialized in the history of international organizations and served for six years as president of the Society for the Study of Internationalism. His publications include *Collective Insecurity: The United States and the League of Nations During the Early Thirties* (Bucknell University Press, 1979), and *The League of Nations: From 1919 to 1929* (Avery Publishing Group, 1996). He has taught at Vassar College and the University of Pennsylvania, and presently holds the Margaret and Barbara Hagar Chair in the Humanities at Alfred University. Ostrower has won numerous teaching awards. He has served as a village official in Alfred since 1981. He is married and the father of two children.

THE EDITOR

Akira Iriye is Charles Warren Professor of American History at Harvard University and visiting professor of history at the International University of Japan. His most recent publications include *China and Japan in the Global Setting* (1992), *The Globalizing of America: United States Foreign Relations, 1913–1945* (1993), and *Cultural Internationalism and World Order* (1997).